Learning Beyond The Classroom

# Engaging the Whole of Service-Learning, Diversity, and Learning Communities

Edited by
Joseph A. Galura, Penny A. Pasque,
David Schoem, Jeffrey Howard

The OCSL Press at the University of Michigan
Edward Ginsberg Center for Community Service and Learning

1024 Hill Street
Ann Arbor, Michigan 48109
mjcsl@umich.edu • www.umich.edu/~mjcsl
(734) 647-7402 • Fax (734) 647-7464

2004

The OCSL Press at the University of Michigan
Edward Ginsberg Center for Community Service and Learning
1024 Hill Street
Ann Arbor, Michigan 48109
mjcsl@umich.edu • www.umich.edu/~mjcsl
(734) 647-7402 • Fax (734) 647-7464

First Printing

Printed in the United States of America

| ISBN | 0-9638136-1-7 | *Praxis 1: A Faculty Casebook for Community Service-Learning* |
| ISBN | 0-9638136-2-5 | *Praxis II: Service-Learning Resources for University Students, Faculty and Staff* |
| ISBN | 0-9638136-3-3 | *Praxis III: Voices in Dialogue* |
| ISBN | 0-9638136-9-2 | *Engaging the Whole of Service-Learning, Diversity, and Learning Communities* |

# Table of Contents

# Introduction

Friday, 1 December 2000

For Joe, the story of this book begins on that date, at a Michigan Community Scholars Program (MSCP) faculty meeting. MCSP is a living-learning program at the University of Michigan. As with many important beginnings, it is often difficult to remember the specific agenda items and only later would Joe name the content as being about service-learning, diversity, and learning communities.

What Joe does recall are some specific innovations, nurtured by David Schoem, MCSP faculty director, and Penny Pasque, program director: encouraging and supporting community partners to team teach academic courses alongside tenured faculty, requiring service-learning or dialogue courses as a condition of students' living-learning community membership, and—probably most important at a research I institution—creating a sense of community so that the faculty and staff implementing innovations could not only talk about their course content but also the particular dilemmas, problems, and/or successes of teaching in a residential setting, in a class of primarily first-year students!

One professor (and contributing author to this book) was honored to teach the students' very first college class. Another struggled with how to make material relevant to today's 18-year olds after decades of instructing graduate students. Yet another wondered if we could, as a faculty and community, even begin to approach higher education's promise: the lived-in and deep practice of democracy.

It was an invigorating and ultimately empowering discussion, and more than one faculty member commented that this meeting was so very different than the discipline-centric meetings he so often attended—which tended to be about "defending our turf" and departmental prestige. Rarely, if ever, did meetings outside of MCSP center around the joys and challenges of teaching undergraduates or how best to prepare today's first- and second-year students to engage thoughtfully and effectively in an increasingly complex and diverse world.

The following day Joe met with Penny and David and told them that he thought we had the makings of a great book. But like the earlier question about naming the content, it was not clear how that would happen—yet.

In a related effort, David and Penny wrote a proposal, funded by the Edward Ginsberg Center for Community Service and Learning, for an ambitious cycle of faculty development. Over the course of an academic year, MCSP would:

- Host two retreats for faculty, community partners, students, and staff
- Feature national experts as keynote retreat speakers: Edgar Beckham (diversity) and David Maurrasse (university-community partnerships)
- Organize bus tours for staff, faculty, and students to visit MCSP community partners onsite in Ann Arbor, Ypsilanti, and Detroit

- Arrange classroom visits for community partners and MCSP faculty to MCSP seminar courses
- Provide stipends for teams of community partners, students, staff, and faculty to co-write articles about how they combine service-learning and multicultural education at MCSP
- Facilitate a series of luncheons for writing teams to present articles-in-progress to peers and the editorial team

This book is, in a sense, a final report, of not only the yearlong cycle of faculty development, but also the story of MCSP, a learning community at the University of Michigan striving to engage the whole of diversity education and service-learning.

# Engaging the Whole

We have entitled this book, *Engaging the Whole of Service-Learning, Diversity, and Learning Communities* because we believe that much of higher education's future in this country is connected to these three innovations to the curriculum. Moreover, these innovations can and should be connected to one another, to achieve a synergism, which broadens and deepens our educational agenda.

We also acknowledge that "engaging the whole" in this manner—that is, considering service-learning, diversity, and learning communities together in an attempt to integrate these innovations—is relatively new thinking within the academy. Often these innovations are considered separately, and it should be noted that individual editorial team members have participated in various aspects of "the whole" over the past decade.

Joe and Jeffrey are the series editors of *Praxis*, a nationally distributed set of "how-to" books on service-learning at the University of Michigan. This book is the fourth volume in that series, which began in 1993. In 1994, Jeffrey launched *The Michigan Journal of Community Service Learning*, and continues to serve as the editor of this only international and peer-reviewed multidisciplinary journal on academic service-learning. In 2000, foreshadowing one aspect of this book, Joe contributed a chapter to Carolyn O'Grady's *Integrating Service Learning and Multicultural Education at Colleges and Universities* with Stella Raudenbush, a faculty member in the School of Education at the University of Michigan.

Penny has worked over 10 years in various types of learning communities at Cornell University and the University of Michigan, connecting students and faculty. Educative themes through these learning communities have been social justice and social change issues. Her most recent national presentations have been on higher education for a diverse democracy, and student social identity development as connected to leadership through civic engagement. These latest presentations have been through the American College Personnel Association, PaperClip Communications and National Association of Student Personnel Administrators leadership conference series, and the American Association for Higher Education. Some of this thinking is present throughout this book.

David has published extensively on the issue of diversity, including *Inside Separate Worlds: Life Stories of Young Blacks, Jews and Latinos* (1991), *Multicultural Teaching in the University* (1995), and *Intergroup Dialogue: Deliberative Democracy in School, College, Community and Workplace* (2001). He also has a long history in leadership roles with learning communities, is a National Learning Communities fellow, and has written a chapter "Sustaining Living-Learning Programs: Ideals and Challenges" in Jodi Levine Laufgraben and Nancy Shapiro and Associates' *Expanding and Sustaining Learning Communities* (2004). His most recent publication in *Change* magazine (2002), "Transforming Undergraduate Education: Moving Beyond Undergraduate Initiatives," helps lay the foundation for this book.

It is the collaborative work *between* the editors that "engages the whole." Much of the work described in the pages that follow is enacted at Couzens Hall, the physical location of the MCSP living-learning community. However, conceptually the work is transacted in the hearts and minds of faculty, University staff, students, and our community partners who serve and learn about diversity together—both at Couzens and in the surrounding community. Thus the message of "engaging the whole"—that service-learning, diversity, and learning communities can and should be considered together—is not limited to Couzens, or even the University of Michigan, but is a call to action for all of higher education and those communities where those institutions reside.

## Contents

The book has four parts. The first part is entitled, "National Trends in Higher Education: Service-Learning, Diversity, and Learning Communities."

These articles, written by national experts, provide a theoretical context for the chapters that follow, which are more practice-oriented. Edgar Beckham, writing eloquently from a lifetime of professional leadership and experience in higher education with issues of diversity, argues that "diversity should become first and foremost, an intellectual pursuit." David Maurrasse, who brings insight and research expertise to bear on university-community partnerships, states that "Higher education is particularly positioned to design and embrace transformational learning communities both internally—through diversifying students, staff, and faculty as well as cur- riculum and programming—as well as externally, through community partnerships and service learning initiatives." John O'Connor is uniquely positioned, through his dual role as national organizational leader and local campus faculty scholar/practitioner, to assess the current progress and successes of community-based teaching, learning, and research, and its linkage to higher education's efforts for a diverse democracy; and to bring clarity to some of the key challenges and disagreements in the field. Nancy S. Shapiro, director of learning community projects throughout K-16 and editor of the leading texts on learning communities, explains that "Because learning communities educate for democracy," they are "particularly well-positioned to take the lead in bringing a generation of young adults into civic awareness." Nancy E. Thomas, consultant to higher education leaders across the country and director of the Democ- racy Project, points us to the urgent need for a new kind of leader to provide colleges and universities the means to "intentionally structure an environment that is likely to enable bound- ary-crossers and foster the kind of creative thinking and action profiled in this book."

The next section is "Innovative Programs that Engage the Whole." Schoem and Pasque describe the conceptual underpinnings, vision, practice, success, and challenges of MCSP, the program that lies at the heart of this book and this ideal, the integration of service-learning and diversity within a residential learning community. One example of this ideal is LUCY: The Lives of Urban Children and Youth Initiative. Nested within MCSP, LUCY is a two-year pathway, which includes a four-course sequence and an AmeriCorps internship (among other co-curric- ular activities), preparing students to interact effectively in a complex and diverse world. The article has three parts, each co-written by different teams of authors: the LUCY instructional team, Galura, Stella Raudenbush and Jen Denzin; the LUCY community partners, Njia Kai, Nancy Balogh, Kate Brady, Jean Klein and Yvonne Mayfield, interviewed by Jen Denzin; and LUCY program evaluators, Professor Gregory B. Markus and graduate student intern Carmen Wargel. Student feedback is represented throughout.

The third section is "Integrative Course Models: Collaborations of Faculty, Students, Staff and Community Partners." Composition faculty member George Cooper collaborates with community partner Marti Rodwell and students Zach Abramson and Kevin Pereria on chal- lenging students to get "Out of Their Comfort Zones" through practical community engagement exercises and reflective writing about these experiences. In "Collaborative Learning about Unsustainability," James Crowfoot, faculty emeritus in the School of Natural Resources and Susan Santone, executive director of Creative Change Educational Solutions, a nonprofit, discuss the "background on the problem of unsustainability and challenge of sustainability, and the reasons why higher education urgently needs to address these topics." Crowfoot and Santone also provide a description of an interdisciplinary first-year seminar focused on "this growing global and local program that threatens life as we know it." "Living and Learning through Community Service: A Reflection on Michigan Community Scholars Program Sections of Sociology 389" is written by graduate student instructor Annalissa Herbert, and MCSP student leaders Amy Borer, Stephanie Brown, Kristen Joe, Sheyonna Manns, and Chibuzo Okafo. Sociology 389 is one of the nation's oldest, continuously running service-learning courses and one of the few that employs undergraduates to facilitate the learning of their peers. Through his article, "Promoting Diverse Democracy in Health Care," Terence A. Joiner, a faculty member in the medical school and physician, provides insight into teaching first-year students for the first time. He includes contemporary movies and readings into the curriculum to make the issues salient to students' lives. Louis Nagel's "Music in Our Lives" tells the engaging story of a music professor's "experiment" with composing a first-year MCSP seminar. Nagel muses, "I do not know if these young people experiencing college for the first time sensed how uneasy I felt." Faculty member Kelly E. Maxwell and staff members Aaron Traxler-Ballew and K. Foula Dimopoulos provide concrete qualitative research results from MCSP and non-MCSP students who have engaged in the Program on Intergroup Relations. The theoretical and practical underpinnings of the nationally recognized intergroup dialogue program is described along with a discussion of the importance of collaboration between university programs in "Intergroup Dialogue and MCSP: A Partnership for Meaningful Engagement." Pasque, Carly M. Southworth, and two student facilitators, Danny V. Asnani and Alefiyah Mesiwala, discuss the conceptual framework and the practical implementation of "Integrating Social Identity, Community Development, and Service-Learning" into the MCSP introductory course that every first year MCSP student enrolls in during the fall term. Santone and Crowfoot collaborate again in "Collaborative Learning about Sustainability" to discuss the significant community partner role in the first-year seminar and reflect on the major course projects that empower students to *think* and *act* on relevant issues. In "Teaching and Learning about Democracy, Diversity, and Community," Schoem and his students, Dorian Daniels, Erin Lane, Jeff Nelson, Byanqa Robinson, and Vanessa Vadnal, offer both the faculty experience of teaching this course and the personal experience of students from three different years who have experienced taking a class that attempts "to engage students in thinking critically about diverse democracy in the United States and practice deliberative democracy in the classroom."

The final section is "Participant Voices of Insight and Experience." In "The Michigan Community Scholars Program and Its Community Partners: Developing a Service Strategy as a Volunteer Organization," Richard Carter provides an extraordinarily useful and practical conceptual model. The volunteer organization is presented as a model for understaffed programs and initiatives such as learning communities, service-learning, and diversity programs, which is based on Carter's higher education experience working with nonprofit organizations. In "A Community Partner Looks at Mentoring Practices," Mary Ann Dunn, a longtime supervisor of MCSP students, reflects on the program's cumulative effects over several student generations. Cassie Lapekas' chapter, "From Student to Community Partner," recounts the author's remarkable journey—from being a student in an MCSP seminar to supervising MCSP students as a community partner! Pasque and MCSP student leaders Sedika F. Franklin and Sarah A. Luke bridge theory, observation, and personal narrative while sharing some of the challenges of building a strong, student-empowered, and inclusive living-learning program. They describe leadership opportunities and student empowerment, diversity in student leadership, community service learning and the challenge of transforming theory into practice. Finally, Schoem, graduate researchers Josie Sirieno and Stefani Salalzar, and interim MCSP program director Carly Southworth provide in their chapter "Program Evaluation and Research Design: Integrating Service-Learning, Diversity, and Learning Communities," the actual assessment tools for MCSP, including surveys and interview guides for its program evaluation and planned research design.

We invite you to engage these issues with us. Joe quoted Browning (1864) to our continuing LUCY students but we think the sentiment applies here as well.

*"Grow old along with me!*
*The best is yet to be..."*

We welcome your feedback and commitment to "engage the whole" along with us.

# Acknowledgements

We wish to thank all the authors for their chapters and ongoing commitment to the mission of MCSP and for working so productively to engage the whole of service-learning, diversity, and learning communities. We also thank them for modeling the scholarship of teaching through their work in MCSP and by authoring these chapters. These chapters truly reflect the art of bringing theory to practice, and practice to theory. All of the contributors—experienced faculty, community partners, and staff as well as talented undergraduate students—speak openly and honestly about the successes and challenges of the teaching and learning in this program.

We are very proud that most of our chapters are co-authored by various combinations of faculty, students, community partners, and staff. This book represents one specific intentional effort to practice the values of collaboration and partnership that MCSP and LUCY so highly value. For many of us and for most people on our campuses, co-authored chapters across boundaries, between faculty and students, faculty and community partners, and faculty, staff, and students represent unchartered territory, neither a skill nor a virtue typically taught in graduate or undergraduate school.

At the University of Michigan, we want to thank the College of Literature, Science, and the Arts and University Housing for their continuing support of MCSP, and the School of Education, Office of the Provost, Edward Ginsberg Center for Community Service and Learning and MCSP for support of the LUCY Program. Thanks also goes to the Office of the Vice President for Student Affairs for their support of the Ginsberg Center.

We extend great appreciation to the OCSL Press for support of this project: Aileo Wienmann for copyediting, Nick Bowman and Nate Daun Barnett for their wordsmithing, and Cris Shankleton and Robyn Skodzinsky for format and design assistance, and distribution coordination.

Many staff, faculty, community partners, and students at all of these programs deserve our thanks. In particular, we want to acknowledge the tireless work of Rosa Maria Cabello, Christopher MacDonald-Dennis, Takisha Lashore, Kourtney Rice, Carly Southworth, and Wendy Woods, as well as Matt Brown, Al Hearn, Anne Kohler-Cabot, Sylvia Orduño, Laurel Park, Chavella Pittman, Josie Sirineo, Stefani Salazar, at MCSP. Many of the faculty and students to whom we are deeply indebted are mentioned throughout the book and/or are contributors to the book. We also want to acknowledge Jen Denzin and Rodolfo Palma at LUCY, and Sean de Four at the Ginsberg Center.

Finally, each of us wishes to thank those closest to us for their support during this project. Joe wishes to thank Cathy for her commitment, devotion and love, and our children, David and Genna, the next generation "engaging the whole." Penny extends her appreciation to her mother, Suzanne Haberstroh, for a lifetime of support and wisdom; to her partner, Frank Kamisky, friends, and family for continual encouragement; and to all who continue to ask difficult questions and strive to engage the whole of our lives. David is forever thankful to Karyn for her steadfast love, support, and inspiration, and Adina and Shana for giving hope for the future through their modeling of the very best values and leadership of service, community, and learning for a just, diverse democracy. Jeffrey thanks his wife and lifetime friend, Janet Miller, and his son Adam, and daughter, Rachel, who are the best kids he could ever imagine.

# SECTION ONE

## National Trends in Higher Education: Service-Learning, Diversity, and Learning Communities

# Chapter 1

## DIVERSITY: AN EDUCATIONAL IMPERATIVE

Edgar Beckham

According to fading memories at Wesleyan University, a group of professors and administrators participated in a series of meetings some fifty years ago at which they engaged in deliberation of the state of the College. Their meetings were part of a self-study funded by the Ford Foundation.

At some point, their discussion turned to the composition of the student body, at the time all male, and in the perception of some, light-haired, corn-fed Protestants who were eager to obey President Victor L. Butterfield's imperative that they become leaders in their communities "out of proportion to their numbers."

One member of the committee, Robert Cohen—Wesleyan alumnus, professor of physics and philosophy, banished from Wesleyan in the mid-1950s for reasons of political ideology, Wesleyan Trustee, revered mentor to many—argued that Wesleyan could improve its intellectual atmosphere by changing the composition of its student body.

According to another member of the committee, Carl Schorske, eminent professor emeritus of history who once observed wryly that Wesleyan was "better than its national reputation, but not as good as it thinks it is," Cohen was probably thinking more about adding "Jews from the Bronx" than about admitting women or students of color.

But the point to remember is that Cohen made the profound connection between diversity of people and the quality of intellectual life, that is, this early impulse toward demographic change was rooted in an educational aspiration. If there is a single message in this paper, it is that accountability for diversity must begin with educational mission.

By the mid-1960s, this educational impulse was largely lost in the fervor of the Civil Rights Movement. Wesleyan had concluded that along with all other historically white institutions of higher learning, it had been complicit in denying educational opportunity to the sons and daughters of slavery. Social justice entailed the affirmative obligation that this be changed, deliberately, systematically. And so, in 1965 Wesleyan began a program of affirmative admission of black students.

To its credit, Wesleyan attempted quite early in the process to move the discourse on its affirmative admission policy from the realm of social justice back to education. That's when the term "diversity" was introduced. Black students were being admitted because they enriched Wesleyan's diversity, and diversity-as was well known-was good for education. In an address to a group of Wesleyan alumni, the Dean of Admissions put it succinctly. "Wesleyan needs black students," he said, "in order to educate white students."

As one might imagine, his comment was not popular among black students. In fact, they were offended by it. What a perversion of the social justice impulse it was, they thought, to bring black students to Wesleyan for the benefit of privileged white students.

Their resentment became a strength as they learned how to create and assert a strong black presence at Wesleyan, to transform themselves into a black group while at the same time preserving their individual black identities. That created quite a dilemma for many white faculty and administrators at Wesleyan who had expected an aggregation of black individuals, but not a black group. Some quickly learned to respond to black students in terms of their assertive group identity only to learn abruptly that that response was also inadequate. It required a long period of edifying trauma for Wesleyan to learn that its black students' assertion of militant group identity did not diminish their sense of individual personhood. They insisted on both.

One of the enduring legacies that continue to burden the term "diversity," at least in higher education circles, is this tension between the educational value of diversity and its value to the pursuit of social justice. While I shall argue that our rationale for diversity should be embedded in our educational mission, I do not mean to suggest that we should abandon social justice or any other moral foundation of our lives and work. On the contrary, I believe that attention to the moral basis of our enterprise is more urgent now than at any time I can remember.

The challenge is to align the educational and social justice arguments in a manner that makes them complementary.

Before we attempt that alignment, let's look at some of the other legacies that seem to burden the term "diversity." First, there is the suspicion that diversity is used to avoid a tough confrontation with racism. Many people want that confrontation, some because they want to vent their righteous anger; some because they hope for a catharsis that will clear the soul as well as the air, and create a platform from which we can launch initiatives aimed at healing, reconciliation, and mutuality.

The second deficit that "diversity" still carries is the suspicion that it serves as a prism that deflects our focus completely onto those newly admitted into our midst. Diversity viewed through this prism is not all of us; it's those of us who are not like the real us. Our students of color give us our diversity; we do not. This is the more severe distortion, for it makes of diversity a term that divides, that reifies separation and builds barriers between people who belong together.

Some advocates of social justice argue that efforts in behalf of diversity should be targeted to benefit only those who have been oppressed, deprived, and disadvantaged by the discriminatory practices of the past. The historically privileged may indeed benefit, but mainly by acknowledging their guilty responsibility for the original injustice. The notion that diversity education should benefit every learner is offensive to some who think of social justice as a correction of past wrongs. That was a primary source of the anger of black students at Wesleyan over the suggestion that they were there to educate white students. That is, they were offended by the suggestion that they were there to do what they were indeed doing.

This tension between the educational and social justice aims of action in support of diversity continues to this day, and in my view, it is one of the most serious impediments to progress on diversity. The tension is most pernicious when it leads an advocate of one aspiration to discount the value of the other. Take, for example, the observation, made to me just a few months ago, that instruction on diversity should be aimed at the disadvantaged, not the privileged. Creating that kind of a division is perverse not merely because it transposes advantage and disadvantage in an almost vengeful way, but rather more importantly because it construes education as a zero-sum enterprise incapable of contributing to the growth and development of diverse students in differentiated ways.

The third deficit has its source in the specific social history of the United States. We know that the American past created the present problem, which gives the problem a decidedly American cast. We are inclined to urge, therefore, that we address diversity as a domestic challenge: one that belongs in our American house, a challenge that ought to define American identity. And we have grown skeptical of those who would locate the diversity challenge in a world of global concerns. Global citizenship, we fear, is a vehicle for skipping blithely over the unfinished business of finding and realizing America.

Some observers have suggested that the term "diversity" is so burdened that it should be abandoned in favor of pluralism, multiculturalism, global citizenship, inclusion, or perhaps a neologism not yet invented. I disagree, and I would argue—along with an old teacher of mine—that abandoning a good word like diversity impoverishes the language and diminishes our capacity to communicate. I advocate a different course. Let us take control of diversity and its definition; let us make it mean what we mean. And while we are at it, let us wipe out its deficits and replace them with constructions of meaning that serve as assets to understanding; not merely passive assets, but performing ones that build our capacity to pursue our moral aspirations.

So let me propose an experiment. Let's turn to speculating about what might have happened if the intellectual foundation for diversity, evident at Wesleyan in the 1950s, had not been submerged in the social justice fervor of the 1960s. What might "diversity" mean today?

First of all, Wesleyan would have admitted black students as assets to a community in need of change. It would not have ignored the history of oppression visited upon black people, but it would also have seen in that history an opportunity to advance the education of all students. It would have noted that oppression is an experience shared by the oppressors and the oppressed, albeit from different perspectives, and that each of the diverse perspectives challenges all the others, and that the reciprocal challenges create the opportunity for the development of critical thinking.

The edifying trauma that Wesleyan suffered might have been even more edifying, and perhaps less traumatic had critical thinking led to the insight that diversity denotes difference, and at the same time, connotes inclusive, and potentially unifying context. Thus, describing Wesleyan students as diverse, defines Wesleyan. Ironically, the dictionary doesn't help us much with this analysis. Usage helps us more. If I suggest that Americans are different, I may mean that they differ from Indians or South Africans. But if I say that Americans are diverse, it is clear that I mean two things: they differ from each other, and they are all Americans. I think we need to work harder to emphasize these two dimensions of diversity simultaneously: to insist on both the denotation and connotation of the term, to reject the notion that it focuses simply on difference.

I think the educational implications of this observation are quite far-reaching. If we neglect diversity as inclusive context, we are very likely to neglect the educational needs of some of our students. We may justify our neglect by invoking the need to redress past wrongs, to focus on the needs of the historically oppressed, but that, in my judgment, simply introduces a new form of oppression. Exchanging one target for another is not a proper aim of diversity education.

But even more importantly, or perhaps more ominously, the neglect of context can blind us to the productive complexity of the teaching-learning process. Let's suppose we are teaching African American history and are seeking thereby to enrich the self-understanding of our African American students. That is indeed a worthy goal, but it is not the only goal, even if all our students are African American. Our students, regardless of the racial/ethnic mix, will position themselves differently in relation to the subject matter. Their positionality will affect what and how they learn, and what they do with that learning subsequently. If we neglect positionality, ignore where people "are at" and where they "are coming from," we drastically diminish the potential power of education.

But let's continue the experiment. What about "diversity" as avoidance of confrontation with racism? I think that if our model were an intellectual one, diversity would lead us directly into the confrontation by asking insistently about the character of our diversity, its dimensions, its historical context, its social consequence, its implications for the future of our polity. Indeed, our diversity would become the vehicle that would drive our discourse about these matters. Diversity would become education.

In the latter part of the 1990s, the Ford Foundation sponsored the second in a series of three seminars on diversity in higher education that involved representatives of India, South Africa, and the United States—at that time the largest, the youngest, and the oldest democracies in the world. All were grappling with the ominous challenge of diversity. The seminar was held in South Africa, and at one of its most memorable sessions we heard an address by Albie Sachs, a justice of South Africa's highest court. Justice Sachs talked about his life, about growing up in a family of radical social activists, a Jewish family that taught him early in life that he was different and the same. He described his work in opposition to apartheid, and the bombing that crippled his body and strengthened his resolve to help build a new South Africa in which everyone could be different and the same. He returned again and again to that phrase until it was imprinted on the minds of his listeners that we are all different and the same.

Justice Sachs' pronouncement that we are different and the same has deepened my conviction concerning the value of diversity and the meaning we should attach to it.

In our diversity, we are different and the same. In South Africa, apartheid arranged society so that difference was in an unequal war with sameness—and difference won. And its victory was so lopsided that even the basic understanding of diversity as a concept suffered a grievous defeat. The notion of a unifying South African context was submerged. The triumphant understanding glorified what it called cultural difference by imposing a rigid hierarchy of access to rights and resources. To this day, some South Africans are suspicious of the term diversity because of the perverse way in which it was used to support oppressive separation.

In other words, the pursuit of social justice does not, by itself, protect us from this kind of distortion of the meaning of diversity. On the contrary, if we view social justice exclusively as redress of past wrongs and not as an inclusive condition in which, to quote Maxine Greene, we all seek to live a world in common, we run the risk of defeating ourselves and creating new injustice. We must remember two things—that diversity is inclusive of difference, and that inclusive education pursues justice.

In our intellectual model, the focus is on all of us and the worlds we inhabit and construct. Our diversity students are all our students. We not only respect and celebrate their positionality, we also seek to know them and to put them to intentional use as assets in the educational process. That may even mean that they take more responsibility for educating themselves. It certainly means that they share responsibility for educating each other. Black students at Wesleyan might still have resented being asked to help educate white students, but because it was a burden, not an affront.

Another element of the negative legacy that still attaches to the term "diversity" is the tension between domestic and global diversity. Now part of this tension is ordinary and probably permanent. It's the simple and straightforward competition for resources. It's important, it needs to be dealt with, but it will most likely not be overcome. What we need to do is acknowledge the competition and manage it productively.

But the competition for resources is not the issue I wish to address today. I am much more concerned about our failure to appreciate the complementarity of domestic and global concerns, and about our tendency to discount the value of one in our effort to promote the other.

As I have suggested, some advocates of attention to the American context fear that global considerations will be at best a distraction, most likely a drain, and at worst a vehicle for avoidance of urgent American concerns. On the other side, advocates of global engagement suspect that the focus on American concerns is yet another example of American incapacity to see beyond its navel. The argument is often made that Americans think their way is the only way, and that their efforts to craft approaches to American diversity really seek to manufacture yet another American export. This tendency was evident in the tri-national discussions at the three seminars I mentioned earlier. Throughout the meetings there was an undercurrent of suspicion that what the Americans were really after was hegemony of their vocabulary, their formulation of the problem, their approach to solutions.

The Americans tried to defend themselves, but we often sounded like white people saying they are not really racists. In other words, we were defending ourselves personally against a structural accusation. Now I won't go so far as to suggest that personal racism is irrelevant, but I will say that I would be prepared to tolerate lots of it if I could rid our American institutions and structures of the racism embedded in them. And I am also prepared to acknowledge that whether or not I personally want my American values and understandings to prevail throughout the world is trivial in comparison to the overwhelming influence of the United States in the world, and its structural tendency to impose its values, tastes, products, and predilections unthinkingly and insensitively on a world without the power to oppose them.

But there is confusion here, and, I think, an intellectual error. An international business consultant once asked me to explain the difference between a multinational corporation and a global one. Knowing that I would politely ask him for the answer, he paused only briefly and provided it. A multinational, he explained, is viewed as multinational only in the country of its origin; everywhere else it is viewed as national. A global corporation, on the other hand, has learned that it must understand the character of its original national culture in order to enter into respectful and productive relationships with global partners.

If our understanding of diversity were influenced more by our educational intentions, I think we would see more clearly that diversity is not merely a matter of getting to know the other, but rather most likely begins with knowing ourselves. What has been the most insistent American question since September 11, 2001? It has been, what does it mean to be an American? I would argue that that is the first iteration of an ultimately global question, and that if we insist on polarization between the domestic and global dimensions of diversity, we will miss the developmental process that the international business consultant was referring to. We will miss the need to know ourselves, indeed, to proceed from self in the direction of wider worlds in which we can be different and the same.

If we want to create institutional accountability for racial and ethnic diversity in the university, we should begin where Robert Cohen did at Wesleyan in the 1950s. We should invoke the educational mission of our institution and ground our endeavor there. We should assert the educational value of diversity, test our assertions through research, assess the outcomes of our educational interventions, and make them part of the learned discourse of the academy. In other words, diversity should become first and foremost, an intellectual pursuit.

The first accountability question we raise should be, "Who has responsibility for leading the discourse?" My answer would be that the leadership role should be shared. It should include faculty who think about these matters intensively and professionally, but it should also include the senior leadership of the institution, and it should draw students into the discourse as partners in the inquiry.

Let me conclude by advancing two arguments in support of my appeal for an educational rationale for diversity. First, the educational rationale proceeds from our publicly recognized expertise. We are educators, and what we advocate takes on greater credibility to the extent that it represents our best educational thinking.

Second, we need to remember that we are accountable for our deployment of resources that come to us from external sources. If we fail to justify everything we do in terms of the purposes for which the resources have been provided, our stewardship of those resources becomes suspect.

If we align our arguments properly, we can preserve the moral underpinnings of our work and at the same time make our advocacy of diversity educationally persuasive.

Education serves our moral purposes. Diversity serves education.

# Chapter 2

## LEADERSHIP, STRATEGY, AND CHANGE: CHALLENGES IN FORGING TIMELY AND EFFECTIVE LEARNING COMMUNITIES

David Maurrasse

Learning communities that enable dialogue and cooperation between groups that don't ordinarily communicate, or may share opposing interests, could be essential to the development of truly democratic, socio-economically just, and pluralistic societies. Higher education is particularly positioned to design and embrace transformational learning communities both internally, through diversifying students, staff, faculty, along with curriculum and programming, as well as externally, through community partnerships and service-learning initiatives. Other institutions can become key venues for such learning as well. But it is important to address the unique aspects of institutions of higher education, as they are designed for dialogue and debate and the shaping and certification of future leaders and overall responsible participants in societies. Moreover, institutions of higher education house expertise in numerous areas, and remain the training ground for most career paths. This is simply to say that this wealth of resources, combined with a social mission, makes higher education a particularly strategic area in which to forge learning communities that can bring about long-lasting societal improvements.

As the world rapidly changes, adapting to new realities emerges as one of the great challenges facing communities, institutions, and industries. What they say about old habits holds true, as we struggle to grapple with shifting from outdated methods to innovative strategies that recognize and embrace undeniable contextual forces or even change those forces themselves. For example, addressing diversity and the dynamics of race, culture, ethnicity, and language may be more complex than living in a world of homogeneity. However, the contextual reality is that working with (as opposed to against) diversity is a matter of acknowledging the essence of today's demographics in the United States. The same would hold true for working with withering boundaries between nations as well as sectors, or with the pace of technological development.

But change is a struggle. The dynamism of human beings simultaneously enables us to adapt to and resist change. This is only facilitated by structural and hierarchical systems that nurture opposing interests. If one group has been systematically denied opportunities, it seeks change, and the group that has wielded the power to determine life chances resists change, as it has grown comfortable with privilege. This shouldn't suggest that less powerful groups or communities do not require change. In fact, adapting to new abilities to wield power and influence require significant change. First of all, the quest for a common good that simultaneously benefits multiple groups remains elusive. Second, a number of compelling efforts to forge partnerships and dialogue between groups signify the potential to birth mutually beneficial scenarios.

While there are multiple opportunities to diversify the composition and nature of higher education and extend the roots of cooperative and mutually beneficial relations between institutions of higher education and communities, the challenges to the flourishing of these concepts remain. In terms of honest and genuine multi-racial and ethnic inter-group dialogue and community partnerships, I see challenges in three areas: leadership, strategy, and change. What kind of leadership is necessary to make the best possible use of inter-group dialogue and community partnerships? Which types of strategies can be effective in this respect? What kinds of changes are required of people and institutions in order to facilitate these efforts and remain relevant as new circumstances arise?

# Leadership

Effective community partnerships and inter-group dialogue both require effective leadership. When large institutions form partnerships with community-based organizations and residents, the question of what truly constitutes an institutional partnership always arises. Corporations may have community relations divisions, universities might have community affairs offices, and hospitals may have clinics. However, a truly institutional commitment likely transcends particular units or divisions, especially when not embraced at the highest levels of decision-making.

It may take an internal coalition to influence major decision-makers, however, because without the commitment of those wielding the power to set policy, the units, divisions, and initiatives lack the philosophical and, often, fiscal support necessary to thrive. Complex organizations are able to support multiple agendas under one roof, but, in the end, those agendas that are embraced by key decision-makers are distinctly positioned to grow and, possibly influence the overall fabric of their environments. In terms of higher education/community partnerships, for example, it has become quite clear that the support of higher tiers of central administrators can make the difference. Inter-group relations within large institutions, in some cases, can be little more than interesting conversation, without leadership committed to addressing diversity and challenging inherent hierarchies and prejudices.

Leadership, however, is critical at all levels. One significant recent change has been the greater incorporation of the ideas of community residents in decision-making, from domestic urban planning to rural international development. A greater willingness has emerged among large foundations, local governments, development agencies, and other institutions to promote community participation in the initiatives that have been designed on their behalf. Because many of these voices have not been solicited in the past, residents need to adjust to such higher expectations. Community participation in such efforts has not come without its critics (1). However, it will be more effective with practical and appropriate leadership development.

The need to enhance the ability of residents to impact their surroundings, both at the ground level and in the halls of decision-making, is only one of many cases for increasing the capacity of community residents and organizations. The growth of the nonprofit sector, and the subsequent creation of an entire industry designed to improve the performance of the many organizations engaged in social activity (2), is more evidence that more skilled and effective leadership is expected at the community level.

The increasing diversity of the United States begs the question of the potential leadership role of new immigrants, and their relationship to populations with longer roots on the American mainland. For many of these communities, the nonprofit sector is the avenue for self-governance. However, as ethnic-specific organizations proliferate, one of the great leadership challenges rests in partnerships across racial and ethnic communities. Community based organizations may be able to facilitate such collaboration. But the challenges of inter-ethnic and inter-racial cooperation, even in shared geographical spaces, cannot be ignored.

Overall, whether within neighborhoods, among community-based organizations, across geographical areas, or between communities and institutions, partnership and collaboration are among the most important leadership concerns. Given the very real interdependence across these various entities, partnerships can maximize opportunity. Among scarce resources, partnership can also be economical and strategic, sharing structures and systems toward common goals.

As the corporate social responsibility movement has grown, so has the need to raise the stakes, by both enhancing the positive contributions of business to society, and by deepening the commitment to social responsibility into the very fabric of corporate expectations and behavior. In 1990, the Prince of Wales International Business Leaders Forum (IBLF) (3) was created in order to encourage corporate CEO's around the world to take leadership around business practices, and collaborate with the public sector and civil society around sustained social, economic, and environmental development. Being truly international in the composition of its staff, and affiliates throughout the world, the IBLF is playing a significant role in forging cross-border dialogue and shared lessons around the potential of corporate resources to be targeted toward addressing some of the world's most pressing social concerns. This is one example of how institutional leadership can transcend traditional approaches, and take greater responsibility for a common good.

## Strategy

If leadership can identify the need to adapt, and develop strategies accordingly, the road to change is paved. Strategic thinking is often informed by environmental concerns in combination with the current status of organizations, groups, or individuals. Issues that once were not considered central to strategic plans, such as community partnerships and inter-group dialogue are now more critical to institutions' ability to do business than ever. A corporation cannot survive if it cannot communicate with diverse markets, and major institutions in general will be at a disadvantage if they are disliked by their surrounding communities.

Similar dynamics hold true from a community perspective. Strategically, it makes sense for communities to leverage local assets, but also seek out resources from institutions that may be perceived as external, but have a great deal to provide in order to bring about community impact. The challenge for many communities, especially those that are low income, is that partnerships with well-resourced institutions have sometimes resulted in limited benefits to residents. Strategically, communities will need to enhance their abilities in developing partnerships and ensure that they are gaining from their endeavors with institutions of higher education, corporations, hospitals and other large institutions. The more communities can strategically articulate the issues which they confront, and ensure that resources and information from their partners are being targeted accordingly, the healthier partnerships will become.

However, strategic collaboration is relevant both between communities and institutions, as well as within them. How does any community develop a representative voice? Coalitions of organizations, community boards, neighborhood councils, no matter the formation, everyone's voice will not necessarily be heard, and voices are not uniform. Homeowners and renters in the same neighborhood, for example, may articulate different perceptions of a neighborhood's needs. This is all to say that perfection is elusive, however, community partnerships that involve multiple parties in forming a uniform platform are closer to representation than a singular organization or individual speaking for an entire community. It is too easy for an institution to say it is in partnership when it only works with one organization, or one particular sector within a community. Efforts that are strategic in ensuring the inclusion of various needs within communities are more likely to secure some sense of buy-in from a wider audience.

Institutions that recognize the value of community partnerships to their survival are increasingly seeing local communities as important stakeholders in their futures. Community partnerships, and a willingness to address diversity and the challenges presented by historical and embedded forms of discrimination, can help a major institution design strategies that are far-reaching, yet within the parameters of essential core aims. The social responsibility industry has created a climate where corporations must pay attention to where they are ranked on various socially conscious indexes, and institutions of higher education wish to be recognized as genuine community partners. As the language in various industries becomes more tailored to ethics and responsibility, more strategic agendas that make note of communities, philanthropy, and service have emerged. Nevertheless, designing and articulating strategies are easier than implementing them. An institution can create as many projects and "charitable" initiatives as possible, but a willingness to change is essential in order for any partnership to become genuine or any inter-group dialogue to transcend historical forms of oppression and festering tensions.

Despite the end of Apartheid in South Africa, the need to provide economic development for the country's majority remains a priority. Strategically figuring out how to address such a challenge within the concept of existing market systems became essential. Shared Interest, a social investment fund exclusively focusing on economic development in South Africa, created the Thembani International Guarantee Fund (4), which grants guarantees to local South African banks. These banks, in return, provide credit to community development financial institutions, community-based intermediaries, and NGOs. This creative approach has led to increased affordable housing, improved micro-enterprises, and greater rural development.

## Change

Complex organizations do not change overnight, nor do people. External forces ultimately drive change in institutions, and what appears as traditional and set in stone ultimately seems more like clay. Change management scholars have identified multiple steps involved in institutional change (5), underscoring the difficulty and time consumption involved in any process that leads to new projects, new approaches, and new ways of thinking.

Higher education, like many other industries, often wears the face of permanency, but historically, the priorities in the industry have been driven by, largely economic, external conditions (Maurrasse, 2001). One of the more critical challenges to higher education/community partnerships has been the limited available rewards. Within many institutions of higher education, community partnerships might be praised for the positive public relations they can bring to colleges and universities. However the recognition often ends there, particularly in major research institutions (Maurrasse, 2001). Although some other types of institutions of higher education, that place a stronger emphasis on teaching and research, may be more sensitive to the significance of partnerships, limited resources hinder the potential of community partnerships in places such as community colleges to broadly impact our overall expectations of higher education.

Ernest Boyer (1990) challenged higher education to reflect upon its priorities and the limitations of extant rewards systems. As the movement to promote civic engagement in institutions of higher education grows, so do the critics of traditional systems of review, promotion, and tenure (6).

Despite the growing sentiment, much more can be done in order to make institutions of higher education more conducive to effective community partnerships. If an institution creates multiple initiatives designed to work with communities, it is a mistake to imagine that those initiatives can persist effectively without institutional change. In a genuine partnership, both parties should be willing to change—to adapt to circumstances in order to spawn a mutually beneficial arrangement. Too often low income and urban communities are perceived as recipients of services, who remain in need, rather than valuable contributors with something to teach. Large institutions such as universities bring extensive resources and knowledge to the table, but community wisdom can be helpful to institutions of higher education as well, as evidenced in the numerous research projects that have been conducted on urban residents, and low-income people. The reality, as David Cox often argues, is that partnerships create new knowledge, only furthering the mission of higher education.

With respect to community partnerships, the question remains: will major institutions do what it takes to adapt (7) in order to facilitate genuine initiatives? In the case of higher education, what will be done to address the obstacles to community partnerships due to narrow reward systems? In some institutions, the mere mention of *service-learning* brings visions of *vocational* enterprises that lack scholarship. Applied research in some settings, may be seen as *practice* as opposed to *scholarship*. This dichotomous thinking is a remnant of higher education's near past. Although resistance will persist, the societal context suggests that it is in higher education's best interest to firmly identify with its surrounding communities, support applied research that can lead to concrete benefits in communities, and educate students in a fashion that builds their skills as well as their ability to work in diverse communities.

The conditions of surrounding neighborhoods do effect all types of institutions of higher education. Some institutions may need to recruit locally to survive, while others need to reside in healthy communities in order to recruit. Local residents will more likely cooperate with the aims of institutions of higher education (from research projects to real estate development) if they receive some gain from those efforts.

A growing sentiment outside of higher education calls for more "real world," solution-based approaches. In the eyes of a growing number, higher education is only valuable for certification, but less so for practical learning. The new generation entering higher education is increasingly seeking out efforts that provide new, hands-on, learning experiences that may, on the one hand, be marketable in job searches, but on the other, provide meaningful processes that transform thinking and break down stereotypes and misperceptions. Future leaders will require a certain sensitivity and empathy for various cultures and life circumstances.

Social issues are increasingly integrated, yet higher education remains segmented. As institutions of higher education further delve into community partnerships, they see the potential of interdisciplinary teams and the limitations of narrow disciplinary lenses. The nature of research is often perceived as useless, unreadable, and inaccessible. In a sputtering economy, such as the present recession, more critical eyes will turn toward what appears to have little use and impact. We will all witness the salivating as the federal government finds its way into large endowments, often thought of as sacred and untouchable at some of the most reputable universities. If well-endowed nonprofit institutions are forced to spend more of their endowment funds, what better way to do so than through community partnerships? This could simultaneously release funds and provide solutions that benefit citizens and create knew knowledge and educate compassionate and civic-minded students. As previously mentioned, external forces will lead to change within higher education and other major institutions. In observing the societal trends and sentiments it makes more sense to prepare to change in accordance with the times than to resist change in order to hold tightly to anachronistic "traditions".

Some of the slowest institutions to change, institutions of higher education, are actually well positioned to lead change, as their focus on scholarly debate surfaces new ideas. Unfortunately, new ideas don't always lead to institutional change. Sometimes institutions are pushed to alter old practices because of reality.

As many urban areas began to deteriorate, and resources began to move to surrounding areas, an urban location became viewed as a liability rather than an asset among many colleges and universities situated in such setting. The University of Milwaukee at Wisconsin is one example of an institution that had not been taking full advantage of its urban location. Upon the arrival of a new president in 1998, Nancy Zimpher, the university began to change that perspective, realizing that it could simultaneously improve the overall surrounding community and enhance its relevance as an institution of higher education. As a result, the university created the Milwaukee Idea (8). This sweeping effort changed the core curriculum to emphasize multiculturalism and service learning, improved partnerships with local public schools, instituted new technical assistance efforts around economic development, and improved the local environment, among others.

We can expect the kind of learning communities that widely disperse benefits within multiple environments. They will have leadership that recognizes changing realities and the potential role of particular sectors or groups in forging a more humane and relevant society. They will develop strategies that are genuine, extensively beneficial and timely, and will demonstrate a willingness to change in order to adapt to today's needs as well as forge social, economic, and political improvements throughout the world.

## Notes

1. A couple of examples of articles that explore the various dynamics of the role of community participation in planning include: Margerum, Richard D. "Collaborative Planning: Building Consensus and Building a Distinct Model of Practice" in *Journal of Planning Education and Research*. Volume 21, pp. 237-253, 2002. Booher, David E. and Judith Innes. "Network Power in Collaborative Planning" in *Journal of Planning Education and Research*. Volume 21, pp. 221-236, 2002.

2. The Alliance for Nonprofit Management has created its own learning community of organizations and individuals committed to increasing the effectiveness of the nonprofit sector. More on the Alliance can be found at allianceonline.org.

3. More information on IBLF can be found on its website, IBLF.org.

4. Thembani is a Zulu word for "We give hope and encouragement." More on Shared Interest and this particular effort can be found at Sharedinterest.org. Shared Interest was founded in 1994, and is based in New York City.

5. One example is Harvard Business School professor, John Kotter's 1996 Harvard Business School Press book, *Leading Change*, which suggests that successful change is an eight step process, moving from establishing a sense of urgency to creating the guiding coalition to developing a vision and strategy to communicating the change vision to empowering broad-based action to generating short term wins to consolidating gains and producing more change to anchoring new approaches to culture. This process is clearly diagramed on page 21 of this well-known book.

6. The American Association for Higher Education's Forum on Faculty Roles and Rewards has attempted to expand academic rewards to be more inclusive of service and outreach. Their guide, *Making Outreach Visible* (1999), by Amy Driscoll and Earnest Lynton captures various examples of faculty who are deeply involved in service and outreach, and how they articulated the scholarly contributions of these efforts.

7. In their 2000 book, *High Performance Nonprofit Organizations* (Wiley), Christine Letts, William Ryan, and Allen Grossman introduce the concept of "adaptive capacity", where organizations are able to stay focused on a mission, but can be flexible enough to adapt to change.

8. A compelling history and analysis of the Milwaukee idea can be found in the Department of Housing and Urban Development's second volume of its "Lasting Engagement" series, entitled, *The Milwaukee Idea: A Study of Transformative Change*.

## References

Boyer, E. (1990). *Scholarship reconsidered: Priorities of the professoriate*. Princeton, NJ: Carnegie Foundation for the Advancement of Teaching.

Bradley, B., Jensen, P., and Silverman, L. (2003) The Non-Profit Sector's $100 Billion Opportunity, *Harvard Business Review*. vol 81, 5 (May 2003) pp 94-103.

Letts, C.W., Ryan, W.P., & Grossman, A. (2001). *High performance nonprofit organizations: Managing upstream for greater impact*. New York: John Wiley & Sons.

Maurrasse, D. (2001). *Beyond the Campus: How colleges and universities form partnerships with their communities*. New York: Routledge.

# Chapter 3

## SUCCESS AND CHALLENGES OF COMMUNITY-BASED TEACHING, LEARNING, AND RESEARCH: A NATIONAL PERSPECTIVE

John O'Connor

### Moving from the Backwater to the Mainstream

Metaphors for change often involve water. There are the slow drips of change, hurricanes and tsunami, whitewater rivers, and tidal shifts. A glass is half full or half empty. Each image alludes to the fluidity and rate of change. Each of these metaphors has been used over the past score of years to describe the engagement of colleges and universities with their communities. They have shifted, however, from references to disengaged students and campuses (Campus Compact formed in 1985 as a response to this disengagement) to a recognition that while civic or community engagement is happening on individual campuses, it is still too often a backwater or small pools-not the mainstream-and could dry up.

From some perspectives, it appears that the wave of community-campus relationships has swelled enough to change the landscape in higher education. Others, however, believe this wave too will wash away, leaving the fundamental landscape unchanged. Living-learning programs, such as The Michigan Community Scholars Program (MCSP, highlighted in this book) and The University of Maryland Civicus program that focus on public and community issues are being developed at a number of campuses around the nation. Service-learning programs have grown dramatically over the past dozen years. Federal programs such as Learn and Serve America and Community Outreach Partnership Centers (COPC) that fund community-based teaching and learning have weathered the ebb and flow of political changes in the White House and the Congress. Community-based research networks are forming, and the "scholarship of engagement" has become a recognizable term on many campuses.

This article briefly surveys some of the activities, programs, and projects developing on campuses through the support of higher education associations. It is a partial update of earlier surveys done by the Campus Compact and the Surdna Foundation (www.compact.org), and Elizabeth Hollander's and Matthew Hartley's fine chapter, "Civic Renewal in Higher Education: The State of the Movement and the Need for a National Network" in *Civic Responsibility and Higher Education*, edited by Thomas Ehrlich (2000).

### Meaning and Usage of Terms

While much is happening, fundamental disagreements still arise about what we are doing or talking about. The terms used in this field are contested. *Civic* is sometimes used in contrast to political; sometimes political is a subset of civic, and other times they are used interchangeably. In addition, civic has a connotation of elitism and exclusion for some. *Citizen* is used interchangeably, and confusingly, as both a legal and moral concept, with the emphasis varying regionally around the country. *Community* can be used so broadly that it becomes meaningless. In addition, community is not always a positive term; needing to add adjectives such as "diverse" or "inclusive" before community reflects a history of exclusion and repression. *Civic competence* has received considerable attention recently, but it also faces contention. *Competence* carries the baggage of past attempts to limit who can vote—the landless or poor, women, and minorities have been excluded on the basis of supposed lack of competence. As an overarching phrase "community-based teaching, learning, and research" seems to be more explicit, inclusive, and neutral than some commonly used terms. While keeping the term community, the rest of the phrase avoids historical connotations, emphasizes learning grounded in experience, and connects faculty roles of teaching and research. The phrase is also growing in currency as a way of describing reciprocal campus-community partnerships rather than one-directional outreach programs.

Whatever the terms, disagreements about language reveal strongly held differences about the relationship between politics, morality, and education. Colby (2003) presents a helpful argument about these differences in the opening chapter of *Educating Citizens*. An instance of this debate has been the differing views about service-learning, resulting in a hyphenated phrase to indicate both service and learning are important and are interrelated, though some point to the implicit inequality in the notion of service. Any discussion of Dewey and education is likely to reveal significant differences in opinions about experiential education, teaching values, and politics in the classroom. Adopting the "teach the differences" perspective, definitional debates can be used in our classrooms and communities to explore the intersection of politics, morality, and education.

For example, a number of colleges and universities are setting explicit learning goals for civic and/or citizenship skills and knowledge and assessing whether teaching and learning are meeting those goals. Colleges and universities as different as Alverno, California State—Monterey Bay, New Century College at George Mason, Portland State, and Tusculum have attempted to define a competency for citizenship. These programs include components such as a self-reflective/reflexive element that recognizes the context and connotations that the language choice entails.

## Survey of Current Initiatives

Whatever the terms, many national higher education associations are deeply committed to various forms of civic engagement or community-based teaching, learning, and research. Most of these projects employ the strategy of organizing a cohort of schools to support change on campus. Since forming in 1985, Campus Compact has been a leader in community-based teaching and learning. A Presidential organization, Campus Compact "promotes community service that develops students' citizenship skills and values, encourages partnerships between campuses and communities, and assists faculty who seek to integrate public and community engagement into their teaching and research" (http://www.compact.org). Member campuses foster a supportive campus environment for the engagement in community service so that they can prepare their students to be "active, committed, and informed citizens and leaders of their communities" (http://www.compact.org/aboutcc/mission.html). Campus Compact programs, publications, and meetings are the first that look for broadly defined community-based teaching, learning, and research with an explicit linkage to political engagement.

The American Association for Higher Education (AAHE) also has a continuing involvement in campus-community relationships through a series of conferences dating back to 1985 and a 20-volume publication on *Service-Learning in the Disciplines*. Most recently, AAHE has begun a project on The Engaged Campus for Diverse Democracy. The project goal is to identify pedagogies that promote student citizenship and responsibility for the public good, and mend the disjuncture between individual learning and public work in a pluralistic society. Initiatives undertaken as part of this project will result in powerful models—such as faculty and staff development for deliberative discussion and dialogue, good practices for integrating community-based teaching and scholarship, and linking separate campus initiatives to support diverse democracy—for what can be done in higher education to teach and practice civic participation in a diverse democracy. The University of Michigan, with MCSP as the team leader, is one of eight colleges and universities partnering with AAHE and the Ford Foundation in developing this project.

Carnegie Foundation for the Advancement of Teaching and Learning, primarily through research by Ann Colby and Thomas Ehrlich, has supported education for responsible, engaged citizenship among college students. The first phase of their project documented 13 higher education undergraduate moral and civic educations. The new phase, the Political Engagement Project, will document and study a diverse collection of 21 academic courses and programs that represent creative approaches to undergraduate political education, including summer institutes on political knowledge and skills, a semester in Washington program, internships, and multi-year living-learning programs focusing on political engagement.

The Association of American Colleges and Universities' (AAC&U) vision of liberal learning includes a sharp focus on developing students' civic capacities, their sense of social responsibility, and commitment to public action. AAC&U initiatives concentrate on the promise and reality of American democracy and the commitment to building more just and equitable communities worldwide. AAC&U publications, *Liberal Education* and *Peer Review* consistently address issues of civic learning and education. Their most recent project, Journey Towards Democracy: Power, Voice, and the Public Good is a national dialogue by seven colleges and universities about putting student learning about democracy and the public good at the center of academic inquiry.

The Association of American State Colleges and Universities (AASCU) has recently initiated a three year American Democracy Project in conjunction with the *New York Times*. This national initiative aims to increase the number of undergraduate students engaged in meaningful civic actions by encouraging participating campuses "to review and restructure academic and extracurricular activities as well as the institutional culture making civic engagement more intentional" (http://www.aascu.org/programs/adp/about/default.htm). 144 AASCU institutions, representing more than 1.3 million students, are involved in the project.

The Society for Values in Higher Education, building on its historic work in values inquiry, has initiated the Democracy Project to explore the role of democratic dialogue in the campus classroom, internal decision-making processes, and partnership with communities. It has drawn upon the new National Coalition for Dialogue and Deliberation to develop models of democratic dialogue as pedagogy and decision-making tools.

The Council of Independent Colleges' program, Engaging Communities and Campuses assists independent colleges and universities to establish partnerships with community organizations that can enhance experiential learning activities through addressing community needs. It has offered workshops and grants to schools to foster institutional civic engagement.

The American Association of Community Colleges, with support from the Corporation for National Service, has been a leader in promoting service-learning. Community Colleges Broadening Horizons through Service Learning, has worked to integrate service-learning into the institutional climate of community colleges since 1994.

There are also projects based in disciplinary organizations such as the Communicating Common Ground program of the National Communications Association, and the Health Professions Schools in Service to the Nation located at the University of California, San Francisco.

## Common Features

Many of these projects offer case studies of individual institutions and research data from the individual projects, but the results have not been widely distributed nor the collective impact of these projects considered. As Barbara Holland (2001) has noted "A synthesis of these important projects would immediately generate broader, deeper, more compelling information that could accelerate our work on implementation and documentation."

What are some of the common features of these programs and projects?

## Student Focused

Even those programs that address the institutional level often see the product as curricular. The programs have implications for faculty and professional staff roles as educators, but less frequently confront their roles as citizens, researchers, and public scholars. The knowledge generated by faculty on college and university campuses is disconnected from the growing need for applied knowledge in a society increasingly dependent on its citizens' intellectual capital and capacity to learn. More fundamentally (for the academy), community-based research is an epistemological challenge to the more traditional view of scholarship and the dominant way knowledge is generated in the academy. As Gene Rice (2002) has noted,

> *Pure research that is objective, abstract, and analytical is most highly valued and has legitimacy because it can be peer reviewed by cosmopolitan colleagues, in national and international refereed journals, independent of place. Community-based research calls for a new appreciation for the wisdom of practice. It is of necessity local—rooted in a particular time and setting. It also needs to be collaborative, valuing the local community perspective and bringing it into every phase of the research process. It also requires that the learning be multidirectional, not university centered and campus bound (personal correspondence).*

## Discussion and Dialogue

Much of the most recent work has been on discussion and dialogue. This strategy fits well within the strengths of higher education and may be an essential first step to develop understanding before action. The Kettering Foundation has a useful rubric for how civic engagement can be learned:

- Learning By Doing—The Public Service Component
- Learning by Talking—Acquiring Deliberative Skills
- Learning by Practicing—Democratizing the Campus
- Learning by Learning—A Classical Academic Model

Each method of learning has a value and use. The second and fourth models better fit the traditions of campuses and classrooms. They do not challenge the traditional conceptions of knowledge building through reading, writing, and discussing, but they also implicitly diminish the value of "knowing in action" and reflective practice. Too often the distinction is made between academic study in the classroom, taught in a manner that actually undercuts democratic engagement, and the "application" of the academic knowledge in the community. The best of programs (for example intergroup dialogue programs at various colleges and the University of Michigan) combine both ways of knowing. Democratic pedagogies integrate the knowledge, skills, and aptitudes essential for active and democratic civic participation.

## Diversity

Diversity is too often haphazardly addressed in our civic and community projects. AAC&U has a longstanding connection between diversity and democracy through its American Commitments: Diversity, Democracy, and Liberal Learning program among others, and AAHE's current project is Engaged Campus for a Diverse Democracy. But on many campuses and in many national projects, diversity and civic/community/democratic engagement run on parallel tracks. Intersection needs to be made more explicit and intentional as David Schoem (2002) urges in his recent essay, "Transforming Undergraduate Education," in *Change*.

The need to support diverse democracy has become more compelling since the September

11th, 2001, terrorist attacks in the United States as well as longer-term terrorist activity throughout the world in the last decade. Although the recent tragedies and current war have evoked frequently a sensitive awareness of religious and cultural differences in the United States, the misunderstanding, stereotyping, scapegoating, and acts of hatred that have resulted reveal the gap between American ideals of diverse democracy and the ability to enact them. The long-term health of our global society depends on more than military preparation. The United States must increase the ability of people to work together to solve profoundly complex problems. And the ability to work together must recognize that groups and individuals may have significantly different perspectives. College and university campuses provide necessary knowledge as well as opportunities for sustained interaction and spaces for democratic dialogue. As such, they may be the most opportune venue to practice democratic engagement.

At a time when the tide seems to be rising in support of community-based teaching, learning, and research, many of the large national foundations—notably Ford, Hewlett, Kellogg, Pew, and Atlantic Philanthropies—have backed away from funding higher education projects in favor of direct support for community development and K-12 initiatives. A common explanation is that higher education is a system that is hard to change; the tide comes in and goes out, but the landscape stays the same. Another explanation is that direct support to communities allows them to decide how to call upon the resources of colleges and universities rather than being dependent upon higher education's decisions. And K-12, another seemingly immovable system, has more compelling needs.

While subject to the shifting currents of partisan politics and White House ideology, the federal government has continued to support campus-community activities in a variety of forms and programs. The most notable programs are Community Outreach Partnership Centers (COPC); the Corporation for National Service, which includes Learn and Serve America and AmeriCorps; and the new "We the People" initiative at National Endowment for the Humanities. Each of these programs encourages connections between campuses and communities, and between analysis and practice. Some on campus and in the community are concerned about the ideological bias the Bush administration is imposing upon these departments, and as the continuing battles for funding support—especially for AmeriCorps—makes clear, many a conservative politician or think tank would love to be rid of these federal programs. Still, three years into this administration, the guidelines leave some room for variety and innovation in community partnerships.

# Conclusion

So, half full or half empty? Is the tide coming in or going out? Are we moving into the mainstream or are we in a backwater? The rise in numbers and quality of community-based academic work suggests the positive. The most recent survey of political beliefs and activities by the Harvard Institute of Politics points to increasing student engagement in their communities and in politics. A 2002 Campus Compact publication *The New Student Politics: The Wingspread Statement on Student Civic Engagement* describes how current student political and civic engagement does not fit our past categories and conceptions. In addition, as the projects described in this chapter mature, surveys and studies will have to consider political and civic involvement at the local, community level. There is much to be hopeful about, and to be done.

## References

American Democracy Project. (2003) Association of American State Colleges and Universities. (http://www.aascu.org/programs/adp).

Campus Compact. (2002) http://www.compact.org.

Colby, A. and T. Ehrlich, E. Beaumont, and J. Stephens (2003). *Educating citizens: Preparing America's Undergraduates for Lives of Moral and Civic Responsibility.* San Francisco: Jossey-Bass.

Hollander, E. and M. Hartley (2000). Civic renewal in higher education: The state of the movement and the need for a national network. In T. Ehrlich (Ed.). *Civic responsibility and higher education* (pp. 345-66). Phoenix, AZ: Oryz Press.

Holland, B. Progress toward Strategies to Evaluate Civic Engagement: paradoxes and conundrums." *Campus Compact Reader*. summer 2001.

Rice, G. personal correspondence.

Schoem, D. (2002). Transforming undergraduate education. *Change*, vol 34,6. (Nov-Dec 2002) pp. 50-55.

# Chapter 4

## LEARNING COMMUNITIES: RENEWING A COMMITMENT TO CIVIC ENGAGEMENT

Nancy S. Shapiro

## Introduction

Back in 1996, when the residential learning communities at the University of Maryland were only two years old, the university administration asked if the *College Park Scholars (CPS)* program would help them out of a jam. At the time, massive construction projects were disrupting traffic patterns around the campus, and the campus anticipated mayhem on freshman move-in day at the end of August. CPS was asked to move in 500 freshmen one day early, and then take them far away from campus the next day to ease some of the gridlock congestion around the residence halls. Little did we know that this request, made out of expediency, would have implications far beyond that orientation week and lead to a fundamental, mission-driven, curricular innovation for the program and the university.

"Necessity is the mother of invention," and we planned a one-day community service project, which involved sending 50 groups of 10 students, with faculty members and a residence counselors, out to the community to paint school playgrounds, clean up trails in the parks, and plant flowers in the median strips around town. We gave out yellow T-shirts and box lunches, piled everyone on busses, and dropped off our freshman service "platoons" at pre-arranged locations around the town of College Park. Six hours later, we picked them up again, brought them back to campus for a "reflection" session with ice cream and sodas. We also asked the Freshman Composition instructors give students an option of writing about their experience for the first diagnostic essay of the semester—thus, we ended up with an un-scientific, but relatively broad-based set of informal evaluations of the project.

The response to the "day-of-service" was beyond all expectation. Students bonded with each other by working and sweating together in the August heat. They bonded with faculty and residence counselors who rolled up their sleeves and got dirt under their fingernails. The bus drivers gave impromptu tours, and the new freshmen learned a little about the way the town was laid out, where the parks are, where to get hair cuts, and fresh bagels. But most remarkable of all, in just one day, they were transformed from 500 nervous freshmen into a community that had already made a positive contribution to their new "home town." They were tired and proud and happy.

One student summed up the experience: "I came here from New Jersey and I've only been here for one day, but I'm going to change my voter registration to Maryland, because I want to make sure the city of College Park keeps up the maintenance on the recreation area we cleaned today!"

What happened here? This was not curriculum-based service-learning (1)—but every journey begins with a single step. This was not sophisticated civic engagement—but commitments, like buildings, are built one brick at a time. This was not an integrated learning community (2)—but bonds were formed which would provide the foundation for such a community. As a result of this serendipitous solution to a campus traffic problem, Orientation Service Days have become a standard activity initiation activity for our integrated, authentic service-learning curriculum. Service-learning is built into every learning community through credit-bearing colloquia and capstone experiences that go far beyond the day of service, but that first "day-of-service" is an important strategy that raises students' awareness of the responsibilities of public service and civic engagement in their communities.

# Higher Education and the Tradition of Civic Education

If one were to examine the missions of institutions of higher education across the country, one would find that most of them include a word or phrase referring to educating for citizenship. American public education was founded on such a premise. In a letter written in 1820, Thomas Jefferson tied the endurance of a civil society to the education of its citizens. He wrote: "I know of no safe repository of the ultimate powers of the society but the people themselves; and if we think them not enlightened enough to exercise control with a wholesome discretion, the remedy is not to take it from them, but to inform their discretion by education" (Jefferson, 1820).

What was true in Jefferson's time is no less true today. Frank Newman, past president of Education Commission of the States, wrote in 1985: "If there is a crisis in education in the United States today, it is less that test scores have declined than it is that we have failed to provide the education for citizenship that is still the most important responsibility of the nations' schools and colleges" (Newman, 1985).

While educators at every level are responsible for civic education, higher education has a special responsibility. Today we have a society where close to 70% of our high school students go on to college—and we know that college students are developmentally ready to make great leaps in their critical thinking abilities and their personal commitments. College is the right time for students to embrace civic values and participation. National studies, such as those undertaken by the Association of American Colleges and Universities (*Greater Expectations,* 2002) confirm that colleges and universities are committed to graduating citizens who understand and accept their individual responsibility for democratic government.

Yet, in spite of the obvious connections between college attendance and political participation, not only has voter turnout in American elections plunged in recent years, but the drop has been particularly pronounced among the young. In the recent election in November 2002, as has happened over the past decade, fewer young people exercised their right to vote than any other year in our history. According to the *Washington Post,* voter turnout in the 2002 election was only 35% nationwide, and among young people between the ages of 18 and 24, the turnout was a mere 12% (Hill and Robinson, 2002).

The Pew Charitable Trust established a National Commission on Civic Renewal, chaired by Sam Nunn and William Bennett. In their report, they addressed the civic health of the nation:

*Too many of us have become passive and disengaged. Too many of us lack confidence in our capacity to make basic moral and civic judgments, to join with our neighbors to do the work of community, to make a difference. Never have we had so many opportunities of participation, yet rarely have we felt so powerless. In a time that cries out for civic action, we are in danger of becoming a nation of spectators (National Commission on Civic Renewal, 1998).*

If we compare today's young adults, not with today's older adults, but with young adults of the past, we find increasing evidence of diminished civic attachment. In the early 1970s, about half of the 18-25 year-olds voted in presidential elections. By 1996, less than one-third did. The same pattern holds for congressional elections—about one-third voting in the 1970s, compared to less than one-fifth in 1998. In 2002 we see a decline to one-eighth (Battistoni, 2002).

We can look at the dismaying trends charted by the annual UCLA Higher Education Research Institute survey. Their studies conducted since the mid-1960s and involving roughly

250,000 matriculating college freshmen each year found that over the three decades since the initiation of this survey, every indicator of political engagement has fallen by at least half.

- Only 26 percent of freshmen think that keeping up with politics is important, down from 58 percent in 1966.
- Only 14 percent say they frequently discuss politics, down from 30 percent.

Traditionally, as the median level of education rises, we expect the median level of political knowledge to rise. Yet recent studies show just the opposite. According to a famous study by Robert Putnam, *Bowling Alone* (1995), for many categories of political knowledge, today's high school graduates are roughly equivalent to the high school dropouts of the late 1940s. At the same time, today's college graduates are roughly equivalent to the high school graduates of the 40s.

But higher education's responsibility to engage young people in pursuit of a civil society goes beyond basic voter behavior. Scandals and lawsuits involving companies like Enron, and Microsoft have eroded confidence and trust in American business and government as well. Two hundred years ago, James Madison suggested that republican government presupposes more trustworthy human qualities-more virtues-than does any other form of government. Throughout our history movements for better government, civil rights, and real democracy thrived on the efforts of young people.

## Learning Communities and Civic Awareness

Why are learning communities particularly well positioned to take the lead in bringing a generation of young adults into civic awareness? One reason is that learning communities depend on a more participatory involvement from all the diverse members of that community, than traditional curricular structures (such as majors, or departments). Learning communities neatly weave together academic, residential, student affairs, and co-curricular components toward a common goal. By their very nature and structure, learning communities require participation and many learning communities incorporate service learning as the curricular vehicle to move toward that goal.

In *Civic Responsibility and Higher Education* (2000), Thomas Ehrlich challenged higher education to take to heart John Dewey's philosophy that our democratic society requires civic engagement of our citizens, and that civic engagement requires an educated citizenry. A very concrete outcome of Ehrlich's work has been the validation, and subsequent significant increase in service-learning opportunities on our campuses. The National Center for Educational Statistics defines service learning as "curriculum-based community service that integrates classroom instruction with community service activities." Over the past decade, we have experienced the most rapid growth in this curricular innovation. As of last year, 32 percent of all public schools had incorporated service learning into their curricula, including a remarkable 46 percent of high schools and well over half of the college and universities in the U.S. have signed on with the Campus Compact.

While overall the evaluation of specific service-learning programs yields mixed results, a massive study of more than 22,000 college students the CIRP Freshman Survey found that the positive effects of service by individual students are amplified by discussion of service experiences among students. Service learning is especially effective in generating positive attitudes and behaviors toward civic engagement, because it is structured to encourage such student-to-student discussion (Sax, 2000, p. 5).

In addition to the curricular innovation of service learning, our institutions of higher education provide "diversities of many kinds," as the Boyer Commission Report characterized them (Boyer 1998). Colleges and universities pride themselves in being safe havens where students grow in tolerance and respect for diversity, learn to transcend social and economic boundaries, and become responsible citizens ready to participate in a multi-cultural society. Our challenge is not to invent civic renewal from scratch, but rather to find ways in which higher education, and in particular, learning communities can build an expectation among our students to continue to participate in civil society after they leave our campuses.

Service Learning has proven to be a robust component of learning communities. But service learning by itself will not necessarily result in fostering the broad-based, sustainable civic engagement we so urgently need. In fact, The National Commission on Civic Engagement (1998) found that young people are not apathetic. Their findings revealed that young people were volunteering in their communities more than ever. But, as the Pew-supported researchers discovered, although more students are volunteering, fewer are voting. "On the one hand, young people are volunteering their services in record numbers," said director William Galston. "On the other hand, young people are disengaging from the institutions through which binding public decisions are made" (Galston, 2002). This is a troubling trend, with long ranging consequences.

In *Bowling Alone* (1995), Robert Putnam talked about the "norms and networks of civic engagement" that knit a community together. According to Putnam, people who come together in formal and informal associations—like clubs, or community service groups, or neighborhood networks—learn the benefits of collective action toward shared goals. These "networks of interaction" broaden the participants' sense of self, developing the "I" into the "we." Learning community leaders recognize that Putnam has described one of the most predictable outcomes of a learning community. In the most successful learning communities, egocentric, dualistic "I's" become altruistic, inclusive "we's." But Putnam has triggered a new twist on our familiar developmental model. Putnam's work draws from the perspective of sociology, rather than the perspective of psychology. His research suggests that civic stances shaped during the teen and early adult years persist throughout adult life.

Beyond the formal structures that bind linked classes, shared living arrangements, and dedicated advisors, learning communities intentionally builds "informal associations" for students as they work toward shared goals. It is the informal associations that sociologists link to increased civic engagement in the broader population. The challenge is to persuade leaders in higher education that they should make civic engagement an essential student learning outcome, bringing it back to the core mission of the institutions. Mission statements drive strategic plans, and strategic plans determine priorities for funding and staffing. Investing in learning communities can be interpreted as part of a larger, mission-driven strategic plan, consistent with the larger mission of developing engaged citizens. Learning communities contribute to the development of good citizenship among students, while investing in the long term welfare of the larger society: Learning communities can do *well* by doing *good*.

While each campus and institution must make its own determination of priorities and program elements that reflect mission-driven commitment to civic education and engagement, the suggestions below offer a range of possible implementation strategies:

1. Invite political candidates and public official to campus and create venues for debate and discussion.
2. Create internships and opportunities for students to shadow public leaders.
3. Create awards for public service.
4. Create high level advisory boards on your campus to work closely with non-profits and link to national centers.
5. Raise money from corporate sponsors to send student leaders to national meetings.
6. Partner with public schools to make them part of the larger "learning community" on campus.
7. Publicly commit to increased civic engagement as an outcome for the community and alumni, and then include it in curricular planning, strategic planning, and in models for

program accountability and assessment.

# Conclusion

The heart of the American conception of civil liberty is that it offers citizens the power to act to improve the conditions of their lives, and thus strengthens their conviction that they can make a difference. Urgent times make special demands on those who help shape the goals and purposes of higher education. In the wake of current events-9/11 terrorist attacks, the anthrax scare, the sniper shootings, and the damaging reality of corporate corruption, it is time to revisit a more visible and public role for higher education. It is time to put the goal of civic engagement at the forefront of our institutional missions, and learning communities can lead our universities and colleges toward this goal. As more and more young people go from high school to college, academic leaders should take advantage of the opportunity to build our capacity for democratic principles and values.

Why should higher education invest in learning communities? Because learning communities educate for democracy.

## Notes

1. Service-learning is the various pedagogies that link community service and academic study so that each strengthens the other. The basic theory of service-learning is Dewey's: the interaction of knowledge and skills with experience is key to learning. Students learn best not by reading the Great Books in a closed room but by opening the doors and windows of experience. Learning starts with a problem and continues with the application of increasingly complex ideas and increasingly sophisticated skills to increasingly complicated problems. (Thomas Ehrlich, "Foreword" (pp.xi-xii) in Barbara Jacoby and Associates, *Service-Learning in Higher Education: Concepts and Practices*. San Francisco, CA: Jossey-Bass. 1996)

2. In higher education, curricular learning communities are classes that are linked or clustered during an academic term, often around an interdisciplinary theme, and enroll a common cohort of students. A variety of approaches are used to build these learning communities, with all intended to restructure the students' time, credit, and learning experiences to build community among students, between students and their teachers, and among faculty members and disciplines. (Definition from National Learning Communities Project website: http://learningcommons.evergreen.edu/)

## References

Association of American Colleges and Universities. (2002). *Greater expectations*. Washington, DC: Author.

Battistoni, R.M. (2002). *Civic Engagement across the Curriculum*. Brown University Providence, RI: Campus Compact.

Boyer Commission on Educating Undergraduates. (1998). *Reinventing undergraduate education: A blueprint for America's research universities*. Stony Brook, NY:

Colby, A., Ehrlich, T, Beaumont, E, & Stephens, J. (2003) Bringing Moral and Civic Learning to Center Stage, in *Educating Citizens*, Ch. 10.p 276-287. San Francisco, CA: Jossey Bass, p. 276-287.

Dewey, J. (1916). *Democracy and education*. New York: Macmillan.

Ehrlich, T. (Ed.). (2000). *Civic responsibility and higher education*. Phoenix, AZ: Oryx Press.

Ehrlich, T. (1996) "Foreword" in Barbara Jacoby and Associates, *Service-Learning in Higher Education: Concepts and Practices*. San Francisco, CA: Jossey-Bass. 1996.

Galston, W. A. (2002, September 11). Truths of civic life [Electronic version]. *Education Week*, p. 1-3.

Hill, S., & Robinson, R. (2002, November 5). Demography vs. democracy: Young people feel left out of the political process [Electronic version]. *Los Angeles Times*. Retrieved November 25, 2002, from http://www.fairvote.org/op_eds/ lat110502.htm.

Jefferson, Thomas. Letter to William C. Jarvis, 1820, from Thomas Jefferson on Politics and Government, ME 15:278, from http://etext.lib.virginia.edu/jefferson/

National Commission on Civic Renewal. (1998). *A nation of spectators: How disengagement weakens America and what we can do about it*. College Park, MD: University of Maryland.

Newman, F. (1985). *Higher education and the American resurgence*. Princeton, NJ: Princeton University Press.

Putnam, R. D. (1995). Bowling alone: America's declining social capital. *Journal of Democracy, 6*(1), 65-78.

Sax, L. J. (2000). Citizenship development and the American college student. In T. Ehrlich (Ed.), *Civic responsibility and higher education* (pp. 4-18). Phoenix, AZ: Oryx Press.

Schneider, C. G. (2000). Education, missions, and civic responsibility. In T. Ehrlich (Ed.), *Civic responsibility and higher education* (pp. 98-123). Phoenix, AZ: Oryx Press.

# Chapter 5

## BOUNDARY-CROSSERS AND INNOVATIVE LEADERSHIP IN HIGHER EDUCATION

Nancy L. Thomas

The pedagogies profiled in *Engaging the Whole of Service Learning, Diversity, and Learning Communities* did not evolve by accident. They defy the typical pattern in higher education of new programs remaining invisible, disconnected from what really counts (theoretical research and student career advancement), or lasting as long as the original organizer or funding. As programs that appear to be "sticking," they stand out as models of best practice in terms of both substance and process. They help us understand not only what works but what campuses need to do to foster and sustain equally creative initiatives.

Innovative pedagogies usually emerge from a confluence of circumstances that include a compelling need or rationale, resources, timing, and the commitment of a specific kind of leader. These leaders, what I call *boundary-crossers* are people who work with others to craft a vision, and in doing so, create the compelling rationale that will attract resources and create a sense of urgency and timing. Boundary-crossers can initiate projects without every element necessarily in place already. Conversely, absent the commitment of boundary-crossers, initiatives will fail, even if the rationale, resources, and timing are there.

Who are boundary-crossers and what role do they typically play on campuses and in society? How can colleges and universities intentionally structure an environment that is likely to enable boundary-crossers and foster the kind of creative thinking and action profiled in this book?

## Boundary-Crossers: You Know Them When You Seen Them

You know this person. S/he (for the sake of this example, we'll say "she") is the person who hangs back at meetings and then summarizes a conversation with remarkable accuracy, connecting seemingly disconnected perspectives and giving closure to a topic that seemed to have mushroomed just minutes earlier. Walking across campus, she talks briefly to many people from the gardening staff to the newest hire in the English department, often knowing details such as a hobby or a child's interest. As someone who is frequently invited to serve on a task force or committee, she may be labeled "one of the usual suspects" on campus. When there is a crisis, she may be consulted by campus leaders for advice. And she is known as someone repeatedly linked to faculty development initiatives, innovative curricula, a new center or institute, or a community-university partnership.

Her title and discipline are irrelevant—she can come from the history department, the engineering school, or the provost or president's staff. Twenty years ago, "she" was a "he." Ten years ago, she was a tenured professor. Today, she may be tenure-track, although if she is at a tenure-granting institution, she is probably not part-time, adjunct, or under an annually renewed contract. She was hired for her substantive expertise—her other attributes went unnoticed in the hiring process and remain virtually invisible for the purpose of promotion and tenure. If she is administrative staff, she also teaches a course. If she is faculty, she has served as department chair. She is a popular teacher.

Why not identify this kind of person as a "leader?" "Boundary-crossers" may not be the term others would use to describe this individual, but the term "leader" seems slightly off. Leaders are in charge or take charge. They hold or seek positions of authority, and they exercise that authority drawing from a variety of leadership styles employed to meet the needs of a situation: top-down, authoritarian, consult-decide-announce, collaborative, or participatory. Leaders often seek to "fix" a problem. Campuses clearly need leaders, but I am arguing that campuses need something else as well.

A number of attributes make boundary-crossers something other than characteristic institutional leaders. They act with or without authority. They move fluidly in and out of official leadership positions.

Most boundary-crossers have a "day job" in that they are tenured or tenure-track faculty members or administrative staff members who work in another capacity for the institution. Sometimes, they develop an idea and then move into an official leadership role to sustain it (e.g., director of a center or program). Usually, they start out in an existing teaching or administrative unit with a full-time position.

Boundary-crossers are careful listeners who remember details and can connect one person's view with another's and with their own. They like to think out loud and brainstorm ideas with many people. They view diversity as an asset and seek contrasting views and ideas. They enjoy robust conversations, and dialogue is their "way of being" on and off campus. Comfortable in conversations that are either informal or structured, boundary-crossers facilitate conversations, network, and lobby quietly. Throughout this complex, intrinsically political process, they are listening and refining their ideas and perspectives. In the end, the actual initiative may not resemble the original idea. It is an initiative that is more community than individually driven, responsive to many views.

As an initiative evolves, boundary-crossers focus on three things: building the idea into something long-term, forming relationships along the way, and following a process that is inclusive and dialogic. Their work is not just about outcomes. They work (not necessarily consciously) toward a small, short-term vision (e.g., the new project with the community) and a larger, long-term vision (e.g., better community-university relations and a reciprocal, respectful process for developing projects).

They have an innate capacity to see connections. When boundary-crossers have an idea, they know whom to call to brainstorm with or get buy-in because they are acquainted with many people, and, when the time is right, know how to bring those people together to build something special. They are holistic thinkers.

Boundary-crossers are advocates, usually verbally gifted, and able to communicate an engaging vision of the future. They are charismatic. People like them. They like others. There is a warmth and charm that draws others to them. One might call them a bit "contagious."

Boundary-crossers are entrepreneurial. Their ideas may not always be new, but they draw from many other ideas on campus and on other campuses, repackaging those ideas to match the institution's culture and needs.

Boundary-crossers' motives are outward rather than inward—they are passionate about the institution and making it a better place, about the institution's mission and improving student learning, about an issue and using their sphere of influence to bring about change regarding that issue, and about bringing out the best in others in the process.

They do not mind mess and are not afraid of failure. Going through life as "trial and error" is a perfectly comfortable way of being for them.

# Fostering a Culture of Creativity and Collaboration

Years ago, after several exhausting days away from my young children, I was anxious to get home and did not relish the thought of a long flight from the west to east coast. Traveling standby, I could not believe my good fortune when I was not only allowed to board but was also bumped up to first class, a rarity for anyone in the nonprofit world. In exchanging pleasantries with my new travel companion, I learned that he was an integrative coordinator for a large corporation headquartered in the northwest, with subsidiaries throughout the United States and Europe. He was traveling to one of the company's plants to work on a productivity issue that was troubling the local management.

He explained that, about six years earlier, the corporation was mired in litigation, most stemming from a series of management decisions that had raised the fur of environmentalists, politicians, employees, and board members alike. After a change in leadership, a new CEO settled the many lawsuits, fired the lawyers, and touted "corporate ethics" as his mantra. Nearly all employees—more than 1,000 in lumber mills, mining facilities, and manufacturing plants—participated in mandatory workshops that took place over several years on topics such as ethical decision-making, teamwork and group process, and conflict resolution. Simultaneously, about 20 employees were trained to run internal workshops and facilitate discussions on any issues of concern (e.g., strategic planning, productivity, difficult decisions such as downsizing). Any employee could initiate conversations on almost any topic and my travel companion or others similarly trained would facilitate the discussions. Since the program began, he explained, the corporation's "capacity for innovation and transformation has been remarkable." Morale, creative thinking, and productivity were up; conflict and employee turnover were down. "And the skills I learned in the process saved my marriage and helped me be a better father," he added. When I asked him where he had earned his MBA (he was incredibly articulate and knew all the B-School buzz words), he responded, "Oh, I never finished high school. I started out in the mines."

I wondered whether this kind of program would work in higher education? Could campuses intentionally carve out space for conversations on difficult issues, a perceived community or social need, an exploration of values, and collective problem solving? Would structured time and a democratic process for campus conversations foster innovation, or would "managed dialogue" be met with the same resistance shown toward the perceived "commercialization" of the academy.

Colleges and universities generally fancy themselves as places where open inquiry and discussion are commonplace. And they are, at least regarding knowledge and the pursuit of it. But few campuses systematically and permanently provide space for faculty and staff to explore what they care about and how to act on it. To the extent that that kind of exploration takes place, it takes place in response to a crisis, a change in leadership, or invisibly and informally. This, despite the fact that it is *precisely* this kind of exercise that often leads to innovation. Yet repeatedly, the work of creating and implementing new initiatives is left to independent individuals and small groups, an approach that indeed has yielded many positive results, including the pedagogies reviewed in this book. Yet if campuses acted more deliberately, if they systematically structured opportunities for collaborative exploration, would more powerful programs result?

Colleges and universities, like most bureaucracies, rely on their "muscle systems" to function: the muscle of the faculty senate, curriculum, task force on diversity, senior staff, and trustees. We could complement this muscle system with an additional way of operating, one that resembles the body's nervous system—a system of nerves that operate simultaneously and next to the muscle system. These "nerves" are the boundary-crossers. They work with and without the "muscle system" of the institution.

Imagine a campus that intentionally recognizes and supports those who contribute to the institution's nervous system. There is a campus hub, an office, committee, or person charged with the authority to create opportunities for dialogue across campus, encourage innovation, facilitate conversation and collaboration, ensure that disconnected programs work toward common ends, and work with the boundary-crossers to assess an initiative's effectiveness. This person or unit would act as the "brain" does for the nervous system. It would gather, analyze, and disseminate data on innovative programs, and individual and organizational capacity for new programs. It would explore new ways to increase involvement of many across campus in decision-making. It would organize and facilitate conversations across campus on personal and institutional views and values (e.g., diversity, student learning, academic freedom) or issues that generate conflict both on campus and in greater society (e.g., sexual harassment, promotion and tenure standards, affirmative action, and more public issues such as foreign affairs and public education). It would broker relationships, encourage participation, and bring together individuals interested in similar issues and ideas. It would utilize and protect open and transparent intergroup dialogue processes to generate trust and constructive action. It would build the institution's capacity for innovation by understanding and drawing from the power of collaborative action.

Campus "hubs" for organizing the work of the boundary-crossers' would adopt a rhythm that includes assessment (Where is the campus right now on this issue? What are people thinking about this issue?), framing (What is the nature of the problem? What language do we use to describe it?), visioning (Where do we want to be? What do we want our campus to look like regarding this issue?), collaborative planning (What can we do about it? What are others doing?), reflection (time between meetings and activities), celebration and public acts (town meetings, action forums), and quiet, one-to-one networking. People in these positions understand that collaboration is a luxury, often viewed as an add-on or burden, and that collaboration only works when those involved agree that, without each other, they can't accomplish what they want to accomplish. This work requires a culture shift away from the American axiom, "if you want something done right, do it yourself."

In his article *Strategies for Change*, Arthur Chickering (1999) highlighted the three fundamentals for innovation on campus: educationally sound, financially feasible, and politically acceptable. The "hubs" for organizing boundary-crossers serve as coaches to ensure that ideas have been adequately researched, that there is financial support for an idea, and that problems (e.g., turf issues) are addressed early.

I am envisioning this coordinating office, person, or committee as expert in institutional change strategies. One explicit role for this "hub" could be to find ways to widen the circle of participants (e.g., renaming the problem or bringing people together to act on something before taking on a new task). It could look for ways to pilot initiatives and reproduce successes. Boundary-crossers usually test out a new initiative or idea, at first, in their "free time" or on their own. As their ideas evolve and grow, it helps if the institution provides them with additional support or insulates them from other administrative responsibilities. This too can be a critical role for a coordinating hub.

# Conclusions

The ideas and language in this chapter are not drawn from business schools or leadership programs. They come from the work of community builders. People associated with Public Agenda, National Issues Forums, Study Circles Resource Center, the Center for Community Change, and the National Community Building Network often speak of "border-crossers" and "boundary-crossing communities." David Mathews, president of the Kettering Foundation, describes the critical role in society of "boundary-spanners." He describes them as individuals and organizations who provide opportunities for others to engage in conversations about the well being of the community as a whole. They bring together people from different sectors of society to experiment with new ways of working together. This, he says, is the civic version of Noah's Ark.

Several years ago, I facilitated a public forum on the role of colleges and universities in American society. One participant, a community activist and educator, maintained that, in its approach to educating students, higher education needs "a whole new way of thinking." He explained:

> *We know that we can train social workers. We have good, for example, child welfare workers. But there is this absolute zone that I do not think has been thought through yet. Where and how is the preparation for people whose job is not social work in the classic sense as it is social and economic engagement of people? It is waiting to happen . . . It is crosscutting and interdisciplinary. It follows the trends of community builders. It makes the connection between human capital strategies and place-based strategies. Currently, the people who train people for jobs are not the same people who are doing, for example, affordable housing or welfare reform. They are in separate camps. One is accused of building a ghetto. The other is accused of only looking out for individuals who have no sense of community. The more advanced educational organizations are trying to break down that barrier. They are trying to do both.*

Not surprisingly, *Engaging the Whole* initiatives in community-based learning, intergroup dialogue, and learning communities are the kinds of programs likely to produce the next generation of boundary-crossers, people who build community, make connections between "camps," and see the link between their work and a more extensive engagement of society.

What this chapter advocates for is that colleges and universities not only rethink their academic programs, but also *practice* a whole new way of *being*. Colleges and universities can take concrete steps to recognize and support entrepreneurial, committed individuals in ways that will significantly increase the likelihood that new programs and activities emerge and last. I am not making the case for a new bureaucratic structure or even a particular end product, but for a commitment to an exploratory process. It is not intended to be prescriptive, other than to press for a lot of trial and error. My hope is that some campuses will take on this challenge and place a premium on connected, boundary-crossing thinking and process.

## References

Chickering, A. (1999). Strategies for change, academic workplace. Boston, MA: New England Resource Center for Higher Education, *10*(2), 3-6.

Mathews, D. (1996). *Is there a public for public schools?* Dayton, OH: Kettering Foundation Press, pp 52-55.

## Resources

Center for Community Change, www.communitychange.org

Kettering Foundation, www.kettering.org

National Community Building Network, www.ncbn.org

National Issues Forums, www.nifi.org

New England Resource Center for Higher Education (NERCHE), www.nerche.org

Public Agenda, www.publicagenda.org

Study Circles Resource Center, www.studycircles.org

# SECTION TWO

## Innovative Program Models
## that Engage the Whole

# Chapter 6

## THE MICHIGAN COMMUNITY SCHOLARS PROGRAM: ENGAGING THE WHOLE OF SERVICE-LEARNING, DIVERSITY, AND LEARNING COMMUNITIES

David Schoem and Penny A. Pasque

## Introduction

The Michigan Community Scholars Program (MCSP) is a unique residential learning community. We have conceptualized MCSP to resemble a small, experimental liberal arts college (located within a large, public research university) in the spirit of both the more traditional Oxford University scholarly community (Ryan, 1992) and the more progressive Meikeljohn experiments (Nelson, 2001). We have attempted to create from ground-up the very best principles and practices in higher education (Boyer, 1987; Gabelnick, MacGregor, Matthews, & Smith, 1990; Guarasci & Cornwell, 1997; Jacoby, 1996; Association of American Colleges and Universities [AACU], 2002), with a particular emphasis on learning, community, civic engagement, and diversity. Indeed, the literature indicates that much of the successful reform in higher education has taken place in intentional, focused educational initiatives such as MCSP (Washington Center, 1994).

MCSP is sustained by its ideal vision, but it functions with a keen sense of realism. It is certainly clear to all that the size and resources of MCSP prevent it from encompassing the broad, comprehensive features of even a very small liberal arts college. Nevertheless, in the many areas that are covered by the program, it does represent a principled model of historic and cutting edge reform.

The mission statement of the MCSP states:

*The Michigan Community Scholars Program (MCSP) is a residential learning community emphasizing deep learning, engaged community, meaningful civic engagement/community service learning, and intercultural understanding and dialogue. Students, faculty, community partners, and staff think critically about issues of community, seek to model a just, diverse, and democratic community, and wish to make a difference throughout their lives as participants and leaders involved in local, national and global communities.*

The goals underlying the mission statement speak of 1) deep learning, 2) engaged community, 3) meaningful civic engagement/community service learning, and 4) diverse democracy, intercultural understanding, and dialogue. They are explained as follows:

- *Deep Learning* - engagement with ideas; ways of knowing; transition to college; academic success; learning about community.
- *Engaged Community* - a scholarly community; a safe and accepting environment; an involved, participatory community; a focus on the individual and group.
- *Meaningful Civic Engagement/Community Service Learning* - high quality service-learning;

reflection; leadership development; sustainable partnerships; long-term commitment.
* *Diverse Democracy, Intercultural Understanding, and Dialogue* - a diverse community; participation in intergroup dialogue; commitment to strong democracy; reflection on social justice; modeling good practice (1).

This chapter will first overview MCSP's underlying the conceptual foundations. It will do this first with a brief look at the national discussion relating to MCSP's central goals and how MCSP specifically thinks about these concepts. Next, it will examine the context encompassing MCSP, the University of Michigan as a large, public, research university, and how MCSP utilizes resources and faces challenges within that context. Third, the chapter will describe MCSP's specific program features, to give the reader a good sense of what MCSP looks like in practice and why these particular program features have been developed as part of the program. Finally, the chapter will discuss some of MCSP's successes and challenges.

# Conceptual and Programmatic Foundations

## Learning Communities

From the Oxford model (Ryan, 1992) to the Meikeljohn experiments (Nelson, 2001), from the Harvard House and Yale Residential College systems (Ryan, 2001) to the alternative residential colleges of the 1960s (Gabelnick et al. 1990; Shapiro & Levine, 1999; Smith & McCann, 2001; Wunsch, 1966)), from the Boyer reports (Boyer, 1987; McDonald, 2002) to the most recent Association of American Colleges and Universities' Greater Expectations report (AACU, 2002), there has been a consistent theme of joining together learning and community. Fundamental to this notion is the ideal of faculty and students coming together in a scholarly community, both inside the classroom and out, learning and engaging together as a community.

MCSP takes the concepts of learning and community very seriously. It is certainly the case that every institution of higher education is by definition about the business of learning, and clearly, in the most common usage of these terms, one would be hard pressed to find critics of the good feeling of community. In the learning communities (and residential learning communities) national movement, the models that have been developed offer the structure and promise of bringing those two concepts together in a rich and meaningful manner. As with any movement, however, the practice on the ground only occasionally rises to the promise of the highest goals.

In MCSP, we see it as a valued challenge to think critically about the broader dimensions of these concepts, learning and community, and how to put them into practice in a way that is both meaningful and has significant impact on people's lives. Our first commitment is to bring together our students, faculty, community partners, and staff with respect, and view each one as educators and learners. At a minimum, we expect our students to stay in college and graduate at a level that is equal to, or better than, a comparable cohort of students. But our goals far exceed that objective. We want our students to be part of a community in which faculty and students engage with ideas, become critical thinkers and active learners, exchange with peers who hold differing viewpoints, strive to make change in the community, and develop a love of learning and a desire for life-long learning. We recognize that we all want to become effective learners in various dimensions, through traditional means, experiential learning, across disciplinary boundaries, individually and collaboratively, and in and outside the classroom. We hope that our learning environment in the college setting and community will allow students to make a smooth transition from high school to college and feel they have access to, and ownership of, the wider university resources. Finally, we hope that with the support of our learning community, each individual student will be able to get what they want most from their college education, and each faculty member, community partner, and staff person will continue to grow intellectually, personally, and socially through their association with MCSP.

Our MCSP community is also comprised of people from diverse social backgrounds who hold, and are encouraged to express, different views and perspectives. We emphasize intercultural understanding, interaction, and dialogue across diverse groups. Many of the students in the program speak of MCSP as the place where they feel personally connected to a diverse group of peers; our faculty often report that MCSP is a more welcoming intellectual and interdisciplinary scholarly community than their home departments. We expect commitment and responsibility from MCSP participants and, in return, the MCSP community cares deeply about each individual and group in the community.

## Community Service Learning

The national studies documenting the dramatic disenfranchisement and disengagement of young people from participation in civic life provide a worrisome picture for the strength of U.S. democracy (Barber, 1998; Dionne, 1998; Putnam, 2000; Skocpol & Fiorina, 1999; West, 1994). The trend is one of significantly reduced voting patterns, lower participation in civic organizations, and lack of interest in public affairs. Some have argued that one of higher education's goals is to prepare students for participation and leadership as educated, capable, and productive participants in society (Campus Compact, 1999; Wingspread, 1999). John Dewey's (1900/1990) view is that building an engaged citizenry begins when students are engaged in real world problem-solving activities that move between action and reflection.

Our students are needed as engaged, involved members of society, and MCSP believes they can learn these "habits of the heart" (Bellah, 1985) in their college years. The MCSP approach is to place students in a community that holds these values as a commitment, and students who engage in community work must make a commitment to the highest quality service to the community. Reflection on service (MacGregor, 2003) is an essential component of community service and civic engagement activities and, in addition, service itself must fit community needs. Students and faculty must be properly prepared to participate effectively in the community (Zlotkowski, 2002).

Universities and their neighboring communities, in too many cases, have histories of conflict often linked to feelings of exclusion and privilege. At the same time, all parties recognize that the opportunity for partnership and mutual benefit is possible. Attention to university-community partnerships is crucial, in terms of mutual respect, mutual benefit, and meaningful, long-term, sustainable commitments (Maurrasse, 2001).

Leadership opportunities are critical for students to provide them with needed skills and to empower them to be active participants and leaders in civic life. At the same time, faculty also need to learn how to work effectively in the community, and serve as leaders in the university, on behalf of the community partnership. Community partners can also provide additional leadership for their own community agencies through their association with a university, when that relationship is structured to be mutually beneficial.

## Diversity and Dialogue

School and residential segregation in the United States continue to be persistent and significant social problems today, 50 years after Brown vs. Board of Education (Massey & Denton, 1993; Orfield, 2001). Students arrive on college campuses having grown up in segregated neighborhoods and attended segregated schools. Upon completing college, most will return to those same segregated environments.

Apart from the military, the one opportunity for young adults (in this case, 18- to 22- year olds) to live in a diverse community and engage with one another across difference often takes place during college. And, for most college students, this opportunity takes place the year they live together in campus residence halls. Once students leave the residence halls, they are most likely to find apartments to share with students from the same homogeneous background.

The University of Michigan's legal defense of affirmative action makes the compelling case for the educational value and deeper cognitive understanding that results from attending a diverse campus (Gurin, 1999). But it is not the demographics of diversity by itself that make the compelling case for diversity; it is intentionally engaging students across their different social identities in safe and welcoming environments, as well as in structured dialogues, that is particularly significant (Hurtado, 2001; Schoem & Hurtado, 2001).

In MCSP, diversity begins with the demographic diversity of its students and faculty, but that is just a starting point. The program seeks to make every student, from every background, feel welcome and important to the community. Student leaders are trained to emphasize the broader, diverse community while giving caring attention to each individual. Groups of students across different backgrounds are brought together from their first day on campus to build bonds and begin the process of engaging one another in substantive issues. This process continues in all MCSP classes and co-curricular offerings, and is structured formally in the intergroup dialogue courses (offered through the Program on Intergroup Relations, and the Departments of Psychology and Sociology) that many MCSP students enroll in as part of their curricular requirements.

Throughout all these activities students find themselves participating in grassroots democratic deliberation. They consider questions of social justice and begin to model the values they are discovering and reflecting upon in the community. Hopefully, in MCSP, they experience a diverse and just democratic society where behavior, attitudes, and interactions can be modeled throughout their lives.

### Integration of Undergraduate Initiatives and Capacity Building

MCSP uniquely brings together what are often distinct and separate undergraduate initiatives—service-learning together with diversity and dialogue in a residential learning community. Higher education is well known for its many high quality undergraduate initiatives, but they are historically stand-alone or parallel platforms of program offerings (Schoem, 2002). As a small unit with little bureaucracy, the integration of different initiatives is much more feasible within MCSP.

The learning community concept allows for an emphasis on both learning and community, where both of those concepts call for attention to diversity in learning styles, pedagogies, and the diversity of social identities and communities. The notion of community clearly calls for linkages beyond a university community, with communities outside the university boundaries, who have much to offer the campus, its students, and faculty. By envisioning these broad notions, it then becomes much easier to imagine the range of specific programmatic initiatives that can be included under this broader umbrella, and which are outlined later in this chapter under "Program Features."

In addition to integrating undergraduate programs and concepts, MCSP has made an effort to build capacity, or social capital (Senge, 1990), among MCSP participants by making similar linkages. Students, faculty, community partners, and staff have all come together in a concerted effort to identify common bonds with MCSP, what each group and individual has to gain from its association with MCSP, and what each group has to offer the program. By building this connected network of program participants, and by each group feeling a sense of ownership of MCSP, the greater whole of the program benefits enormously as does each individual participant and cohort.

# MCSP in the Context of the University of Michigan

MCSP is obviously not a stand-alone institution, but rather it is a program that is situated within the structure of a large, public, research university. This contextual relationship defines the program parameters while MCSP makes use of the resources of the larger university. MCSP must demonstrate that it also serves the larger university needs. MCSP is directly funded and situated within the College of Literature, Science, and the Arts and University Housing. Some of the features of MCSP within the university context are mentioned below.

## Learning Communities

MCSP is part of a University of Michigan network of 12 programs it designates as the Michigan Learning Communities (MLCs), which offer the following: 1) faculty-student interaction and intellectual engagement, 2) individual attention, lasting friendships, and diverse communities, 3) learning inside and outside the classroom, 4) student involvement and student leadership, and 5) transition from high school to college (Michigan Learning Communities, 2002). While they have much in common, many of these programs are supported and organized differently, emphasizing a variety of intellectual and social themes. MCSP is distinctive in its focus, but shares many features with other programs and works very closely with its learning community program counterparts.

## Community Service Learning

MCSP is also one of a loose confederation of service-learning programs on the campus, but is the primary entry point for first-year students entering college with experience and interest in this area. There are numerous service-learning programs, ranging from comprehensive campus-wide centers, programs with a particular focus, such as arts and community, and others built around a single course (though some of these courses enroll hundreds of students each term). There are undergraduate and graduate professional school programs with service-learning opportunities. In addition, MCSP is part of the Provost's Committee on Education for Diversity and Democracy, which is attempting to build closer linkages among the programs. In addition, MCSP is part of a Ford Foundation planning grant, "The Engaged Campus in a Diverse Democracy" coordinated by the American Association of Higher Education, whose University of Michigan focus is to construct a "pathway" through the curriculum and co-curriculum for civic engagement and diverse democracy efforts.

## Diversity and Dialogue

The University of Michigan is most recently known for its defense of affirmative action policies before the U.S. Supreme Court. Since the late 1980s, diversity has been a high institutional priority. Further, the University's intergroup dialogue program, the Program on Intergroup Relations (IGR), is well-known as the leading program of its type in the nation. This institutional context provides a supportive climate for MCSP's efforts in these areas. MCSP collaborates with IGR and other units working on diversity, and is involved with numerous other institutional diversity and dialogue initiatives. MCSP has an intentional emphasis on diversity in its community life, its community-based learning, its courses, and its demographics, and it works actively to engage students across different social identity backgrounds into a cohesive community.

## Small Undergraduate Program

MCSP and the other MLCs advertise themselves as the "best of both worlds," providing students the experience of a small liberal arts college with the resources of a large research university. MCSP is a counterforce to the impression of Michigan as an impersonal university where an undergraduate student could remain anonymous amidst the 23,000 other undergraduate students. The program takes that mandate seriously and makes a commitment to know personally, honor, and value each student in MCSP. MCSP helps students access resources in the wider university in a manner that will help them get what they desire from their college education.

## Teaching Emphasis

The University of Michigan is a world class research university, and faculty achieve tenure primarily on the basis of their excellence in research, although they must also be very good teachers and participate in service activities. In MCSP, excellence in teaching is the highest priority and faculty are selected who love to teach, have established reputations as outstanding teachers, and are interested in being part of a faculty-student (and community partner) scholarly community. They have a common interest in community issues and seek to share teaching experiences across intellectual and interdisciplinary backgrounds. MCSP is known at the University for gathering together some of the very best teaching faculty on campus.

### Student Leadership

Michigan, like all colleges, has an enormously talented student body. The University of Michigan has a history of student activism and leadership both within the traditional modes of university structures and departments as well as outside those traditional frameworks. Students serve on various university committees, organize, and lead a vast array of student organizations, are officially honored for their leadership roles, and organize periodic protests and demonstrations. MCSP sees every student as a leader and creates a climate in which students are empowered and challenged to feel program ownership through numerous leadership opportunities. New students are mentored by student leaders and enroll in classes facilitated by their peers. Sophomores, juniors, and seniors are provided numerous opportunities to be trained, and demonstrate leadership and responsibility for MCSP. Many MCSP students go on to leadership positions across campus.

# MCSP Program Features

### The MCSP Community

MCSP takes the "community" aspect of a learning community very seriously. A learning community in a university setting is obviously most fully enriched when it has both students and faculty together as part of the community. Similarly, a program that focuses on community service learning is best served when the community members are invited and acknowledged as part of the learning community. Program staff, too, contribute extensively to the community learning and life, and MCSP recognizes them as fully contributing and participating members.

Each of these various MCSP community constituencies is essential and makes the program particularly vibrant and unique. Further, in the 21st century, one simply cannot conceptualize community without acknowledging individual participants' diverse backgrounds, histories, and ideas, and their social identities and the benefits that such diversity offers to the learning community's vitality and strength. MCSP, therefore, actively seeks to build a diverse community and engage participants in the diversity of the community through dialogue and discussion.

The learning community that is MCSP focuses on all of the following: it is student-centered, faculty-centered, community partner-centered, and staff-centered. It is MCSP's philosophy that each individual and constituent group learns from one another. Each group has a commitment to being engaged in creating and sustaining the larger MCSP community, developing a safe and accepting learning environment for a diverse set of ideas and perspectives, and individuals and groups from diverse social backgrounds.

Finally, MCSP is comprised of people who have made an intentional decision to participate in this community. Everyone who participates in MCSP has made a choice to participate based on MCSP's values, people, and programs. Students come because they have participated in community service prior to college and want to make a difference in the world, and they seek to be part of a diverse and engaged small learning community at college. Faculty participate because of MCSP's emphasis on innovative, high quality teaching and learning inside and outside the classroom and in the wider community off campus, and because they share its commitment to a diverse, interdisciplinary, scholarly community that takes the very notion of community very seriously in both an intellectual and practical approach. Community partners join the MCSP community because of the shared values, the quality of student and faculty service in the community, and the commitment to sustained partnerships. Staff participate in MCSP because they value the ideals of the program and enjoy working together with the diverse students, faculty, and community members who are attracted to the program.

## Students

MCSP each year has served about 120-160 students, small enough to create a personal, close community, yet large enough to have a vibrant diversity of ideas and backgrounds. About three-quarters are first-year students and one-quarter is returning sophomores and upper class students. In the first years of the program, about 60% of the students have been Students of Color or International students, and about 40% White students. Students are enrolled in all schools and colleges and come from Michigan and throughout the United States and other countries.

One of the first MCSP students to graduate from the University of Michigan was Takisha La Shore. Takisha, a first generation college student, knew few students on campus when she first arrived and, literally, her voice was rarely heard. Over time, however, Takisha became one of MCSP's foremost vocal student leaders and, at an end-of-year banquet, told of how she would never have stayed in college in her first year had it not been for her experience in MCSP. Takisha is just one of hundreds of student leaders who have made extraordinary contributions to MCSP and who have also gained enormously from their experience.

## Faculty

MCSP has about 10-15 departmental faculty linked to MCSP each year. About 80-90% of the faculty return to the program each year. Faculty come from a wide range of schools and colleges, including the College of Literature, Science, and the Arts, School of Natural Resources and the Environment, Education, Music, Medicine, Information, as well as departments such as Afro-American Studies, American Culture, Asian Languages and Culture, Communication, English, Film/Video Studies, Psychology, Spanish, Sociology, and University Courses Division.

One example of MCSP's dedicated faculty is Jim Crowfoot, an MCSP faculty member who is highly accessible to students and eager to chat either in the MCSP faculty office or the residence hall cafeteria over lunch. Jim teaches on Environment, Sustainability, and Social Change, involves his students in community sustainability projects, and regularly participates in MCSP co-curricular activities at night and on weekends.

## Community Partners

Community partners are individuals or community agency representatives who seek to participate in the MCSP community in an ongoing partnership. The community partners participate in seminars with the MCSP faculty, are invited to contribute ideas to the program, and help guide student learning at community sites and in the classroom.

There are about 10 community partners each year. Community partners predominantly fall into two primary and often overlapping categories: community agencies where MCSP students participate in community service learning projects, and agencies that assist faculty in teaching their courses. Examples of community partners include people from several elementary and middle schools, Community Organization for Urban Revitalization and Sustainable Environments (COURSE), Focus Hope in Detroit, Homeless Empowerment Resource Organization (HERO), HIV/AIDS Resource Center (HARC), and the Peace Neighborhood Center. A third category of community partners are nonprofit organizational leaders who provide advice and counsel to MCSP, as well as community leaders and donors who provide access to financial, media, and human resources.

Susan Santone, MCSP's very first community partner, has helped the program shape community partnership. Susan works in the area of sustainability and curriculum design, and has recently started her own nonprofit organization. She assists a faculty member in teaching one of MCSP's first-year seminars by leading class workshops and simulations, helping students on research papers, and meeting individually with students. She also serves on MCSP's Advisory Board.

## Professional Staff

There is a small professional staff, including a faculty director, program director, and administrative assistant. There is a half-time community coordinator funded on soft money. There are also hourly graduate students hired as an academic support services coordinator, and a program evaluator.

Rosa Maria Cabello, MCSP administrative assistant, reflects the commitments of the MCSP staff. She has created a welcoming atmosphere in the MCSP office in which students and faculty come to sit, talk, and informally socialize together as a community. This comfortable atmosphere has allowed the office to become a hub of information, connection, and programmatic activity and meant the difference for some students in their retention and ultimate graduation from the University of Michigan.

## Student Leadership Staff

Student staff are hired on an hourly basis as resident advisors, program advisors for community service, program advisors for programming, and a peer mentor coordinator. Many sophomore students volunteer each year as peer mentors. (For a glimpse of their many outstanding contributions, please read and note the many student co-authored chapters in this book.)

## Advisory Board

An MCSP Advisory Board meets once each semester. It includes representatives from the College of Literature, Science, and the Arts' Dean's Office, University Housing, faculty, students, community service learning and diversity units on campus, department chairs, community partners, and MCSP staff.

## MCSP Courses

MCSP has given careful attention to the "learning" aspect of learning community. There is a genuine concern and commitment to each and every MCSP student's success. MCSP gives considerable attention to transition issues from high school to college. For instance, the MCSP introductory course, University Course 102 (UC 102), and the MCSP first-year seminars are recognized as important positive factors in student retention. In addition, these same courses emphasize intensive faculty-student engagement through small class size and required student visits to faculty office hours. MCSP courses are taught in the MCSP residence hall and many faculty hold office hours there as well (2).

MCSP courses demand active and deep student engagement through developing critical thinking and writing skills, exploring new perspectives, and encouraging consideration of different viewpoints. Through MCSP courses, students also learn through various approaches, through traditional, experiential, discovery, and other innovative means. Students and faculty alike approach topics across disciplinary boundaries and recognize the value of learning both inside and outside the classroom. The MCSP faculty have a genuine interest in teaching and pass along to students the contagion of excitement and joy of learning.

MCSP students not only build community in the program, they study about community in their first-year seminar courses and in introductory composition courses. Then, in their service-learning courses, MCSP students participate in community service projects and reflect upon those experiences through readings, discussions, and papers. Many MCSP students also elect to participate in intergroup dialogue courses, central to the MCSP's core mission, in which they engage with other students in intensive, structured conversations across different social identities. A new initiative will integrate the service-learning courses with the intergroup dialogue courses.

Many of these courses emphasize peer facilitation. Discussions in UC 102, service-learning, and intergroup dialogue are led by trained undergraduate peers who are often current or former

MCSP students. The MCSP leadership course offers students yet another opportunity to develop their leadership skills and understanding of issues facing leaders.

**UC 102.** The MCSP introductory course, UC 102: The Student in the University, is a one-credit expectation of all first-year students entering the program, offered in the fall term. The program director teaches the lectures, while resident advisors facilitate weekly discussion sections. Sophomore peer advisors collaborate with the resident advisor facilitators to offer a community service learning component to the course. The goals for the course reflect the overall goals of MCSP and include transition from high school to college, academic excellence, social identity exploration, community development, and community service learning. Each topic builds upon the other and progressively challenges students to probe deeper into the construction of identity and community engagement. (Please see the chapter in this book on the UC 102 course.)

**First-Year Seminars.** These three-credit content courses, organized by the College of Literature, Science, and the Arts, are comprised of 20 students, each specifically designed for active student engagement and close faculty-student contact. MCSP seminars are taught by faculty from various disciplines, schools and colleges, but all focus on community issues. MCSP students are required to enroll in one MCSP seminar. Approximately 15 seminars are offered each year. (Please see the many chapters in this book discussing specific first-year seminars.)

**Service-Learning Courses.** These are three-credit courses emphasizing reflection about service that require weekly student service (4-6 hours) in the community, often for after school tutoring or mentoring in schools or agencies. The larger course is organized through the Sociology Department in conjunction with Project Community of the Ginsberg Center for Community Service and Learning; MCSP provides its own sections of this course. The MCSP faculty director oversees this course together with an MCSP graduate student instructor, and undergraduate peers facilitate discussions. MCSP students are required to enroll in this course or the intergroup dialogue course. In the spring/summer terms, MCSP students participate in Americorps internships at Focus Hope in Detroit, or serve at the HIV/AIDS Resource Center (HARC) of Washtenaw County. (Please see the chapters in this book discussing service-learning courses.)

**Intergroup Dialogue Courses.** These are two-credit courses offered through the Program on Intergroup Relations, for Psychology and Sociology credit. They emphasize engagement across social identity groups, with students focusing on topics such as men and women, White students and Students of Color, gay and straight students, etc. MCSP students are required to enroll in this course or the community service learning course. (Please see the chapter in this book discussing the intergroup dialogue courses.)

**Introductory Composition Courses.** A four-credit writing course offered through the English Department is required for all students in the College of Literature, Science, and the Arts. MCSP faculty teach composition courses with an emphasis on issues of community. (Please see the chapter in this book discussing specific introductory composition courses.)

**Leadership Course.** MCSP first-year students who are interested in holding leadership positions as sophomores are offered a course on leadership development. A myriad of issues are discussed, such as knowing yourself as a leader, decision-making, and leading for social change. (Please see the chapter in this book discussing student leadership.)

**Spaces in Calculus Courses.** MCSP reserves spaces in introductory calculus courses for MCSP students. It allows students to more easily form study groups and be in classes with other students they know from MCSP.

## MCSP Community Life

MCSP's expectation is that, in addition to studying about community and doing community service, students and all MCSP community members will model their highest ideals about community as they live, work, and study together as a community in the residence hall, community, and all of their activities.

Active participation, involvement, and engagement are key words in the MCSP vocabulary, whether relating to learning, service, or diversity and intergroup relationships. In the area of learning, there is an expectation that students will collaborate in study and support one another's academic interests and success. In community service, the expectation is that MCSP students will provide high quality service and critically reflect upon their service experiences, and that the program will sustain its commitments to community agencies and commitments. MCSP students are well-supported in their interest to take on leadership roles in the classroom, co-curricular activities outside of class, and the community.

These same expectations hold true for students (and all MCSP community members) in their daily lives and interactions. They are expected to engage one another constructively across the diverse backgrounds of program members, stretch their social and intellectual comfort zones, gain experience in democratic practice, and reflect closely on issues of social justice and injustice. In doing all of this, it is hoped that students will develop their individual visions of a just, diverse democracy and model practices in their lives at MCSP that can be replicated in the short-term and their lives beyond college.

***Leadership Opportunities.*** MCSP offers a number of student leadership opportunities for students to continue to develop leadership skills and take on additional responsibility in their second and third years with the program. MCSP student leaders serve as resident advisors who build community on the residence hall floors and facilitate the sections of the UC 102 introductory course. Peer advisors are selected to create and organize the student programming board and community service events within the program. The peer mentors and peer mentor coordinator serve as mentors to aid in the first-year students transition from high school to college. Together, these student leaders create the welcoming climate within the program. (Please see the chapter in this book on student leadership opportunities.)

***Residence Hall Life.*** MCSP is situated within a residence hall operated by University Housing. A strong working relationship with the residence education staff including the hall director, manager of building operations, housekeepers, and office coordinator is vital to the program's success. The first-year students experience life in Couzens Hall as a seamless college experience, and the living-learning staff and the University housing building team often work quite closely to provide a positive residence hall and living-learning environment.

***Faculty and Classes in the Residence Hall.*** The MCSP courses are taught within the residence hall where MCSP resides. The lounge areas have been equipped with couches and/or tables and chairs, chalkboards, and all the material necessary for a classroom to function. The overstuffed couches, large windows, carpet, and oak walls often create a relaxed atmosphere in the classroom that often enhances in-depth discussion during the first-year seminars. Many faculty also hold office hours in the residence hall.

***Programming Board.*** The MCSP programming board is a student-driven organization where first- and second-year students come together to organize MCSP programs and events. The programming board and its events are often what first-year students associate with the program. Events organized are community service learning events, volunteering opportunities, a speakers series, and various social events. The students organize multiple events each month, and at high points during the year they organize multiple events each week. Numerous leadership positions are offered through the programming board, and during the 2002-2003 academic year it was elected as the University of Michigan Student Organization of the Year.

***Community Service Projects.*** The MCSP programming board, through the efforts of the MCSP peer advisors for community service and our first-year students, offer a number of community service learning events and volunteer opportunities throughout the year. Events include: building houses and play-houses for children with Habitat for Humanity, hosting a parents' night out for University family housing, creating a drama troupe to teach drug and alcohol education in the local schools, and organizing a 30-hour famine on local and national hunger issues.

**Academic Support Services.** MCSP provides academic support services in order to support our academic excellence initiatives. The coordinator of academic support hires tutors for popular first-year student courses, creates e-mail connections between MCSP students who may be enrolled in the same classes but in different sections in order to facilitate study groups, and helps MCSP students connect with academic support resources on campus. The coordinator of academic support visits each student in the MCSP introductory course to provide resources and information about services and personal connections with the students. Office hours and various academic programming are offered on a regular basis.

## Affiliated Links

MCSP has sought to help initiate and support more expansive, structural program links with other units that share similar values. The LUCY program (Lives of Urban Children and Youth) shares many of MCSP's same broad goals, but provides a more focused and intensive experience for a small subset of students that MCSP cannot offer its larger numbers. The two programs work in hand-in-hand with many of the same students, share similar resources, and each benefit from the close partnership.

Similarly, a fledgling linkage is developing with the Program in Environment, a new academic program focusing on issues in the environment. Its commitment to active learning, close faculty-student interaction, experiential and service-learning, sustained community partnerships, and co-curricular programming makes for a natural fit for an interested subset of MCSP students and faculty.

**Lives of Urban Children and Youth (LUCY).** The LUCY program is one of MCSP's great and successful partnerships. LUCY is an independent program of about 20 students each year that is "nested" within MCSP, with support from the School of Education, the Provost's Office, and the Ginsberg Center for Community Service and Learning. LUCY gives students from all academic fields and broad professional interests an opportunity to learn and develop a focus on urban issues regarding children and youth. LUCY has its own faculty director and staff who have an office and teach in MCSP, and work very closely with MCSP. Academic requirements for LUCY have been constructed to simultaneously meet the MCSP requirements. (Please see the chapter in this book discussing the LUCY program.)

**Program in Environment (PIE).** A more recent affiliation is developing with the Program in Environment, a partnership between the College of Literature, Science and the Arts and the School of Natural Resources and the Environment. MCSP, in conjunction with PIE, seeks to provide about 20 students each year who are interested in environmental issues with an opportunity to enroll in a first-year seminar on issues of the environment and the community, a community service-learning course focusing on environmental issues, and to participate in field trips, outings and, service projects with environmental themes in conjunction with the PIE student club and the MCSP programming board.

## Miscellaneous Projects and Activities

**Student Recruitment.** MCSP has a number of student recruitment efforts including high school visits, a letter writing campaign, and collaborating with the office of admissions. In almost every stage of recruitment, MCSP students are the spokespersons about the program. Current students and MCSP alumni tend to be the strongest advocates for MCSP.

**Faculty Recruitment.** There has been a very high level of faculty retention in MCSP, and faculty commitment and involvement in the program grows deeper each year they stay with the program. However, some annual faculty turnover causes the faculty director to seek new faculty to teach in MCSP. The primary reasons faculty teach in MCSP are for the faculty collegiality with peers interested in issues of community, the MCSP community diversity, and the commitment to MCSP students and community concerns. MCSP also provides faculty with a small research stipend, a fund to draw upon for innovative teaching practice, a shared faculty space for office hours and office use, and free meals to eat with students in the residence hall dining hall. Faculty are expected to teach in the program residence hall and attend MCSP faculty-community partner seminars, and are encouraged to hold office hours in the residence hall and take part in various educational and social programs as time permits.

*Assessment.* In the past year MCSP has developed a program evaluation and a research design. The program evaluation will 1) record base-line data about the program that can be compared from year to year, 2) measure MCSP student GPA and retention data compared to cohorts of students with similar demographic characteristics upon entrance to the University of Michigan but who did not participate in a learning community, and 3) gather student impressions of various program aspects through a survey/focus groups. The research design will survey students annually, with a control group, to measure the program impact on individual student attitudes and behavior toward engaged learning, civic commitments, and diverse democracy measures. There also will be a longitudinal study of students through college and beyond using in-depth interviews. The research design will require external funding to complete. (Please see the chapter in this book on assessment and research.)

*Development.* MCSP works to strengthen its program offerings through external funding opportunities. There are ongoing efforts to work with individual donors, corporations, foundations, parents of current students, and program alumni to raise additional funds to support programs, speakers, student travel to conferences, Americorps opportunities, etc. The program has participated, and continues to participate, in a number of grants and grant proposals.

*Publications and Presentations.* In the short life of the program, MCSP has been written about or mentioned in national publications and presentations. The news media have highlighted MCSP students, faculty, staff, and the program in stories and photos in *Newsweek*, the Associated Press, Detroit area newspapers, "CNN's Anderson Cooper 360 Show," and on the Detroit CBS-TV affiliate on the "Making a Difference" segment. Journals such as *Change* magazine, and the AAHE/PEW National Learning Communities Monographs have included discussion of MCSP. The book in which this article is being published, *Engaging the Whole of Service-Learning, Diversity, and Learning Communities*, is another noteworthy example of MCSP's public face and recognition. MCSP is participating in the eight-campus AAHE/Ford Foundation planning grant, "The Engaged Campus in a Diverse Democracy," and has been a co-sponsor of the Politalk US-European On-Line Student Dialogue on Iraq. Presentations on MCSP have been delivered at organizations including the Association of American Colleges and Universities, American Association of Higher Education, American College Personnel Association, National Conference on Residential Colleges and Living Learning Programs, and PEW National Learning Communities Fellows.

*Distinctive Program Features.* MCSP stands out in a number of respects. First, it integrates program initiatives of learning communities, service-learning, diversity, and dialogue. Second, it provides meaningful faculty involvement with students. Third, it is a highly diverse unit demographically. Fourth, it provides substantial opportunities for student leadership. Fifth, it promotes faculty collaboration across disciplines. Sixth, it brings together students, faculty, community partners, and staff and holds a faculty-community partners seminar. Seventh, it collaborates with numerous campus offices, programs, and departments. Eighth, it addresses well-known student engagement and successful practices such as: (a) serving as a living-learning program, (b) offering first-year seminars, (c) providing community service learning activities and intercultural understanding workshops and dialogues, (d) requiring student visits to faculty office hours, (e) offering a first-year student transition course, (f) providing opportunities for student-faculty involvement, and (g) involving students in a wide range of student leadership opportunities.

# Successes, Challenges, and Lessons Learned

The idea of MCSP, a learning community with a focus on community, was created through conversations between the Dean of the College of Literature, Science, and the Arts and students in spring 1999. An administrative assistant, program director and faculty director were hired that summer and students arrived September 1, 1999 with barely anything in place. The program developed its substance and structure through an ongoing, evolving process, while students were already participating in the program, and that process of ongoing evolution and development continues today.

The conceptual underpinnings of the program, outlined earlier in the chapter, have found a receptive audience on campus and in the national higher education community. Linking undergraduate initiatives such as learning communities, service-learning, and diversity and dialogue make a lot of sense to most people in higher education locally and nationally, but MCSP is the among the first to do so; and we believe, quite successfully.

MCSP's original vision has been a major reason for its success. In addition, MCSP's dedicated commitment to learning and community has paid enormous dividends in the quality of students, faculty, programs, courses, and community service projects that have emerged from MCSP. The various constituencies of MCSP, students, faculty, community partners, and staff feel ownership of the program, are empowered by the program, and it is by intentional choice that they seek to become members of the MCSP community. All participate in the program with a spirit of innovation, experimentation, and creation.

MCSP students and faculty engage one another across different social identities, growing and learning, confronting and celebrating the differences and commonalities represented within the community. Students come with a commitment to community and service, and that commitment deepens over their experience in MCSP. They become leaders in the program, on campus and in their wider circles beyond campus. The faculty are enormously dedicated and effective teachers and appreciate having a home on campus that shares their commitment to teaching, community, and to the engaged, scholarly community of students, faculty, community partners, and staff. It is not typical on this campus, even among living-learning programs, for faculty to teach and hold office hours in a residence hall.

The first years of MCSP were critical to establishing a vision, partnerships, and structures upon which to build the program. MCSP continues to work to build strong linkages across its constituents of students, faculty, community partners, and staff. This past year, with support of a grant from the University of Michigan's Ginsberg Center for Community Service and Learning, MCSP held a year-long series of activities designed to build capacity among these groups through retreats, class visits, community agency tours, and co-authoring the chapters in this book. Such close and sustained partnerships are not typical of traditional university business, and thus this work is new, challenging, and highly rewarding when successful.

The future holds great opportunity for building upon the foundational structures, vision, and partnerships of the program, and for renewing and strengthening the quality of each facet of the program. Certainly the effort to strengthen the partnerships among faculty, students, community partners, and staff remains an ongoing opportunity and challenge. How does the program build ongoing and structural linkages for faculty and students to learn together outside of class, and how will community partners remain invested in the program's continuing growth and development?

The program has created a formal MCSP-Community Agency agreement to ensure shared expectations and high quality, one of the first of its kind for undergraduates on this campus, but it would be also be helpful over time for the program to strengthen its oral history and legacy to help new generations of students, faculty, and community partners sustain a tradition of good relations.

There are numerous opportunities to give students more occasions to model their community ideals and visions of a just, diverse, democratic society through their experience in the residence hall. Decisions on such matters as discipline, quiet hours, artwork and decorating, cleanliness, etc. could all be developed.

In the same spirit of modeling the vision, MCSP would benefit by developing some sort of community forum in addition to the student-led programming board and community gatherings, to regularly provide greater opportunity for input and decision-making from the various program constituencies. Already in the works is a weekly "Tuesday Night is MCSP Night" by which students' calendars are open on Tuesdays for programming and community gatherings.

Another effort to make conceptual linkages is now underway to integrate MCSP's community service learning courses with its intergroup dialogue courses. Working with the various units and departments that support these courses, MCSP hopes to offer a single course where its students will engage in intergroup dialogue while participating in service-learning activities. It is clear that dialogue and diversity are a central aspect of the service-learning experience, and it is also apparent that many students are better able to engage in dialogue when they have an experience working on common projects together with participants from other social identity groups.

Time constraints are an ongoing challenge. In many respects, MCSP is everyone's secondary association, and people give of themselves to MCSP beyond any formal agreement precisely because of their commitment to the program's ideals and values. The staff is very small, students have the full joy and responsibility of being involved in courses and co-curricular activities across the entire campus, faculty have their departmental and scholarly obligations to attend to, and community partners are working full-time in their budget-stressed, high demand agencies. At the same time, for many associated with MCSP, it is this connection that is among the most meaningful and rewarding in their lives.

There are distinct developmental issues that the program has yet to fully understand. In terms of service-learning, it certainly seems that there may be a developmental sequence of activities that make most sense for students in their first semester of college which are different from those that may be most useful and challenging for students who are juniors or seniors. At what point do students move from thinking about service as volunteer work to being able to participate effectively in community-based research projects or community social change efforts? MCSP is working with other units on campus to consider a pathway through the curriculum and co-curriculum to help guide students through the rich resources available on campus for engagement with community and diversity in a meaningful and more developmentally meaningful path.

The program is looking forward to beginning a much needed program evaluation in the coming year and for years to come. It hopes, too, to secure outside funding to conduct longitudinal research about the experience and impact of the program on students throughout college and into their professional lives. More discretionary funding would be of great value to the program to encourage ongoing innovation, experimentation, and program change and development.

Finally, while MCSP is having an impact on campus culture through its student, faculty, and administrative messengers spreading out in leadership roles across the University, its greatest impact may very well be as a small but effective model of a different approach to college education that deeply touches the program participants. MCSP provides a vision for students, faculty, community partners, and staff alike that models and teaches that college can be a place for close faculty-student interaction, engagement with diverse people in meaningful and substantive dialogue and friendship, and commitment to civic life and a just, diverse democracy that they can carry with them in their daily lives and into the future.

### Notes

1. MCSP Mission and Goals

   *The Michigan Community Scholars Program (MCSP) is a residential learning community emphasizing deep learning, engaged community, meaningful civic engagement/community service learning, and intercultural understanding and dialogue. Students, faculty, community partners, and staff think critically about issues of community, seek to model a just, diverse, and democratic community, and wish to make a difference throughout their lives as participants and leaders involved in local, national and global communities.*

1. Deep Learning
- Engagement with Ideas: critical thinking; intellectual exploration; active learning; joy of learning; long-term commitment to learning; exchange of differing viewpoints.
- Ways of Knowing: learning and teaching through traditional, experiential, discovery, and other innovative means; learning across disciplinary boundaries; learning collaboratively; learning in the classroom and outside the classroom.
- Transition to College: successful academic and social transition from high school to college and throughout their years with MCSP; academic and social support services and mentoring; providing an orientation to the resources of the wider university.
- Academic Success: each student getting the most of what he/she wants from a college education; GPA performance of students equal to or better than a comparable cohort of University of Michigan students.
- Learning about Community: developing complex understandings about community and social issues in society; learning about self, social identities, and a wide range of socio-cultural groups and histories.

2. Engaged Community
- A Scholarly Community: close faculty-student-community partner-staff interaction; respecting each community member as both educator and learner; a focus on community members coming together to teach, study, learn, understand, and engage with ideas from different disciplinary perspectives and people from different backgrounds.
- A Safe and Accepting Environment: comprised of people from diverse social backgrounds and with diverse perspectives; intercultural understanding, interaction and dialogue across groups. A place and set of people who enjoy being with one another.
- An Involved, Participatory Community: high levels of commitment, short- and long-term, to building and participating within the community.
- A Focus on the Individual and the Group: a community that cares for each individual yet fosters a sense of responsibility to community; exploration of personal and social identities of self and others.

3. Meaningful Civic Engagement/Community Service Learning
- High Quality Service-Learning: providing service fitting community needs; preparation of students to participate effectively in the community; participation in the community through long- and short-term projects, including service-learning, internships, social change efforts, political participation, volunteering, and fundraising.
- Reflection: reflective learning about democratic processes, civic life, social problems and social justice, self, and society.
- Leadership Development: preparing students to be active participants and leaders in civic life; training for students through courses and workshops; student leadership through peer facilitation of courses, peer advising and mentoring, peer control of student program planning and budget; leadership roles for faculty, community partners, and staff.
- Sustainable Partnerships: meaningful, mutually beneficial, and long-term partnerships between university and community.
- Long Term Commitment: develop long-term commitment to civic engagement for the

public good; broad dissemination of experience and insights from MCSP community.

4. Diverse Democracy, Intercultural Understanding and Dialogue

- A Diverse Community: a commitment to maintaining a diverse community among students, faculty, community partners, and staff; a commitment to working with diverse individuals and communities outside MCSP.
- Participation in Intergroup Dialogue: deep intercultural engagement; understanding and dialogue across groups; broadening students' social and intellectual "comfort zones" beyond their own social identity groups.
- Commitment to Strong Democracy: developing a commitment to strengthening democratic practice and participating in public life and civic organizations locally and globally.
- Reflection on Social Justice: linking notions of diversity with democracy; reflection on issues of social justice and injustice, equality and inequality (including historic legacies of inequality).
- Model Good Practice: developing a vision of a just, diverse democracy; modeling diverse democratic community practices in the short-term that can be replicated long-term beyond college.

*\* This is a working document of the MCSP Mission and Goals. We view it as a living document, offering us an opportunity to educate and engage one another in discussions about the values of this statement, and to make changes to the document when the community deems appropriate.*

2. Sampling of First-Year Seminar Course Titles by University Department
   1. Asian Languages and Culture
      - Food, Identity, and Community in Modern Japanese Culture
   2. Communication
      - People, Politics, and Intergroup Relations in Global Perspective
   3. Economics and Center for Afro-American and African Studies
      - Community Economic Development
   4. Education
      - Lives of Urban Children and Youth: Schools, Community, and Power
   5. English
      - Writing Life: Placing Yourself in Cultural Context
      - Defining Community
      - Poetry in Everyday Life
      - Home-less, Home-more: Quality of Life and Urban Development
      - Writing in the Community
   6. Film and Video Studies
      - Documentary Film and Community Cultures
   7. History and Center for Afro-American and African Studies
      - The Local and the Global in the African American Search for Community
   8. Information
      - Virtual Community: Exploring Home, Identity, and Place
   9. Medicine
      - Health Care, Privilege, and Community
   10. Music
      - Music in Our Lives

11. Natural Resources
    - Environment, Sustainability, and Social Change
12. Psychology
    - I, Too, Sing America: A Psychology of Race and Diversity
    - Urban Youth, Self-Regulation, and Motivation
13. Romance Languages and Literatures (Spanish)
    - From One Community to Another: Our Journeys
14. Sociology
    - Democracy, Diversity and Community
    - Community Service Learning
15. University Courses
    - Arts and Community
    - The Student in the University
    - Leadership, Decision-Making and Community Arts and Community

## References

Association of American Colleges and Universities. (2002). *Greater expectations: A new vision for learning as a nation goes to college* [Brochure]. Washington, DC: Author.

Barber, B. (1998). *A passion for democracy.* Princeton, NJ: Princeton University Press.

Bellah, R. (1985). *Habits of the heart.* Berkeley, CA: University of California Press.

Boyer, E. (1987). *College: The undergraduate experience in America.* New York: Harper and Row.

Campus Compact. (2000). *Introduction to service-learning.* Providence, RI: Campus Compact.

Dewey, J. (1990). *School and society.* Chicago: University of Chicago Press. (Original work published 1900).

Dionne, E.J., Jr., (Ed.) (1998). *Community works: The revival of civil society in America.* Washington, DC: Brookings Institution Press

Gabelnick, F., MacGregor, J., Matthews, R., & Smith, B.L., (Eds.). (1990). Learning communities: Creating connections among students, faculty, and disciplines. *New Directions for Teaching and Learning, No. 41.* San Francisco: Jossey-Bass.

Guarasci, R., & Cornwell, G. (1997). *Democratic education in an age of difference.* San Francisco: Jossey-Bass.

Gurin, P. (1999). Expert witness report, "The Compelling Need for Diversity in Higher Education." Presented in *Gratz et al. v. Bollinger et al.* No. 97-75231 (E.D. Michigan), and *Grutter et al. v. Bollinger et al.*, No. 97-75928 (E.D. Michigan).

Hurtado, S. (2001). Linking diversity and educational purpose. In Gary Orfield (Ed.), *Diversity challenged.* Cambridge, MA: Harvard Education Publishing Group and The Civil Rights Project, Harvard University.

Jacoby, B. & Associates. (1996). *Service learning in higher education.* San Francisco: Jossey-Bass.

The Washington Center (Producer) (1994). *Learning communities: Constancy and change.* [Video Production]. Washington Center for Improving the Quality of Undergraduate Education. Olympia, WA: The Evergreen State College.

MacGregor, J. (Ed.) (2003). *Integrating learning communities with service learning.* Washington, DC: AAHE/PEW National Learning Communities Monograph.

Massey, D., & Denton, N. (1993). *American apartheid: Segregation and the making of the underclass.* Cambridge, MA: Harvard University Press.

McDonald, W. (2002). *Creating campus community: In search of Ernest Boyer's legacy.* San Francisco: Jossey-Bass.

Maurrasse, D. (2001). *Beyond the campus.* New York: Routledge.

Michigan Learning Communities: A Place for You. (2002) [Brochure]. Ann Arbor, MI: University of Michigan Marketing Communications.

Nelson, A. (2001). *Education and democracy: The meaning of Alexander Meiklejohn, 1872-1964.* Madison, WI: University of Wisconsin.

Orfield, G. (2001). Schools more separate. *Rethinking Schools, Fall,* pp.14-18

Putnam, R. (2000). *Bowling alone: The collapse and revival of American community.* New York: Simon and Schuster.

Ryan, M. (1992). Residential Colleges: A Legacy of Living and Learning Together. *Change, September/October,* pp.26-35.

Ryan, M. (2001). *A collegiate way of living: Residential colleges and a Yale education.* John Edwards College, New Haven, CT: Yale University.

Schoem, D., & Hurtado, S., (2001). *Intergroup dialogue: Deliberative democracy in school, college, community and workplace.* Ann Arbor, MI: University of Michigan Press

Schoem, D. (2002). Transforming undergraduate education: Moving beyond distinct undergraduate initiatives. *Change, 34*(6), pp.50-55.

Schoem, D. (2003). Learning communities at the University of Michigan: The best of both worlds, In B.L. Smith & J. O'Connor (Eds.), *Learning communities in research universities.* Washington, DC: AAHE/PEW National Learning Communities Monograph.

Shapiro, N., & Levine, J. (1999). *Creating learning communities: A practical guide to winning support, organizing for change, and implementing programs.* San Francisco: Jossey-Bass.

Skocpol, T., & Fiorina, M. (1999). *Civic engagement and American democracy.* Washington, DC: Brookings Institution Press.

Smith, B.L. & McCann, J. (2001). *Reinventing ourselves.* Bolton, MA: Anker Publishing.

West, C. (1994). *Race and social justice in a multicultural democracy.* Washington, DC: American Association of Colleges and Universities.

Wingspread Declaration on Renewing the Civic Mission of the American Research University. June, 1999.

Wunsch, E. (1966). The Pilot Program - An Attack on Impersonality and Academic Isolation in a Large College. *Memo to the faculty.* Ann Arbor, MI: Center for Research on Learning and Teaching, University of Michigan. No. 20

Zlotkowski, E. (Ed.). (2002). *Service-Learning and the first-year experience: Preparing students for personal success and civic responsibility.* Columbia, SC: National Resource Center for the First Year Experience.

# Chapter 7

## LUCY: THE LIVES OF URBAN CHILDREN AND YOUTH INITIATIVE

Joseph Galura, Stella Raudenbush, Jen Denzin, Njia Kai,
Nancy Balogh, Kate Brady, Jean Klein, Yvonne Mayfield,
Gregory B. Markus, and Carmen Wargel

## Introduction

Today's colleges and universities face a growing need to prepare undergraduate students to interact effectively in a complex and diverse world. Studying the lives of children in urban settings provides an excellent intellectual context for this process. Students have the opportunity to prepare themselves intellectually and personally, through their college experience, to engage actively in the intellectual, ethical, economic, scientific, and justice-seeking challenges of contemporary society and its urban centers. The current curricular and co-curricular pathway created by LUCY, the Lives of Urban Children and Youth Initiative, asks students to make connections between their academic inquiry, and civic engagement.

This chapter is the story of LUCY, told in three parts and from multiple perspectives, with student voices woven throughout the narrative.

Part One explains the LUCY Initiative within the Michigan Community Scholars Program (MCSP). Written largely by the LUCY instructional team, this section describes the components of the LUCY pathway, and directly relates LUCY's challenges and successes to MCSP's four goals: deep learning, engaged community, meaningful civic engagement, and intercultural understanding and dialogue.

Part Two is about University-Community Partnerships. This section opens with a brief professional history of the instructional team but is primarily a dialogue between LUCY program associate Jen Denzin and agency staff from our four community partners: Cultural Arts Media Production (CAMP) Detroit, Logan Elementary School, University Preparatory Academy (UPA), and Bellevue Elementary School/Boulevard Harambee.

Part Three evaluates LUCY's curricular and co-curricular aspects. An independent evaluation of LUCY, drawing from students in University Course 151 and Sociology 389, was done by UM Political Science Professor Gregory B. Markus, a research scientist at the Institute of Social Research. In addition to Markus' findings, Part Three also includes Carmen Wargel, a graduate student who examined the impact of participation in LUCY-related co-curricular activities on students during the 2002-2003 academic year.

The story of LUCY is still unfolding, with its spirit of high adventure, risk-taking, and challenge, as the Initiative's students, instructional staff and community partners cross back and forth between social and intellectual frontiers, with an emerging sense of community, diversity, and civic engagement.

Welcome to the adventure.

## Part One: The LUCY Initiative within MCSP

The LUCY Initiative was conceived as a two-year curricular and co-curricular pathway for first- and second-year students interested in examining the lives of urban children and youth as a topic of serious academic inquiry. Service-learning is the instructional methodology, with a special interest on university-community partnerships. Specifically, the idea was that students would be able to serve at the same agency for up to two years. The intent here is that extended involvement in the community would both broaden and deepen the students' learning objectives, while increasing the quality of service delivered to our community partners.

Our hope is that as LUCY students work more systematically with asset-based views of children and their community, their work becomes more about improving the life prospects of children in urban settings (in the case of LUCY, Detroit) than about college students feeling good about "helping out those poor kids." The concomitant issue in reflection is that LUCY students move from thinking about working in Detroit to *how* they are thinking about Detroit. In LUCY, meta-cognition is a central developmental thrust.

With these concepts in mind, we developed the following course sequence:
First term - University Course 151: Schools, Community and Power
Second term - Sociology 389: Social Justice
Third Term - Education 310: Child Study
Fourth Term - Education 310: LUCY Capstone

We also developed these co-curricular activities:
AmeriCorps paid summer internship - 450 hours placed with our community partners
Images of the Possible Speaker Series - six lectures, each featuring a national expert and local practitioner known for their work with urban children
Campus Day - LUCY students host a visit to Ann Arbor for urban children and youth

Although the first course in the sequence is taught at Couzens (the residence hall where MCSP is located), non-MCSP students may enroll. However, to continue in the LUCY sequence a student must join MCSP. The benefits and challenges of nesting LUCY within MCSP are discussed in the next section.

The LUCY pathway has its origins in adventure education where education, both formal and informal, is put to immediate use in service to one's community. However, the parties involved define that community. There is a spirit of high adventure, risk-taking and challenge throughout the program. The key elements of service-learning are planning, preparation, design, meaningful service, reflection, and celebration. Each course follows this design, as well as the overall sequence.

## MCSP Goals and LUCY's Challenges

### MCSP's First Goal: Deep Learning

The LUCY instructional team emphasizes the MCSP "way of knowing" objective. When researching LUCY through a case-study lens, Penny Pasque (2002), former MCSP co-director noted that a single seminar featured LUCY faculty director Stella, a Nia instructor, leading the students in a warm-up exercise involving music and motion; Joe, the LUCY co-director, facilitating a class discussion based on his reading, responses and theme analysis of students' weekly assignments; and Jen, the LUCY program associate, providing essential information about each community partner, both to improve weekly service on-site and to frame the term paper about community asset-mapping. Our aim here is to promote learning collaboratively in the classroom and community. Our team approach emphasizes learning across disciplinary boundaries, as well as learning and teaching through experiential, traditional, and other innovative means. Our students sometimes ask how we, as an instructional team, ever started working together, given our diverse teaching styles. One student in this class concluded that her seminar was "a real gem" among the courses she had taken during her first year.

Two major challenges have emerged from our commitment as an instructional team to the MCSP "way of knowing" objective. This first is that sometimes we simply lose students, conceptually, when we attempt to link community service with academic learning.

Early every semester in UC 151, one weekly assignment is for students to describe their prior community work, and then compare these experiences with the definition in Dunlap's (2000) *Reaching Out to Children and Families*. In one respect, the response is almost always unanimous— students have participated in community service in high school, perhaps as part of a school requirement, or through a civic or religious organization, or because of their parents' beliefs.

However, when asked if this work in the community is intentionally linked to any educational objectives, the answer is very rarely yes.

**Expectations and Grading.** The second and related challenge, perhaps more directed at the instructional team than the students, is about expectations and grading. Academic service-learning often is an alternative to our students' prior experiences, either the traditional classroom-bound instruction, or community service without intentional educational objectives. However, alternative does not mean that academic rigor is compromised.

The instructional challenge becomes how to create an educational environment of high adventure—and even fun—while concurrently setting expectations that all class aspects are being graded?

To this end we have developed a grading scale, which actually weights campus and community participation more heavily than the formal papers. Unfortunately, because participation, particularly in the community, is hard for the instructors to evaluate beyond whether or not students are present, often grades are determined by which students came into the class prepared by their high school curricula with the best writing skills.

This is a particularly vexing challenge to the instructors because to some extent the inequalities between urban and suburban education that students are studying about in the class are also being reproduced in our grades. During LUCY's two years of existence, our sense is that the majority of our students, like the majority of the University, are graduates of segregated, suburban high schools. It is not uncommon, however, for a few urban high school graduates to also enroll in the seminar. These urban graduates may have greater familiarity with the neighborhoods in which our students serve, however, it is also our experience that these same graduates enter our classrooms less equipped to articulate their thoughts, feelings, and experiences in writing. The irony of teaching about the inequalities of urban and suburban education, often along racial lines - then seeing the same inequalities reenacted in the classroom is not lost on the instructors.

**The Value of the MCSP-LUCY Relationship.** This is the point at which being part of MCSP has real value to the LUCY team. We have raised this concern at faculty meetings, identified resources we might refer student writers to, and even shared LUCY students—and assignments—with other MCSP faculty, particularly in English. This is clearly a benefit for both the students and the instructors. Because of their membership in MCSP, LUCY students have access to academic advising and writing-specific support that simply may not be available to other students. Our guess is that there may be few other places at this or other research I universities where concerned first-year faculty actually attempt to implement solutions to this challenge.

From the faculty perspective, this expressed concern about how best to teach first-year students is refreshing and often does not take place within our home departments. Moreover, the hope that a student, perhaps struggling with the writing requirements in our class is receiving support from numerous sources and faculty in more than one course is both reassuring and helps us to become better teachers.

Finally, we must note that it is difficult to codify, if not judge, the personal transformation that takes place when individuals begin to confront their unexamined notions of race, class elitism, and social segregation, and to explore who taught those ideas to them—and why. This once again raises issues for us as an instructional team—what is developmentally appropriate and how do we guide, without judging, through these first steps toward principled actions as urban scholars and workers?

Despite this stated difficulty, there are genuine benefits to the LUCY-MCSP relationship. We have touched briefly on how faculty and staff may combine to support LUCY students in MCSP. Because LUCY is a pathway within MCSP, this has a cumulative effect. LUCY students, because of their membership in MCSP become more skilled in a number of MCSP venues, including the sequence of LUCY courses and the AmeriCorps internship. Because of this cumulative effect, the community partners hosting our students benefit. Not only are they getting the same students over a two-year period—and in the case of the internship—for a concentrated immersion experience, but they are also getting students better equipped to identify and respond to community need.

## MCSP's Second Goal: Engaged Community

Here LUCY emphasizes the MCSP "scholarly community" objective: close faculty-student and community partner-staff interaction, with different perspectives and different backgrounds. In the previous section, we have outlined some of how the instructional team functions. In addition to the office hours Stella, the faculty director, and Joe, the co-director, keep at MCSP, Jen, the program associate, is there up to 20 hours per week, often interacting with students, and these conversations are often where much of the deep student learning occurs. Our community partners are also a vital part of the extended instructional team. Sometimes they come to campus to help orient our students to their agencies. Sometimes they are featured as speakers in the Images of the Possible series. Interviews with specific community partners are required as part of the LUCY Capstone.

We include elders as community partners throughout the two-year pathway to mirror patterns of community life in many communities of color. The intent here is to ground our students' community engagement in a larger historical and community-wide context—elders are the individuals who teach care in the community. They are also the community's keepers of memory and holders of their people's dreams (Somé, 1993).

However, a clear challenge emerges out of this "scholarly community" objective—who is in charge?

Particularly at the beginning of a term, some students may be confused as to which member of the on-campus instructional team to ask about a particular aspect of the LUCY Initiative. We confess that at least once the instructional team has misplaced (and sometimes misgraded) assignments turned into the wrong team member at an odd time.

In general, implementing the principles of good practice with regard to an academic service-learning course is a time-consuming and labor-intensive process. In the case of LUCY—where three members of an instructional team teach four courses, coordinate co-curricular activities over a two-year period, including a summer internship, and manage community partnership with four agencies—these demands on our labor and time grow exponentially. The MCSP faculty director often smiles reassuringly to staff. "I think you're doing great work," he says, "but be careful you're not doing too much."

***What's Really Important in this Class?*** For students, this question of who is in charge of what is ultimately a deeper question—what's really important in this class? In a typical semester, usually students' first experiences in the community—and their interactions onsite with our community partners—are so engaging and vivid that students often speak effusively (and uncritically) in class about their site visits.

Combine this tendency with what is often students' previous conceptions of involvement in the community—disconnecting the service from educational objectives—and frankly, the instructional team struggles with how to bridge this perceived gap between students' experiences and academic readings, between just-lived practice and written theory.

One student questioned why the class would study the history of racial inequality in Detroit when she saw her task each week as only tutoring one specific student. Responding to this particular student, again, raises the value added benefit of LUCY being nested in MCSP. Typically our first-year students have been taught to view the world on an individualistic level—it's the tutee's fault he can't read, or his family's, or maybe even that particular school's. The idea that any of these explanations might be connected to the Detroit area's longstanding history of social inequality may be something that simply may not have occurred to our students to think about before. And it really helps to know that this individualistic worldview, and the novelty for many first-year students to even think about social structures, is not simply LUCY's challenge, but endemic to many first-year seminars.

It helps to know that by continuing to press students to connect what they see in the community with what they're reading about, to think about psychological and sociological explanations, the LUCY experience is transformative for at least some of our students. "I love the liberal nature of this class! If I had something like it in high school, I'd be a better person today" (course evaluation, 2003).

Finally, this challenge allows the instructional team to review our intellectual scaffolding so that students own their internal learning processes in order to become more effective in their service. We often remark, "Please don't tell us what the book says—we read the book! Tell us what you think and how it might help the children at your site."

For many of our students this is a big change from high school, where rote memorization and repetition of assigned information often ensured a good grade. Here, the learning process is mediated by the instructors and we wish to convey that college students are undertaking a serious commitment when they sign up to teach someone else's child—and to do that work well requires every tool they can muster.

## MCSP's Third Goal: Meaningful Civic Engagement

With regard to LUCY, the MCSP "sustainable partnerships" objective—meaningful, mutually beneficial, and long-term partnerships between university and community—is the bedrock of our programming.

As an instructional team, we chose to partner with only four community agencies, with the idea that on the program and student level, LUCY would demonstrate long-term commitment. One of our goals is to make partnerships mutually productive, and respectful of community needs, strengths, and limitations. We grapple with the difficulty of making our collaborations reach beyond that of an urban laboratory for our students, to a space where university and community students work and learn together, meeting community needs.

Among the challenges to this vision are the inability of some students to see beyond their own learning objectives, and the inherent structural differences of the University and the community. Sites report that students miss their weekly sessions, or send last minute e-mails stating that they will not be mentoring the after-school program because "I have a really important exam to study for today," or "my study group can only meet today." During the community asset map exercise in the first semester, students have returned to class insisting that they were unable to get material for their papers because cooperating teachers were "too busy to talk about my part of the assignment," or "we drove around and couldn't see any assets in the community." These interactions bring up one of our repeating questions: how can we get students to look beyond themselves?

*Structural Differences between University and Community.* Structural differences in the schedules and procedures of the University and the community create additional challenges to our progress and understanding community work. Three of four sites follow school calendars that begin before and end after the University's academic calendar. In the fall session, students begin traveling to site the third week of September, a full month after the beginning of the Detroit school year, and complete their semester the second week of December, four to six weeks before the end of Detroit's semester. This means we are asking teachers and after-school facilities to alter their schedules to meet, train, and assimilate our students in the middle of their own semester.

These structural differences spread into meeting times and locations with our community partners. Because three of our site coordinators are part of school communities 40 minutes from campus, it is essential for us to make the effort to meet with them onsite. In the MCSP semester this need was clear when our site partners were not able to attend many of the Ann Arbor sessions, but were able to be part of the Detroit activities. This also means that meetings during regular school hours are difficult to manage, and communication via e-mail is frequently the most effective. For our grassroots partner, the concern is usually flexibility. This is where our first question for students comes back to us: can we remember to look beyond ourselves? While meetings may seem terribly important to us, we must remember that our efforts and partnerships are only spokes in the wheels that run our partner institutions.

*Strengthening the Partnerships.* To strengthen these partnerships, both between the University and the individual agencies, and strengthen the links between the agencies themselves, we have created a community consortium, conceptualizing our combined service-learning activities as a multiple-action pathway for urban children and youth within a defined geographic area. Although initiated by grant-seeking activity, the consortium is in effect whether or not any one particular grant is funded—with the understanding that the overall concept, the University working in partnership with multiple agencies on a committed and long-term basis on issues affecting urban children and youth, is eminently fundable. From the perspective of the instructional team, the bottom line is that the consortium is a vehicle to mobilize a flow of resources directly to the over 600 children served by our community partners.

On this goal, the value added is the mutual benefits to various campus and community partners. Because of LUCY's relationship to MCSP, MCSP has now added an AmeriCorps internship program, strengthening MCSP's relationship with two additional community partners and using the LUCY model of linking the internship with Sociology 389.

Not only does this double the number of AmeriCorps members serving with our community partners, but it also of the UM-based AmeriCorps program, which, before its involvement with LUCY, almost exclusively recruited students from our graduate and professional schools.

## MCSP's Fourth Goal: Intercultural Understanding and Dialogue

As will be noted later, the director of the Program on Intergroup Relations (IGR) was a member of the 2000 Association of American Colleges and Universities (AAC&U) delegation where many of LUCY's foundational principles were discussed. In a similar fashion to nesting LUCY within MCSP and building the course sequence around a paid AmeriCorps summer internship, the Soc 389: Social Justice seminar represents the input of intergroup dialogue principles to LUCY. Because of MCSP's commitment to diversity and community service, MCSP students are required to elect either a service-learning or intergroup dialogue course. LUCY's social justice seminar was an attempt to integrate these two curricular innovations, which will also be discussed in the chapter by the IGR staff.

**The First Year.** In LUCY's first year, we required students to participate in IGR's First-Year Interest Groups (FIGs), a series of six events designed to help students become aware of their multiple social identities. Combined with a digital dialogue, our LUCY students thought the overall experience was beneficial, but presented certain challenges.

First, the events focused on social identity but were not designed for students currently engaged in service to the community. Our students reported that many students had not been in more diverse settings, or had not experienced being out of their comfort zone. One student wrote, "One thing I did ask this particular girl was what she considered diverse. I think that in order for her to feel she is in a 'diverse' place, she needs to be surrounded by all black people, which obviously isn't diverse. She mentioned that she didn't want to come to Michigan and 'be around all those white people.'" It seemed our students felt that their time in MCSP and LUCY classes had over-prepared them for the dialogues causing other students in their groups to rely on them to lead and direct the discussions. Another student wrote:

*I feel like, in my experience at the University of Michigan so far, I have talked about everything that we're talking about or have talked about in FIGs. From being in MCSP, UC 151, and Soc 389, I sort of feel like a broken record when I have to keep going over the same issues again and again. I do realize that these are very important issues that people need to continually talk about if we want to makes any changes in the world, but I still feel like the way we're doing things and what we are doing is getting very redundant.*

Another student concurred, "There were a lot of students who did not wish to speak on topics concerning other races or their own. I could see some of the students looking at me funny because I was speaking my mind on all of the topics regardless of if I could relate or not."

Second, the timing of these events required release time from seminar often at crucial points in the semester when critical incidents at site arose and needed prompt attention. A tutee's family may suddenly decide to move, for example. The LUCY student would then feel the need to process this abrupt change and plan for her next site visit before the tutee's last day, however the timing of the dialogues made this impossible. Additionally, dialogues every other week in the middle of the semester made it almost impossible to reconnect class discussions, or stay on top of our own readings. Students began to feel disoriented and confused over which part of the class was the focus, their service or dialogue groups.

**The Second Year.** In the second year, we built the syllabus around many of the core readings in the IGR syllabus, particularly related to White privilege. However, this semester raised another challenge.

Despite relatively diverse enrollment in UC 151, the Soc 389 LUCY students tended to be overwhelmingly white and female. Although some evidence seems to indicate that this demographic is typical of leadership in service-learning programs, it is, nonetheless, troubling in an Initiative within a living-learning community that values diversity.

To address this, we started the semester with readings focused on identity formation and awareness. One of the earlier readings, Peggy McIntosh's (1986) "White Privilege and Male Privilege," elicited powerful journal responses that spoke of our students' increasing awareness, such as

*After reading McIntosh's article, I really started to think about the many privileges that I have due to my social identity. It seems that being a white person of middle class has many advantages that I may not have recognized before reading this article,*

and, "I was sheltered my whole childhood. I thought this was the norm. I was completely and utterly oblivious."

Initial responses from the preliminary identity work was limited to the desire to help others: "I think it is important to recognize these privileges, and try to help others around you who may be less fortunate," "I do know that I want to do everything I possibly can to learn about the racial situations in the world. I want to one day support and help them as best I can," "Even if I can only help one child in some small way, I will feel like the time I spent at University Preparatory Academy was all worth it."

As the semester continued, reactions of guilt, embarrassment, confusion, and anger were exhibited through students' awareness of privilege and oppression, "It is not very comfortable to be faced with these privileges. It makes one feel uneasy because we don't want to think that we are better than anyone else, or that we are given automatic advantages just because of the color of our skin." Students' responses to Lena William's book, *It's the Little Things* (2001), opened the door for this discussion: "I felt ashamed at some of the things people of any race may do to discriminate, and angry that my race was being attacked," "I just feel like no one can ever win I think it is so sad that color divides people. It is completely unnecessary."

**Making Progress.** Despite many unanswered questions at the end of the semester, students generally believed they had made progress in their identity formation, awareness, and understanding of privilege and oppression, and felt their time on-site was an essential part of this ongoing process. Part of this semester's success appeared to be facilitated by the open and safe environment for dialogue:

*In setting guidelines and stressing that no one would be judged in our setting, we all learned to feel comfortable expressing our opinions to each other without being judged. Our discussions all semester have felt very safe and therefore, we have all been able to speak freely, allowing our discussions to be very deep and substantial. I feel as if the discussions we have had in this class are the most honest, thoughtful discussions I have ever had.*

Finally, we note that once again LUCY has a value-added benefit here because we are part of MCSP. We are part of the discussion between MCSP and IGR about how to best integrate service-learning and intercultural understanding within the existing MCSP, IGR and LUCY courses. Our hope here is not only for continuous improvement in the Soc 389: Social Justice seminar but also to expand the number of courses in the LUCY pathway, particularly those which resonate with and build on our initial concept.

# Part Two: University-Community Partnerships

## A Professional History of the Instructional Team

Stella, the faculty director, Jen, the program associate, and Joe, the co-director, have a significant professional history together prior to the LUCY Initiative's installation within MCSP during fall 2001.

During winter 1999, Stella and Joe team-taught Education 310, "Service-learning with multicultural elders" and later published an article about this class in *Integrating Service Learning and Multicultural Education in Colleges and Universities* (O'Grady, 2000).

In subsequent academic years, they taught variations on this service-learning course, and in March 2000, co-hosted Our hope: A conference on the multidimensions of urban children on the Ann Arbor campus.

Later in 2000, Stella and Joe were part of a UM delegation to a 10-day AAC&U Institute on Diversity and Democracy. This delegation also included the directors of UM's AmeriCorps and Intergroup Relations Programs, Marian Krzyzowski and Theresa Brett, Renee Bayer from the School of Public Health, and David Schoem, the MCSP faculty director.

Prior to the Institute, Stella developed a concept paper which she later refined with Joe Galura, David Schoem, and Penny Pasque into a proposal to pilot LUCY over a two-year period.

Stella's concept paper was prompted by her Dean's concerns regarding an immediate and very pressing need: how does the School of Education prepare and recruit early undergraduate students to teach in urban settings, recognizing that most UM undergraduates have little or no meaningful urban experiences? The LUCY pilot was funded by the Provost, College of Literature, Science, and the Arts, School of Education, and Edward Ginsberg Center for Community Service and Learning, and would be implemented during fall 2001.

When the LUCY proposal was funded, Jen Denzin was hired as the program associate, to coordinate logistics and develop our community partnerships. Jen had previously worked for Joe two semesters as a Project Community peer facilitator, then as the transportation coordinator for all the programs at the Ginsberg Center. Jen had just returned from a Peace Corps assignment, teaching English in Kenya. We could not have asked for a better synthesis of service-learning pedagogy, combined with proven administrative acumen and demonstrated intercultural competence.

## LUCY Community Partners

LUCY's four partnerships represent a wide range of ethnic, cultural, and economic backgrounds in Detroit. Each site provides our students with unique opportunities for learning and engaging in the day-to-day practices of their organization. The common ground that ties all of the sites is their goal to improve the life prospects of urban children and youth. Either through direct instruction, innovative education, after-school enrichment, or community programming, leadership at these sites believe that the future is dependent upon youth, and their goal is to provide their young citizens with the experiences and skills to make a difference in the world.

***CAMP Detroit.*** CAMP Detroit, a grassroots organization housed in the First Unitarian Universalist Church on Cass Avenue, stemmed from the community's need for a safe, creative, and inexpensive after-school program for families with working parents. A group of mothers came together to lay the framework for a program that supported the arts (which had been cut by the Detroit Public Schools), and was based on an inclusive African-American community. Njia Kai, one of the founders, and a professional filmmaker and producer, led the program as its visionary and main supporter.

***Logan Elementary School.*** Logan Elementary School, part of the Detroit Public Schools, Is situated on Cicotte Street off of Livernois in southwest Detroit. Logan is a neighborhood school in a community that, within the last ten years, has gone from predominantly Polish to Latin American. 90% of the students come from Spanish speaking homes; 70% of the students qualify for Title I benefits. LUCY's onsite instructor is Nancy Balogh.

***University Preparatory Academy (UPA).*** Doug Ross founded UPA, a charter school in Detroit's museum district, in 2000. Based on the MET school in Providence, Rhode Island, UPA is grounded in experiential learning through community internships, and individualized, project-based classroom instruction. Like CAMP Detroit, UPA spent its first year in the First Unitarian Universalist Church on Cass Avenue before its move in 2001 to a renovated building on St. Antoine. LUCY's onsite instructor is Kate Brady.

***Bellevue Elementary School/Boulevard Harambee.*** Bellevue Elementary is a small neighborhood school in Northeast Detroit, just blocks from Belle Isle off East Grand Boulevard. Of the predominantly African-American student population, 95% lives below the poverty line, and the school had recently been threatened to close because of cuts in the Detroit Public Schools. The school had recently been ranked one of the lowest in state test scores, and adopted the Open Court reading program to address the school's literacy needs. LUCY's onsite instructors for the Bellevue site are Jean Klein and Yvonne Mayfield.

## Conversations

As part of the MCSP semester, Jen held a series of conversations with LUCY's community partners in order to highlight the role of community expertise and voice in LUCY students' learning, and the program's ability to provide and maintain mutually productive partnerships.

**Jen:** What community, school, or organizational needs do the LUCY students fill?

**Njia:** The LUCY students provide a direct connection between the children we are working with here, between the ages of 6 and 12. They provide a direct connection to the idea of higher education and notion that college can be fun. They also provide an obvious and specific example of combining service with getting an education. For our program needs, they often fill the gap between the amount of money we have and the number of people we can hire, as opposed to the number of people we can really use in order to maintain a certain level of quality for our program. The students come and can be held responsible to play with the youth, work the desk, or run errands.

**Nancy:** We have the LUCY students working with our ESL students, and that is always a big problem here at Logan. We just don't have enough staff to work one on one with limited English students so, we have two people doing that...actually, more than two, probably four people doing that. And then we have an after-school program that we also have trouble staffing. So we are using students for after-school programming which is very important to us. And we also have LUCY students working with at-risk students, troubled kids who need time one-on-one. So they work in three different ways right now.

**Kate:** I think the most obvious one is giving some of our students who come in with lower math and reading scores more direct attention. We ended up using more LUCY students in our sixth-grade classes this year because we felt it was a better fit for them—especially because our kids are so uneven coming from so many different primary schools. Certainly the students who have had the opportunity to work with us for a longer period of time have expanded the roles they fill. They have chosen to come and work with the after-school program maintaining relationships with adults in a mentoring role, which is obviously very important with this age group.

**Jean:** Right now they are filling the needs of people by working for our summer program, since we do not have the money to pay or hire people to do that. The LUCY students are fulfilling some really important needs because they are college students and they have the ability to organize things, and make connections that some other people we might hire would not. We also began a partnership with the neighborhood school, Bellevue Elementary, and were not really sure which way to go with that. It was supposed to be an after-school program, but they already had an after-school program. Then, when we became connected to LUCY, we realized that we would be able to use UM students during the day at Bellevue, and we were then able to fulfill our commitment to them. That was really helpful.

## Positions

**Jen:** In terms of your role in our partnership, we consider you onsite instructors for our students. Does this role fit and is it a role you wish to have?

**Kate:** I would say the role fits 50% of the time because I probably share that responsibility with the actual classroom teacher that I place them with. They certainly come to me first—because some of the issues they have were about things in the classroom. For the classrooms where things went really well, those were the classrooms where I had much less to do with your students' learning and their time here on site. The teachers that I know are great, that I know I can count on, they learned a lot. I wouldn't want to say that it was my role, as much as it was in situations where it was more of a challenge, or where your students needed extra guidance.

**Nancy:** To be honest, the first year that they came, I was more involved in other projects with Schools of the 21st Century grant and my time was extremely limited. I was pulling my hair out, running around the office. They would come in and I would say, 'Hi!, How are you doing?' and out they would go. I always felt bad, that I was not giving them enough attention.

But, now, this year particularly, I have more time and so I have. If I have the time, I will be there and be more than happy to be there and to work with them. I have been more involved this year because time has allowed me to actually observe them more, which is step number one: taking the time to observe them and check up on them to see how they are doing and not just this 'Hi, how are you doing' kind of superficial thing that goes on when they come and sign in and out.

**Njia:** One of the things that are very clear to me right now is that CAMP Detroit, after five years, is now a thing, a real thing. It has a basic structure whether it has been written or articulated or not. There is a basic structure and philosophy. I've found that I am basically that person right now to translate that methodology and those perspectives that we have developed, and therefore there is a training aspect to what I am doing right now—with the hope that persons can take it on and develop it further. And so we are conscious of the fact that when these students come here, part of their educational process, and the community portion of it can and should be a significant part of the experience in the program. I take that title. I think it is appropriate to what we are doing. I also take it with pride because I think it is important that all persons have some reality training in the midst of an educational pursuit where you tend to get very theoretical and often believe your theory so deeply that when you encounter a reality you are not ready to adapt to the obvious reality or your reality. We appreciate the opportunity and responsibility. We think eventually some of these people we go into the world. They are University of Michigan students, so there's potential for them to be in influential places and we hope their experiences here will lend something toward their attitude, toward the way they approach running our society and the carrying out its laws or its day-to-day functioning.

## Challenges

**Jen:** Have you experienced any challenges working with our students?

**Yvonne:** None at all. They are very dependable, self-initiating. We introduce them to the staff, and then place them in classes. They come in, sign in, and then head right to their classrooms. They have been really helpful.

**Nancy:** Their lack of experience. Some of them come in very enthusiastic, they have a really Good Samaritan kind of view-point, and that's nice. But what ends up happening is that they end up being too nice in a way, and the kids seize on that and take advantage, and they end up having behavior problems where it is kind of difficult—maybe because of their age and experience does not allow them to separate themselves as teacher vs. student and they are more like a friend.

**Kate:** I think most of the challenges are the types of challenges you are going to have with any college students. There is a wide variety in terms of their preparation to assume adult roles and the things that go along with that—appropriate dress, calling more than five minutes before your scheduled time to say that you will be late. There are going to be times when they do not show up, and that is definitely a challenge. But I think you will find that with any college student—underclassmen in particular.

**Njia:** I've spoken before about the very first time they came and our thinking that they were of a mature level and that they could actually replace a staff person and, as far as a body is concerned, they could, but in terms of maturity, you can't just dump that responsibility on them. There is also the notion that you have to see them as students; to know that they are young people in pursuit of a knowledge that they may not have. The assumption cannot be made that they have any clear perspective or experience in working with younger kids, teaching environments, or the safety and other concerns that are needed here. So we recognize that and try to provide the support in developing those skills and experiencing those situations, and either mentoring or role modeling for them the possible response that can bring about positive results.

**Jen:** Have you experienced any challenges working with the LUCY staff? Do you feel that there is enough support and communication to make the partnership work?

*Yvonne:* You know, it is like a well-oiled engine. I feel that the students are coming, and they are dependable. Unless there is something major being planned, as time permits, if things come up, everyone is so flexible and agreeable, I don't see any great challenges with that.

*Njia:* Absolutely. I don't think there has ever been a time where I have had communication with you, Joe or Stella when it did not result in an action—a call back, letter, or whatever was required. I hope to set up a situation where I am able to train a person to become the official trainer so they would be on the lookout for all of my new staff persons—whether they been volunteers, university students, or hired staff. Then we could be a little more unified in the perspectives and structures of the CAMP Detroit way of hosting after-school program.

*Kate:* I think the level of communication is good. Sometimes it is hard to get a hold of people, but I am sure that I am just as hard to get a hold of too. I think if there is any support we would need, it would be creating materials for our teachers about what the LUCY students can and cannot be used for, and the program goals and curriculum. I am sure that if the school was sending student teachers here, the classroom teachers would get much more material and support for the process. I don't think that I need any more support, but our teachers need more for what their roles are in the partnership.

*Nancy:* Yes, there is still a slight problem, when students don't show up and I don't find out until that moment. Like, I had somebody not come this week, and I had somebody not come last week and there is no explanation, or forewarning. That communication needs to be better.

## Goals

*Jen:* LUCY strives to look at two sets of goals in each part of our program: student and community. As the community coordinator, are we doing enough to meet community goals?

*Nancy:* Absolutely, absolutely. I often feel like I hope they are getting as much out of it as we are because it is very helpful what they do here. It is very valuable.

*Jean:* I think you are doing a really good job of that. At least from our perspective, you are extremely sensitive to our needs.

*Njia:* I don't have an issue with that here. When the students come here they follow the CAMP Detroit parameters. That is all that I have to have happen. I just need people who want to walk in and become a part of what we do here, a part of the processes that allow us to functions. The young people take on the names, they learn the African words we have for things, they join in the classes we have, and never once has anyone come here and been a hindrance to any part of our program.

*Kate:* I think that is hard to answer. I certainly think that working toward the grant with Stella is a way to help meet some of our needs, and I think that grant fits with a lot of our personal goals and wants here at the school. I guess that is what I would point to—the grant with Stella.

*Jen:* One of our main goals is to help students become effective practitioners in urban communities. In your opinion, what do students need in order for this to happen?

*Nancy:* I think it is a really individualistic thing. In some cases, it might actually steer someone to a career in education. I think in some cases it might just be an experience, a learning experience, a personal kind of growth on the part of having some experience outside of what you have known all of your life. And then there are students who genuinely care about working in an urban setting and will probably come back to that.

*Jean:* I think that they need to see themselves as part of a team that includes the whole community. They need not to see themselves as someone who goes into a needy place from somewhere else, but someone who is part of the indigenous community that is part of the movement to help the entire community.

*Yvonne:* When you really get into an urban setting, I think everyone can improve the educational process by learning about brain-based learning and learning styles—why certain people respond to certain lessons. In urban settings, just like anywhere else, to meet the needs of children, you have to look at the total child: the emotional aspects, and their learning style. So many children in urban settings lack prior knowledge, and that is critical to learning—connecting new learning with the old. You have to make learning exciting for them, and bring resources to them so that they meet people from a variety of professions and experiences. You know, when you think of elementary school children, what does it mean to know a college student? I used to always take my fifth-graders to a university for an open house. You know, a picture is worth a thousand words. Urban children do not have the variety of experiences that other children have—and I think that is the greatest deficit there is.

*Kate:* I think it is hard to say. The only way I would know is when I had the opportunity to work with your students last summer more directly. And, through that experience I feel like I have a better sense of where they were as urban practitioners. I think if they go looking for it, they know where to go, and who to ask questions of, and certainly being placed in a classroom is an opportunity—but there is a difference between an opportunity and actually being sure that students had the experience. If they don't know to ask those questions, or if they don't know to say, "Hey, why do you do that?" or "Why does this seem to happen so often?" I think it is very possible for them to just come here and have a good experience in the classroom, and have a good time, but not actually build the skills towards practice. The variation is just huge, and a lot of that is coming from where they are before they walk through the door.

*Njia:* I think that, clearly, and very pointedly, we have to think about this race issue in the United States, and not by melting everybody into some kind of multicultural pot so that now you can't distinguish the rose from the daisy without being politically incorrect. I appreciate the fact that we are able to have the young people come down and, without having sermonettes about race, they are able to experience African American people doing positive things, being positive productive people, their children being intelligent and bad, and good, and able to watch people from various backgrounds walk in and out of our space and be our friends, and mentor the program. I think the race issue is buried in the word urban—and maybe not so deeply. And that notion of urban and the Black race or the Latino race, or whoever is the urban minority, that is something we are helping to at least cause and disruption in otherwise assumed mythologies about the urban environment and the people in it. It is good for young people to come into an environment where basically intelligent folks are doing a thing that has structure and a flow to it, because it allows everyone to just get into it. It is very effective. All the preaching in the world is great, but it is nothing like a positive experience to cause you to change what you think.

## Outcomes

*Jen:* What successes have you experienced through this partnership?

*Yvonne:* One thing I want to say about Bellevue is sometimes it takes our students a little longer to focus on their purpose here, but I always think they are better off when they leave us. We try to mold character, as well as teach them skills, so a lot of my old students do better. Even this thing about how to get along and conflict resolution, you have more problems with second-graders because they do not understand the expectations. We need this partnership and the help. We have children with needs. We want them to know that there is a bright future, and we will do our best to prepare them for it.

*Njia:* The number one success is that there has been positive reinforcement of the benefits to completing college amongst the children here. There is a foregone conclusion by most of the children here that they will be attending college, and I am sure that the LUCY program and the students have been part of helping them to have that positive attitude.

I also think we have been successful in creating a positive environment for the LUCY students...I think advancing to meet the abilities and interests of the different age groups would be the major change I would make for my program. I consider the LUCY students the next level, like right now I don't have that 17-25 year-old group covered, and so they are that group for me. As far as I am concerned, we have been successful in providing a positive, creative, and safe environment for them, and a wonderful way for them to enter this community.

**Kate:** I felt the summer [AmeriCorps] program was really successful for all of the students involved. I think a lot of our teachers feel like the students who went through the summer program came out of it with a much more positive attitude, and increased math skills. I know a lot of the LUCY students didn't want to spend that much time on the math sessions, but that is where we saw real jumps. That is a major one.

Another area of success was with the kids who worked one-on-one with a LUCY student tutoring and completing the "Who am I?" project. That was really important for them. The teachers tended to pick kids who had not had a lot to be rewarded for, and so that attention and the final products were really a success. I'm thinking, in particular, about one sixth grader who worked with one of the LUCY students and they made such a huge decorated book for the project. When they brought that back, the kids were so excited. She got to show it off to her class. That work is really important.

**Nancy:** I think the greatest benefit is to our children and our students here at Logan, particularly the ESL students, who just really need the attention. I am especially thrilled to see UM students coming here with a background in Spanish. That is very exciting to our building. It is very hard to find volunteers and professionals that have that background and I think it is a wonderful, mutually satisfying thing because they get to practice a skill they have been working on, and put it into action. I watch them as I walk by in the hallway and I hear them speaking in Spanish, and I kind of chuckle. It's not always the best Spanish, but it's working! Both parties are really getting a lot out of it.

## Reflection on University-Community Partnerships

How LUCY students come to answer questions about their place in society is central to the LUCY experience? Who is the other? How do we connect to the other? How do we differ? Am I the Other? When? How? Why? The border-crossing into Detroit neighborhood organizations helps students begin to systematically address the core question of how one understands one's place in a diverse society. Implicit in our approach is a commitment; we teach young adults about how to care the other and one's own self. The instructional team recognizes that as members of modern American society, we and our students had been taught multiple and often contending perspectives on race, gender, and social class. On the one hand some narratives characterize the city and her citizens as an endless list of deficiencies, defining most problems as matters of individual will and bad choices. On the other hand there are narratives that reject deficit beliefs in favor of recognizing and building on the assets, resources, and capacities of citizens who are engaged in their communities.

The dilemma we, as experienced learners, faced was how best to support our students' exploration of the contending narratives. We constantly asked just what experiences would enable our students to provide skilled, respectful service to children and youth in urban areas.

Drawing on the teachings of bell hooks (1994), Paolo Freire (1970), John Kretzmann (1993), John McKnight (1994) and others, we were certain that contending narratives about social inequalities would be carried out in the approaches to community organizations, and social service agencies used within the community organizations themselves. Some locate the problems in individuals, blaming them for shortcomings, while others would work to hold the economic, social, and political structures accountable to the promise of equality and justice for all. We wanted students to have a wide range of experiences that would give them first-hand knowledge of these contending perspectives. We also wanted to give them plenty of practice under the tutelage of community practitioners that held strongly to the belief that community development flows from educated, empowered community members, and that the community knows what's best for its members.

We chose four community partners whose practice best represented longtime political activist and community elder Grace Boggs' perspective. Boggs gave a speech at the first MCSP Gathering of Elders in September 2001 as part of a discussion of how UM undergraduates can best contribute to the well being of diverse communities through service-learning. She spoke about strategies for re-spiriting Detroit after 40 years of economic decline. She said, "classes of children K-12 should be taking responsibility for maintaining neighborhood streets, planting community gardens, recycling waste rehabbing houses, creating healthier school lunches, visiting and doing errands for the elderly, organizing community festivals, painting public murals." It was this perspective that offered the best guidance for not only what community partners we would work with, but how we would work with these partners.

We had worked with these partners for years in various roles, but were now working to formalize their roles as a type of community organization mentor. These partners clearly put in to practice understanding that children and adult allies are powerful agents for social good.

As we worked alongside of the partners with our own focus on UM undergraduates, we began to examine reciprocity as a principle of good practice in service-learning pedagogy. Simply put, reciprocity is the win-win attitude and commitment between partners to achieve mutual goals. We recognized that community benefit could not be simply a by-product of our students' community work. Community good, as defined by our community partners, had to be central to work for social justice. We were acutely aware of the perceived power of a research I institution such as the University of Michigan in contrast to small schools and grassroots organizations who were our community. We had learned from history how easily community-university partnerships could reproduce inequality and extend the social injustice that individuals had intended to change. The last things we wanted to model for our students were relationships leaving class and racial privilege unexamined and unchallenged. We therefore began to develop dual related course objectives. Our community partners' goals were to be as valued as the UM student learning objects. Our challenge is to revisit the progress toward these goals throughout the term with both our community partners and our students and make adjustments if community goals are not adequately addressed. This unfolding dynamic has begun to create a higher level of student commitment to community work. Developmentally it is consistent with adolescent development theories to place youngsters in the heart of caring organization to learn caring or civic engagement.

The development of the Urban Children and Youth Consortium is another step in equalizing the power dynamics between the university and smaller community organizations. The Consortium goals are two-fold. The first is for the community organizations and the LUCY Initiative to create a large scale interdisciplinary and cross-organizational youth development model that can have a positive impact on hundreds of Detroit children and youth. By joining together, the partners will leverage community knowledge and experience the creative energies of children, teachers, and allies to envision and embrace practices that would hold public and private institutions accountable for the well-being of Detroit children. The second goal is to create effective models for organizations serving children and youth in which participants gain competencies that will generate proactive community youth leadership throughout the city. These are intellectual contexts in which to train UM students as future urban workers.

# Part Three: Evaluation
## The LUCY Program

As part of LUCY's two-year funding cycle, we hired Political Science Professor Gregory B. Markus, a research scientist at the Institute of Social Research, to conduct an independent evaluation of LUCY. Markus concludes: "LUCY is a thoughtfully designed and carefully implemented service-learning initiative. It is substantially succeeding in achieving its intended objectives."

## Discussion

Although the entire report is too extensive, we include Markus' findings on one objective below, "Increase participants' knowledge and understanding of the lives of urban children and youth and the social, economic, and political factors that affect them."

In the questionnaire distributed at the end of the winter semester, all but one of the participating undergraduates (94 %) judged that LUCY increased their understanding of "the challenges that urban children face," and all but two (88 %) agreed that the courses increased their understanding of "the positive qualities and assets of urban communities." The students were unanimous in agreeing that the community service they performed "contributed significantly" to what they learned in the course, although students in University Course 151 emphasized that more than students in Sociology 389. Ninety percent of the University Course 151 students agreed "strongly" with that proposition, as compared with 50 % of the Sociology 389 students. That difference may be due to the fact that the topics and readings in Sociology 389 tended to be more conceptual or abstract than those in the introductory course (see Table 1).

Solid majorities of students in both classes also agreed that the community service they performed: (1) broadened their knowledge and interests, (2) made good use of their skills and knowledge, and (3) "fulfilled a sense of personal responsibility or obligation." Students were somewhat less enthusiastic in their endorsement of course readings, discussions, and writing assignments, although their overall assessment of that aspect of the courses was nevertheless quite positive (see Table 1).

The favorable summary assessments students provided in the feedback survey are corroborated by written reflections they submitted during the semester. For example, a first-year student from suburban Long Island who was volunteering at Logan Elementary School wrote:

> *I had heard many horrible things about the Detroit public school system. I was expecting the facilities to be worse than they are, the teachers to be less capable than they are, and the students to be much less eager to learn than they are. Yes, many of the students in my fifth-grade class are not up to fifth-grade level in many academic areas. Yes, it bothers me how poorly some of the kids read for their age. However, the most important part in the whole equation is there. Every single kid in my classroom has a tremendous desire to learn. Every student loves coming to school.*
>
> *...I feel as though I have truly been given a special gift. My experiences have subjected me to people and situations that I normally would not be exposed to in my sheltered life at the University of Michigan....Not only is what we do by going to Detroit beneficial for everyone involved, it is a lot of fun as well!*

## Data Analysis

**Table 1.** Undergraduates agree that LUCY increased their knowledge and understanding of the lives of urban children and youth and the issues affecting them.*

| This course increased my understanding of... | Agree Strongly | Agree | Neutral | Disagree | Disagree Strongly |
|---|---|---|---|---|---|
| The challenges that urban children face. | 33 | 61 | 6 | 0 | 0 |
| The positive qualities and assets of urban communities. | 44 | 44 | 11 | 0 | 0 |

| The community service that I performed as part of this course... | Agree Strongly | Agree | Neutral | Disagree | Disagree Strongly |
|---|---|---|---|---|---|
| Contributed significantly to what I learned in the course. | 72 | 28 | 0 | 0 | 0 |
| Broadened my knowledge and interests. | 56 | 39 | 6 | 0 | 0 |
| Made good use of my skills and knowledge. | 56 | 44 | 0 | 0 | 0 |
| Fulfilled a sense of personal responsibility or obligation. | 56 | 39 | 6 | 0 | 0 |

| The on-campus component of the course (readings, discussions, writing assignments)... | Agree Strongly | Agree | Neutral | Disagree | Disagree Strongly |
|---|---|---|---|---|---|
| Contributed significantly to what I learned in the course. | 33 | 61 | 6 | 0 | 0 |
| Increased my understanding of social or political issues. | 44 | 50 | 6 | 0 | 0 |

*Entries are percentages, N = 18.*

## Concluding Reflections

A UM student from rural Michigan wrote:

*In the two communities where I have worked over the past months, I have...witnessed a true endeavor for change. At CAMP Detroit the people involved in the program are striving for improvement in their community. CAMP Detroit provides children with an academically and socially encouraging environment. UPA is also playing a positive role....In studying the history of Detroit in class, we have learned of the racial prejudice and separation that has long existed there. After the "white flight" of the 1960s and 1970s, many of the neighborhoods in the center of the city became predominantly black. This is very visible today in that all of the children are African-American at both of these sites. I think that both of these sites do a good job with the resources they have to celebrate the common heritage, while also educating children about cultures other than their own.*

LUCY's impact was not limited to out-of-state or from rural students. Even undergraduates from Detroit learned a great deal from their experience in LUCY, as the following excerpt demonstrates:

*I grew up in Detroit and went through its public school system, ...but it was not until I came to work at UPA and learned some of the history of Detroit that I came to realize some of the real problems of the city and the communities that make it up. I have learned about the past hardships of Detroit that have led to its current state. I have also learned, from listening to the children at UPA, about some of the hardships that they are still up against today. ...But the city and its people are not beyond help or hope.*

## Co-Curricular Activities in LUCY

Carmen Wargel was a graduate student who did her social work internship with LUCY during the 2002-2003 academic year. Following is her evaluation of the program's co-curricular activities.

*Methodology.* The co-curricular piece of the LUCY Initiative was developed in formal and informal integration with the academic and service components. The AmeriCorps internship, for example, was formally developed and integrated into the Initiative during the first year of the pilot, just as the Images of the Possible lecture series was during the second year. Informal co-curricular development also began during LUCY program's first year. For example, when a staff member published the first LUCY News and students expressed a desire to generate subsequent issues, the staff supported them. In these ways, the co-curricular opportunities with LUCY developed over a two-year period to include the activities described above as well as facilitation of discussions after the lecture series, screening student-made documentaries, a student organization, a movie and discussion series and other assorted events, such as dinners hosted by one of the instructors.

During the second year of the pilot, we wanted to examine how building a co-curricular program around community organizing principles would and would not be different than student development/student leadership programs, such as the one offered by MCSP. One reason we came to this question was because two of us approach work with college students from the perspective of community organizers. We did not seek to establish or support any hierarchy of values between the two fields. We wanted to understand if or how a community organizing approach with LUCY program students would facilitate their integration of program goals, and increase participation and sense of community. Some ways that we have come to understand the difference between the two approaches include who sets the structure and goals of the co-curricular activities for students and the value placed on outputs, outcomes, and process. Given the descriptions of the events above, it is easy to see which components of the program fall under a student leadership model vs. a student-organizing model. The student organization is the prime example of the organizing model, while the other activities follow the student leadership model.

In order to understand the impact of our co-curricular program elements on students, we administered a survey in the final class of each LUCY course with the course evaluation. We received 21 surveys back. Nine surveys are from students from the first course in the LUCY sequence, six are from students in the second course in the sequence, and six are from students in the fourth course in the sequence. The returned surveys reflect what we know about our program in that it is predominantly white and female (four respondents were male and five were non-white) particularly for the second, third, and fourth courses. The distribution shows strong representation across the different experience levels in the LUCY Initiative. The pool of students in the first course of the sequence is much larger than that of the other two courses, which means that there is a higher percentage representation of the second and fourth classes than there is of the first course. The data we collected asked students to reflect on only their activity during the 2002-2003 academic year, but that does not mean that students were able to easily separate their responses to the questions by year rather than responding based on their overall feelings of the program. Still, we were pleased with the survey and response rate, and believe it is a good base from which to draw preliminary findings.

Students were surveyed to measure how the frequency of their participation in co-curricular activities impacted their integration of program goals, sense of community, and desire to increase participating in LUCY co-curricular activities. Additionally, surveying allows us to measure differential impact of types of events to see if there is a difference between how attending a lecture or planning a documentary screening affects students. With this data, we analyzed the impact of the different types of events as well as on the quantity of events in which the students participated, including a control analysis with all respondents' data. We begin with the aggre-

## Table 2

| | Community | Participation | Goals |
|---|---|---|---|
| 0-5 events | Strongly Agree (SA): 0<br>Agree (A): 71.4% or 5<br>Neutral (N): 28.6% or 2 | A: 71.4% or 5<br>N: 28.6% or 2 | SA: 0 SA: 57.1% or 4<br>A: 42.9% or 3<br>N: 0 |
| 6-10 events | SA: 14.3% or 1<br>A: 57.1% or 4<br>N: 28.6% or 2 | SA: 57.1% or 4<br>A: 42.9% or 3<br>N: 0 | SA: 42.9% or 3<br>A: 42.9% or 3<br>N: 14% or 1 |
| 11-20 events | SA: 85.7% or 6<br>A: 14.3% or 1<br>N: 0 | SA: 100%<br>SA: 100%<br>N: 0 | SA: 100%<br>SA: 100%<br>N: 0 |

gate results, and then discuss how participation levels impacted results, followed by how the type of event in which participation occurred impacted results. Finally, we close with suggestions for further research.

***Analysis.*** Analyzing all responses shows that participating in LUCY's co-curricular activities has the strongest impact in facilitating the integration of program goals. Ninety-five percent (20 respondents) of students responded that they agreed (28.6% or 6 respondents) or strongly agreed (66.7% or 14 respondents) with the statements measuring integration of program goals. The one student not represented in these numbers responded that they felt neutral about the impact of co-curricular events on their integration of program goals. In particular, the students felt that attending the events enhanced their ability to develop mutually beneficial relationships with urban children and youth, sense that they can make a difference on issues they care about, and that they can provide the necessary leadership to improve the lives of urban children and youth. Ninety percent of students agreed (38% or 8 respondents) or strongly agreed (52% or 11 respondents) that participation in the co-curricular program elements made them feel like an active participant who wanted to participate in and/or plan future events. Nine and a half percent (or two) students felt neutral about the role that participating in co-curricular activities had in this area. Eighty-one percent of students said that they agreed (47.6% or 10 respondents) or strongly agreed (33% or 7 respondents) that participation in co-curricular events strengthened their relationships with students in the same LUCY course, with students in other LUCY courses or with LUCY staff/instructors. Nineteen percent (or four respondents) were neutral in this area.

The gap in percentage of agreement between students who saw their participation enhancing program goals (95%) and those who saw it contributing to a sense of community (81%) is further explored by examining student comments on a short-answer section of the survey. When asked why they chose to participate in LUCY co-curricular events, 52% (or 11) students indicated that they based their decision on a desire to gather information. As one student said, the events "gave me extra insight into different issues," while another said, "they were fun and filled with new information." The remaining students were split between those motivated by generally valuing the program (19% or four) as demonstrated by comments like "I love the kids and the program," and those who saw participation as generating community. The latter group was made up of 29% (or six) students who shared comments like "I believe [the events] help in community building," and "I like the people and [the events] help me feel connected to them." However, in response to a question as to how their participation in LUCY's co-curricular activities helped or didn't help them feel more a part of the program, 57% (12) students commented that their participation did increase their sense of community. One student noted that the events "create greater sense of community," while another noted that the activities "brought our group together and helped us to bond in our common goals." In particular, one comment emphasized the benefit of the student organization saying that it, "is so small and personal you can't help but feel involved." On the flip side, another comment reflected the remaining voices saying that participation "helped to open my eyes to other important aspects of service learning but didn't necessarily make me feel more connected to other students."

In order to understand the aggregate information above in more detail, we divided the respondents into groupings based on how many events they participated in during the 2002-2003 academic year. We wound up with three groupings of seven students each. They are those with low participation (0-5 events), medium participation (6-10 events) and high participation (11-20 events). We thought there might be a point of diminishing returns where participation in events beyond a certain point did not yield increasing benefit. However, we found a positive correlation between more participation and self-reporting of integration of program goals, sense of community, and desire for increased participation. The frequencies are detailed in Table 1 below. Most strikingly, we noted that 100% of students in the high level grouping strongly

agreed that the events increased their integration of program goals and desire for more participation. The lower score on the measurement of community for this grouping (85.7% or six
students strongly agreeing and the remaining student agreeing) possibly demonstrates the complexity of developing relationships and community, and inevitably generating "insiders" or
"outsiders." The pattern in the high level of participation group is reflected in all groups. That
is, the scores for development of community are lower (or in one case equal to) the scores for
the other variables, and for all groupings, the more events attended, the higher the overall scores.
The news from the data in Table 2 is really good for the LUCY Initiative. It tells us that nearly
all students find a direct benefit from their co-curricular participation to their sense of community, desire to participate more, and integration of program goals, and that the increased
participation leads to positive benefits of community, participation, and program goals.

An even more detailed data analysis is possible as we break down the information based on
participation in certain kinds of events. We measured for five different event categories, but since
nearly all of the 21 respondents participated in at least one event for two of the categories
(Images of the Possible lecture series and a catch-all category of "Other"), we will focus our
analysis on the responses in the remaining categories. Eleven students participated in at least one
viewing and discussion of a movie addressing social identity issues and 11 helped to plan or
attended screenings of documentaries that students produced during their AmeriCorps summer
internship. Twelve students participated in at least one student organization meeting. These
three events represent a continuum between the student leadership and the student-organizing
model with the movies on one end and the student organization meetings on the other. LUCY
staff planned and facilitated the movie and discussion events. Students, with staff support,
planned the screenings as a part of their AmeriCorps internship. Finally, students set and organized student organization meetings with staff support as requested.

Despite thinking that different events, especially those representing different ideologies, might
have different results, as shown in Table 3, there is no major difference in the numbers. In fact,
the difference between the scores of the three categories described is less than the differences
between the three categories and the group as a whole. Consistently, the students who participated in a screening, organization meeting, or movie/discussion had the highest scores in the
participation area. That is, the students who participated in these events were more likely to
report strongly agreeing (67 or 64%) that doing so increased their desire to participate in, or
plan other events, compared to the whole data group (which had a rate of 52%). Significantly,
all students who attended one of these events agreed or strongly agreed that it increased their
desire for more participation. The students in these categories also had higher scores on the community scale. Most notably, those attending the movies/discussions reported a 55% strongly
agree rate where the whole group reported the same response at only 33%. Surprisingly, the students in these groupings had lower scores on integration of program goals (55 or 55% strongly
agree) than those of the whole (66%). Still, we find again that Table 2 produces good results for
the program in that all responses are in the neutral to strongly agree categories, with most as
strongly agree.

After reviewing all of the above data, we decided to explore the responses by those students
who had completed the AmeriCorps internship. The AmeriCorps internship is the most
demanding co-curricular activity in terms of time commitment and responsibility offered in
LUCY. Most students doing the internship do it between their second and third LUCY course,
which is generally between their first and second year of college. While we did not directly ask
about the AmeriCorps program in the survey, we can filter the responses by those who did the
internship and those who did not, and begin to understand the internship's impact. Those students completing the internship are also students who participated in more LUCY classes and
co-curricular events than other students, so it is impossible for us to determine which of those

**Table 3**

|  | Community | Participation | Goals |
|---|---|---|---|
| Screenings | SA: 36.4% or 4<br>A: 36.4% or 4<br>N: 27.3% or 3 | SA: 63.6% or 7<br>A: 36.4% or 4<br>N: 0 | SA: 54.5% or 6<br>A: 36.4% or 4<br>N. 9.1% or 1 |
| Student Organization Meetings | SA: 41.7% or 5<br>A: 33.3% or 4A: 33.3% or 4<br>N: 25% or 3 | SA: 66.7% or 8<br>A: 36.4% or 4<br>N: 0 | SA 54.5% or 6<br><br>N: 9.1% or 1 |
| Movie with Discussion | SA: 54.5% or 6<br>A: 27.3% or 3<br>N: 18.2% or 2 | SA: 63.6% or 7<br>A:36.4% or 4<br>N: 0 | SA: 54.5% or 6<br>A: 36.4% or 4<br>N: 9.1% or 1 |

factors caused their responses to be different (or in one case not different) from the group as a whole.

Interestingly, the AmeriCorps interns had much higher scores on participation. Where they had a strongly agreed rate of 83%, the group as a whole reported they strongly agreed at a rate of 52%. However, the AmeriCorps interns reported almost the exact same rate of agreement with integration of program goals as the group as a whole, and had substantially lower agreement with statements measuring sense of community. The AmeriCorps interns strongly agreed that participation in co-curricular activities generated a sense of community at a rate of 17% as compared to the aggregate groups 33% in the same area. While the scores between the two groups even out if we look at the composite scores of agree and strongly agree (84% for interns and 81% for the aggregate), it is important to see the difference in the strongly agree category because it reflects some real difficulty in developing community, that the interns experienced with each other, as well as some they experienced getting to know LUCY students in other classes.

***Conclusion.*** This preliminary data on the impact of LUCY's co-curricular events on our students is very positive and provides an overall message that we are moving in the right direction with our work in this area. Further, the data on how different events are more likely than others to produce a sense of community, desire to increase participation, or integration of program goals gives us solid information on which to base our programming decisions for the future. If time and money was no object, however, and we were able to delve deeper into the impact of co-curricular elements on our students, we would definitely want to do more qualitative analysis. For example, to see how students are differentiating the impact of the classes from the impact of the co-curricular events, to know why they choose certain events to participate in over others. Additionally, it would be wonderful to have more data to analyze in order to make hypothesis testing a more substantive choice. However, the surveys here represent most of the active students in the program at this time, so this was not an option.

# Conclusion

We agree with Professor Markus' evaluation that LUCY "is substantially succeeding in achieving its intended objectives." We are also following up on some of the issues raised in each section of this chapter.

LUCY is committed to co-developing the new MCSP course, which would train intergroup dialogue facilitators in service-learning pedagogy. Raised as an issue in Part One, this development would simultaneously strengthen LUCY's curricular ties to MCSP, while contributing directly to both MCSP's and IGR's understandings of University-Community Partnerships.

As mentioned in Part Two, LUCY is also co-creating, with its community partners, an inter-agency consortium, which would envision a broad spectrum of services to urban youth in a spirit of multi-organizational cooperation, rather than a scarcity model of competition for limited resources.

Carmen Wargel's evaluation in Part Three underscores the importance of well-integrated co-curricular activities. To this end we have hired two MCSP peer mentors (both graduates of the initial LUCY class) specifically to bring LUCY student programming closer to the heart of MCSP. The $1,000 stipend for these two students is shared jointly between LUCY and MCSP.

Our hope is that these adjustments in programming will make an innovative and high-achieving Initiative even better.

The adventure continues.

## References

Dunlap, M. (2000). *Reaching out to children and families.* Lanham, MD: Rowman & Littlefield Publishers.

Freire, P. (1970). *Pedagogy of the oppressed.* New York: Continuum.

hooks, b. (1994). *Teaching to transgress: Education as the practice of freedom.* New York: Routledge.

Kretzmann, J., & McKnight, J. (1993). *Building communities from the inside out: A path towards finding and mobilizing a community's assets.* Evanston, IL: Institute for Policy Research, Northwestern University.

McIntosh, P. (1986). *White privilege and male privilege.* Originally from www.departments.bucknell.edu/res_colleges/socjust/Readings/McIntosh.html.

McKnight, J. (1994). *The careless society: Community and its counterfeits.* New York: Basic Books.

O'Grady, C. (2000). *Integrating service learning and multicultural education in colleges and universities.* Mahwah, NJ: Lawrence Erlbaum Associates, Publishers.

Pasque, P.A. (2002). *The lives of urban children and youth: A case study.* Unpublished manuscript, University of Michigan.

Raudenbush, S., & Galura, J. (2000). We made the road by talking: Teaching Education 310, "Service-learning with multicultural elders," at the University of Michigan. In O'Grady (Ed.), *Integrating service learning and multicultural education in colleges and universities.* Mahwah, NJ: Lawrence Erlbaum Associates. 153-167.

Somé, M. (1993). *Ritual: Power, healing and community.* Portland, OR: Swan/Raven and Company.

Williams, L. (2001). *It's the little things: Everyday interactions that anger, annoy, & divide the races.* Fort Washington, PA : Harvest Books.

# SECTION THREE

## Integrative Course Models:
## Collaborations of Faculty, Students,
## Staff, and Community Partners

# Chapter 8
## OUT OF THE COMFORT ZONE

**George Cooper, Zach Abramson,
Kevin Pereira,** and **Marti Rodwell**

Marti Rodwell, executive director of the Homeless Empowerment Relationship Organization (HERO), a non-profit agency seeking to help homeless people empower themselves, advocates getting beyond one's comfort zone. Marti says this to a group of students in an introductory composition class, my class, taught in conjunction with the Michigan Community Scholars Program. Marti's mission is to empower not just homeless people, but everyone she comes in contact with, and her collaboration with my writing course involved her in empowering some very comfortably "homed" students, as we met twice a week in the Couzens Residence Hall library.

Marti came up with the assignment. Students were given a scenario to live out: *You are a twenty-six year old male. You graduated college with a Liberal Arts degree. You are a chronic drug abuser and recently you lost your job because of absenteeism and inappropriate office behavior. All of your savings and income have been spent on drugs. Your rent is paid up until the end of this month. You view yourself as being in control of your drug use—though you are, in reality, an addict. Any income you get, you immediately spend on drugs.* My students were to accept a scenario such as this, each scenario different, examine it to determine what kind of choices the scenario presented, and then play the role suggested, identifying and contacting the public resources available to restore themselves to a place in the community. Following their research, students wrote first person narratives from the perspective of their case study.

Yes, this took students out of their comfort zone. Kevin Pereira said that his experience began with frustration:

> *Despite a frustrating beginning to this assignment with the phone calls, my perspective on help for the homeless changed. It dawned on me that if I was feeling frustrated in my warm, comfortable room, what must the homeless out there in the cold without a roof over their heads be feeling?*

Kevin's frustration turns to appreciation as he realizes that the difficult process he has been assigned is actually much easier from his position of relative security than it would be were he homeless or at risk of being homeless. Zach Abramson presents it in another way:

> *The physical challenge of trying to find myself a home brought the situation into reality for me. It is one thing to think that you may not have found a place to stay, or in my case not fulfilling the assignment, because of nasty people on the phone telling you that there is nothing they can do. It is a completely different story, however, when you actually go out there and try, and still come up with nothing.*

Though the people answering requests over the phone do not mean to be nasty, too often they can sound nasty. There is help for people at risk, but the help does not automatically appear, nor does it come without compromise, sacrifice, and a sometimes dehumanizing intervention into a difficult and conflicted life.

# The Purpose of a Writing Course

The obvious purpose behind a writing course is to help students write better, prepare young people to write in the many venues they encounter at the university, and do so with some linguistic expertise. At the University of Michigan, this task is undertaken every term in numerous ways, but the generic goals are stated as follows:

> Basic Course Requirements: 20-30 pages of revised, polished prose, and other (often ungraded) writing at the instructor's discretion. Educational Goals: At the end of the course, students should be able to: 1. Revise argumentative/expository writing in order to improve correctness, appropriateness of expression, and development of ideas 2. Organize essays of varied lengths—from one paragraph to seven pages 3. Use outside sources correctly and effectively in developing ideas 4. Set appropriate individual goals for improving writing and devise effective plans for achieving those goals, and 5. Collaborate with peers to define revision strategies for particular pieces of writing and to set goals for improving writing.

This statement of goals is a clinical and objective description of what a writing course can be. In this way it is useful to an academic community in its communication to students that written work flourishes with objective standards. "Fluffy stuff" is not allowed here. There is an emphasis on process—revision, organization, research, and collaboration—without any allusion to the emotional, intuitive, subjective factors involved in the writing process. Affective references suggested by words such as "appropriate" or "improving" are countered and forged more securely in a sense of objectivity by references to "correctness." Nowhere is there any suggestion that a student might enjoy their writing. This description of writing goals subordinates the rhetorical purposes of writing, i.e. that writing might somehow make a difference to someone, to the mechanical purposes of writing, i.e. that good writing is about improvement toward correctness.

The less obvious path to that purpose is to give students difficult thought-problems that provide new and important wrinkles in a young person's perspective. The new and more complex perspective then, gradually but surely, inflicts itself on the written composition process, making the student a better thinker and writer. In other words, undertaking every writing exercise should involve taking the writer out of a comfort zone, while no writing exercise is ever about just the writing. A good writing exercise should engage a writer both emotionally and mechanically, where efforts at correctness are complicated (and sometimes hindered) by the ferocity of critical and affective thought. Marti's assignment achieved such goals in a clever way. It gave students a topic to write about and a form to write in, and it forced them to think about security measures they possessed in their own life. In being presented an individual subject so greatly in conflict, the assignment demanded students recognize the relative luxury afforded them as participants in a university community. The personal nature of the essay, and inversion of its perspective—our students writing through the eyes of another—contributed to the depth of student learning and their experience in a community poised or not-so-poised to support its members.

The first person essay is not new to college writing. Composition teachers have employed it more frequently as an accessible way to initiate students' writing and thinking. Moreover, teachers have found the genre interesting to read, stimulating even, as students are often invigorated to tell stories about their lives. The first person essay provides writers with familiar subject matter and, as such, provides them a welcome and reasonable opportunity to succeed in writing with vivid detail. Such beliefs are not asserted without controversy, however. Critics of the first person narrative argue that students do not know enough to write and reflect effectively on their experience (Harris, 1996). Others complain that the emphasis on personal essay comes out in the "personal" to the loss of the "essay," making the end result heavy on confession and light on reflection. Dana Elder (2000) asserts that, "If students do write personal essays, teachers find they're as likely as not to substitute a tagged-on 'moral' rather than incorporate the reflective qualities many readers look to find in the essay"(as cited in Bishop, 2003, p. 270).

Such assertions are accurate, though they do not hold force over every student example. A general lack of reflection or deep thought, the tendency toward exhortation rather than contemplation, is sampled in all kinds of student writing, from essay writing to argument, and in all disciplines. The uneven standards of good writing across institutions make it possible that such writing is even rewarded in some cases (1). Moreover, we are all guilty of a lack of deep thinking at some point in our lives, for most of us at some point in our daily lives. In our tel-evangelized, Internet-focalized society, tagged on morals are the norms, not the anomaly. We celebrate quick and easy solutions. Why then should we think them oddities when easy solutions and moral lessons are paper-clipped additions to the convoluted dilemmas at the heart of a personal narrative? At some point, such endings find their way into the churn and plunder of all academic enterprise. We should not single them out for criticism only at the helm of the personal essay.

The above criticisms of the personal essay can be directed at a vast amount student writing, the fault of which is as much the writers' age and frame of mind (and the writers' culture) as it is the genre of writing. On the other hand, the benefits of personal writing, though applicable to writing at large, must also be considered unique and appropriate to the experience chosen as a subject for reflection and extrapolation. Scott Russell Sanders (1995) argues that "Writing is a way of discovering what you don't already know, of clarifying what you don't understand, of preserving what you value, and of sharing your discoveries with other people" (as cited in Root, 1999, p. 129). This statement can be said of all writing: it is personal, expressive, expository, and argumentative. But apply this statement to personal experience and the subject matter and its "discovery" carry with them the potential for life management and change, self-improvement, and community enrichment, and when employed at the college level, this process engages change at young and impressionable ages. Thomas Newkirk (1997) writes that, "the desire to make sense of what we see and do does not suddenly come upon us in midlife. I have always believed that students appreciate the chance to write about their lives and interests" (p. 39). Wendy Bishop (2003) celebrates Newkirk's position, saying Newkirk views his students as individuals "with an insistent need to make meaning of [their lives] as it is unfolding and as individual[s] who will evolve, rather than as individual[s] who should wait until [they are] 40 or 50 before [they are] able to understand the events of [their] young adulthood" (p. 258-9). Teachers often promote student-centered education and student empowerment, and they talk about how narratives of growth contribute to self-understanding. The pressure of evaluation and objective standards, however, even in the ambiguous world of written ideas, resist full-fledged student acceptance as insistent meaning-makers.

Composition teachers converse energetically about various academic forms of writing, the most celebrated among them argument—the dialectic interchange among viewpoints and ideas—especially as such interchange involves analysis of some particular objective topic. The personal expressive essay gets criticized a little in these conversations, flowing as it does on the subjective, even emotional, tributaries of the writer's experience. In the face of such criticism, I have tried to address some of what I think to be the genre's overarching value. Now, using two student examples, I would like to discuss how the personal narrative can be the keystone to a learning experience more complex than a single writing opportunity can represent. Moreover, the collaboration between my class and our community partner, joined under the aegis of a living-learning community, contributed to a synergy not ordinarily found in the academic classroom.

# Community Lessons

The Michigan Community Scholars Program has stated goals of "deep learning," "engaged community," "meaningful civic engagement/community service learning," and "diverse democracy, intercultural understanding, and dialogue." Underpinning these phrases is additional language that attends to matters of knowing and the transition to college, addresses concepts of success and learning, and characterizes relations between the individual and the group: commitments, sustainability, and justice. As a teacher I want to believe that I am mindful of, and even achieving, these goals every day. Even being so mindful does not make it so, though I was not aware of this until my community partner made her first visit to our class. We had been reading *Nickel and Dimed* by Barbara Ehrenreich (2002) and *Down and Out, On the Road* by Kenneth Kusmer (2002), books that I thought were excellent in bringing to life aspects of homelessness and empowerment. Texts being what they are, students have a tendency to argue with them. That is their job and what they are trained to do. Sometimes, however, and I had a sense of this happening at the time, the academic challenge and adventure of critiquing texts may overshadow the real knowledge that the text provides. My students thought that Ehrenreich's participant-observer research was biased, due to her upper middle class status and the cushion that her status provided her. The criticism of Kusmer was more basic: he was boring.

Our community partner was neither biased nor boring, and even if she had been, her real life presence, her ethos of lived experience helping the homeless, and those at risk of becoming homeless, gave her immediate credibility and influence. The influence was not to persuade students so much as it was to draw their attention. Unlike what they do with a written text, my students' first impulse was not to break down our community partner and analyze her into contradictory pieces. Their impulse was to listen. Let me consider for a moment that the presence of one woman in my classroom for one day contributed to achieving programmatic goals of "deep learning," "engaged community," "meaningful civic engagement/community service learning," and "diverse democracy, intercultural understanding, and dialogue," contributed more powerfully than what I had been trying to do each week for months. It sounds like an overstatement, but there is also a degree of truth.

HERO's mission is to "Empower people who are homeless to achieve maximum self-sufficiency." Among the program's most difficult objectives is to get its clients to think critically about the circumstances that have led to homelessness, or the threat of becoming homeless. These circumstances have their sources both internally, in the heart and mind of each person, and externally, in the social, economic, and political forces that striate our culture. In presenting HERO's objectives to my students, Marti Rodwell also tried to get my students to examine their own circumstances (though much more privileged than those of her usual cliental) and examine them critically. "It takes great courage to see beyond the comfort of your own situation," she would say, "especially when the comfort and entitlements of college students are so profound. And before the courage, seeing the circumstances of your own good fortune requires a tremendous shaking of the trunk and spading of the roots."

Marti's interest was not primarily in my students, however. She wanted to make the situation of the homeless real and tangible for them, but she also hoped that the narratives they wrote would be useful in helping the nonprofit support organizations act less like organizations and more like interested individuals. In this way, the students would be performing a service for Marti, contributing to the conversations among nonprofit organizations in Washtenaw County. In turn, the work of the assignment would help the students better understand the myriad variables among people and associations that contribute to, and result from, homelessness in our culture. Marti cited Louis Anderson, HERO founder, who likes to say of their work, "It's not about money, it's not about organizations. It's about people solving the problems of homelessness in a personal way." Though nonprofit organizations are in most cases humanistic in approaching their work, they are, like for-profit organizations, constructed of hierarchies and consequently prone to the philosophies and behavior consistent with hierarchical structures. Kenneth Kusmer (2002) writes that the history of organized charity reveals an antagonistic relationship between reformers and the people whom they are trying to reform, and the institutional view of the homeless contained a strong element of authoritarianism. Josephine Shaw Lowell, a leading 19th Century charity reformer, said, "Tramps, vagrants or loafers [to be] unhappy beings [who] should be forced into a decent existence or kept in close confinement" (as cited in Kusmer, 2002). Indeed, times have changed, and attitudes toward the homeless have evolved, especially among those people and organizations designed to aid the homeless. But the economic, social, and personal factors that converge upon the homeless identity are far more complex than an institutional framework can efficiently respond to, even as that framework seeks to be benevolent.

Just as the homeless require a hard, invigorating, and empowering examination of self and surroundings before securing themselves a stake of independence in society, and just as my students require the same in order to understand the depth of their privilege, reform organizations require a healthy sense of self reflection to see the degree that institutional assumptions have become institutional reality without anyone noticing it (anyone, that is, from the institutional point of view). The homeless tend to be quite sensitive to, and aware of, the limits presumed upon them by well-intended benefactors at ease in the world of 9 to 5. Marti thought that a set of narratives written through the eyes of homeless clients, might release such a reflection, reminding us all to solve the problems of the homeless in a personal way, and in this way the narratives would serve the community at large. At the same time, my students would be drawn out of their comfort zone and drawn into the Ann Arbor community in ways they had never anticipated.

# How Am I Going To Do This?

*Just take a breath and if you find yourself at a loss for words, read the following intro: Hi. My name is (give your first name only). I'm a student at the U-M and I need your agency's help with a writing assignment. I am supposed to write a first person narrative about being homeless and I have been assigned a specific case scenario. May I speak with a caseworker or intern who could answer some of my questions?*

*(Be silent here and wait to be connected with the appropriate person).*

*Once you get to the caseworker, you will find yourself calming naturally (that is, IF the caseworker is doing his/her job well.)*

Students were nervous about starting their research. It was like nothing they had ever done before. What are the organizations that I would go to for help? Where do I find them? Why does it matter that my scenario says I am biracial? Where is Ypsilanti? Do I have to try to live on a job that pays $8.50? How am I going to get to work if I don't have a car? What do you mean, I can't work from the computer in my room?

Marti wrote encouraging notes to the students, telling them to be confident in themselves. She also sent them a list of supporting questions entitled "food for thought."

- Given the scenario, where are you living while trying to solve your housing crisis?
- How much time do you have (if any) before you are homeless?
- What needs do you have (immediate and/or long term)?
- What services will you seek to meet those needs?
- How many calls did it take to find all the help you needed?
- What are you feeling as you seek out assistance?
- How many places did you have to contact to find the services you need?
- How many times did you have to reveal your personal "story" in order to receive help?

- How did you manage conflicting demands—i.e., you would have to go to the agency to meet with someone but in so doing, you would miss work/school/etc.
- How did transportation factor into your housing crisis?
- How were you treated by the people you sought help from (from receptionist to service provider)?
- Did you receive all the assistance you needed?
- Did you encounter any judgments from others?
- Is your solution to your housing crisis temporary or permanent?
- Did you learn anything from this exercise—has your view of what it means to be homeless changed?

The longer students studied these questions, immersing themselves in their complexity, the better they did in both research and writing. Though students had marveled at the intensity of Marti's community presence, the first week after her visit some found themselves in various degrees of turmoil, and few of them wanted to engage the "food for thought" questions vigorously. The scenarios were generally 50-75 words, leaving many particulars of a person's life unstated. To imagine, for example, where one would stay while looking for a home required a huge leap for a college student never susceptible to any such risk. On the other hand, those few students who had been familiar with such risk, either from their own situation, or more likely from an acquaintances' situation, became defensive and unexpectedly proud of such knowledge and experience. Still others expressed distain for the person in their scenario, possibly disturbed by the close proximity, for example, of a 17-year-old biracial female who became pregnant in 10th grade but insisted on finishing school.

## Reflective Writing: Kevin Pereira

After leaving the classroom on the day that the HERO assignment was given to us, I thought to myself, "This is a really ambitious assignment." It wasn't your typical English paper where you had to analyze some text or approach a topic from a certain perspective. This task was going to require me to make some phone calls and really involve myself in the assignment. My worries about this task were compounded by the fact that I had to take on the role of a pregnant teenager. This was something I was uncomfortable with, as the difference in sex between me and my character would require some extra thought when writing the piece.

I began this assignment by looking at the immediate needs of my character. It turned out that due to car repair payments I wasn't going to be able to pay my rent. As my character had a baby, I thought a logical place to start would be with the Family Independence Agency (FIA). I was quite nervous making my first phone call, as I wasn't quite sure what the reaction would be. To my surprise the person on the line was extremely helpful, giving me details about a 'work-first' program that would help to pay my car repair bills. This was both good and bad news in the context of the assignment. I had solved my character's problem, but I had done it in only one phone call, which didn't give me enough material to write a paper.

I then decided that I would back up into the earlier years of my character's life and start from the causes of the pregnancy. This allowed to me to include organizations that helped pregnant teens through childbirth and other related issues. I then made a new list of immediate needs and set up my story as a prospective University of Michigan student who runs away to the only other place she is familiar with, Ann Arbor. With my character being a student, I felt that it was easier to write a somewhat authentic account of her experience. Being an international student myself, I was able to convey the feeling of being new to Ann Arbor in my piece.

The next organization on my calling list was Ozone House. Expecting a helpful response I was greeted by a monotone voice who seemed rather irritated when I told him that I was a University of Michigan student doing a paper. Despite this, he did answer my questions, albeit keeping his responses rather brief. This attitude was also reflected in most of the other organizations that I called. At first I was frustrated; after all wouldn't these organizations want good publicity? But then I tried to think about the people answering the phones. All they would hear would be tales of woe from distraught teenagers. Trying to be upbeat and enthusiastic to their callers would definitely be very difficult in this context. All the same, if I were a distraught teenager, I would want to have a comforting voice on the other side of the phone. A monotone voice telling me to calm down would probably upset me even further.

In the process of finally sitting down and writing this piece, I realized that in some way I had experienced what my character would have experienced in real life. The frustrating and powerless feelings of making phone calls that would determine where I slept and when I ate. In some small way it actually frightened me. It made me realize what some homeless people may actually go through, especially when we see on television that the budget for social welfare is going up, and automatically assume that the less fortunate are being taken care of. This assignment really made me think about and question that assumption.

## The Argument

It is incumbent upon me to make some kind of claims about the students' writing, if possible to show the nature and degree of the learning that occurred from this collaboration. Above is Kevin's reflective essay on the assignment and his experience completing it. As conclusive evidence, student writing should be considered with some reservation, as should the claims I make about it. I can easily see in student work the qualities that I desire, even when they might not be clearly there. I will, however, admit to not having given too much direction to Kevin (and Zach, following) about "what" and "how" to write this reflective essay, an especially important point because both pieces so nicely suit my needs. It is not, however, the case that I chose these from a group of essays as the best. I asked these students to write a reflection, and accepted it as is. I gave them this direction:

> *From you, we would want two things: a copy of the essay you wrote in response to that assignment and a, say, 500-word composition that searches the depth of your reaction to doing that assignment. I mean, what did you really learn by doing that assignment (if anything)? Did it have any kind of altering effect on your character or sense of self?*

I am aware of how good students try to give the teacher what he wants, and I work against this propensity by drawing attention to the quality of the questions that arise after giving an assignment. I highlight where I think it is best that students answer for themselves, or think of audiences beyond the teacher and purposes more complex than pleasing the teacher. Nonetheless Kevin's reflection is a very teacher-pleasing piece of writing. He says the assignment was not typical. Marti and I, of course, knew it wasn't typical, and its uniqueness supports our contention that some new kind of learning was possible out of the exercise. Kevin points out that he will have to do some real imaginative thinking, because as his scenario was to be a woman, and he would have to try to think like a woman. He is nervous, out of his comfort zone.

More important in these teacher-pleasing reflections is the cultural transposition that Kevin speaks of, himself having come from Hong Kong, and how he can try to use his own experience as a newcomer to Ann Arbor to help imagine his young female counterpart coming to this town for the first time. Most important in this reflection is Kevin's depth of understanding of the homeless and, by association, his identification with people who work with the homeless. Kevin describes it as, "the frustrating and powerless feelings of making phone calls that would determine where I slept and when I ate." I accept Kevin's observations here completely, and resist interpreting this reflection as writing for the teacher. At their age, students don't really have much experience with power, nor do they generally have the experience of being powerless, having to ask for help to get by, and depend on other people and institutions to find a place to lay their head.

# Reflective Writing: Zach Abramson

It felt like just another assignment until I actually had to go out and find the place where I was supposed to live. The physical challenge of trying to find myself a home brought the situation into reality for me. It is one thing to think that you may not have found a place to stay, or in my case not fulfilling the assignment, because of nasty people on the phone telling you that there is nothing they can do. It is a completely different story, however, when you actually go out there and try and come up with nothing. For the first time, when I walked for 45 minutes trying to find the place where I was supposed to live and found only a dog-grooming place and an abandoned warehouse, I felt like I had failed. No matter what or who was against me, no matter if the woman on the phone gave me bad directions, I could not help but feel low and even stupid for not being able to complete the assignment.

The most upsetting part for me was finding out that it would be nearly impossible to continue the type of education that I desired and still be able to make it on my own. I had not even graduated high school yet and even though I had goals of continuing on to college, with the menial jobs that I would have been able to obtain, I would have had to work at least 40 hours a week in order to pay to be living on my own. I could only afford to take night classes. I am a very highly motivated person when it comes to school, but I cannot honestly say that I would find it in myself to get up everyday, go to work, go to school, all for a goal that because of my financial situation, seems very distant and perhaps unreachable. So the question of, "What would Carlos have to do to get through this situation?" suddenly transformed itself into "What would I do?" It is easy for me to be motivated right now because I don't have anything else to worry about, and because the goals I have set for myself seem within reach. When the question was finally turned onto me, the answer became more elusive than I had anticipated.

I never directly answered that question to myself. I just remember thinking how unfair the world must be. If someone who is so highly motivated, and has such high spirits, could be knocked down so many times by poverty that the same spirit that once gave them hope, cannot even get them off the ground any more, then there is something terribly wrong. I realized how much that same energy and motivation in myself goes in to making me who I am, and how I view and feel about myself. If I lost that spark, that energy that gets me up in the morning, I would have lost a part of myself. Deep down I think I knew that the answer to my question was that my so-called strength, my own self-perceived strong will, would most likely surrender to the hopeless injustice that is poverty.

I have always heard and read that poverty strips you of your autonomy and sense of self, but I never actually knew what that meant. This assignment, as corny as this may sound, made me realize all the things I take for granted. It made me realize that I am able to explore opportunities, and therefore myself, my likes and dislikes, interests and hobbies, all because I am privileged enough to do so. Now I always knew that the world is unfair and that not everyone can have everything they want, and I had come to accept the fact that the world distributes goods unequally and unfairly, but I could not accept the fact that people can be deprived of themselves. When I tried to get into the head of my character I felt that he had something to offer the world but couldn't afford to do so. I can only imagine what that must feel like. His personality, his goals and dreams, were stifled by the fact that he could not pay his rent. That is why I had him write that letter to his dead parents. I think he thought that no one in the entire world could see who he truly was, and the only people in the world who knew the true Carlos, not the poor boy, were his deceased parents. That letter was a catharsis in Carlos after many months of being confined emotionally to the world.

## The Argument

Zach's reflection strikes many of the same notes that Kevin's does, but Zach spends a little more time developing what he learned about homelessness, and he writes about it as well as any authority I can think of. Indeed, he is telling back to a teacher what he learned, and he might have learned some of this from his careful reading of Kusmer and Ehrenreich, both of whom explore in some detail the complexities of homeless identity. Noteworthy too is how Zach achieves some of his understanding and uses it as a basis for communicating his own perspective on being a student. Education is extremely important for Zach. He writes that he is highly motivated when it comes to school, but considers that he can maintain that motivation only because he has the luxury of being able to devote all of his time to being a student. More subtly, Zach addresses how poverty and uncertainty of home can be exhausting, and, finally, dehumanizing, making goals that exist beyond the necessities of food and housing seem increasingly distant and impossible. Zach suggests that he too might buckle under such pressure. He writes, "I have always heard and read that poverty strips you of your autonomy and sense of self, but I never actually knew what that meant." And I believe him. His experience advanced and made more concrete a concept that he had learned about before, but understood only in the abstract relationships of words.

Both Kevin and Zach make reference to the people with whom they spoke on the phone. Kevin said he was greeted by "a monotone voice who seemed rather irritated when I told him that I was a University of Michigan student doing a paper." Zach says that "It is one thing to think that you may not have found a place to stay, or in my case not fulfilling the assignment, because of nasty people on the phone telling you that there is nothing they can do." The assignment intersects with real life. Community agency workers no doubt felt it a burden to try to help a college student with an assignment. Kevin's version connects the irritation rather directly to his being a university student. But he further understands the considerable weight and pressure on the people charged with helping others reconcile serious life crises. He writes, "Trying to be upbeat and enthusiastic to their callers would definitely be very difficult . . ." Zach's version emphasizes the harsh reality of when an agency just cannot be of help, for whatever reason. Refusals of help, not out of willfulness but out of impossibility, refusals to help with an assignment, and especially refusals to help with life, are demoralizing. Zach writes, "No matter what or who was against me, no matter if the woman on the phone gave me bad directions, I could not help but feel low and even stupid for not being able to complete the assignment." The phone call, the interchange between people who do not see one another, the phone call that for one person might be intimidating, for the other person is a matter of routine: both Kevin and Zach alluded to the sensitive nature of that interaction.

# My Personal Narrative:

Earlier I considered the merits and demerits of the personal narrative, and how narrative writing is consistent with goals for a writing course. Because they are relatively long, I have not included Zach and Kevin's narratives here, hoping to show the extent of their learning through their written reflections. I think, however, that the assignment's personal nature promoted the crossover of lives apparent in both students' experiences. That they were asked to see the world through another's eyes certainly initiated some of this exchange. Having then to explain the experience, and examine it closely enough to then write about it for others, rhetorically sealed the experience in their consciousness. This is genuine learning. Also important is the connection with our community partner who became the second set of eyes to read the narratives. My students were writing for me, but with the understanding that their work would have a larger function within the community, and in a small way, their high quality writing might influence the homeless support network in Washtenaw County.

This is not to say that everything went perfectly. Some students put off the research, phone calls and investigating resources, which are not tasks that can be done at the last minute. Nor do I think that all of the students spent enough time with the "food for thought" questions that Marti developed, missing the conceptual complexity of their scenario. One particular homeless resource, Ozone House, complained that too many students were calling them with questions, tying up their employees and volunteers needlessly.

A most vivid personal memory regarding the quality of my students' work and the learning from that work came a month or so after students completed this assignment. I had attended a community meeting with three of them, in which there was a presentation by a group of teachers. They were doing wonderful work and made considerable claims about how they were changing students' lives. I can be skeptical about such claims, changing of a life being such a considerable achievement. After the meeting I asked my students what they thought, and they in turn asked me what I thought. I told them I was skeptical about such extravagant claims and said it would be like Marti and I giving a presentation saying that our assignment changed their lives. It was a critical moment. Were they free to respond honestly? "Well," I asked, "Did completing that assignment change your life?" Shyly, as if they were really surprised that I would consider it in any other way, they said yes.

## Note

1. In saying this I do not mean to imply that standards of good writing can be established. The effort, though ongoing, remains futile due to the complex, fluid, subjective nature of words and interpretation. Such futile efforts, however, remain vital to the writing life we hope to inculcate in each new generation of student and teacher.

## References

Bishop, W. (2003). *Suddenly sexy: Creative nonfiction rear-ends composition.* College English, 65, 257-275.

Ehrenreich, B. (2002). *Nickel and dimed: On (not) getting by in America.* New York: Henry Holt and Company .

Elder, D. (2000). Expanding the scope of personal writing in the composition classroom. *Teaching English in the Two-Year College, 27*, 425-33.

Harris, W. V. (1996). Reflections on the peculiar status of the personal essay. *College English, 58*, 934-53.

Kusmer, K. (2002). *Down and out, on the road: The homeless in American history.* Oxford: Oxford University Press.

Newkirk, T. (1997). *The performance of self in student writing.* Portsmouth, NJ: Boynton.

Root, R.L., Jr. (1999). Interview with Scott Russell Sanders. *Fourth Genre, 1*, 119-32.

Sanders, S. R. (1995). The writer in the university. *Writing from the center.* Bloomington, IN: Indiana University Press.

University of Michigan. Student academic affairs: The course guide, fall 2003. http://www.lsa.umich.edu/saa/publications/courseguide/fall/361125.html?f03

# Chapter 9
## COLLABORATIVE LEARNING ABOUT UNSUSTAINABILITY: AN INTERDISCIPLINARY SEMINAR TO HELP ACHIEVE SUSTAINABILITY

James Crowfoot and Susan Santone

Environment, Sustainability, and Social Change is one of several first year seminars available to MCSP and other first-year students at the University of Michigan. This seminar fulfills MCSP students' requirement to complete an academic seminar that includes a focus on community. The seminar's main topic is a contemporary crisis: of rapidly increasing unsustainability and the response to this unprecedented set of interlocking challenges. Unsustainability is of growing concern to local communities, nations, and the rapidly developing international/global system.

This chapter covers two main topics: (1) background on the problem of unsustainability, challenge of sustainability, and why higher education urgently needs to address these topics, and (2) description of an MCSP first-year seminar focused on this growing global and local problem that threatens life on planet Earth.

## What Is Unsustainability?

Unsustainability is increasingly associated with multiple, interconnected, and unprecedented changes in the natural environment and human societies. These environmental changes threaten the sustainability of life on planet Earth. These changes are significantly and negatively impacting Earth and its human inhabitants. They have been documented by scientists (e.g., Board on Sustainable Development, National Research Council, 1999; Vitousek, Mooney, Lubchenco, & Meillo, 1997; Wackernagel et al., 2002); United Nations Conferences (e.g., on environment [Stockholm, 1972], environment and development [Rio, 1994], population and development [Cairo, 1995] and related topics); United Nations operating units (e.g., Environment Programme, Development Programme), and innumerable reports by governments at all levels throughout the world. These changes have also been accepted as significant and threatening by increasing numbers of both public and private sector leaders, nongovernment/nonprofit organizations focused on topics including human rights, environment, poverty, education, and religion (Tibbs, 1999; Todd, 1997; Union of Concerned Scientists, 1993, 2000).

Driving forces behind these serious global and local changes include quantitative and qualitative changes associated with population growth, inequitable economic consumption and production, resource extraction, waste disposal, and rapid technological changes. The growing negative impacts of these human caused changes are being detected in the:

- Atmosphere (e.g., global warming, ozone thinning, acid rain, and disruption of the nitrogen cycle);
- Land (e.g., urban sprawl resulting in loss of agricultural lands and natural areas; deforestation; desertification; degradation of agricultural lands through soil erosion, salinization, and depletion of micro organisms and other nutrients, and rapid and extensive species extinctions);

- Fresh water (e.g., growing demand, overuse, and pollution);
- Oceans (e.g., loss of species, rising sea levels, growing "dead zones," habitat destruction, and other widespread pollution);
- Human health (e.g., nutritional changes leading to increasing malnourishment, hunger, and obesity; new widespread diseases such as AIDS and SARS: presence of endocrine disrupting chemicals in animals including humans that lower fertility and increase birth defects; elevated radioactivity levels causing cancers; and genetic mutations and increasing unhealthy impacts from lead, mercury, PCBs and other toxic substances);
- Human social conditions (e.g., increasing economic and social inequities between and within nations with attendant poverty contributing to suffering and reduced life expectancies; increased cultural and economic interdependencies with additional vulnerabilities; growing violence and threats of violence from inequities; ethnocentrism; and threats including weapons of mass destruction, terrorism, and new technologies such as genetically modified foods) (Board on Sustainable Development, 1999; Hinrichsen & Robey, 2000; Lee, 2002; Roberts, 1999; Vitousek, et al., 1997).

With increasing local, national, and international attention to these problems, there is a growing awareness that human civilization's future sustainability can no longer be taken for granted. As public concern and expert analyses about the possible future for humans, it is urgently necessary that teaching and learning be redirected to the topics of unsustainability and changes needed to achieve sustainability (Wheeler & Bijur, 2000).

# Sustainability

Since the mid-1980s the United Nations has been the most influential organization to identify the challenges of unsustainability, increasing international awareness. In 1987, the World Commission on Environment and Development concluded pioneering investigation, analysis, and recommendations by publishing *Our Common Future*. The report calls for an intensive and ongoing international effort to address environmental degradation, poverty, population growth and economic development. "Sustainable development" is advocated, which is defined as "meeting the needs of the present without compromising the ability of future generations to meet their needs" (World Commission on Environment and Development, 1987, p. 8).

This report and subsequent United Nations commitment to sustainable development has been the focus of a series of major United Nations conferences. In one of the most important such conferences, the 1993 Earth Summit in Rio de Janeiro, Brazil, participating governments made commitments, and adopted treaties and a broad and comprehensive set of goals and objectives titled "Agenda 21" to guide sustainability initiatives. Subsequently, many international government bodies, private organizations, and businesses developed and adopted new policies and implemented programs that respond to the Agenda 21 plan. Ten years later, in 2002, in Johannesburg, South Africa the United Nations convened a follow-up conference to examine progress and problems in working toward the goals adopted at Rio. At the most recent conference—largely ignored by the United States—governments did not take bold new actions or even remedial actions in response to the successes and failures since the Rio conference. In Johannesburg, public-private partnerships undertook the boldest initiatives, although more limited changes were committed in specific regions. This conference generally concluded that despite many new initiatives and ongoing programs, unsustainability was still ongoing and increasingly threatening. This is due to cumulative environmental and social damages and a shrinking window of opportunity before potentially critical thresholds are exceeded in fundamental biophysical processes that are vital globally or in specific regions.

## The Use and Misuse of the Term "Sustainability"

While there are many approaches to sustainability, most reflect the belief that the current patterns of ever increasing consumption accompanied by ever increasing damage to the biosphere and its ecosystems along with every increasing inequities among and within nations cannot be sustained. Consequently many people, groups and organizations believe that individuals, communities, organizations, societies and global systems must find new ways to meet needs based on maintaining and restoring the natural environment and more equitably distributing resources including power.

Shifting to more sustainable practices will involve significant changes in the fundamental belief systems underlying many current economic policies-especially the ideas that unlimited growth is both desirable and possible, that unregulated markets are both desirable and possible, and that poverty is inevitable and is only to be ameliorated by means of continued economic growth the benefits of which accrue mainly to people above the poverty level.

While some interest groups are taking the lead in advocating greater eco efficiency, use of renewable energy, more equitable and environmentally focused taxation, and needed regulations the most powerful interest groups are advocating the status quo or worse still, policies that degrade the natural environment and increase economic and social inequities. While some businesses are taking a lead-for example, by reporting on their 'triple bottom line' of economic, environmental and social progress toward greater sustainability-most industries continue to operate under the 'profits-first' paradigm that includes maximization of externalized costs to be paid for by others often the public and acquisition of subsidies from the public purse.

So how do such businesses try to gain a place under the PR-friendly 'sustainability banner'? One approach is to co-opting the term, "sustainable" by using it frequently to describe their organization. For example the phrase "sustainable growth" has become popular in some circles to describe a business-as-usual approach to sustaining only profits. Other industries now pepper their marketing with the term "sustainable" along with visual images of pristine nature while behind the scenes they resist policy initiatives that would truly advance environmental sustainability. The practice of green washing a company's environmental practices and record has become so widespread and profitable that PR firms specialize in it and watchdog groups devote themselves to exposing it.

In attempting to sort out the meaning and validity of phrases such as 'sustainable growth' or 'sustainable development,' scholars and policymakers have emphasized a critical distinction: 'Development' refers to an increase in the quality of an output-product or service, while 'growth' implies an increase in quantity of whatever is produced and concomitantly an increase in the energy and other resource inputs. As economist Herman Daly (1996) notes, "when something grows it gets bigger. When something develops it gets different" (p. 193).

In this spirit, the term 'sustainable development'-an increase in the quality of life within ecological limits along with more equitable distributions of costs and benefits-is considered by many to be a valid goal, while 'sustainable growth'-perpetual increases in quantitative output while maintaining or increasing inequities-is dismissed by critics as an inherent contradiction.

In assessing and making sense of the use of the term "sustainability" in different contexts, then, the reader is encouraged to consider, to what extent does this emphasize qualitative over quantitative, and more equitable over inequitable improvements?

## Why Should Higher Education Be Involved?

To fulfill its responsibilities to students, nations, humanity, and future generations, higher education must refocus its teaching, research, and operating activities. Higher education should place highest priority on efforts to identify and understand unsustainability and develop means to achieve sustainability (Cortese, 2003; Fiho, 2000; Rees, 2003). Calder and Clugston (2003) concluded,

*These institutions [colleges and universities] are vested by society with the task of discerning truth, imparting values, and preparing students to contribute to social progress and the advancement of knowledge. They have a profound responsibility to impart the moral vision and technical knowledge needed to insure a high quality of life for future generations (p. 42).*

Furthermore, higher education's responsibilities should reflect its exclusive areas of expertise, research, and teaching capabilities, which are needed to understand unsustainability. Colleges and universities have the capabilities to develop innovations and other changes required to achieve sustainability, and train teachers and other leaders to be active and effective in working for sustainability (Moomaw, 2003). Increasingly, faculty members and college students world-wide want to study the topics and issues of unsustainability, and develop strategies, innovations, and resources needed to achieve sustainability.

Higher education is just beginning to recognize this challenge, and initiate some needed changes (Calder & Clugston, 2003; Fiho, 2000; Shriberg, 2002). According to Clugston and Calder (2000), "the two major factors controlling the structure and functioning of academia—disciplinary structure and economic forces—have moved very little toward sustainability" (p. 45). Because the overwhelming majority of students graduating from U.S. universities and colleges are ignorant of this challenge and needed responses, many higher education institutions still contribute more to increasing unsustainability, rather than its solutions.

At the University of Michigan in 1997, a small group of faculty and administrators from the School of Natural Resources and Environment and the School of Business, initiated and implemented a major event to increase visibility and understanding of the challenges of unsustainability. Positive examples of responses to this unprecedented problem were presented. The event was a semester-long "Lecture Series on Sustainable Development, Community and Business," held in winter 1998. Many University units and a major business corporation sponsored and funded this series. Attendees included many undergraduate and graduate students, members of the public, faculty, and research scientists. Lectures were broadcast locally via educational television. Visiting experts and speakers were nationally recognized scientists, professional practitioners, and activists working to understand different aspects of the unsustainability problem and the changes needed to accomplish sustainability. These lecturers came from diverse backgrounds including ecology, agricultural science, economics, political economy, architecture, landscape planning and design, business, environment, social activism, public policy, and politics.

## Seminar Development by Students, a Professor and an Expert Community Partner

Two faculty members on the planning committee for the lecture series, Crowfoot and Gladwin, decided to respectively teach an undergraduate and a graduate course in conjunction with these lectures. Their goal, subsequently realized, was for a group of students to regularly attend these important lectures while studying related issues and discussing the lectures.

In Crowfoot's course, an undergraduate student, Kathryn DeGroot, chose as her course project the need for universities to offer ongoing undergraduate courses focused on understanding unsustainability and means for achieving sustainability. Her final paper recommended topics which merit coverage. In class discussions leading up to the students' final papers, other students offered their ideas and support for the ideas that DeGroot developed. Crowfoot had begun to develop a first-year seminar focused on learning about unsustainability with examples of initial responses to the problem. Crowfoot's work to develop a new course for incoming undergraduate students was inspired by the lecture series, students' serious interest and work in conjunction with these lectures, and his own increasing attention and involvement with sustainability. DeGroot expressed interest in being involved, enrolled in an independent study course with Crowfoot and began planning the new seminar.

Based on its first-year students' growing interests in the environment, the Residential College—a long established living-learning community—wanted a first-year seminar focused on environmental issues. Crowfoot was invited to teach the course. Based on an understanding and commitment to environmental studies, the Residential College was interested in making the new seminar interdisciplinary, focused on sustainability, and inclusive of field trips. Because of the Residential College's long commitment to innovative undergraduate education, there was an established practice of senior undergraduate students participating with a faculty member. This model emphasized a learning experience in some aspect of course teaching related to an area of the student's knowledge and interest.

This precedent further supported Crowfoot's supervision for DeGroot's independent study. A major in environment and natural resources, DeGroot brought with her interest, creativity, and environmental knowledge relating to sustainability, previous teaching experience, and experience as a peer academic advisor. Crowfoot had not previously taught first-year college students, but wanted the opportunity to expose them to this urgent and widespread problem. He also believed that interdisciplinary teaching and learning needs to happen as early as possible for undergraduate students. He welcomed DeGroot's rapport with undergraduates and her experience, good ideas and commitment to motivating and challenging first-year students to learn about unsustainability and possible solutions. She and one other student from the course based on the lecture series, Paul Siersma, led small group discussions that were used extensively in this seminar. They also helped lead other learning activities, including field trips and student projects. This three-person team, with seminar participants in fall 1998 created an exciting, challenging, and successful seminar that laid the groundwork for continuing to develop and offer this seminar. Based on positive student and faculty evaluations, the Residential College also offered the opportunity for the course to be taught again.

At this time, David Schoem, faculty director of MCSP, invited Crowfoot to move the seminar to MCSP. MCSP was a highly attractive setting because of its focus on community and community service, and its ability to attract and challenge a highly diverse group of first- and second-year students. MCSP was innovating a new teaching role, "community partner" for its academic seminars and service-learning courses. Crowfoot was becoming involved in local off-campus sustainability initiatives, recognizing a source of rich learning resources. The community partner's role offered an opportunity to bridge this academic seminar and community-based expertise and sustainability work being pioneered in Ann Arbor and Washtenaw County. Susan Santone was a leader in these activities. Washtenaw County hired her to lead efforts to engage local K-12 systems in sustainability education. Independently of these responsibilities, she had developed a high school curriculum on sustainability. This provided Santone, a skilled and committed community-based professional working for sustainability, the opportunity to join Crowfoot as a community partner for the seminar. Santone brought to the seminar in-depth knowledge of sustainability, new learning activities, community-based student project opportunities, new and more structured student involvement in developing projects, and her professional expertise in planning and conducting selected seminar sessions. Working together, the authors further developed and taught this seminar based on different but complementary academic backgrounds, community practice experiences, and strong commitments to empowering education to further community, societal, and global changes.

Throughout subsequent semesters of this seminar, student evaluations and suggestions, and participation in class and other activities has continued the strong tradition of student involvement, influence, and experience. Seminar members often provide instructors with anonymous midterm written evaluations of the seminar. This results in explicit commitments to changes that frequently involve both students and instructors. Sometimes individual seminar sessions are evaluated through structured discussion to identify seminar members' positive and negative impressions and describe suggested changes to make improvements.

Special student participation opportunities have emerged, such as when previous first-year participants returned as upper-class students to lead seminar discussion groups, give guest presentations, and join seminar service-learning activities. For example, in the fall of 2002, Ethan Orley and Alex Wolk—seniors and former seminar students—spent a semester leading small group discussions, presenting some of their international project experience working for sustainability, and contributing to weekly seminar planning. At the end of their experience, Orley and Wolk provided Crowfoot with extensive written feedback on their own learning and on ideas for strengthening the seminar. Many of these ideas are being used successfully.

Within some seminars, students have been proactive in taking on presenter and panelist roles, and shaping requirements that better met their learning styles and interests. A recent seminar discussion, triggered by instructor criticism on a prior written assignment, focused on what the students considered the best ways to learn. One student asked for the current requirements to be expanded to include the option of examinations in addition to papers. Several students agreed and the instructor offered a midterm take-home examination. This option was in lieu of a required paper. After handing in their examinations, students reported better understanding the connections between different topics. In reviewing for the exam, valuable information crystallized, which they had missed in earlier readings. These outcomes would have been less likely if the paper requirement had not changed. The syllabus subsequently changed to reflect student learning needs and requests to change the requirement.

## Seminar Content

Several factors influence seminar content, including:
- the topics of unsustainability and sustainability, and related academic work and social practice;
- students' precollege academic and life background, and their learning skills and current interests;
- teaching staff's commitment to interdisciplinary based learning in relation to major contemporary problems;
- commitment to critical thinking, collaborative learning, independent study, service-learning, and active participation and listening in discussions and problem solving.

Sustainability embraces concepts and information from many traditional disciplines, from biology to political science to ethics, and involving many other subjects, from natural and social science to the humanities (Board on Sustainable Development, 1999; Milbrath, 1989). Sustainability education is an interdisciplinary activity, to identify and understand processes, problems, and interactions involving both biophysical and social systems. This requires a new perspective that incorporates breadth while focusing on interactions and connections driving human and institutional change that affect biophysical processes and resources.

For example, students learn from information about earth's biophysical systems to understand climate change, species extinctions, the ozone hole, and pollution of aquatic and terrestrial systems (Meadows, Meadows, & Randers, 1992; Roberts, 1999). Economic changes require attention to the dynamics of growth and different perspectives including development, international trade, inequality, and unemployment (Daly & Cobb, 1994; Nadeau, 2003; Williamson, Ibroscio, & Alperovitz, 2002). Social systems are examined to understand unprecedented changes, including emerging global organizations, and changes in local geographic communities (Anderson & Cavanagh, 2000; Roseland, 1998). Contrasting social theories are introduced, emphasizing the importance of conflicting perspectives, and responses to the aforementioned changes (Harper, 2001). To further appreciate these changes it is important to learn from environmental, economic and social history. Ethics and other analyses of cultures and cultural evolution are equally important (McNeil, 2002; LaDuke, 1997; Lazlo, 1999).

Interdisciplinary course materials selected for this seminar include journal articles (e.g., *Science*, *Harvard Business Review*, *The Ecologist*, *American Psychologist*); book chapters (e.g., *Beyond the Limits*, *Sustainable Community Development*, *The Ecology of Hope*); general interest texts (e.g., *The Atlantic Monthly*, *Hope, Human and Wild*) and diverse Internet materials. This interdisciplinary seminar also draws heavily from the emerging new policies and practices from organizations, governments, and communities committed to sustainability. These groups are found throughout the world, ranging from localities to nations. International organizations are becoming ongoing global structures of decision-making and implementation.

Initially, it is necessary to help students grasp the complexity of course material in a way that includes specialized information, expertise, and motivated, self-reflective social practice. The authors therefore sought a text that was well written, interesting, and focused on the topics of unsustainability/sustainability. Bill McKibben's *Hope, Human and Wild* (1995) is an excellent fit. McKibben reflects critically on environmental restoration in his home region—northern New York State and, more broadly, New England. McKibben visits and learns from substantial sustainability accomplishments—environmentally, socially and economically—in Curitiba, Brazil, and the Kerala region in southern India.

Generally no more than two or three students have heard about sustainability as a public issue, at the beginning of the semester. In the six times the seminar has been offered, only one student began the seminar familiar with the concepts of sustainability or sustainable development. These students who come to the University of Michigan with excellent high school academic records, often community service work experience, and sometimes-extensive travel experiences, generally know shockingly little about global environmental, economic, and social conditions. They are, however, highly motivated to learn about these conditions, sometimes disappointed and puzzled that they have not been aware previously of this information.

Most students in the seminar came from high schools without environmental science or an environmental studies course. Some students have been exposed to such topics through their high school biology class or school/community based youth organizations. Occasionally, summer camp and work experiences have provided students with information about the natural environment.

While many students have studied economics in high school, this did not include environmental and ecological economics, economic unsustainability, or contrasting economic theories. Students bring initial economic perspectives commonly informed by TV news and home based political discussions. Most students seem very confused about economics and lack interest in the topic.

Major social problems of poverty, inequality, discrimination, violence, wars, etc. are generally understood through the lens of dominant historical narratives that favor the affluent, United States, and status quo. Exposure to specific information about global conditions in these areas and major structural inequalities comes as an unpleasant surprise to most first-year students electing the seminar. Commonly expressed student beliefs include: "the poor will always be with us," and, "if people just worked hard they wouldn't be poor," etc.

Despite little previous background for this seminar, almost all students who elect it are highly motivated to learn about fundamental and difficult realities. While students are disappointed not to know more than they do, and discouraged about the state of unsustainability, they are willing to do substantial reading, discussion, and learning to come up to speed. Critical thinking that includes reflections on their own privilege, lifestyles, institutions, and values helps to understand their personal involvement in unsustainability. This process of introspection is a great challenge for students, who are struggling with many issues at the beginning of their college experience.

The MCSP's central theme—the study and practice of community—is integral to this seminar's content and process. The ideas that unsustainability occurs locally, nationally, and globally and that sustainability must be rooted in local changes (along with national and international changes), has given rise to many urban and rural community-based initiatives (Roseland, 1998). While the United States has lagged behind some nations in pursuing sustainability, some U.S. cities and larger local areas such as counties and metropolitan regions have initiated their own sustainability projects (Shuman, 1998).

One such city is Olympia, the capital of Washington. Olympia is located in Thurston County. Olympia's definition of sustainability states that a sustainable community continues to thrive from generation to generation because it has:

- ...a healthy and diverse ecological system that continually performs life-sustaining functions and provides other resources for humans and all other species.
- ...a social foundation that provides for the health of all community members, respects cultural diversity, is equitable in its actions, and considers the needs of future generations.
- ...a healthy and diverse economy that adapts to change, provides long-term security to residents, and recognizes social and ecological limits. (http://www.olywa.net, October 10, 2003).

Over the past decade, Olympia city government has pursued new policies and practices focused on sustainability, along with various local organizations. The Roundtable for Sustainability, a nonprofit organization staffed mostly by volunteers, has provided critical leadership for sustainability initiatives.

Typical goals for these local sustainability projects include:

- Maintaining and increasing biological diversity and healthy ecosystems through preservation, using conservation and restoration.
- Increasing human well-being and local and regional self-reliance within the locality and regional ecological carrying capacity, while minimally utilizing the carrying capacity outside the region, to more equitably share the planet's ecological carrying capacity.
- Increasing ecoeffiency to conserve resources and achieve zero waste, separating all biodegradable waste from closed-use system for nonbiodegradable wastes.
- Increasing stakeholder group participation and influence in decisions, paying attention to groups with different backgrounds with regard to: income and wealth, race and ethnicity, gender and sexual orientation, and nationality and religion.
- Balancing short- and long-term needs.
- Meeting basic human needs including safety and human rights, water, food, housing, education, health care, and a living wage with meaningful work.
- Stabilizing and/or reducing human population.

Students read descriptive and conceptual information about local geographic communities, and consider written and video case studies of community change in pursuit of greater sustainability (Bernard & Young, 1997; Hoff, 1998). Students draw on their own community experiences to compare and contrast these experiences with readings about local communities different from their experiences. Ann Arbor is used to illustrate unsustainable practices and the early stages of actions to pursue sustainability.

The seminar also focuses on international organizations such as the United Nations, World Bank, and World Trade Organization. Students generally know very little about these organizations and how they impact personal, local community, and global conditions. Most students pay little attention to in-depth news coverage. Therefore, to understand current events requires exposure to new media including the independent media to supplement mainstream media.

The seminar has included different subtopics. These have been determined by the availability of field based learning opportunities. For example, fall offers great opportunities for outdoor activities including sustainable agriculture and ecosystem restoration. The University of Michigan annually hosts a winter Martin Luther King celebration that provides many rich opportunities to examine the social unsustainability of racism, classism, and sexism, and responses to these hegemonic conditions.

Typical seminar topics include:
• Environmental and social problems contributing to unsustainability
• Sustainable agriculture and food security
• Sustainable land use
• Sustainable local communities
• Sustainable consumption
• Sustainable economy and business
• Sustainable global policies and practices

The time allotted to different subtopics is influenced by the students' interests, availability of guest speakers, field trips, and service-learning opportunities.

# Seminar Processes and Activities

Sustainability education's goal is to assist students as lifelong learners in creating a sustainable future for themselves and future generations. This assistance is partially cognitive, requiring new perspectives that are supported with theoretical background. Commonly accepted assumptions must be challenged, encouraging "outside of the box" thinking.

But sustainability education is also emotional, involving issues about which we are passionate and need to be involved. Involvement, connection, and intimacy are required to pursue sustainability. Sustainability education can be said to be about nurturing life in the present and for the future. This philosophy values all people, not just for now, but for all children of generations to come. It also includes respect for other species and their protection.

It is therefore easy to see why sustainability education can involve spirituality, and other subjective experiences and realities, and shared experiences and knowledge. Respectful, open, collaborative inquiry and problem solving among socially diverse individuals and groups is required for sustainability education.

Sustainability education is first and foremost about inquiry—questioning, examining, discovering what is not obvious either individually or collectively. As such it is an intensely topical-centered activity, yet always pulled along by emerging and future issues. Sustainability education gives rise to vital competencies including: deep inquiry and integration of what can be known through science, local knowledge, spirituality and the intellectual, emotional and practical commitments to caring for life. With this comes enhanced decision-making and problem-solving skills that include collaborating with others, to develop plans and actions to achieve sustainability.

This seminar is planned and implemented to develop a collaborative teaching-learning community in which each member is both teacher and learner. Responsibility is shared for doing the collective and independent reading, and participating in group discussions and written assignments. These assignments receive both peer and instructor evaluation.

The requisite pedagogy required by sustainability education is very much at home in the MCSP program because it emphasizes collaboration, learning process, teacher and learner roles, self-reflection, assessment, and community engagement.

## Collaboration

By definition this seminar is a small group activity in which 15-20 participants may constitute the small group, or subgroups may have as few as 3-5 participants. Within these small groups, collaborative relationships are encouraged, in which everyone listens, speaks, and learns. Everyone has something to offer and everyone is respected. When these small inquiry groups are functioning effectively the whole is greater than the sum of its members. Ideally, small groups have members from diverse backgrounds, and with diverse interests and life experiences. Mutual learning objectives are developed through collaboration. This collaboration is characterized by respectful interactions and honest exchanges of ideas and opinions. Seminar members both give and receive support and other resources, mutually working in the interest of overarching values and goals.

## Learning Process

Keeping with the tradition of academic seminars as a learning experience, this seminar emphasizes every member participate. There is mutual responsibility to learn through discussing assigned materials, self-selected materials, and individual presentations. This mode of inquiry contrasts an academic mode that is expert dominated, one-way communication based on memorization and student subordination. In sustainability pedagogy, inquiry, discovery, application, evaluation, and reformulation are emphasized over rote memorization. Discussions take place in groups of various sizes. Sometimes part of the seminar constitutes the active discussion subgroup and the other seminar subgroup sits outside of the active group, observing, listening, and providing focused comments when the active group discussion is finished.

## Teacher and Learner Roles

In the seminar the primary teacher role includes being a facilitator, resource, supportive co-learner, and model for leadership in shared learning. Not only the instructional staff acts in this role; students are encouraged and enabled to assume this role. In this seminar, as in MCSP, learning relationships among community partners, students, and faculty members are collaborative. No one is the lone expert and learning flows in all directions. Everyone teaches and learns, sometimes collectively and sometimes individually, but with mutual accountability achieved through evaluative but supportive critical feedback.

## Self-Reflection

Students use personal life experiences in seeking to understand how and why unsustainability occurs. As they learn about what is required to achieve sustainability, students evaluate necessary changes through personal and community experiences. Such seminar reflection is congruent with MCSP's emphasis on continually learning about "self, social identities, and a wide range of sociocultural groups and histories." Such learning is not a one-time event, but an ongoing process of continual reflection and evaluation.

## Assessment

In the sustainability seminar, learners practice and demonstrate their skills in inquiry, problem-solving, interdisciplinary analysis, creativity, and cross-cultural exploration through discussion, writing, and leadership responsibilities. The seminar regularly utilizes self-evaluation, peer feedback and instructor evaluation. Students are interested and willing to utilize such feedback toward learning about sustainability, and improving their skills in writing, speaking, discussing, and leading in small groups. Common questions in this seminar, as in the MCSP program, are: What is in the public interest? What will advance the local common good? What will advance the global common good?

## Community Engagement

This seminar continuously focuses on communities, including the community of the seminar and other communities in which the participants are. Other communities are engaged as well, via field trips, readings, videos, and guest speakers. Some of this engagement involves the entire seminar, but an important aspect of engagement happens when individual seminar members pursue independent projects. The seminar also emphasizes outside learning events in the larger university and surrounding community, encouraging members to attend events that are of particular interest to them, and report them to the larger seminar. These experiences and presentations greatly enrich the seminar and support an active, independent, and at the same time collaborative learning style.

As the University of Michigan has begun to recognize its own unsustainability and potential to contribute to sustainability, rich learning resources are available to students. Sometimes students independently seek to learn more about these initiatives or focus on them for their seminar project. Examples have included residence hall-based energy conservation, recycling, and information boards focused on sustainability and its connections to student lives. Field trips provide examples of local sustainability initiatives in the Ann Arbor area. Such field trip sites include sustainable businesses, housing communities, farms, and meetings for the Washtenaw County project, Sustainable Washtenaw. These field trips have included service to assist in an ecological restoration project within a nature preserve, or farm work for a sustainable agriculture.

Sometimes guest presenters from these initiatives or campus sustainability projects participate in the seminar. Field trips involving service-learning are particularly important to the seminar. These learning activities provide the growing awareness about unsustainability, the responses to this complex problem, and many opportunities for individuals, groups, organizations, and communities to adopt more sustainable behaviors. These positive examples provide needed hope and optimism in the face of the extensive and daunting information describing the negative impacts of current unsustainable practices.

Throughout the seminar members are required to critically examine their own behavior, and behaviors of their families and social background groups, to determine how, why, and how much they contribute to unsustainability and sustainability. This reflective analysis is respectful and supportive, so as to avoid blaming, denial, and other forms of distancing from the behavior patterns on which the seminar focuses.

A major seminar learning activity of the seminar is individual and group projects in which students pursue a topic of interest related to sustainability. They develop and complete this project to teach what they have learned to other seminar members. The chapter in this book titled, "Collaborative Learning About Sustainability: Independent Projects as a Significant Course Element," describes why these projects are so important, how they have been developed, and what we have learned and continue to learn in facilitating these learning-teaching experiences.

## Conclusion

Teaching and learning that focuses on unsustainability and sustainability, is in the early developmental stages. Already a small number of innovative states and localities recognize the issue's importance, including it in the K-12 curriculum. Over the six semesters in which this seminar has been taught, only one enrollee has come from such an earlier educational experienced focused on sustainability. This student completed her secondary education in Germany where attention to sustainability is found throughout educational institutions.

U.S. colleges and universities are currently not ahead of K-12 education in including sustainability in the curriculum. Attention to interdisciplinary learning opportunities for undergraduates provides a positive opportunity for expanding undergraduate education explicitly focused on unsustainability and sustainability. The seminar described in this article, in fact, is the first such freshman seminar at the University of Michigan that fulfills an interdisciplinary requirement.

Environment, Sustainability, and Social Change has benefited from being offered through MCSP, and from support of both the College of Literature, Science, and the Arts, and the

School of Natural Resources and Environment. MCSP's recognition and development of community partnerships has made possible our collaboration on this seminar.

What we have reported here would not have been possible without University of Michigan's ongoing improvement of undergraduate education. This seminar's development has been strongly supported by the development of the innovative Michigan Community Scholars Program and the new interdisciplinary Program in the Environment, a collaboration between the College of Literature, Science, and the Arts and the School of Natural Resources and Environment. We are grateful that these programs have provided us the opportunity to teach about the important and urgent challenges of unsustainability and the opportunities to bring about the much needed changes that will insure a sustainable future for human life and all that it depends on in order to survive and thrive.

## References

Anderson, S., & Cavanagh, J. (2000). *Field guide for a global economy.* New York: New Press.

Bernard, T. and Young, J. (1997). *Ecology of hope.* Gabriola Island, British Columbia, Canada: New Society Press.

Board on Sustainable Development, Policy Division, National Research Council. (1999). *Our common journey: A transition toward sustainability.* Washington, D.C.: National Academy Press.

Calder, W., & Clugston, R.M. (2003). International efforts to promote higher education for sustainable development. *Planning for Higher Education, 31*(3), 23-29.

Clugston, R., & Calder, W. (2000). Critical dimensions of sustainability in higher education. In Walter L. Fiho (Ed.), *Sustainability and university life* (pp. 31-46). New York: Peter Land Publishing Group.

Daly, H.E. (1996). Sustainable growth? No thank you. In Mander, J. and Goldsmith, E., (Eds.). *The case against the global economy and for a turn toward the local* (pp. 192-196). San Francisco, CA: Sierra Club Books.

Daly, H.E., & Cobb, Jr., J.B. (1994). *For the common good: Redirecting the economy toward community, the environment, and a sustainable future.* Boston: Beacon Press.

Cortese, A.D. (2003). The critical role of higher education in creating a sustainable future. *Planning for Higher Education, 31*(3), 15-22.

Fiho, W.L. (Ed.). (2000). Sustainability and university Life. New York: Peter Lang Publishing Group

Gallopin, G.C., & Raskin, P. (1998). Windows on the future: Global scenarios & sustainability. *Environment.* April. 7-11, 26-31.

Harper, C.L. (2001). *Environment and society: Human perspectives on environmental issues* (2nd ed.). Upper Saddle River, NJ: Prentice Hall.

Hinrichsen, D., & Robey, B. (2000). Population and the environment: The global challenge. *Population Reports: Special Topics, 28*(3), 1-28.

Hoff, M. (Ed.). (1998). *Sustainable community development: Studies in economic, environmental and cultural revitalization.* Boca Raton, FL: Lewis Publishers.

LaDuke, W. (1997). Voices from white Earth: Gaa-waabaabiganikaag. In H.E. Hannum, (Ed.). *People, land and community* (pp. 22-37). New Haven, CT: Yale University Press.

Lazlo, E. (1989). *The inner limits of mankind.* London: Oneworld Publications.

Lee, M. (2002). State of the planet. *The Ecologist, 20*(7), 6-11.

Meadows, D., Meadows, D., & and Randers, J. (1992). *Beyond the limits: Confronting a sustainable future.* White River Junction,VT: Chelsea Green Publishing.

McKibben, B. (1995). *Hope, human and wild: True stories of living lightly on the Earth.* St. Paul, MN: Hungry Mind Press.

McNeil, J.R. (2002). *An environmental history of the Twentieth Century: Something new under the sun.* New York: W. W. Norton.

Milbrath, L.W. (1989). *Envisioning a sustainable society: Learning our way out.* Albany, NY: State University of New York Press.

Moomaw, W.R. (2003). Aligning values for effective sustainability planning. *Planning for Higher Education, 31*(3), 159-165.

Nadeau, R.L. (2003). *The wealth of nature: How mainstream economics has failed the environment.* New York: Columbia University Press.

Rees, W.E. (2003). Impeding sustainability? The ecological footprint of higher education. *Planning for Higher Education, 31*(3), 88-99.

Roberts, Leslie, (Ed.). (1999). *World resources: A guide to the global environment, 1998-1999.* New York: Oxford University Press.

Roseland, M. (1998). *Toward sustainable communities: Resources for citizens and their government.* Stoney Creek, CT: New Society Press.

Sale, K. (1997). The Columbian legacy and the ecosterian response. In H. Hannum (Ed.). *People, land and community* (pp. 13-21). New Haven, CT: Yale University Press.

Shriberg, M. (2002). Institutional assessment tools for sustainability in higher education: Strengths, weaknesses and implication for practice and theory. *Higher Education Policy, 15*(2), 153-167.

Shuman, M. (1998). *Going local: Creating self reliant communities in a global age.* New York: Free Press.

Tibbs, H. (1999). Deeper news. *Global Business Network, 3*(1), 1-42.

Todd, J. (2000). An ecological economic order. In H. Hannum (Ed.). P*eople, land and community* (pp. 265-274). New Haven, CT: Yale University Press.

Union of Concerned Scientists (2000). World scientists' 1993 warning to humanity. P*opulation Press, 6*(1), 6-7.

Vitousek, P.M., Mooney, H.A., Lubchenco, J., & Meillo, J.M. (1997). Human domination of Earth's ecosystems, *Science, 277*, 494-499.

Wackernagel, M., Schulz, N.B., Deumling, D., Linares, A.C., Jenkins, M., Kapos, V. et al. (2002). Tracking the ecological overshoot of the human economy. *Proceedings of the National Academy of Science*, June 27, 2002.

Watson, G. (1999). The wisdom that builds community. New Village, 1, 18-21.

Wheeler, K.A., & Bijur, A.P. (Eds.). (2000). *Education for a sustainable future.* New York: Kluwer Academic/Plenum Publishers.

Williamson, T., Imbroscio, D., & Alperovitz, G. *Making a place for community: Local democracy in a global era.* New York: Routledge.

World Commission on Environment and Development. (1987). Our common future. New York: Oxford University Press.

# Chapter 10

## LIVING AND LEARNING THROUGH COMMUNITY SERVICE: A REFLECTION ON MICHIGAN COMMUNITY SCHOLARS PROGRAM SECTIONS OF SOCIOLOGY 389

**Annalissa Herbert, Amy Borer, Stephanie Brown, Kristen Joe, Sheyonna Manns,** and **Chibuzo Okafo**

*For the 5,000 first-year students who annually descend upon the University of Michigan's Ann Arbor campus, the first year of university life begins what is often considered a great adventure. Attending college involves an entirely new way of thinking and acting, a new way of living independently and understanding intriguing ideas and diverse individuals. How well one manages this transition may well define the rest of the college experience, and quite possibly one's life (A. Borer, personal communication, 2003).*

At the University of Michigan, selected first- and second-year college students have an opportunity to live, learn, and build community through the Michigan Community Scholars Program (MCSP). For these students, the concept of building community extends first as residents of Couzens Hall and to the local Ann Arbor community that is their home during college. Not all the residents of Couzens Hall are part of MCSP; students in the program take MCSP courses that emphasize: deep learning, deep community, civic engagement, and diverse democracy in a living-learning environment. This program allows students to grow as individuals and build leadership skills, while contributing tangibly to the greater communities in which they belong during their college years.

MCSP students are expected to participate in a close faculty-staff-student-community partner interaction. This allows all to contribute their skills, knowledge, and expertise in a safe and accepting environment comprised of people from diverse social, and racial backgrounds. These MCSP students are provided many opportunities to create and build community. They make a commitment to take MCSP courses in their first years that emphasize deep thinking about community building. Furthermore, student clubs, and MCSP events and programs allow students to further their leadership skills and knowledge base about community.

One required MCSP course students can take for college credit, but not for a letter grade, is Sociology 389/Project Community (1). This course places students as community service tutors and mentors in after-school programs at local elementary, middle, and high schools. On the surface, this interaction benefits both parties. The local schools have free access to highly skilled college students who serve as tutors and role models for their students. In exchange, the college students gain a tangible way to interact with the community outside the college classroom. This community interaction contributes in meaningful ways to learning, allowing students to observe in "real life settings" what they are learning about in the classroom. Though many students have reported amazing moments of self-actualization and deep learning through this course, some have observed its flaws. This article will reflect on the course successes and challenges from student perspectives.

Every year, the Ann Arbor Public School system faces budgetary constraints on hiring teachers, support staff, and needed services such as tutoring. Local community response to this situation has included asking for volunteers, local corporations, and other interested groups to fill the void. This concept of the local community pulling together is the bedrock of American civil society. Through this unique living-learning program, MCSP students are able to perform community service at these sites for college credit, and understand more deeply issues of social justice, community engagement, and service learning.

# Pedagogy of the Project Community/ Michigan Community Scholars Program

The MCSP sections of Sociology 389 are designed to accomplish four main goals of the MCSP program: deep learning, deep community, civic engagement, and diverse democracy. Like many of the MCSP courses, Sociology 389 is taught in Couzens Hall where many MCSP students live. This class provides critical linkages between academic engagement, critical thinking, and practical knowledge of real life issues, through a community service placement. Furthermore, the ability to engage in a living and learning environment allows student class discussions to spill naturally into other similar discussions in the residence dining hall, and student dorm rooms. The classroom is located down the hall from where the students live, creating an intimate and casual class atmosphere.

In Sociology 389, the students holistically live out MCSP goals. This allows for interesting cross conversations and deep thinking about issues such as deeper meanings of service-learning, and personal versus public responsibility. Such discussions may not naturally occur in other college seminars. As students see each other more frequently in the residence hall, they form strong bonds and friendships that continue in the classroom and at the community service sites. Another class goal is to foster and develop student leadership skills through peer-led weekly class discussions. Students also contribute individually and collectively at the community service sites through creative suggestions, and projects addressing specific community needs. The entire process allows students' "deep learning" by reflecting on their service and engaging in discussions about class, race, and social and educational justice.

### Class Requirements

Students who enroll in Sociology 389 MCSP sections are required to perform service work approximately five hours weekly at preassigned tutoring sites in an Ann Arbor elementary, middle, or high school. These students attend a weekly seminar that MCSP undergraduate student coordinators teach and lead. The coordinators attend weekly training meeting with a graduate student instructor (GSI). The GSI creates a class syllabus, which incorporates class readings on education, tutoring issues, and social justice. The student coordinators are required to lead the class discussions. Students enrolled in the course write 1-2 pages of a weekly reflection journal and a three-page midterm paper and a 10-15 page final paper analyzing their experiences at the community service site, course readings, and class discussions. Upon successfully completing of course requirements, these students receive credit on their college transcript—no letter grades are recorded for regular students. However, student coordinators do receive letter grades for the class based on the extra work and leadership they contribute to the course. The core of the "deep learning" occurs at the community service site placements where college students tutor and mentor in after school programs.

Student feedback has prompted course changes several times over the years to be more relevant to the community service site. For example, if college students report challenges working with children at site who lack discipline and motivation to learn, the class GSI would respond with class readings to supplement those issues (see class syllabus in the Appendix). Student feedback has been instrumental in tweaking the topics and the course requirements to make the class more useful to the next group of students working at the same site the following semester. This student feedback has also been instrumental in identifying issues that aid MCSP in building a more conducive working relationship with community partners, thus improving the experience for all. Consequently, students bring their "real life" experiences into the classroom and improve the class for the next group.

Much of the learning happens through experience at the community service sites. Over the last three years, MCSP has built relationships with an Ann Arbor high school, elementary school, and two middle schools. For various reasons, we have chosen to concentrate on working with a local elementary and middle school, and an after school program in a residential housing neighborhood. At each site, the college students experienced working with elementary and middle school students of different racial and ethnic backgrounds, and often with students who often come from lower socioeconomic backgrounds than the MCSP students.

What makes this course unique is that undergraduate students facilitate a seminar with their peers. MCSP class peer coordinators are selected through interviews with previous MCSP coordinators, faculty, and staff. This interview process occurs before peer coordinators lead a class. Before the semester starts, peer coordinators attend a one-day mandatory training, which the GSI and faculty director supervise. Throughout the semester the student coordinators meet weekly with the GSI to discuss class issues and receive ongoing training. Coordinators are not only responsible for leading class discussion based the course readings and site observations, but also are assigned readings specific to leading a class. Class coordinators receive letter grades for Sociology 395, which the MCSP faculty director and GSI supervise.

Class coordinators are required to lead seminars, write weekly journals, and generally participate at the community service site with their students. The GSI is responsible for the class syllabus, and training class coordinators in weekly sessions, through modeling different exercises and teaching techniques. The GSI also occasionally sits in on classroom discussions and visits the community service sites to observe student progress. The GSI and faculty director maintain relationships with community partners and troubleshoot administrative issues that may come up.

The course structure allows student coordinators a great deal of responsibility for the class. However, coordinators work closely with the GSI to resolve any issues related to teaching, personality conflicts, or the community service site. Student coordinators generally do an excellent job running the courses. In many cases coordinators begin as undergraduate students who completed the course and have demonstrated leadership skills in other aspects of the MCSP program. After the interview process mentioned above, selected students are offered coordinator positions for the following semester. Student coordinators are encouraged to show initiative and enhance their leadership experience by being innovative and creative within all levels of the course structure. Often, coordinators enjoy the experience so much that they take the course again or pursue other opportunities to lead class discussions.

Because most student coordinators have previously lived in Couzens Hall or are current residents, they tend to know students in the course more intimately than would normally be expected. Primarily in their first and second years of college, students in the course generally are getting to know each other adjusting to college life and living away from home. This level of intimacy often leads to heightened trust, openness, and honesty in classroom discussions between students and class coordinators. While there are advantages to extending learning opportunities and discussions to the cafeteria or dorm rooms, for example, the situations can also make maintaining individual levels of privacy difficult because many coordinators and students live in the same residence hall. Some coordinators report difficulty maintaining classroom authority among peers who they may have been "acting silly" in the dorm just the night before. Some coordinators may be younger than their classroom peers and fear their authority will be questioned. Other coordinators report that living near their students was convenient if they needed to talk about missed assignments, arranging rides to the community service site, or if students needed to contact them about other issues. Time is spent in weekly training sessions to address these issues and help the coordinators feel confident in their leadership role.

Almost every semester, both students enrolled in the course and class coordinators report making strong friendships through the class, and taking on other leadership positions because they developed confidence through the course. In the weekly training meeting, coordinators often share different techniques and exercises they use to elicit deep thinking about various topics related to race, gender, class, and working with children and teenagers. In many ways the coordinators serve a resource to one another in these meetings.

In addition to discussion, coordinators use exercises to explore class, gender, race, and other privilege. Exercises are drawn from the Project Community resource binder developed by the Edward Ginsberg Center for Community Service and Learning. The resource binder contains information on running a class, and exercises that sociologists, psychologists, and other professionals developed. The exercises are designed to start deep conversations about class, race, and gender hierarchies, and start conversations on multiculturalism, privilege, and team building as well as other issues in a safe but thought provoking way. Class coordinators have used various activities to elicit a deep discussion, the most popular tends to be the fishbowl exercise, and the privilege walk.

In the fishbowl exercise, students are asked to self-segregate based on various social identity groups. Then the group that is considered to have less societal power sits in the middle of the room to discuss issues, while everyone outside of the circle remains silent and listens intently to the conversation. After the conversation, the groups can switch places. After the exercise, the coordinators lead a class discussion about what students learned inside or outside the circle.

The privilege walk demonstrates spatially students' socioeconomic positions in society. The exercise begins with students standing in one straight line and moving a step forward or backward in response to various questions based on race, gender, socioeconomic categories, and financial resources. Through the exercise the students reveal perceived privilege. Class coordinators then lead a discussion about student feelings during the experience and how it impacts perceptions of each other. This exercise often begins a difficult conversation about assumptions that students may have about each other based on race, gender, and class. Coordinators ask the class to think about their assumptions regarding children at the community service sites and how to work around those assumptions.

# Voices of Undergraduate Student Class Coordinators

For undergraduate student coordinators, running their own class is an opportunity to grow personally and enhance their leadership skills. It can also be scary to face peers as an authority figure. Many coordinators initially report being nervous and later growing into the authority position. As Sheyonna Manns explains in her journal entry, being class coordinator put her in the awkward position of being both peer and authority figure:

*... I am a facilitator and a peer to many of the students. A thin line of respect draws the separation of the two. Along with setting ground rules, I will also establish a firm foundation of respect and camaraderie with the students. Through the mutual respect we'll have for each other my position in the class will easily be seen. I am aware that some of the decisions I'll have to make may not be well liked, however if respect is established in the beginning it matters not if they like my decision ...*

*Cooperation is key to a successful work relationship. Kristen [her co-coordinator] and I haven't had much time to exchange facilitator techniques and habits. We will, in the near future, set a time for us to meet and set the plan of action or agenda for discussion. We both have strong leadership skills, such as being able to react quickly to [unforeseen] situations. As we work together we'll be able to compliment each other's weaknesses and strengths. This will strengthen our role as co-coordinators and also hone each other's leadership skills. While cooperating with each other we will exercise our active listening skills, facilitation qualities, and compromising skills. These skills that we will utilize will aid us when we tutor at site (S. Manns, personal communication, 2003).*

According to class coordinator Chibuzo Okafo, although running a class may have initially been scary it is an intense growth experience. As he explains:

*I remember when I was first approached to facilitate Sociology 389. I was very skeptical about 'teaching' a class. I had no prior experience and absolutely no real training. I thought there was no way I would be able to facilitate a class and have the students take me seriously. It was very interesting to me when I found out that I would have a co-facilitator. Interesting and calming, [it made] me feel better about facilitating because I wouldn't go it alone. Looking back now, even I would admit that we were sloppy. We had a "training session," but nothing we did at training actually prepared us for the second week of class where we met with the students by ourselves. The first week had been easy because the GSI and professor were with us to introduce the course to the students. As fall semester progressed, I could tell that my co-coordinator and I had definitely grown as facilitators and we both felt that we understood what it took to be good coordinators. This helped our decisions to facilitate classes again this semester. We both had new co-facilitators. I thought this semester would be a breeze because I had facilitated upperclassmen, mostly seniors and juniors and had no problem. Facilitating freshmen would be easy, right? I felt that I had the facilitation thing down pat. Little did I know that my greatest challenge as a facilitator would just be around the corner (C. Okafo, personal communication, 2003).*

As can be seen from Okafo's journal entry, the coordinators' growth process can be quite impressive. Even with the training and experience of running a course, each semester brings new challenges.

Building trust can be difficult, especially in the beginning stages. Building trust with children or teenagers at the community service site, who may initially distrust college students who they will only see for a few weeks, can especially be difficult. Class coordinator Kristen Joe illustrates this point in her journal reflection:

*The only issues that are beginning to come up are different things regarding individual [children at the site.] We had one incident where we did not think that a [child at the community service site] was reading well enough for her age. We found this our while playing a game. This was kind of a tough situation because we did not know exactly what we should do. We did not want to embarrass her because we were in a large group with [MCSP] volunteers and other [children]. We also did not just want to let it pass and not acknowledge the situation at all. I also felt a little uncomfortable because it was still very early in the semester and the relationships between us and the [children] were really just starting to form, so they were not quite totally comfortable with us yet (K. Joe, personal communication, 2003).*

As Chibuzo Okafo explains, trust is important for coordinators to establish quickly to make undergraduate students comfortable working with one another:

*Trust is something very few people give away lightly, including me. Establishing trust between people takes time, which is something that very few college students have much of. To establish trust in my seminar, we, my co-facilitator and I have established methods in which [the college students] would get to know each other quicker and ...getting to know the kids more. As a class, we only get to meet once a week, and that is a short amount of time to really get to know a person. During class, we decided to do icebreakers that would allow everyone in the class to know something about us that wouldn't normally be apparent. We used the two truths and a lie.[Each student gives two truths and one lie about themselves and the class guesses the lie.] It allowed people to see an in-depth aspect of the other. It was nice in that it was revealing without being too revealing. It also gave an inner look to the person and allowed you to see the way that they think... i.e., what lie did they use? We also had people check in and then check out at the end of class. It gave us a feel of what and how people felt when coming into class and then how they felt when they left at the end of class. Since everybody left class feeling somewhat better than when they came in, it makes one realize that the class is beginning to feel comfortable ... and it makes me feel good to know that in such a short time, we are becoming friendlier and friendlier and this will make it easier for us to find common ground to be able to spend more time establish trust amongst ourselves and the kids (C. Okafo, personal communication, 2003).*

## Facing Race and Class and Gender Issues

Because the program is designed for first- and second-year college students, many are unfamiliar with addressing issues of race, class, gender, or social and educational equity. For many students, college is the first time interacting with people significantly different from themselves. Adjusting to college life can be a traumatic and life changing opportunity. The MCSP structure allows students to explore emotions and feelings safely through classes, residence hall activities, and various student clubs. Sociology 389 challenges college students to be effective tutors to children who may come from different economic and racial backgrounds than themselves and who have not mastered basic grade-level skills.

In one class section two African American women lead a class of five African American males and two white females. The coordinators knew some students well through other clubs and activities. Initially, the class coordinators worried that these students might take advantage of their friendship and attempt to abuse the class requirements. The coordinators and GSI spoke at length in the weekly staff meetings about it and discussed methods to prevent it from happening. The GSI advised the class coordinators to impress on their students from the beginning that they would enforce the rules and would not allow anyone to slack off. When students challenged the coordinators' authority, the coordinators employed techniques from the training meetings. According to one of the class coordinators:

*Our group of students isn't very diverse. It is dominated by African American upperclassmen. ...Also the size of our class is below average. We have about seven students, and rarely [do] all show up for class. Attendance has slowly become an issue in our section. It's not just missing seminar but it's also being absent from site. Though the site absences are largely due to sickness and transportation issues, the students aren't as passionate about attendance as they should be.... I want them to see the effects of stereotypes, gender roles, race, class, and privilege outside of the textbooks and in reality... (S. Manns, personal communication, 2003).*

Kristen Joe, who co-coordinated this section with Sheyonna Manns, contrasted in her journal that how students in this section treated her and Sheyonna may have been based on age differences between the students and the coordinators:

*There are many personality differences with this semester's class and last semester's class. The dynamics of the entire class are totally different. I find this to be for a few reasons. The first is that three of the boys in the class are good friends and have known each other for three years, so they are already very comfortable with each other. They have also known me for three years, and I feel that they feel comfortable in the class. My only concern with this is that sometimes they do not look at Sheyonna and I as having equal power in the class. When they turn in journals my name will be on it, and they tend to direct their questions to me also. This could also be because they are juniors and she is a freshman. I am sure that it is not intentional, they probably just feel more comfortable with me right now. I am sure as the semester goes on that this will change.*

*Another reason that the dynamics in our class are so different from last semester is that we have four guys and three girls in the class. And the four boys are black and two of the three girls are white. At first I was feeling like it might be overwhelming to them, especially because these are outgoing, almost rowdy boys, and that [others] might feel a little intimidated by them. But this is not the case, they all seem to get along well, and we have good discussions in class and they all interact well at site (K. Joe, personal communication, 2003).*

In another class section, lead by a white woman, lack of class diversity negatively impacted discussion. The lack of diversity meant that the students who came from similar socioeconomic and racial backgrounds tended to have similar opinions. Class discussion tended to drag or stop all together.

*Comparing my current section to my section from last semester is quite difficult; the two have very little in common. I have to admit, I was a little disappointed when I walked into class on the first day of this semester only to meet 13 Caucasian students. Now, after the add/drop deadline, my class has nine white college students and one Indian student. They do, however, come from many midwest states, so we have some geographical diversity. A few students went to private schools, which gives us a good comparison for what we read and experience at site. As far as I can tell, most of them come from a similar socioeconomic status. These aspects are a huge contrast to my extremely diverse section of last semester. Having such a varied group of students last semester made my job as a coordinator easier than I anticipated. They were very eager to share their opinions with each other. I think all of my students last semester recognized that having such a diverse class was unlikely to occur again over their four years at U-M, and they took full advantage of the opportunity to learn about very different cultures.*

*This semester my students are much more passive. I really have to coax them to elaborate on their ideas and they rarely voice controversial opinions. Last semester, I would come up with detailed agendas every week, only to discover that we discussed only one of the items. Now, I feel I must have a database of questions to ask them or else they will stop talking. One of my goals for the semester was for the students to gain a greater understanding of each other's differences, but as far as I can tell, their differences are not as obvious as I would have imagined. It is now my new goal to discover what differences they do have, and then work from there (A. Borer, personal communication, 2003).*

## Using Multimedia to Supplement Discussions on Race, Class, Gender and Privilege

In conjunction with the GSI, class coordinators use video clips of documentaries, movies, and television shows to illustrate a particular course theme of class, race, gender, or educational equity. Video clips used have come from movies such as *White Man's Burden, Bamboozled, Higher Learning,* and documentaries on race, class, and gender. The GSI discusses with the coordinators which movies clips are appropriate given course themes and discussions the coordinators want. Video is used to engage students in illustrating ways that race, class, gender, and other factors have stratified society implications in the public school system. For many students, this is the first time confronting these complex issues directly, and seeing the issues illustrated through film often elicits passionate discussion.

As Kristen Joe explains, using movies such as *Bamboozled* and *White Man's Burden* helped illustrate how racism operates:

*I am glad that these movies were able to reach the students in our class. I am also very glad that we were able to take the time to show them to the class. They really have had the effect on them that I was hoping that they would; I kind of wanted them to be offended by the videos. ... Many of the students have not experienced any outright discrimination, and I wanted them to see how offensive it was.*

*We only have about 30 more minutes of the video to watch, but overall I am pleased with the effect that it has had on the class. We are going to have the discussion about* Bamboozled *in class next week. I am really looking forward to what the class has to say after they have seen the entire movie. I also want to hear what has changed since their last reaction from the beginning of the movie.*

## Student Expectations vs. Entitlement Issues

Many University of Michigan and who apply to MCSP come from middle- and upper middle-class communities. They often report having previous community service and student leadership experience that fits the model of service as charity. They have rarely, if ever, deeply thought about the underlying reasons for service or understand the concepts of service-learning, or social justice. Furthermore, these students tend to resist to thinking about how privilege operates in their own lives. The course is structured to create a forum for students to question how privilege operates in society and observe through community service site placements how privilege, or lack of it, is implied in public school students' lives. The course allows for a deep interrogation of social and educational equity, and the differences between service as charity and service-learning.

Furthermore, many Sociology 389 students report coming from communities where they have associated with very few people outside of their own socioeconomic and racial background. Coming to the University of Michigan and living in the residence halls is frequently their first experience meeting and living with significantly different people. It is therefore important that the class coordinators establish classroom trust and model appropriate behavior in a multicultural setting to prepare students for their community service.

*This semester is different. Last semester I started off with fears about whether or not I would be able to facilitate a class. I was worried about whether or not my students would like me. Also as some of them were older, I was scared that they wouldn't pay attention to me. This semester, I feel a lot more confident this semester. I feel that I can control the class, plus also I have a co-facilitator that I feel comfortable with. Last semester, my co-facilitator was someone I was acquainted with, but didn't really know. This semester it is different because it is so much easier to plan class with a facilitator that lives down the hall from me. Also, when it comes to emergencies that require either one of us, it is easier for me to get a hold of her. This is pretty much the thing that is different in the way I will facilitate the class. Everything about the way I facilitate will stay the same because from what I perceived, I think that the way I facilitated the class worked well. I feel that if I do things the same way, the level of trust will rise really quickly in my class and it will help us be able to speak openly about the readings and discussions in general. Check in and check out really helped and I think it is a tactic that will be used again (C. Okafo, personal communication, 2003).*

Chibuzo's co-coordinator Stephanie Brown explains that trust, and teaching students to listen to each another and the children at the community service site is the most productive way to work together.

*Establishing trust in the seminar is a key thing because it's the only way that my students are going to willingly open up to me in discussion. Trust comes easier to some than it does to others, so I have used and plan on using some of the icebreakers to break the ice. Icebreakers are the best way for everyone in section to begin to open up and get to know each other. They are also a way for quieter students to get noticed without having to jump right into "discussing" during that initial day of class... Having an open ear and being trustworthy in discussion will help my students when it comes to them establishing trust with the kids at site. I think that making it known to the students that we can be trusted is a step to getting that trust. I also think that being a good listener and being consistent will make the kids at site more comfortable and therefore more trusting of us. However, there needs to be some way of letting the kids know that although they can trust us, if they tell us something that we feel needs the attention of a teacher or someone, we will have to tell someone. This way my students won't feel obligated to hold on to information that needs to be addressed by someone that can do something to help (S. Brown, personal communication, 2003).*

## Student Responses to the Course

Both student coordinators and undergraduate students in Sociology 389 write final papers analyzing their community participation, combining site observations theory from course readings. Undergraduate student responses to the course vary. Those who entered the course with high motivation for community work tend to write papers stating high satisfaction for the course in general, and their individual participation. These students tended to reflect on the impact of course and the class discussions on their thinking about real world problems. The class is often cited as inspiring them to continue being involved with the community. These typically note personal experiences at the community service site as illustrating personal growth and insight achieved through the course. Furthermore, these students tend to see themselves continuing to engage in these issues as problem solvers. These students also tend to be more likely to have formed bonds with the children at the community service site that they wanted to after the course.

On the other hand, some students had a more ambivalent attitude toward the course. Undergraduate students that indicated ambivalent motivations toward community service, tend to write papers concentrating on community service frustrations. These students generally rely more on course readings for analysis and tend to write that the complex problems inherent within public education were too difficult to solve. It was also common for these students to blame either the school system or parents for problems. These students tend not to use as many personal examples from the community service site, indicating either an inability to form bonds, or some distance between themselves and the children at the site. These students did not project themselves as potential problem solvers and were generally more fatalistic in analyzing public education problems. Some of these students were uninterested in taking a particular stand on public education. This group of students also tends to complain more about the amount of community service time required, often indicating that they were "useless" at the community service site because students did not ask them for help. The GSI makes grading decisions for the final papers based on coordinator evaluation of the students, and successful completion of writing assignments, site, and class participation.

After the class, some students continue working at the site, even without getting academic credit, staying in touch with their community service sites. Other students choose to retake the class two or even three times. Still others interview to become class coordinators and leaders. Many maintain an ongoing relationship with the children or teenagers where they worked, sometimes for months or years after the class. Other students see the experience as positively enhancing their career and academic goals.

## Final Thoughts from Graduate Student Instructor's Perspective

The three years that I have been fortunate to be associated with this course has been a very meaningful experience for myself, the many class coordinators I have worked, and college students in the course. At the end of every semester, I often meet students who personally thank me for the course and usually relay a personal growth moment they experienced through the program. They often tell me they are committed to doing future community service because of the MCSP experiences. Some have chosen a career path leading toward some kind of service. I have worked with students who will go on to work in teaching, business, and community service, for example. I have also dealt with students every semester who express disappointment and intense frustration with the course structure and community service site. These students leave the class disappointed with the course or their experience with the course organization. They often recommend important changes for improvement. At the end of every semester, I welcome both positive and negative feedback, and work with the faculty director, new student coordinators, and others in MCSP to improve the course. We have listened carefully to student feedback and responded by changing readings, restructuring the syllabus, and meetings with community site leaders to improve the course. Like a favorite family recipe, we tweak the course every semester to make it better for the next group of students. Though the course is not perfect, feedback from college students, community partners, and the MCSP faculty and staff is essential to building community.

## Note

1. Project Community is an innovative course at the University of Michigan and was started by Professor Mark Chesler more than 30 years ago. Hundreds of students from various disciplines take the course each semester and participate in community service areas such as health, prisons, and education. The MCSP program focuses on after-school enrichment programs in the local Ann Arbor community.

## References

Borer, A. (Fall, 2003). Personal communication.

Brown, S. (Fall, 2003). Personal communication.

Jansen, Joann F. and Hellerman, Paul (Producers), Nakano, Desmond. (Writer/Director). (1999). White man's burden [Motion picture]. United States: HBO Home Video.

Joe, K. (Fall, 2003). Personal communication.

Kilk, John and Lee, Spike (Producers), Lee, S. (Writer/Director). (2000). *Bamboozled* [Motion picture]. United States: New Line Cinema.

Manns, S. (Fall, 2003). Personal communication.

Okafo, C. (Fall, 2003). Personal communication.

Schoem, David, Ximena Zuniga, and Biren (Ratnesh) A. Nagda, 1995. "Exploring One's Background: The Fishbowl Exercise" In Multicultural Teaching in the University , ed. David Schoem, Linda Frankel, and Edith A. Lewsi. Westport, Conn.: Praeger.

Singleton, John and Hall, Paul (Producers), & Singleton, J. (Writer/Director). (1995). *Higher learning* [Motion picture]. United States: Columbia Pictures.

# Appendix

Class Syllabus
**Winter 2003**
**Project Community Sociology 389- (Sections,500,501,502)**
MCSP: Elementary/Middle School Tutors/Mentors
Sections 500, 502  Mondays 6:00-7:30pm Couzens' Hall
Section 501 Meets Tuesdays 3-4:30pm Couzens' Hall
Office Hours: By appointment
Course Homepage: http://www.umich.edu/~mserve/ProjectCommunity

## Class Requirements:

• Attendance in weekly seminar meetings
• Class readings
• Weekly journal 1-2 pages Due each week at seminar (to be collected by class coordinators)
• Attend and participate at service site every week Approximately 5 hrs a week
• Fill out student contact sheets at site that summarizes the contact you have had with you mentee.
• Midterm reflection paper - 3 pages (to be collected by GSI) due Week 7
• 8-10 page Final paper reflecting class readings, and experience gained from the service project. (to be collected and graded by GSI)

## Required Texts:

• Coursepack: Available at: Ulrich's South University.
• Rabow, Jerome et. al. *Tutoring Matters: Everything you always wanted to Know about how to Tutor* Temple University Press 1999.
• Johnson, Allan G. *Privilege, Power, and Difference* Mayfield Publishing 2001.
• **Not required, but highly recommended:**
   A Kaplan Guide to public school curriculum such as: Drew & Cynthia Johnson *"Homework Heroes"* Simon & Shuster. These guides cover Middle School, Elementary school curriculum and are a great review if you are unsure about the curriculum of the students you are working with.

## Expectations of the Course

• **Class Credit:** This class can not be taken for a grade. Students will be assigned a grade of credit/no credit based on the successful completion of written assignments, attendance in seminar and participation at the project sites.
• **Time Commitment:** Students are to attend section once a week for approximately 1 1/2 hrs. Students are to volunteer at their sites for approximately 5 hours a week (not including travel to and from the site.)  Students should plan on attending the site about twice a week. Students are responsible for getting themselves to and from the site either by providing their own transportation or using cars provided by the Ginsberg Center.
• **Journal Requirements:** Students are to turn in a thoughtfully written, 1-2 page response journal weekly to the section coordinators that respond to that week's readings, class discussions and site observations your interaction with your mentee should be at least one paragraph of the 1-2 page total.
• **Papers:** In addition to keeping weekly Journal Assignment due at the beginning of class, students are to turn in two papers, a three page paper to be collected at the middle of the term and a final 8-10 page paper which will be graded by the GSI.
• **Students behavior:** Each student is expected to participate in the sections fully by coming prepared to discuss the readings, and to incorporate experiences, and observations from the

volunteer sites. Each student is expected to conduct him or herself in a respectful manner to others. Section is meant to be a safe place where everyone feels free to talk. Behavior that offends, belittles, or is hurtful to others will not be tolerated. Each student is responsible for contributing to the discussion by being active and should freely express themselves in a respectful manner to others. Students should also behave appropriately at site. Please bring a positive attitude with you and consistently attend your site. Remember your tutees/mentees are counting on you to come to site consistently! *Students are responsible for getting themselves to and from site by either providing each other rides or using public transportation or using the cars available through Project Community. Only licensed drivers who fill out the paperwork can borrow transportation. Students who borrow cars are responsible for paying for any tickets, or damage done to the Project Community cars while in their possession.*

- Attendance policy: Unless there is documented proof of a family emergency or illness, students who *miss more than one section meeting or one scheduled appointment at the site* for any reason other then severe illness or family emergency *run the risk of not receiving credit* for the course.

## I. ORIENTATION TO PROJECT COMMUNITY
Week 1
January 6th / 7th Couzens Hall
- First Class Meeting.
- Introduction to the Course.
- Field Assignments Students should come with their schedules so that they can be placed in site assignments.
- Course Pack Reading: Ganon, Geoffrey. "A real world education in real world problems" The Michigan Daily 11/27/01.
- Course Pack Reading: Joseph Kahne and Joel Westhemer - "In the service of what? The Politics of Service Learning."

## II. GETTING TO THE SITE, BUILDING RELATIONSHIPS
Week 2
Jan. 13th / 14th
- In class training: How to begin a Tutor/Mentor relationship with your tutee/mentee.
- Reading: *Tutoring Matters*, Chapter 1 Attitudes, Anxieties and Expectations pp 1-29.
- Coursepack: Lesson 3 Coaching Tutees to Win, & Lesson 4 Organizing a Tutoring Session.
- Coursepack: *The Power of their Ideas* Chapter 1 In Defense of Public Education & Chapter 4 Myths, Lies and Other Dangers.
- Journal Assignment due at the beginning of class: What does community service mean to you? Whom do you hope to serve? What do you hope to accomplish in this tutoring/mentoring project?
Week 3
Jan 20 / 21nd
- In class training: Building Relationships with your Student.
- Reading *Tutoring Matters* Chapter 2: Building Relationships pp30-70.
- Coursepack Reading: *Real Boys:* Epilogue: Mentoring Boys and Creating Safe Spaces: A 15 Step Program.
- Coursepack Reading: "A Delicate Balance: How Teachers Can Support Middle School Girls' Confidence and Competence."

- Students should begin attending their sites this week.
- Journal Assignment due at the beginning of class: What are your expectations, fears and hopes regarding tutoring/mentoring students? What kind of relationship do you hope to develop?

## III. EDUCATION AS SOCIAL INSTITUTION

Week 4

Jan 27th / 28th

- Reading: *Tutoring Matters* Chapter 3 : Teaching Techniques pp 71-103.
- Coursepack: Bowles, Samuel & Gintis, Herbert. *Schooling in Capitalist America* Chapter 4: Education, Inequality and the Meritocracy.
- Journal Assignment due at the beginning of class: You have by this time attended site a few times. You have also had several readings about the debates in public education. Do you feel that the students you are working with are being served by the Ann Arbor School system? Why or why not?

Week 5

Feb. 3th / 4th

- Coursepack Reading: Friere, Paulo P*edagogy of the Oppressed* Chapter 2.
- Coursepack Reading: Oakes, Jeannie. *Keeping Track* Chapter 6 Classroom Climate.
- Journal Assignment due at the beginning of class: Though some of students you are working with are much younger than these students in the articles, do you notice ways in which the children are socialized into their identities along the lines of race, gender, class? If so, in what ways is it manifested in how the adults yourself included relate to the kids.

Week 6

Feb 10th / 11th

- Coursepack: Oakes, Jeannie. *Keeping Track* Chapter 7 Student Attitudes: The Legitimation of Inequality.
- Coursepack: Bowles, Samuel & Gintis, Herbert. *Schooling in Capitalist America* Chapter 9: Capital Accumulatioon, Class Conflict , and Educational Change.
- Reading: Johnson, Allan G. Chapter 1 *Privilege, Power & Difference*: Chapter 1 & 2 pp 1-14.
- Midterm Reflection paper- 3 pages DUE FRIDAY February18th by NOON at Annalissa's box at MCSP Office: Does the public school system allows some students to fail and others to succeed? Use as evidence for your argument observations from site and at least two articles from weeks 1-6. Why or why not?

## IV. GENDER ISSUES IN SCHOOL

Week 7

Feb 17th / 18th

- What boys are really saying.
- Coursepack Reading: Excerpts from *Real Boy's* Voices Chapter 1 - The Secret Emotional Lives of America's Boys, Chapter 3 - The Mask of Masculinity and the Double Life: Suppression and Bravado & Chapter 15 Friendships and Romances with Girls (replaces the weekly journal).

*February 21st - 28th - Winter Break*

Week 8

March 3th / 4th

- Girls in School/ Gender Issues.
- Coursepack Reading: O'Reilly, Patricia "Learning to be a Girl."
- Coursepack Reading: Orenstien, Peggy , Introduction: The Bad News about Good Girls

- Coursepack Reading: Macintosh, Peggy White Privilege and Male Privilege: A Personal Account of Coming to See Correspondences through work in Women's Studies.
- Journal Assignment due at the beginning of class: Gender issues are often difficult especially for young people. What do you notice about the differences between how the boys and girls act at site? How does this impact how the tutoring sessions go?

## V. SYSTEMS AT WORK, SOCIAL CHANGE
Week 9
March 10th / 11th
- Understanding Privilege Part I.
- In class training: Connecting Larger Issues of American society with classroom experience of your mentees/tutees.
- Reading: Johnson, Allan G. *Privilege Power and Difference* Chapter 3 The Trouble We are In.
- Reading: Rabow, Jerome. *Tutoring Matters* Chapter 4.
- Journal Assignment due at the beginning of class: Using the students at site as a example, Do you think some students are set up to fail in the United States Public School System? Why or why not?

Week 10
March 17th / 18th
- Understanding Privilege Part II.
- Reading Johnson, Allan. Chapter 4 Capitalism, Class and the Matrix of Domination Chapter 5 Making Privilege happen.
- Journal Assignment due at the beginning of class: Privilege can be a hard thing to discuss however, we have all experienced it in different ways at one time or other. Reflect on a time in your life, either with family or at school when you felt someone was given unfair privilege over another. What was the situation? Who was given an advantage and why? Who was not? Describe what that moment meant to you personally.

Week 11
March 24th / 25th
- Understanding Privilege Part III.
- Reading: Johnson, Allan. *Privilege Power and Difference*, Chapter 6 The Trouble with Trouble Chapter 7 Privilege, Power Difference and Us.
- Journal Assignment due at the beginning of class: We are often unaware of the many different privileges that we have in everyday life over others because we see it as normal. Think of someone at site who is entirely different from you in gender, race and economic position. Make a list similarly to Macintosh's of at least 10 things that you are be able to do and take for granted that this person can not. Ask this person to make a similar list of things they do on a regular basis. What did you notice about the two lists?

Week 12
March 31st / April 1st
- In class training: Creating Lasting Solutions.
- Reading: Johnson, Allan. *Privilege, Power and Difference* Chapter 8 How Systems of Privilege Work Chapter 10 What Can We Do?: Becoming a Part of the Solution.
- Journal Assignment due at the beginning of class: In many ways, it is overwhelming to think about all the problems with the school system. However, what do you think would be some of the small ways that individuals or organized groups can help improve the school system.

Week 13
April 8th/ 9th
- Coursepack Reading: Excerpt from *The Power of Their Ideas* Chapter 1 In Defense of Public Education & Chapter 4 Myths, Lies and Other Dangers.
- Journal Assignment due at the beginning of class: The reading this week encapsulates many of the debates surrounding public education. The author gives evidence that public education has actually improved slightly over the generations. Where do you think the staff at your site stands on the debate over state funding for public and private school? Do you agree or disagree with their positions?

## VI. SAYING GOODBYE
Week 14
April 14th/ 15th Last Class Meeting
- In class discussion: How to come to closure and say goodbye to your mentee/tutee.
- Reading: Chapter 6 *Tutoring Matters:* Saying Goodbye.
- Journal Assignment due at the beginning of class: How do you plan on bringing closure to the relationship you have created with your mentee/tutee? What activities will you do? What do you plan to do on your last day at the site?

Final papers (8-10 pages double Spaced 12 point font) *Due no later then Friday April 18th at 12 NOON at MCSP Office* Topic: TBA

# Chapter 11

## PROMOTING DIVERSE DEMOCRACY IN HEALTH CARE

Terence A. Joiner

It is ironic that the legal community has profoundly influenced my life's ambition to be a responsible member of the medical community. In 1978, the United States Supreme Court ruled that, although racial quotas could not be used as a factor in medical school admissions, public universities could use race as a factor in admissions (Davidson, 1997). In 2003, the Court again decided that race could be used as a factor in the admissions process to a public university.

These two momentous Supreme Court decisions have provided bookends for my career in medicine. As an African American pediatrician, diversity has been extremely important to me throughout my academic and medical career. It has also been a major part of my personal life. This is why I welcomed the invitation to teach in the Michigan Community Scholars Program (MCSP).

In my 25-year career as a student and physician in medicine, I have worked with colleagues from all the continents and dozens of countries including England, South Africa, Nigeria, China, Iraq, Iran, Israel, France, and Germany, to name a few. My roles as a student and physician have been intertwined as my career has offered lifetime learning.

One of the goals of the MCSP is to promote a diverse democracy. Accordingly, 57 percent of the 140 participants in the program are minorities. The opportunity to teach a class in the MCSP appealed to me as a chance to discuss the importance of diversity in health professions. MCSP goals were reflected in the course.

It is important for me to teach in the MCSP to watch diversity work. I have benefited from diversity as a physician, and others have benefited by knowing me as a doctor and faculty member. As a teacher, biomedical researcher, and clinical practitioner, diversity has enriched my career.

## About the Course

### Educational Goals

The goal of the Health Care, Privilege and Community course is to provide undergraduates an opportunity to understand the evolution of American health care in a multicultural context. The course examines how medical care has been delivered to different ethnic communities in the United States focusing on issues of racism, patient rights, civil rights, and health disparities. This historical perspective examines changes in the health professions over the past century and establishes a foundation for understanding current inequities in health care.

### Course Content

The course begins by discussing our national demographics. As the United States population evolves from a Caucasian majority (63 percent) in 2000 to a minority (less than 50 percent) in 2050 (Smedley, 2001), students of the health professions must be aware of the consequences involved in this transition. In the first weeks of the course, our discussions focused on cultural identity and multiculturalism. We also discussed how different diseases impact different ethnic groups.

The next topic was discussing the different health professions. In addition to the medical profession, we discussed the allied health professions, including nursing and public health. However, most discussion focused on the medical profession and evolution of the "western medical-industrial complex" which is very much dominated by American values, including individualism and man's mastery over nature. The western medical system often is not accommodating or accessible to minorities, especially groups that have not assimilated into the American system (Julia, 1995).

After painting a sociopolitical landscape of our country and providing a glimpse of the medical world, we next moved into health disparities and inequities in the health professions. We discussed the disproportionate burden of disease in minority populations (Hogue, 2002). Although a student course evaluation commented that there was "excessive discussion" of these disparities, it is important for students to realize that American medical care does not provide equal opportunity for all citizens. I tried to challenge students to be a part of a positive change— a type of civil rights movement—in health care.

Finally, the course concludes with discussions of cultural competency. Cultural competency can best be defined as "a set of practice skills, knowledge and attitudes that encompasses 1) awareness and acceptance of difference; 2) awareness of one's own cultural values; 3) understanding of the dynamics of difference; 4) development of cultural knowledge; and 5) ability to adapt practice skills to fit the cultural context of the client" (CCP Website, 2003). These are some of the necessary tools the health professions will need to correct the injustices in medicine. The students learned how to assess the level of cultural competence in an organization. This may include their sorority or varsity athletic team. They also had a chance to apply the lessons learned in cultural competence to health organizations. Part of this application was a field experience in which the students visited an agency and assessed its level of cultural competence. In the fall semester, there were three projects—HIV/AIDS awareness, access to health services for International students, and prenatal care—at the University of Michigan Health System. The descriptions findings of these projects are included in Table 1.

## Teaching Methods

During the course of the semester, the class met twice a week. The class was primarily a seminar format, which encouraged discussion. After establishing a few simple ground rules, including the expectation that students would be prepared to discuss the assigned readings, the discussions were relatively easy. Frankly, the readings—more than 400 pages, were a bit excessive. I received feedback (more than I wanted at times) about the readings. The students preferred Anne Fadiman's book *The Spirit Catches You and You Fall Down* (1997). This book is a vivid and sensitive account of an immigrant family's struggles with the American health care system seeking care for their epileptic youngest daughter. The book also relates many lessons about the level of cultural competency at the hospital where the family received their health care. The book also recounts how the health care workers' lack of cultural competence impaired their ability to care for Lia Lee, the epileptic daughter, and meet her family's needs.

It was perhaps easier to have the discussions in this class because the students got to know each other during the semester. With this knowledge there was an acquired respect for each other's views and perspectives.

It also helped that I made a point to get to know each of the 18 students individually. I tried to meet with each student at least once early in the semester. I also responded to students' questions promptly and tried to work them through their questions.

I used movies and other media to illustrate course topics. These movies helped stimulate discussion. I was inspired to use contemporary movies when I saw an ad for *John Q* (2002) midway through the Winter 2002 semester. That semester was my first experience teaching in the MCSP. Since *John Q* was a story about medicine and Denzel Washington was the star of the movie, I felt I had nothing to lose by treating the students to an afternoon matinee at a local cinema.

Actually, this adventure was a turning point. This story about a working class couple's struggle to get a heart transplant for their young son touched on many topics we discussed in class. It included ethics, equity, personal dignity, and medical technology. I was ecstatic that the students were discussing the movie on the way back from the theater.

Recently, Glenn Flores (2002), a pediatrician whose work has focused on language barriers in medicine, published an article that discussed the portrayal of minorities in movies. Most of the physicians are white, young, and surgeons. Minorities tend to be portrayed negatively in these movies.

Modern cinema offers a great opportunity to educate students about health care. Movies also allow discussions of sensitive issues. Students were able to vicariously express their feelings about racism and xenophobia without having to actually experience these personally. In addition, some movies, such as *Schindler's List* (1993), moved us to appreciate the struggles of oppressed minorities. This was why I selected *Schindler's List* as the first movie of the Fall 2002 semester.

Comments about the movies were revealing. Students were asked to complete a movie critique. About Schindler's List one student, I will call him Josh, explained to me that he had a deeper understanding of his own Jewish heritage and greater awareness of the struggles his ancestors faced.

Other movies provided similar insights. The class also viewed *And the Band Played On* (1997). This movie was based on Randy Shilt's book about the evolution and spread of HIV. The movie also recounts the scientific and political barriers that prevented recognition and containment of HIV. Some class comments included:

- The significance of the movie title.
- If AIDS had not been a "gay issue" would things be different today?
- Why did the President not address the issue sooner?
- Why is it difficult for homosexuals to receive good health care?
- Has AIDS brought homosexuals together or split them apart?
- What effect does AIDS have on America's youth?
- The bathhouses, what was their purpose: besides the obvious? Were there places like that for heterosexual people? If not, why?
- Why they would not be more specific about elements of the disease?
- Why was the Center for Disease Control was so slow in funding?
- How could they let so many people die before doing something?
- How can Dr. Gallo get away with such fraud?
- Does the government currently have bias in its funding toward research on specific diseases based on which group they most affect?
- What do people think about the current controversy surrounding "generic" AIDS drugs being provided to poor African countries with high AIDS rates vs. companies rights to drugs they produced?
- If Dr. Gallo and other scientists, doctors, and companies were forced to share information and could not have patents on viruses and drugs, would there be enough incentive in the medical field for people to continue trying to discover cures?

I was impressed with such insight about issues related to AIDS and HIV. We also had a presentation about HIV/AIDS from one of our community partners. During the semester, we worked with HIV/AIDS Resource Center (HARC). The community partner, Nicole Adelman, gave an "AIDS 101" talk to the class. She also brought a patient who was HIV-positive into the class. Students appreciated the chance to talk to a "real person" with HIV. Many had never known anyone with HIV or AIDS.

## Class Service Projects

A group of students worked with HARC in doing an AIDS awareness project for World AIDS Day—December 1, 2002. Unfortunately, this day was the last day of the Thanksgiving holiday. Many students had not returned to campus from their visits home. Nevertheless, the students decided to extend World AIDS Day into a week. One student, a varsity basketball player, suggested there should be an acknowledgement of World AIDS day at a basketball game. He sought out permission from the athletic department to pass out information about HIV/AIDS at a game. After running into "administrative indifference," he concluded that the athletic department was not ready to provide an opportunity for HIV/AIDS awareness at one of its events. The official he talked to at the athletic department did not want to use a basketball game as a forum for HIV/AIDS. Maybe this will happen in the future.

Other service projects included prenatal care for Medicaid patients and access to health care for international students. There were three group projects. These "field experiences" included opportunities to work with partners in our community. In addition to HARC, the other partners were the Ypsilanti Health Center (a University of Michigan health center) and the University Health Center (UHC). At the Ypsilanti Health Center, students talked with nurses about issues related to prenatal care for expectant mothers with Medicaid. They also talked to a social worker and nurse at the Washtenaw County Health Department about infant mortality and barriers to prenatal care for low-income expectant mothers.

At the UHC, students worked with a health educator about how to improve access to care for international students at the University of Michigan. They also received information UHC services. Students conducted a focus group about issues related to health care for international students. They asked focus group participants to review and comment on informational videos about health care services.

Descriptions of the service projects are included in Table 1, including some of the student recommendations.

## Participation in Democracy

Since 2002 was an election year, this offered a unique opportunity. This was the first time most of the members of the class were eligible to vote in an election. In addition to elections for Congress and Governor of Michigan, there were elections for dozens of local officials as well as several referenda. I encouraged students to register to vote locally on campus or via absentee ballot in their home districts. This was an exciting chance to show the students how the democratic process works: to see how an election for a senator on congressman in another state affected them, as well as their interest in a career in health professions. Nevertheless, I felt the students were reluctant to express their political views publicly. Instead I gave them the following assignment:

*This is the first time you will have a chance to vote in an election. One candidate is a member of the Spartan party, one of two major political parties. This party's political views are mostly liberal. It supports universal health insurance, gun control, affirmative action, and is opposed to the death penalty.*

*This candidate for the U. S. Senate seat is challenging an incumbent who has over 20 years' tenure in the Senate. The Fighting Irish party has more conservative views and opposes universal health insurance, gun control, affirmative action, and abortion. It is also in favor of the death penalty. The incumbent also chairs the Senate Health Care Committee and is often quoted on C-SPAN for his views. He has even been mentioned as a possible presidential nominee for his party.*

*The Senate election is tomorrow. Discuss how this election may affect your future aspirations to become a doctor.*

*How will you decide how to vote in this election?*

*How will this election impact health care in your community?*

There were many comments on both sides of the political spectrum. One insightful student responded that she was an independent and offered her own candidate for Senator. The students had now participated in a democratic society, whether they realized it or not!

## Personal Reflections

In retrospect, I learned more from teaching the class than many of the students. During my career, I have learned from experiences with diverse colleagues as well as diverse patients. Actually, it has occurred to me that my medical education in diversity began well before I started medical school. Perhaps it started my freshman year of college, when a upperclassman named John Garofalo, an Italian Catholic from Connecticut, took this African American Methodist from Alabama to the Primary Day School to work with Sisters Marita and Evodine on the west side of South Bend, Indiana. For me, this was my only opportunity to retreat from campus. During the four years of college, I kept my weekly commitment to volunteer at the school, no matter what academic (or social) challenges I had.

I still keep in touch with Sister Marita. She is now working with adult literacy in South Bend. Over the years, she has shared with me her struggles and joys with her school. She has been a witness as students such as myself transformed from shy, introverted followers to leaders not only in their campus community but in government, medicine, business, and academia.

It is this milieu of education based in service to the community that inspires me to participate in the MCSP. It is difficult to replicate this experience in our present medical curriculum. I recall as a student, and now as a faculty member, how little time is allotted to life's most important lessons—the lessons of learning to live with and grow in a diverse community. This time amounts to infinitesimal small moments in our lives.

The opportunity to have students for an entire semester, 14 weeks, is a precious opportunity. In addition, having students share their classroom experiences with others is a welcome opportunity. I also had an opportunity to share my experiences. Student comments in their evaluations support this notion. One student commented: "I like(d) the class discussion the best. This allowed me to hear other people's experiences and viewpoints. Also, in some of the readings, I learned a lot. This class opened my eyes to what is really going on in the health care system." Another student added, "I liked that the class was discussion oriented and that we got to participate every day. It wasn't just the teacher lecturing, the class was very interactive." Finally, a student stated, "I really enjoyed this course. I learned a lot and had a good time doing so. Dr. Joiner is a great teacher. He is very sympathetic to student's needs. He was extremely respectful of people's opinions. It was great how he brought in MANY speakers relevant to topics in the class. It was a great class."

## Lessons Learned and Future Directions

At the beginning of this chapter, I mentioned how my interests and goals of teaching in the MCSP were to promote diversity. Gurin (2002) discussed the value of learning in a diverse environment: "Informal interaction remained statistically significant in all but one test when classroom diversity was added as a control" (p. 359). Gurin also found that informal inter-action with diverse peers was consistently influential on all educational outcomes for all (four) groups of students.

Teaching in a diverse environment offers an opportunity to students to learn as they live. The classroom lessons are only a small part of the total educational experience. It is important that what is taught in seminars is consistent with the larger academic environment.

As consistent with MCSP goals of diverse democracy, students who take the Health Care, Community and Privilege course learn what a diverse community means. They also participate in intergroup dialogue and share a commitment to strong democracy. This seminar offers the opportunity for students, as well as faculty, to reflect on what social justice means. Finally, the course hopes to imprint the vision of a just, diverse democracy into students who will leave the undergraduate experience after only four short years.

I have taught the course now for only two semesters. I honestly can say that I am on a steep learning curve. My biggest challenge teaching this class is being flexible. It is difficult to think about this when you are preparing your syllabus and course pack two months in advance. Fortunately in medicine, "life happens." Whether there is a discussion about an affirmative action lawsuit and its impact on medical education or a medical breakthrough such as an artificial heart, there is always material for discussion. The challenge is to make this relevant to 18- and 19-year old college freshman and sophomores.

Toward the end of the semester, a student shared with the class that he had seen *Bowling for Columbine* (2002) during the weekend. Again this was an opportunity for a "road trip." The class met for the late night showing at a theater close to campus. As it turned out, Michael Moore touches on many health issues in the Academy Award-winning documentary. These included welfare reform, gun control, education, and health care politics.

It is also imperative that an instructor in a seminar is available to the students both collectively and individually. I had to be there for them. I think I met with every student outside of class at least once. Sometimes these meetings occurred in the dining room in the residence hall. Not only did the students talk about issues in the class, they also gave me feedback about the class as well as insights into how their lives as college students were evolving.

The MCSP offers a great opportunity to promote community-based service-learning. A barrier to the opportunity is the challenge of getting college freshmen involved in community service opportunities, which allows an appropriate setting for education. Community partners, especially partners in health care, are essential components of the educational service experience.

Time limitations make it difficult to get students off campus to work with community partners. Perhaps it would be advantageous to invite service organizations into the classroom to present information about their programs. It would then be up to the students to determine whether and what kind of service they wanted to do. The students may then decide to keep an ongoing commitment to an organization during their undergraduate, and even graduate, experience at Michigan.

One thing is apparent. Students prefer to talk rather than read, unless the reading material is interesting. The students really enjoyed reading *The Spirit Catches You and You Fall Down* (Fadiman, 1997). Instead of a 450-page course pack, I will attempt to use this book to illustrate the points I am trying to make in the class.

Finally, asking the students to keep a journal of their experiences would be a valuable tool in evaluating and expressing their experiences. Some of the students who tend to be quieter could express their ideas through a journal. The best thing about recording these experiences is the chance to relive them, even after 25 years of "medical education."

I still have my own personal journal from when I was a freshman taking Freshman Seminar

101. On March 2, 1975, I recounted my experience collecting money for the World Hunger Coalition at a college basketball game. "Some people say they would like to wipe out starvation and hunger in the world, but how many would be willing to give up Saturday afternoon and collect money?" After 28 years, I am still learning about diversity and democracy. Today as citizens in an academic community, we must challenge ourselves to make a personal commitment to improve our world.

# References

Brugge, P. (Producer) & Mann, M. (Producer, Director). (1999). *The Insider.* Hollywood, CA: Touchstone Pictures.

Burg, Mark (Producer) & Cassavetes, Nick (Director). (2002). *John Q.* Hollywood, CA: New Line Productions, Inc.

Cultural competency program tools and resources—basic concepts. Retrieved on August 11, 2003 from http://www.med.umich.edu/multicultural/ccp/basic.htm.

Davidson, R.C., & Lewis, E.L (1997). Affirmative action and other special consideration admission at the University of California, Davis, School of Medicine. *Journal of the American Medical Association. 278*(14), 1153-1158.

Douglas, Michael & Reutherr, Steven & Fuchs, Fred (Producers) & Coppola, Francis Ford (Director). (1997). *The Rainmaker.* Hollywood, CA: Paramount.

Fadiman, A. (1997). *The Spirit Catches You and You Fall Down.* New York: Farrar, Straus, and Giroux.

Flores, G. (2002). Mad scientists, compassionate healers, and greedy egotists: The portrayal of physicians in the movies. *Journal of the National Medical Association, 94*(2), 635-658.

Gurin, P., Dey, E.L., Hurtado, S., Gurin, G. (2002). Diversity in higher education: Theory and impact on educational outcomes. *Harvard Educational Review, 72*(3). 330-366.

Hogue, C.J.R., & Hargraves, M.A. (2002). *The commonwealth fund minority health survey of 1994: An overview. Minority health in America.* Baltimore, MD: The Johns Hopkins University Press.

Julia, M. (1995). *Understanding the concepts, multicultural awareness in the health care professions.* Needham Heights, MA: Allyn & Bacon.

Kavagh, D. & Konwise, K. (Producers) & Sargent, J. (Director). (1997). *Miss Evers' Boys.* New York, NY: HBO.

Moore, Michael (Producer & Director). (2002). *Bowling for Columbine.* Toronto, Canada: Iconolatry Productions, Inc.

Shadyac, Tom (Producer & Director). (1999). *Patch Adams.* Hollywood, CA: Universal Pictures.

Smedley, B.D., Stith A.Y., Colburn L., & Evans, C. (2001). *The right thing to do, the smart thing to do: Enhancing diversity in the health professions.* Washington, DC: National Academy Press.

Spelling, A. (Producer) & Spottiswoode, R. (Director). (1997). *And The Band Played On.* New York, NY: HBO.

Spielberg, S. (Producer & Director). (1993). *Schindler's List.* Hollywood, CA: Universal Studios.

# Table 1

## Student Projects for Health Care Community and Privilege, Fall 2002

| Project Title: | Health Information for International UM Students. | HIV/AIDS Awareness on UM Campus. | Barriers to Prenatal Care at Ypsilanti Health Center. |
|---|---|---|---|
| Purpose of Project: | To improve awareness of the issues faced by international students as they seek health care in the United States. | To increase awareness of the HIV and AIDS in the University community. | To increase understanding of the barriers to pregnancy care for low-income patients at a university health center. |
| Contact Person: | Carol Tucker. | Nicole Adelman. | Sue Nehring. |
| Location: | University Health Service. | HARC. | Ypsilanti Health Center. |
| Nature of Student Involvement: | Students will meet with International students and discuss issues related to health care. MCSP students will get feedback from International students on movies discuss health issues. | Students will work with community partner to discuss ways to increase HIV/AIDS awareness on campus. Students will also plan an event to commemorate World AIDS Day in December. | Students will work with an RN to gather information about prenatal care and risk factors for pregnancy outcomes. The information will be obtained by meeting with representatives from several agencies in Washtenaw County. |
| Recommendations: | 1. Orientation should include a video about UHS. | 1. More awareness and education is necessary for students on campus. | 1. A support groups should be set up for expectant prenatal mothers. 2. Materials for low-income prenatal mothers should be more culturally specific. |

# Appendix

## Movies Viewed Fall Semester 2002

*Schindler's List, And the Band Played On, Miss Evers' Boys, The Insider, John Q, The Rainmaker, Patch Adams,* and *Bowling for Columbine*

# Chapter 12

## INTERGROUP DIALOGUE AND MCSP: A PARTNERSHIP FOR MEANINGFUL ENGAGEMENT

**Kelly E. Maxwell, Aaron Traxler-Ballew,** and **K. Foula Dimopoulos**

Collaboration is critical to catalyzing transformative change in both undergraduate education and individual students. At the intersection of innovation and interdisciplinary connection, living-learning programs are natural locations for such partnerships to occur (Schoem, 2002). Together, the Program on Intergroup Relations (IGR) and the Michigan Community Scholars Program (MCSP) have provided inventive avenues of learning for MCSP students. The intersection of deep community and service activities at MCSP combined with the intergroup dialogue model at IGR offers students meaningful civic engagement experience grounded in dialogic practices and social justice education.

IGR and MCSP have a history of mutual cooperation. For many years, two lead faculty in each program have taught first-year seminar courses in both programs. It was a natural evolution, then, for the two programs to invest further in mutual collaboration and link intergroup dialogues with MCSP students. Currently, Michigan Community Scholars have the option of enrolling in either a service-learning course or intergroup dialogues. Roughly half of MCSP students currently enroll in the dialogue course. The chapter, subsequently, describes the important way MCSP students can be impacted by the dialogue experience. It is notable that together with the Ginsberg Center for Community Service and Learning, MCSP and IGR are currently developing an exciting new course to mindfully bring together the service-learning and intergroup dialogues courses to enhance the living-learning component of MCSP and the service-learning aspect of the Ginsberg Center. We see this chapter, then, not only as an explanation of the specific areas of intergroup dialogue that enhance the current IGR/MCSP collaboration, but also as a beginning design for understanding how dialogue may enhance the service experience.

We have identified seven praxis themes that can facilitate MCSP students in their own learning. Praxis, for us, is the interaction between action and reflection. This interaction informs and transforms both theory and practice, as these are considered together in dialectic process. Certainly intergroup dialogues are not the only place that students could or should experience the type of learning discussed below. In fact, the power of the learning community is reflected in students' many opportunities to experience transformative styles of practice. Before we discuss the praxis areas of intergroup dialogue, it is important to provide more information about IGR and the development of each of these theme areas.

## The Program On Intergroup Relations

IGR is a social justice education program at the University of Michigan that works across disciplines in partnership with faculty and staff from a broad range of academic backgrounds. As a collaborative organization in the Division of Student Affairs and the College of Literature Science, and the Arts, IGR administers courses and co-curricular initiatives that work to develop the whole student inside and outside of the classroom. IGR's signature academic offering, The Intergroup Dialogue Program, consists of three distinct courses: Intergroup Dialogue (Psychology 122/ Sociology 122), Processes of Intergroup Dialogue Facilitation (Psychology 310/ Sociology 320), and Practicum in Facilitating Intergroup Dialogues (Psychology 311/ Sociology 321). These courses provide undergraduate students with the opportunity to participate in and facilitate 13-week intergroup dialogues.

Intergroup Dialogues are two-credit courses carefully structured to explore social group identity, conflict, community, and social justice. Each intergroup dialogue involves two social identity groups defined by ethnicity, gender, national origin, race, religion, sexual orientation, or social class background. Each group is represented in the dialogue by balanced numbers of student participants. Trained student facilitators—one from each represented identity group—encourage dialogue rather than discussion or debate. Facilitators and participants explore similarities and differences among and across groups, and strive toward understanding the complexity of social justice issues and building a multicultural democratic community.

The course emphasizes both the process and content of intergroup dialogue, which inform one another to create a synergy between the two. Consequently, there is a specific process/content outline that guides the dialogue process. It is a four-stage model that follows a developmental sequence for dialogue. The stages are: creating a shared meaning of dialogue; identity, social relations, and conflict; issues of social justice; and alliances and empowerment. These stages have been adapted in practice from those created in the early 1990s by IGR founders (see Zúñiga, Nagda, and Sevig, 2002 for a similar framework).

The other two courses, Processes of Intergroup Dialogue Facilitation—the facilitator training course—and Practicum in Intergoup Dialogue Facilitation train and coach undergraduate student facilitators. The training course is structured to increase and deepen students' passion, awareness, knowledge, and skills around social justice issues (Beale, Thompson, and Chesler, 2001). Students also study facilitation techniques and practice facilitating peer interactions. Practicum serves as a continuation of training as well as a supervision course for intergroup dialogue co-facilitators and offers them an opportunity to intensify their own understanding of intergroup relations and social justice.

## Praxis Themes

For the purpose of this chapter, we felt it was important to talk with students about their experiences in dialogue and MCSP. We held three interesting and sometimes provocative conversations with students. One focus group was composed of intergroup dialogue facilitators. Roughly half of the facilitators at this focus group were also MCSP members. Another focus group was composed of MCSP students, most of whom had not taken an intergroup dialogue. This group provided a context for connections between dialogues and MCSP, as well as offered insight into the MCSP student experience. The final group consisted of MCSP students who have taken an intergroup dialogue in the past.

One important task that we asked all three groups to complete was a concept map. Students were asked to draw a map to illustrate relationships between a list of terms associated with either or both MCSP and intergroup dialogues (words such as: dialogue, democracy, civic engagement, leadership, social identity, and self-reflection). This was an illuminating portion of each focus group and some of the responses are included in this chapter. Additionally, students who enroll in intergroup dialogue write a final paper about their thoughts, feelings, and reactions to both the process and content of the intergroup dialogue. For this chapter, we revisited some of the MCSP focus group participants' final papers and integrated that information as well.

The praxis themes addressed below are situated in student experiences. Encouraging students to integrate their personal experiences to make meaning of the course content is a foundation of intergroup dialogues. Just as student experiences drive the dialogue process, they too guided the themes presented here. These themes, then, are a product of the authors' experience with the theoretical frameworks that guide intergroup dialogues, experience in the practice of doing them, and the analysis of student voices from the focus groups and final papers.

The first three praxis areas—an intentional social justice framework, dialogue as a pedagogical technique, and student-centered learning—establish a foundation that fosters the dialogue process. Four additional themes further illuminate the practice of intergroup dialogue: experiential learning, self-reflection, conflict, and power. Because the themes are interrelated and linked to one another, their collective relationship to MCSP will be addressed fully at the end of the chapter. Combined, they enhance the potential for deep learning and individual and institutional thinking about community, democracy, and civic engagement.

## Social Justice Framework

*... We can cut down the tree as much as we want but the problem is that few people realize that we also have to take up the root of the problem because when we don't deal with the roots, the tree will just keep growing back because we just keep the top of it down. I think the work we do is one of those things that will look at the root of the problem. We're not just cutting down the tree. We're also taking out the roots and trying to make sure that these problems don't come back or at least try to get people to realize that they can't just cut down the tree but we need also to take up the root.*

*-Dialogue facilitator, expanding on an analogy of oppression*

In the quote above, the facilitator is making an analogy between oppression in society and a tree. Digging up the roots of the tree involves uprooting oppression in society and, most importantly, within each of us. This requires seeing ourselves in the context of privilege, power, and oppression, an intentional goal in intergroup dialogues. Intention, as defined by Encarta World English Dictionary (1999), is the "quality or state of having a purpose in mind." Being intentional with a social justice framework means that one chooses to pay attention to, and focus on, concepts of social identity, oppression, power, and privilege and the ways in which they operate on individual, systemic, and cultural levels. This involves seeing oneself in this context and expanding one's own thoughts and actions to incorporate this worldview. Further, Bell (1997) suggests that social justice is both a process and a goal. In the case of intergroup dialogues, there is an intentional classroom process which challenges notions of hierarchy, seeks to minimize power differentials, seeks to name issues of privilege and oppression, and does this in a way that compliments the efforts of a social justice curriculum. Ultimately this process supports the long-term goal of living in an equitable world where all can live as "full" selves; where power, privilege, and oppression cease to impact someone's life chances simply because of their social identities.

Within this framework, social identity encompasses one's affiliation with social groups. These identity groups, defined by ability, age, class, ethnicity, gender, race, and sexual orientation, are salient for individuals and have meaning in U.S. society. Agent identities are associated with dominant groups that hold privilege in society through exploiting target groups. Target identities are associated with marginalized groups that are disenfranchised, exploited, and victimized by systems and institutions as well as individual acts of oppression. Systems and institutions of oppression exist through the participation of individuals with multiple target and agent identities—included in all of us (Hardiman & Jackson, 1997; Johnson, 2001).

When students become mindful of their social identities, privilege, and oppression, they are able to confront and release previously held stereotypes, which moves them toward liberation (Freire, 1970). Liberating oneself is not completed in the process of dialogue, but it often begins there. Just as students follow a developmental path for understanding their social identities (Hardiman & Jackson, 1997), intergroup dialogue moves across a continuum of consciousness. Students have the opportunity to discover the meaning of their social identities, realize that oppression exists, and recognize the importance of forming alliances. Dialogue, then, is a catalyst. It helps students be mindful of the concepts embedded in social justice education and exposes them to valuable information that can lead to critical consciousness.

## Dialogue

*...As I became more comfortable with the people in the dialogue I think I was more able to share. And then instead of making them see my side, I would sort of compare it and see that there are actually similarities and differences, and it became easier and there wasn't retreat....*

*-MCSP student, describing her experience in intergroup dialogue*

As a form of communication, dialogue differs from debate or discussion. It is collaborative rather than competitive, and it assumes that ideas and perspectives can enrich one another through honest exchange. In this spirit, assumptions are made transparent while participants listen to others' ideas about truth and reality. Dialogue also affirms emotional responses as valued contributions enriching cognitive and theoretical insights. The context for this exchange is an open environment, which strives to minimize the coercive influences of status differences and hierarchies among participants (Isaacs, 1999; Yankelovich, 1999).

Dialogue involves ways of thinking, speaking, learning, and communicating that differs from most other settings. Working toward and through this communication develops important skills such as active and empathetic listening. Active listening is hearing and receiving a message with understanding (Bidol, 1986). Empathetic listening involves placing oneself in another's shoes, thinking another's thoughts, and feeling another's feelings (Yankelovich). These skills serve as a foundation for dialogue and are further developed through engagement in dialogic communication.

As a pedagogical technique, dialogue differs from traditional "banking" models of education. While banking models consider students as empty vessels into which instructors deposit knowledge, dialogic models view students and teachers as co-learners and co-actors in praxis (Freire, 1970). This praxis is grounded in the notion that teachers and students learn and teach alongside one another and that this encounter, where student-teachers and teacher-students name the world, is simultaneously action and reflection.

## Student-Centered Learning

*Everything is so charged [in the world today] and dialogue was a place you knew you could go every week and talk about the things that affect you more than probably anything.*

*-Former intergroup dialogue participant and current facilitator, discussing features of dialogue*

Teaching methods, style of presentation, and attitudes toward innovative teaching and training impact a faculty member's approach to the classroom setting (Entwistle, 1998). As such, there are primarily two modes of classroom teaching emphases: teacher-centered and student-centered. Typically, a teacher-centered classroom mirrors the banking method described above where "knowledge and methods/techniques [are] transmitted from a knower to the learner" (Terenzini, 1999, p. 36). Probably the most popular form of teacher-centered instruction and still the primary method of university classroom teaching is the lecture, where the faculty member is perceived as the "sage on the stage" providing information for students to absorb (Terenzini).

A student-centered approach is markedly different. It is an environment "designed to take advantage of the multiple opportunities we have to shape or influence student learning" (Terenzini, 1999, p. 38). Also called learner-centered, it encourages active student involvement by allowing students to apply what they are learning in practical ways.

Embedded in the dialogic approach discussed above is a greater emphasis on student-centered learning. Peer facilitation is one feature of this approach. Students often feel more open to learning from classmates and from their own experiences when peers are leading the class. One dialogue facilitator confirmed this notion:

> *I think just the whole process of peer facilitation is in itself very powerful because obviously there's that power that's given to the two people who walk in the room and know what is going on that day...but the fact that we're still students and we can be a little bit more flexible. It's really for students, by students, with students—like that seems very important.*

Intergroup dialogues also take into account different learning styles. In addition to engaging in dialogue with the whole group, students sometimes work in dyad pairs to encourage shy students in one-on-one situations. Students also work in caucus groups where people of specific social identities share information together before coming back to the larger group. Facilitators utilize kinesthetic activity to engage students whose learning happens best through movement. They also show pertinent videos or use other illustrations to engage visual learners. This two-time dialogue facilitator and MCSP student commented, "I like the 3-fold component like the written parts—the journals, the verbal part—the speaking, and then the activities we do which are visual and different people are stimulated in different ways." As an example she adds, "some people don't talk or they don't physically respond but when they write it out you can see all of their emotions in that and so I really like that."

Additionally, student-centered learning promotes the opportunity for students to question one another and receive encouragement within the classroom context. Nevitt Sanford (1967) identified the primary process of learning as confronting something different from what one has experienced in the past. His theory relates to challenging and supporting students in their learning process. The purpose of student-centered learning is to provide the challenge by engaging students in "the Different" while at the same time providing them an outlet for response and support (Terenzini, 1999).

One way students experience challenge and support in the intergroup dialogue is through an activity at the beginning of the term where students name both their hopes and fears for the course. This challenges students to be honest with relative strangers about their own feelings while facilitators support them in this process. By doing this aloud, students often recognize they are not alone in their apprehension to speak about difficult issues. One MCSP and dialogue student noted:

> *The common fear was that we would unknowingly offend people with our remarks...How would I know what is offensive if I do not even know about their culture and beliefs? In a way, I felt assured when I realized that others had the same fear.*

## Experiential Learning

> *I found I was just taking a lot of really disconnected literature classes and science classes and nothing was really connecting...There was no continuity...And then through a bunch of friends, I just found that [they were] living and studying the same thing and that was such an attractive thing to me. It was people who were really motivated by an idea that connected their school and their passions and that was really exciting for me.*
>
> *-Intergroup dialogue facilitator speaking about intergroup dialogues and facilitation*

As the quote above suggests, connecting life experiences with classroom content is an important classroom goal, particularly in intergroup dialogues. While student-centered learning is a broad concept that likely includes experiential techniques, we feel there is an important distinction between the two. Experiential learning engages students in theoretical material by utilizing their own life experiences or experiences created in the dialogue to illuminate concepts like privilege and oppression.

When discussing issues that have a highly theoretical element, such as privilege or institutional discrimination, experiential exercises help make these concepts more meaningful for students. One of the experiential techniques used in intergroup dialogues is testimonials. Students share their story about what it means to be a part of their identity group. This helps students truly connect their experience to the learning process. One MCSP student and participant in the International/U.S. dialogue commented:

> *I felt that the [testimonials] session was very meaningful and successful as everyone bared their hearts, making it easy for the others to empathize with their situations. Although we grew up in different cities and suburban areas, it was interesting to note that many of us had similar points in our testimonials.... Sharing of the testimonials has made me respect [the other participants] much more, not just for who they are, but for what they have gone through.*

Rather than perpetuating dichotomous worldviews, testimonials provide an opportunity for a broader understanding to consider people for their experiences and to see commonalities across different social identities as well as differences within social identity groups.

Additionally, we envision the dialogue as an experience itself. Often experiential learning means only that students bring in outside experiences to inform concepts introduced in class (McKeachie, 1999). However, with issues of social justice, there are some realities that students have not yet encountered in their lives. It therefore becomes imperative that intergroup dialogues give students an experience in class that allows them to make connections with course content. For example, one simulation exercise asks students to build towns and communities with varied access to resources. They build "cities" with tape, index cards, and other materials within a specified area. Groups have different amounts of time, different size areas, and are given differential amounts of building materials to create their communities. They have increasingly more rules and less flexibility as the "land" and resources are reduced (this exercise was developed for IGR by Chavella Pittman, a graduate student instructor). This classroom experience can give students enough of a "real-world" replication of social inequality that they can reflect and learn from what they experienced in the moment. How did they feel building their community while watching others who have less or more resources build theirs? How might the simulation relate to a real-world example? Both emotional and cognitive processes help students make sense of their classroom experience. One facilitator noted the importance of this learning for her dialogue participants stating, "I saw a lot of people who you can talk about it 'til you turn blue and they don't get it, but then if you do an activity like 'Sim City' every time, the visual is just like 'wow.'" Utilizing a variety of classroom techniques is a powerful learning tool that facilitates students making connections between in-class experiences and abstract concepts they have not yet encountered in their lives.

## Self-Reflection

> *... I put self-reflection at the center of mine [concept map]. Then, I put everything else tight knit around it. I think self-reflection is the center of social justice because I feel like without that you can't be working from the most productive place. First, you have to gain an understanding of your self and your social identity, which I put right next to it, before you can understand issues of oppression, which is under that.*
>
> *-Intergroup dialogue facilitator describing the concept map*

If reflection is crucial to critical consciousness (Maybach, 1996), then self-reflection is essential to the praxis of dialogue. Hatcher and Bringle (1997) define self-reflection as "the intentional consideration of experience in light of particular learning objectives" (p. 153). Students use dialogue as a springboard to connect their lives, academics, and the world around them. The process of self-reflection challenges students to critically consider their social identities in order to more fully understand themselves and their relation to systemic and cultural institutions. It further assists students in synthesizing the content and process components of intergroup dialogue by challenging students to examine their ideas, beliefs, and actions in relation to oppression, power, and privilege.

Self-reflection also helps students develop their ideas and voice. This is particularly significant for marginalized groups who often do not have a voice in society, especially at institutional and cultural levels. Self-reflection can also be useful for members of agent groups in assessing the ways they are privileged. The following quote, from an MCSP participant sharing reflections on her multiple identities, illustrates how intergroup dialogue can cause reflection of one's self-concept and lead to deeper self-awareness:

*I had never really looked at the issue of my position as a white woman, compared to the position of women of color. This was not really a comfortable position to analyze. I can express the ways that I am a "minority voice," as a woman and a Jew, but I had never really confronted the plain fact that as a white woman, I undeniably have a lot more privileges than women of color—privileges that I take for granted all of the time.*

Furthermore, as the quote suggests, students are able to critically look at their multiple identities, as members of both privileged and targeted groups. Self-reflection, then, allows students to speak from their experiences and, ultimately, take ownership of their voice in the world.

Journals have been widely regarded as one method used for reflection. Rather than free writing or a mere record of events, reflective journals incorporate Bringle and Hatcher's (1999) five suggested guidelines: activities need to be linked to course content and learning objectives, occur on a regular basis, provide structure in terms of objectives, expectations and assessment criteria, provide feedback to students both in terms of challenges and supportive actions, and be a safe space where students may explore values, ideas, and questions. Furthermore, Rockquemore and Schaffer (2000), explain that it is the content focus of reflective tools, such as journals, that move students to a place of engagement where critical questions and realizations are made.

Intergroup dialogue students submit a weekly structured journal. Journals correspond to classroom activities and reinforce themes and process from in-class discussion. Later in the term, students are given specific questions regarding the week's topic. For example, a structured journal regarding affirmative action may be assigned to students who have spent a week discussing racism. Students receive feedback on their journals from facilitators. In this way, students have the opportunity to experience validation of their experiences, while receiving meaningful challenges. Additionally, journals offer a space where students wrestle with dissonance that may arise from learning new information. For example, as one dialogue participant noted:

*I started to have more reflection in my journals. I started saying, 'Oh.' I remember when I started making a list of my privileges. That's where I started to become more engaged in the class, to really see where/how I fit in....I read the article and from then on it was kind of more reflection. I was more engaged, becoming more and more interested.*

In this illustration, the student not only connects her experiences to the course readings, but also accepts the opportunity to reflect on these ideas, which moves her to a place of engagement.

## Conflict

*I think when we tell people about dialogue, we have to be honest. We have to tell them that there are positives and not necessarily negative aspects of it, but it's a learning experience. You're going to have people who disagree and disagreement is a part of dialogue. So don't just go in there and think that you guys are just going to talk and everyone is going to agree and then you're just going to leave because then the dialogue will not have been productive. But if you go in with an open mind and a willingness to share and respect others, then it will be such a great experience.*

*-Intergroup dialogue facilitator, elaborating on what he would tell future participants*

Conflict is explicitly cultivated during the third stage of intergroup dialogue, where participants address hot topics and issues related to the identity of focus in their class. Here, conflict is handled differently than in other areas of life. It is normalized. This change in mindset removes the mystique and shock of explicit disagreement and dissonance in the classroom by incorporating times of conflict as vital moments within a sustained learning process. Dialogue does not attempt to resolve conflict situations, but instead uses them to uncover deeper truths among participants.

An example often noted in intergroup dialogues involves participant views of discrimination in U.S. society. While some see acts of discrimination as isolated and unimportant, others see such acts severely impacting members of social groups. While many would view this conflict as an interpersonal disagreement between two people, intergroup dialogue works to unveil reasons why the conflict exists. How has each of these participants experienced oppression regarding her/his identity? What group history, background, or beliefs might impact participants' feelings and opinions on this issue? These types of questions help participants and facilitators deepen their learning by examining conflict situations.

Intergroup dialogue can also produce cognitive dissonance for participants as they challenge long-held notions of self and society. The self-reflective aspects of intergroup dialogue help students work through these uncertainties. Structured journals and testimonials, both discussed in other parts of this chapter, encourage participants to reflect upon their own thoughts, feelings, and experiences. The result of this process is rarely, if ever, a fully integrated and cohesive self-concept. Rather, as dialogue produces understanding—more than resolution to interpersonal and intergroup conflict—the dissonance produced by self-reflection promotes self-understanding.

Self-reflection in intergroup dialogue helps participants monitor their involvement in interpersonal and intergroup conflict in the classroom. Course readings suggest multiple ways of coping with emotional responses to challenging conversations. This builds participants' self-awareness and provides language to name emotional responses as they arise in the classroom. One MCSP student accustomed to shutting down in conflict situations described how intergroup dialogue helped her to voice her own opinions:

*At times I would get angry if I heard a comment that I didn't like as far as if I found it derogatory personally or to another group and sometimes I wouldn't talk back because I felt that I would just be angered and my point wouldn't get across. But after being in dialogue it really helped me. It really taught me how to combat that and how to take a stance and just have verbal interaction without your anger showing.*

How conflict is handled in dialogue suggests alternative ways of addressing conflict in society. When perceived as normal and beneficial, conflict is less likely to escalate and much easier to handle. As Gay (1997) suggests, "Without some conflict and the changes it generates, society is stagnant, unproductive, unimaginative, uncreative!" (p. 6). Intergroup dialogue provides tools and experience that help participants realize change, productivity, and creativity through situations of conflict.

## Power

*There's this power that a facilitator seems to have in a room that the participants seem to just give us just because we're supposedly the instructors. For my dialogue we kind of made it clear in the beginning that we were pretty much on equal ground. We did have the authority but it's more like "we're learning from you at the same time"....overall we felt very much like participants and I think that made them really comfortable.*

*-Intergroup dialogue facilitator discussing peer facilitation*

Intergroup dialogue occurs in an environment that seeks to minimize hierarchy and power imbalances. The contact hypothesis in intergroup relations research suggests that interactions characterized by equal status are more likely to lead to improved intergroup relations (Stephan & Stephan, 1996). Intergroup dialogue works to neutralize status and hierarchy in the room through peer co-facilitation and a balanced number of participants with the identities of focus in the dialogue (e.g., a balanced number of women and men in a women and men dialogue). Co-facilitators share power with each other in all of their activities by spending equal time leading in-class activities and debriefings, co-signing and sharing email and written communications, and genuinely collaborating in developing their session plans. Co-facilitators share power with participants by inviting group input when choosing topics and remaining flexible in their planning for salient and pertinent issues that arise through the semester.

Co-facilitators also work to balance voices in the room by providing space for quiet or withdrawn members, maintaining equity in "airtime" among individuals and groups, and introducing the perspectives of groups not necessarily represented in the room (for example, reminding participants of the existence of lesbian, gay, and bisexual people when conversations assume heterosexuality). Readings also incorporate the perspectives of marginalized groups and help to give these perspectives voice and power during participants' reflection and journaling outside of the dialogue.

# Discussion

Our conversations with students and our collective experience with intergroup dialogue, service-learning, and living-learning communities all suggest that the IGR and MCSP collaboration is beneficial for both organizations. The experience and commitment that MCSP students bring to intergroup dialogue is a particularly significant facet of this partnership for IGR. One MCSP student and dialogue facilitator noted:

*MCSP focuses a lot on community building and a lot of the things discussed in the dialogue are discussed in the class that you take with MCSP [UC 102] your first semester. So it just kind of gets you ready for your dialogue...it helps you talk more because you're more knowledgeable about the subjects and you already have personal experiences because personal experience is always a part of dialogue and sharing. So overall it kind of gets you prepared.*

Others in the focus groups echoed this sentiment—particularly in reference to the course mentioned above, University Course (UC) 102. By initiating students to the language and philosophy of intergroup dialogue and social justice education, UC 102 prepares students for the intergroup dialogue experience. In addition, MCSP's service-learning focus brings students to dialogue with a rich background in community service. This can add perspective in dialogue about privilege, power, and oppression in society.

Involvement in MCSP also seems to help prepare students for facilitation. A large number of intergroup dialogue facilitators have come to IGR from MCSP in recent years. These students, like all intergroup dialogue facilitators, make a significant commitment to social justice education during their undergraduate careers and help sustain intergroup dialogues at the University of Michigan. This is one of the clearest ways in which MCSP students enhance and strengthen IGR.

# Relation to MCSP Goals

The praxis themes addressed in this chapter relate to the goals and activities of MCSP in a number of ways. First, deep learning is encouraged in intergroup dialogue through self-reflection, student-centered learning, experiential learning, and an intentional social justice framework. Self-reflection and experiential learning connect students' own lives with course content and process, deepening engagement with the material. Student-centered learning allows students to question one another, developing critical thinking and deep examination of personal and social issues, and encourages multiple ways of knowing by accounting for different learning styles. Experiential learning adds to this a meaningful connection between curricular and co-curricular experience. Further, a social justice framework helps students develop complex understandings of themselves in relation to their community and social issues in society.

Intergroup dialogue also fosters deep community through a safe and accepting environment that encourages people to share their thoughts and feelings even when these conflict with those of other participants. This promotes a strong and deep community capable of managing conflict. Student-centered learning and dialogue pedagogy help further co-learning within a scholarly community and energize cross-disciplinary synergy. Every stage of intergroup dialogue maintains a focus on individuals and groups, furthering this dual focus within community.

Intergroup dialogue contributes to diverse democracy by offering a structured forum for sustained face-to-face intergroup interaction. Schoem, Hurtado, Sevig, Chesler, and Sumida (2001) have described these and other important features of intergroup dialogue, as well as how the intergroup dialogue model relates to diverse democracy. As they note, "Intergroup dialogue is one significant and bold model of small groups of people coming together from various walks of life to build a strong democracy" (p. 4). The way intergroup dialogues frame conflict is particularly relevant. As Schoem et. al. (2001) state, "Our societal task is not to end or resolve all conflicts, but to examine and understand conflict so communities can live together productively, even harmoniously, with conflict" (p. 15). This philosophy helps students view conflict as an inevitable and beneficial feature of life in a diverse democracy.

The intergroup dialogue program contributes to civic engagement by providing facilitation opportunities for undergraduate students. Co-facilitating an intergroup dialogue is an active form of civic engagement on a college campus. Intergroup dialogue also contributes to civic engagement by providing a forum for students to self-reflect and draw connections between their experience, actions, beliefs, and multiple identities. This can be particularly beneficial to service activities in local and global communities as well as life in diverse residence halls. Lastly, intergroup dialogues provide a social justice framework that has important implications for service-learning to be discussed below.

A praxis theme that contributes to all four MCSP goals is dialogue as a form of communication. Dialogue contributes to deep learning by fostering safe and accepting environments that encourage deep and meaningful reflection and communication. Students develop dialogic communication skills as they learn to find meaning in their peers' varied opinions, perspectives, and experiences. Joining students together in a living-learning environment with these skills in hand furthers creating deep community.

Dialogue is also a unique method of civic engagement in a diverse democracy. The connection between democracy and dialogic communication is perhaps clearest in the following quote from Barber (1989) describing strong democracy:

*The kind of talk required by strong democracy is much richer and is characterized by creativity, variety, openness and flexibility, inventiveness, capacity for discovery, subtlety and complexity, eloquence, potential for empathy and affective expression, and a deeply paradoxical character.* *(p. 355).*

While Barber did not use the word "dialogue" here, his words provide an excellent description of dialogue and suggest a broad and important connection between dialogue and democracy.

## Relation to MCSP Activities

Our conversations with MCSP students confirmed what several scholars have advised about the benefits of combining service-learning and social justice education. Rockquemore and Schaffer (2000) suggest that in order for students to be engaged in service-learning, they must first recognize and be confronted with inconsistencies of their worldview and the world as it is. Through this "shock" stage, students are better equipped to analyze the conditions that operate to make community service and service-learning necessary. O'Grady (2000) further suggests that being mindful of integrating social justice within service-learning programs helps students understand in very real ways the roots of social problems and how these problems are perpetuated by privilege, power, and oppression. Students, then, are able to move beyond the idea of doing "good" and helping the "underprivileged," to working toward ending the problems that perpetuate the existence of privilege and the underprivileged.

In our conversations with MCSP students, we noticed marked differences in language use between students who had taken a dialogue and those who had not. Students who had not taken dialogue used phrases that suggest a charity model of service where service providers "give to" service recipients. For example, one MCSP student noted:

> *...We built the playgrounds for them. Then they brought some kids over after and just to see their faces, it was like, "Yeah! I did this. This is for these underprivileged kids." And I know they have somewhere nice to play and they don't have to play with rocks or whatever....It was just a good experience to see their faces.*

MCSP students who had taken intergroup dialogues more often noted the mutual benefit of service activities. One MCSP student described how her perspective on community service shifted after participating in an intergroup dialogue:

> *Sometimes you go with the mindset that you're going to help them but dialogue makes me realize that if you're going to the community with an open mind, they are actually teaching you much more than you are helping them.*

While language usage may seem trivial to some, recent literature (Maybach, 1996; Eyler, 2002) suggests that terms such as "service recipients," "service providers," "the helped," or the "the helper" create an atmosphere of inequity and fail to account for community strengths and insights. While recognizing community strengths and insights is an important part of the MCSP mission, it seems that students who have taken intergroup dialogue are quicker to internalize this philosophy.

Intergroup dialogue promotes this internalization by supporting self-reflection that intentionally incorporates a social justice framework. As Maybach (1996) has suggested, reflection furthers students' understanding of why they do service, why service avenues are needed in the first place, and how collaboration with community partners can further dismantle an inequitable system.

Another aspect of intergroup dialogue relevant in this context is power neutrality, which helps break down the status differences between volunteers and community members. With greater resources, more stability and political clout, universities often hold a position of power over community agencies. Recognizing this and working toward equal status relationships can lead to meaningful, mutually beneficial, sustainable partnerships.

For students, learning in a setting that seeks to minimize hierarchy provides insight and understanding beyond traditional sources of knowledge. Dialogue also helps illuminate the importance of lived experience and local knowledge. This awareness is critical to service-learning where students are asked to learn from community members rather than from professors in a lecture class. In short, dialogue is one place that offers MCSP students an experience to catalyze service-learning and community service in their lives and draw connections between these activities and life in a diverse democracy.

The praxis themes discussed throughout this chapter build upon and cultivate the student experiences. In intergroup dialogues, students are asked to reflect and act in ways that demonstrate consciousness of privilege, power, and oppression, to be receptive to multiple sources of knowledge and understanding, and engage in the pursuit of justice and democracy. This action and reflection reveals a complexity and meaningful connection between self and society. At the intersection of intergroup dialogues and the MCSP living-learning community, students engage in a praxis of active learning, social justice, and meaningful engagement.

## References

Barber, B.R. (1989). Public talk and civic action: Education for participation in a strong democracy. *Social Education, Oct.,* 355-356, 370.

Beale, R.L., Thompson, M.C., & Chesler, M. (2001). Training peer facilitators for intergroup dialogue leadership. In D. Schoem & S. Hurtado (Eds.), *Intergroup dialogue: deliberative democracy in school, college, community, and workplace* (pp. 227-246). Ann Arbor, MI: University of Michigan.

Bell, L.A. (1997). Theoretical Foundations for Social Justice Education. In M. Adams, L.A. Bell & P. Griffin (Eds.), *Teaching for diversity and social justice: A sourcebook.* (pp. 3-15). New York: Routledge.

Bidol, P. (1986). Interactive communication. In Patricia Bidol, Lisa Bardwell, Nancy Manring (Eds.), *Alternative environment conflict management approaches: A citizen's model* (pp. 205-209). Ann Arbor, MI: University of Michigan.

Bringle, R.G., & Hatcher, J. A. (1999). Reflection in service learning: Making meaning of experience. *Educational Horizons, 77*(4), 179-185.

Encarta World English Dictionary (1999). Electronically accessed in Microsoft Word Verson X for Mac. Developed for Microsoft by Bloomsbury Publishing, PLC.

Entwistle, N. (1998). Improving teaching through research on student learning. In James J.F. Forest (Ed.), *University teaching: International perspectives* (pp. 73-112). New York: Garland Publishing, Inc., a member of the Taylor & Francis Group.

Eyler, J. (2002). Reflection: Linking service and learning - linking students and communities. *Journal of Social Issues, 58*(3), 517-534.

Freire, P. (1970) *Pedagogy of the oppressed.* New York: Seabury.

Gay, G. (1997). The relationship between multicultural and democratic education. *The Social Studies, 88*(1), 5-11.

Hardiman, R. & Jackson, B.W. (1997). Conceptual foundations for social justice courses. In M. Adams, L.A. Bell & P. Griffin (Eds.), *Teaching for diversity and social justice: A sourcebook* (pp. 16-29). New York: Routledge.

Hatcher, J.A., & Bringle, R.G. (1997). Reflections: Bridging the gap between service and learning. *Journal of College Teaching, 45,* 153-158.

Isaacs, W. (1999). *Dialogue and the art of thinking together.* New York: Doubleday.

Johnson, A.G. (2001). *Privilege, power, and difference.* Toronto: McGraw Hill.

Maybach, C.M. (1996). Investigating community needs: Service learning from a social justice perspective. *Education and Urban Society, 28*(2), 224-230.

McKeachie, W.J. (1999). *Teaching tips: Strategies, research, and theory for college and university teachers.* (10th Ed.). New York: Houghton Mifflin Company.

O'Grady, C.R. (2000). Integrating service learning and multicultural education: An overview. In C.R. O'Grady (Ed.), *Integrating service learning and multicultural education in colleges and universities* (pp.1-20). Mahwah, NJ: Lawrence Erlbaum Associates.

Rockquemore, K.A., & Schaffer, R.H. (2000). Toward a theory of engagement: A cognitive mapping of service-learning experiences. *Michigan Journal of Community Service Learning, Fall,* 14-25.

Sanford, N. (1967). *Where colleges fail: A study of the student as a person.* San Francisco: Jossey-Bass.

Schoem, D. (2002). Transforming Undergraduate Education. *Change, Nov./Dec,* 51-55.

Schoem, D., Hurtado, S., Sevig, T., Chesler, M., & Sumida, S.H. (2001). Intergroup dialogue: Democracy at work in theory and practice. In D. Schoem & S. Hurtado (Eds.), *Intergroup dialogue: deliberative democracy in school, college, community, and workplace* (pp. 1-21). Ann Arbor, MI: University of Michigan.

Stephan W. G., & Stephan, C.W. (1996). *Intergroup Relations.* Boulder, CO: Westview.

Terenzini, P.T. (1999). Research and practice in undergraduate education: And never the twain shall meet? *Higher Education, 38,* 33-48.

Yankelovich, D. (1999). *The magic of dialogue.* New York: Simon & Schuster.

Zúñiga, X., Nagda, B.A., & Sevig, T.D. (2002). Intergroup dialogues: An educational model for cultivating engagement across differences. *Equity & Excellence in Education, 35*(1), 7-17.

# Chapter 13
## MUSIC IN OUR LIVES
Louis Nagel

## Striking a Chord

In spring 2000, my friend David Schoem invited me to teach a course dealing with music through the Literature, Science, and the Arts school at the University of Michigan. This school's Michigan Community Scholars Program (MCSP) targets first-year students to provide them contact with a professor in a seminar setting. The subject matter deals with some aspect of learning and community, how the classroom and "real life" interact and coalesce. The class size would be no more than 20, and the opportunities for students to interact with faculty would be many and varied.

My initial response was to be greatly flattered and I immediately accepted the invitation. I called the course "Music In Our Lives." Not long after the flush of pleasure sank in, I began to have qualms. After all, my role in music for nearly six decades has been to perform in front of domestic and international audiences, and teach at an advanced level at the University of Michigan, the National Music Camp, and a variety of summer festivals in America and Europe. My solo recitals are of the lecture recital variety—taking a piece or group of pieces, or a concept, discussing the topic, and then performing the music. I am very comfortable talking to audiences. But this sort of performing is a one-time event. I play and then I go home. I have also taught piano literature at the University of Michigan School of Music for years, so I had the experience of sustaining a class from week to week over the course of a year.

But my audiences usually include many knowledgeable people, and my students are often very accomplished. The students I was now invited to teach were not musicians. They were not devoted to music in any way beyond "liking" it. And they certainly were not about to walk into a concert hall and listen to a string quartet or see an opera. It was, in other words, a constituency I had never met as an educator. And the more I thought about this, the more concerned I became. Yes, I know something about music history and how music functions in society. Yes, I can perform for the class. But can I encourage and inspire students whose commitment to music is quite unlike mine or my students at the music school? What would the reaction be from the class when I put on a Haydn symphony and then launched into a discussion of music and its role in Haydn's life? Would these students care? And why should they? Clearly this sort of discussion is far removed from the world of Madonna or rap music.

Subsequent talks with David provided me with some ideas as to how I might structure this experiment. For one thing, we felt that it would be useful if I spent some time discussing the elements of music. And it would be good to spend time on the subject of how to listen to music—the difference between hearing music and listening to it. It would be helpful, too, to bring in community guests to discuss their particular roles in music. It seemed imperative that

I ask the students to attend some concerts and write reviews, basing those reviews on what they were learning from my lectures and those of our guests.

There was a missing link, however. These stratagems all addressed the world of classical music. And that was neither my goal nor the goal of MCSP. We did not want to "convert" the students into classical devotees. Nor was this entirely fulfilling to me. So I modified the course content: there would be three concert reviews, two of which must be about classical music and one about popular music. In the second half of the term, each student would present a 15-20 minute project on music that meant a lot to them. Almost without exception the music would be from the popular field. And it would probably engage their individual interests as well as the collective interest of the class. And believe it or not, I, the stuffy classical professor might actually learn something along the way.

David and I agreed to try this format. In September 2000 I offered my first lecture to a group of freshmen. I do not know if these young people experiencing college for the first time sensed how uneasy I felt.

# Course Content

The intent here is not to give a music lesson so much as to share with the reader some concepts I offer the students concerning the elements of music.

I believe there are nine elements of music—basic building blocks of all music from all time. Not every single piece of music the world over has all of these elements working together, nor are they always comfortably familiar to our Western ears. But all music shares these things in common. In no particular order after the first one, they are as follows.

### Rhythm

Rhythm is not only the most important element of music. It is perhaps the most important building block of life itself. We exist in time, and everything we do has some sort of periodicity about it. We breathe. Our hearts beat. We walk. In music, we have familiar rhythms such as the waltz, march, or tango. We have irregular rhythms and changing rhythms, strong and weak beats, square and unbalanced phrases, but all are varieties of the same basic thing, the so-called beat. I try to illustrate different aspects of rhythm to the students, showing them the difference between music whose beats are grouped into three units (a waltz or minuet) and music whose beats are grouped into two or four beats (a polka or march). I show how a composer from the time of Mozart would write a minuet, and then contrast it with a minuet by Ravel, for example, from the early part of the 20th century. I will play some music by Copland or Schoenberg where there is constant change of rhythm or the pulse is elusive to virtually nonexistent. All these examples are performed on a "boom box" provided by MCSP and I usually walk into class with 10-15 compact disc examples from which I use in this sort of lecture. And every example is from a piece of music that most, if not all, these students are hearing for the first time.

### Melody

While not all music has melody, it is endemic among all musics of the world. Melody is the horizontal juxtaposition of pitches, and more importantly it is the thing we sing. And I believe singing is one of the defining aspects of the human condition. I point out that when the slaves were suffering their most horrible torments in their subjugation, they sang. When the Jews were being marched to the gas chambers, they sang. It is not only a question of making music. It is a question of affirming one's humanity in the face of desperate horror and certain death. Not all melody is as familiar to us as "Happy Birthday" (a tune which I analyze in great detail with my classes), but all melody allows its singer to express something that only words cannot do alone. I bring in melody from Gregorian Chant, Italian Madrigals of Gesualdo, Bach Cantatas, Schubert Songs, and a variety of difficult melodic writing from the 20th century—music of Webern or Varese, for example. Melody need not always be "pretty." I always bring in Elvis singing "Hound Dog." Students are always stunned to hear it blast out of the boom box, and still more amazed when I illustrate how very few melodic notes it has. (Play it for yourself and count the different melodic notes used!)

## Harmony

Harmony is the vertical juxtaposition of notes, and is often the element that particularly attracts a listener. And with harmony comes the basic concept of consonance and dissonance. Students are surprised to learn that harmony, which is supposedly consonant in the eighteenth century was raucously dissonant in the 14th century—in other words, consonance and dissonance are not immutable concepts. In the present century, we are accustomed to so much that clashes and seems dissonant that we are desensitized to what was once wild and forbidding harmonically. Of course I play music from the medieval period, from the Renaissance, and the so-called common practice years from 1700 through the dawn of the twentieth century. But when I put on Schoenberg's magnificent work "Erwartung" I see peoples eyes glaze over. "How can you call this great?" their expressions ask. I sometimes follow it with an example of a Mozart piece, or some popular music where some of the same dissonances are heard. And here I bring up intensively the difference between hearing music—being in the same room with some sounds and coexisting with them as opposed to taking in intellectually what is actually being sounded. I point out that most people hear music, lacking the tools to *listen* to it. When we listen again to something fiercely dissonant, at least I have shared with the class that dissonance is not necessarily forbidding.

## Texture

I spend relatively little time of this particular element—texture is the thickness or thinness of the music. A two-part invention by J.S. Bach has but two lines of music interacting at any time and is thin-textured. The climax of the last movement of Mahler's Symphony Number One, full orchestra blazing forth in triumphal glory, is thick and richly textured. A piece I use to illustrate texture as well as other elements is Ravel's "Bolero," and I am always surprised that rarely is anyone in the class is familiar with it.

## Dynamics

Obviously we are discussing how loud or soft the music is. Here I always point out that dynamics is a relative concept. I ask in a normal tone of voice if they think I am speaking loudly or softly. Invariably someone says loudly. I reply "If we were at a football game?" Or if someone says softly, I ask "In a library?" My point is to urge students to be sensitive to the relativity among louds and softs and shadings in the music they listen to, for it is dynamic variety that contributes so importantly to the quality of artistry in music performance. I point out that often in popular music there is far less dynamic contrast than in classical, and while I am not making a value judgment about this fact, I do want to alert their ears to it. Of course the Bolero, with its 15-minute crescendo from beginning to end is a fine example of dynamic growth, but I also play other examples, again from all periods of music.

## Tone, Color, or Timbre

All music is produced by instruments or voices which have individual qualities of sound. An oboe sounds quite different from a tuba, of course. A violin sounds different from a cello. A violin also sounds different from a viola, but maybe this is harder to distinguish. A soprano and a mezzo-soprano are often very close one to another. But each instrument or voice has a tone quality and range that characterizes and makes it unique. And these qualities are critical to composers as they orchestrate their works. It is inconceivable to me that the theme of the Mendelssohn Violin Concerto could not be played successfully by any other instrument—it was born to be played on the violin. Similarly, it would be all but unimaginable for the opening of the Stravinsky Rite of Spring to be played by any other instrument than the bassoon. The timbre of these two instrumental examples is the music itself.

### Form

All music has form—it is organized in that it begins somewhere and progresses through time to an ending point. It may not be easy to grasp, this formal design. Many people stay away from classical music performances because they are long, and require that the listener sit quietly through what seems to be music of interminable length, and it is easy to get lost. This is a fair complaint for one who does not understand how music is put together. The problem is that this aspect of music requires much study—far more than I can provide for a class of this experience and purpose. While we delve but superficially into the concepts of form, I do try to explain something about a few of the forms that classical composer employ in their organizational processes.

### Performance

Simply put, all music requires performance in order to bring it to life. Few of us will derive much pleasure from sitting in front of a score and trying to hear it in our minds—this for trained musicians only!

### The Ninth Element

The whole is greater than the sum of its parts. This is certainly the most elusive musical element. No amount of explaining can ever equal the music. Analysis describes certain gestures and aspects of music, but does not equal it. The social conditions under which Handel's Messiah were composed are fascinating, but hardly does this knowledge equate with the experience of hearing this mighty music. Knowing that Beethoven was totally deaf when he composed the Ninth Symphony makes hearing it even more galvanizing, but it cannot explain how a totally deaf man could nevertheless have such perfect hearing in his inner ear. It is a miraculous experience every time to hear this symphony I have been performing live for the class throughout these series of lectures, but at the end of my talks, I always play something live. At first it was a lengthy composition, but in recent terms, I have shortened the composition so I can probe more with the class as to their emotional response. And some of the students are able to apply some of the concepts we have explored with startling insight.

# Community Participants

The next few classes, usually two or three, I invite guests from the Ann Arbor or Detroit community to visit the class and talk about their relationship to music and the community. One term I invited a group of delightful senior citizens from a retirement home to share with the freshmen what music meant to them when they were themselves freshmen. That class was one of the truly delightful experiences I have had as a teacher. I was concerned that it would need some "professorial guidance," that the seniors would not be able to hold the class without my help. Nothing was farther from the truth. I kept my mouth shut for over an hour while the class and seniors interacted almost magically. Another pair of guests were David and Jenny Heitler-Klevans, two professional musicians who tour the country with music they compose for very young children—two year-olds, and five year-olds. They do a fabulous show, and I asked them simply to come and perform for the class. I had qualms about this too after I set the date and time. Would sophisticated freshmen, leaving their childhoods far behind as they work their way through approaching adulthood appreciate this "regression" I was bringing to class? Quite the opposite, it was perhaps the best class of the term, and we learned much about how music and body motions can reach even the youngest children. We have had Elaine Simms visit the class— she runs the Gifts of Art program at the University of Michigan Hospitals. Music has healing powers and can be reaffirming in a hospital environment. Many years ago Elaine (as well as her predecessor) asked me to provide music students for this program. I have played often at the hospital myself. The power of music—all types, classical, folk, popular, whatever—is nothing short of amazing, and the Gifts of Art Program is, in my opinion, one of the truly significant aspects of our health care at the University Hospitals. And we have had Betty Lane, from the Michigan Opera Theater. Betty is a classically trained singer, a Juilliard graduate, who in addition to her own professional activities on the stage, oversees a summer music and theater program for young people in the Detroit Metropolitan area. It is a huge undertaking and reaches out to children of all ages, colors, backgrounds, and economic status. Young people actually have experience composing and putting on operatic scenes, or dances. Professionals of stature in the community work intensively with these youngsters, providing them all with an artistic outlet that is unparalleled anywhere in the state.

In a community such as Ann Arbor (and there are few like it in the country) there are many musicians that I can invite to visit our class. But I leave time for the students to present their projects. While most of these projects are short talks with musical examples about current pop stars, some of them have been different. We have learned about the business of music from a young man who was going to intern at one of the popular booking agencies in Hollywood. He not only learned a lot, but also proved to be a fine communicator in coming back to the class to visit after he had participated in his summer experience, and sharing his knowledge with the new group of students. We have had some presentations on music in commercials. We had someone talk about computer generated music. We had a student who was in a small a cappella gospel choir bring the group to class and perform. Some of the projects have dealt with instruments the students themselves play—one in particular that stands out in my memory is a fine discussion/demonstration of percussion instruments by a young man who could have attended the music school of his choice.

## Conclusion

By the time the class is over, at the end of the term, there have been a wide variety of musical experiences that illustrate something of music's range and affects in our lives. It is, of course, all around us, and so easily taken for granted. My hope is that my students learn a little something about listening, experience music in a way they heretofore had not, and all in all enjoy a freshman learning experience. I cannot speak for all of them, but I can assure the reader that their professor has a great time teaching this course!

# Chapter 14

## INTEGRATING SOCIAL IDENTITY EXPLORATION, COMMUNITY DEVELOPMENT, AND SERVICE-LEARNING INTO THE MCSP INTRODUCTORY COURSE

**Penny A. Pasque, Carly M. Southworth,**
**Danny V. Asnani,** and **Alefiyah Mesiwala**

## Introduction

The Michigan Community Scholars Program (MCSP) introductory course, University Course 102: The Student in the University (UC 102) provides a structured place for integrating various theoretical concepts, social identity exploration, community development, and community service-learning, and connects these aspects with daily action in the MCSP community. Through this one-credit expectation of all first-year students entering the MCSP living-learning program, deep living and learning is interconnected and builds upon itself throughout the semester as the course provides a place for linking the various aspects of the program.

The program director teaches lectures, while resident advisors (RAs) facilitate weekly discussion sections. Sophomore peer advisors (PAs) collaborate with the RA facilitators to offer a community service learning component to the course. This article explores the course goals, describes the course structure, and defines the student facilitator training and development process. Resident advisor facilitator (RA) and first-year student perspectives are included to describe how the course materials are actualized in the program. Examples from the classroom and best practices based on four years of our teaching this course are also included. Together, the authors have held the positions of program director, interim program director, RA, PA, and student in the course. These perspectives provide a multi-layered description and analysis of the course, and its foundational nature for the overall MCSP experience.

## Course Goals

The course goals reflect MCSP's goals and included transition from high school to college, academic excellence, social identity exploration, community development, and community service learning. Each topic builds upon the other and progressively challenges students to probe deeper into identity construction as it is connected to community engagement. First year students develop a shared understanding to be utilized in MCSP courses, community living, and toward understanding MCSP's inclusive culture. As each of the five course goals are discussed, course examples are provided.

### Transition from High School to College

As students enter MCSP, many are moving away from home for the first time. They encounter a difference between high school and college academic expectations, while learning to cope with the independence of everyday college life. The first weeks at college are often filled with anxiety, questions, enthusiasm, and excitement. UC 102 provides a timely opportunity to engage first-year students in discussions about college student transition issues. During the first class session, facilitators engage students in a reflective process by asking questions such as: How are you going to achieve a balance between academics and a social life? Where are good places to study on campus? Does your home environment influence how you perceive U-M? What support systems are there for you on campus? How do you connect with faculty members? Information about the University, the residence hall, and the living-learning program are shared. Students are often relieved to discover that other students are encountering similar challenges, such as feeling homesick, developing positive study habits, and having concerns about college life.

John Gardner (1997), faculty member at the University of South Carolina and executive director of the National Resource Center for the Freshman Year and Students in Transition, has identified 21 "persistent factors" or "keys to success" in college, such as learning what helping resources the campus offers, understanding why students are in college, and developing critical thinking skills. UC 102, and MCSP as a whole, attempt to share these "keys to success" to provide students access to this information.

In addition, DeGrauw and Norcross (1989) found that an increase in active coping strategies was positively correlated with self-reported student success. UC 102 provides a structured forum to discuss various coping strategies and to inform students of additional strategies to ensure success. These discussions, in the context of small group sections, help provide all MCSP first-year students with a solid foundation for a successful transition from high school to college. Danny Asnani recalls his first year with MCSP and transitioning from high school to college.

*Being in MCSP since its inception in 1999, I feel as though I have truly grown with the program. As a first-year student that year, I believe MCSP helped me adjust and transition into the University of Michigan. I remember being a first-year student in similar situations in which I use to sit with a diverse group of people in the dining hall. I have developed many friendships with people because of the bond we have created through MCSP. I have had the opportunity to create one-on-one relationships with my students, residents, and other faculty.*

*During my first year, the warm welcome I received from the MCSP staff and faculty swayed me to continue with the program for four years. I have been given the chance to take on various leadership roles in the program. The introductory course was like no other course that I have taken here at the University of Michigan. It is a course where real life issues are brought to the table and openly discussed. The small setting with students in my hall allowed me to create relationships with a diverse group of people. My RA was also my facilitator; we often talked outside of class about identity issues, communities in Ann Arbor, and various organizations in which he was involved. I feel the structure is one in which the student does not feel a great deal of pressure in terms of coursework, but is still learning many essentials of life, like the meaning of social identity and its significant role in community. This is why I chose to facilitate sections of UC 102 as a RA and see the program grow over the years.*

## Academic Excellence

Empirical research at the University of Michigan shows that students participating in a living-learning community had greater levels of interaction with other students and faculty members, more positive perceptions of their residence environments, and stronger academic achievement and intellectual development (Inkelas, 1999). MCSP students demonstrate these results every day. The increased faculty/student relationship outcome is witnessed through interactions in the classroom, in faculty offices, and even in the dining hall. MCSP faculty represents numerous departments and colleges across the University. All faculty teach their MCSP courses in the residence hall and hold office hours in the MCSP office, which make students and faculty accessible to one another. Faculty and staff eat in the dining hall regularly and have continual interaction with students. The program director keeps the faculty abreast of UC 102 course readings, expectations, and community service learning projects. In this manner, faculty may build upon material they know will be covered in UC 102.

MCSP employs an academic support coordinator who hires tutors for first-year student courses (e.g., chemistry, biology, and math), holds office hours for academic support, and connects first-year students to various campus academic resources. The academic support coordinator visits each UC 102 section to share information about tutors and support services available to all MCSP students. This classroom contact aids in bringing the academic support information directly to students, reinforcing all advertising and email information with personal contact. The entire culture of MCSP, in conjunction with resources offered through UC 102, supports first-year student academic success.

The first academic assignment in UC 102, to visit faculty office hours, is an important component of the course. Each first-year student must visit each of their faculty members during office hours within the first two months of class. Some students' groan when they learn of the assignment, but by the end of the semester, most students admit it was one of the most valuable exercises they participated in during those first months. This assignment helps students seek out faculty members or graduate student instructors. It also helps break down some of the barriers between students and faculty, as first-year students often perceive professors as unapproachable and inaccessible.

## Social Identity Exploration

Social identity exploration is at the crux of developing a strong MCSP community, thoughtful leaders for a diverse society, and conscientious, civically-engaged students. Students' social identity development through self-exploration is greatly emphasized in UC 102 to create a solid foundation for future curricular and co-curricular community development efforts. Similarly, emphasis is intentionally placed on this section of the article.

The Gurin, Dey, Hurtado, and Gurin (2002) empirical study conducted at the University of Michigan concluded that diversity education in higher education is crucial for individual development during and beyond the college experience. The U.S. Supreme Court, in *Grutter v. Bollinger* and *Gratz v. Bollinger*, considered this research compelling evidence for racial diversity on college campuses. The decision reinforces the validity of the Gurin, et al. research and connects the findings to policy decisions. Individual learning about diversity has implications for personal change, but as the research and results of the case indicate, diversity also has implications for social change at institutional and systemic levels of society. Therefore, UC 102 utilizes a process for teaching and learning about social identity development, as informed by social identity development theory. The students each learn social identity development theory, explore their personal identity, learn about the identities of people different from themselves, and work to understand individual identity within institutional, systemic, and societal levels. It is through this transformative perspective that issues of equity, justice, education, identity, and community action are approached. This lens aids students in conceptualizing the larger picture of community service learning work, and enhances the sense of community within the living-learning program.

Students identify their own identity, and the identity of people different from themselves, while establishing a common language of understanding. This provides a context for further exploration of self, others, and remaining course material. Theorist Maurianne Adams (2000) has developed a strong model of social identity, which is utilized as a guiding principle for MCSP. Adams defines diversity in two ways. First, social diversity refers to different perspectives, worldviews, modes of communication and behavior, and belief systems and values learned through socialization in different groups. Second, Adams believes social groups are both unequal and different. Here, the groups are not equally valued, and occupy different places in a social hierarchy. Exploration of this second definition of diversity helps build linkages and understanding among different groups to aid in eradicating prejudice, discrimination, inequality, and oppression of one group by another. In addition to Adams' work, the course includes other contemporary social justice educators such as Peggy McIntosh (1992), Martin Luther King Jr.

(1963/1994), and Beverly Tatum (1997).

Social identity is based on categories of difference and commonality of race, ethnicity, language, and culture; gender and sexual orientation; physical and mental ability; and religion and class (Adams, 2000). One's social identity changes over a lifetime. It is important to note that identity groups are socially constructed by each specific culture and situated in a historical context. Many theorists believe these categories are capable of being changed (Friere, 1970/2000; Helms, 1990; Adams, 2000), and that understanding social identity development will help to create positive individual, institutional, systemic and societal change. The terms "target" or "subordinate" refer to oppressed social identities throughout much of the literature (Adams; Obear, 2000; Pincus, 2000; Tatum, 2000). In the United States, target identities include: people of color; gay, lesbian, bisexuals; women and transgender persons; physically disabled; working poor or unemployed; youth and seniors; and non-Christians. "Agent" or "dominant" identities include: White, male, heterosexual, able-bodied, middle-aged, Christian, and upper or upper-middle class (Adams; Obear; Pincus; Tatum). Together, these identities make up what Griffin (1997) calls our "social identity profile," which was utilized in some UC 102 small discussion sections to enable students to visualize their own profile. Table 1 shows the "social identity profile." It is notable that judgment is not made based on the social identity profile. Instead, it is a useful tool for the individual using the profile.

Table 1: Social Identity Profile
Fill out your membership (social identity category) and status (target / agent) in the following columns.

| | Membership/s | Status |
|---|---|---|
| Race | | |
| Ethnicity | | |
| Language | | |
| Culture | | |
| Gender | | |
| Sexual Orientation | | |
| Physical and Mental Ability | | |
| Religion | | |
| Age | | |
| Class | | |

Adapted from "Introductory Module for the Single Issue Courses," by P. Griffin, 1997, Teaching for Diversity and Social Justice, p. 70.

Next, students begin to understand what it means to have multiple identities as members of target and agent identities, and to understand how power is constructed on various levels. Dissecting the internalization of oppression and providing examples of systemic oppression in the real world is imperative to student development at this juncture in the course material. An exercise used to actualize social identity development is the "Dollar Bill" exercise (1). During this assignment, students line up, standing 50 feet away from a dollar bill. The facilitator describes social experiences that acknowledge differences in privilege. These experiences pertain to healthcare, gender and racial identity, family life, financial resources, quality of education, environment, and physical health, etcetera. Those who have experienced privilege (e.g., those who attended private schools, men, White students, etc.) take steps toward the dollar bill, while those who do not (e.g., students from single-parent homes, no insurance, health problems, students of color, etc.) step back from the dollar bill based on the facilitator's instructions. As participants respond to the various statements, they begin to separate from one another based on their own privileges. The first person to reach the dollar bill symbolically "wins" the money; this exercise is followed by discussion to acknowledge the myriad social situations that shape people's lives. The exercise allows students to view the differences that privilege and oppression play in society.

The RAs lead small section discussions that explore this material in greater depth. Participatory exercises help heighten understanding of the complexities of social identity development. One example is the "Who's Here" interactive exercise (2). Facilitators arrange the class in a circle. An identity such as "women" or "men" or "transgender" is called. Every person who wishes to claim the identity (called at the moment) is asked to step into the circle. Students are asked to observe both who is in the circle and who remains outside the circle, reflecting on how it feels to be in either group. Target identity groups, such as "women," have a tendency to vocally and physically support one another when inside the circle. On the other hand, agent identity groups such as, "people who grew up with enough resources" might respond in a fairly quiet and introspective manner. The exercise begins with an intentional introduction and ground rules, including: it is acceptable not to claim an identity to which you belong if you do not feel safe or comfortable in the room.

A few articles that consider the concept of White privilege and group discussions are also utilized when exploring how privilege correlates with understandings of oppression, social justice, and social identities. For example, articles and testimonials from *Critical White Studies: Looking Behind the Mirror* by Delgado and Stefancic (1997) were instrumental in shaping discussions around identity and privilege including, "Growing up (What) in America?" by Jerald Marrs (1997) and "White Privilege and Male Privilege: A Personal Account of Coming to see Correspondences through Work in Women's Studies," by Peggy MacIntosh (1992). These articles help many students think through White privilege for the first time. Students explore definitions of privilege, and reflect on how privilege affects their own lives as individuals and members of social identity groups.

At this point in the course, the multidimensional aspects of multiple identity theory need to be understood and explored, both inside and outside the classroom. Instruction moves students from comprehending relevant institutional policies and practices, toward an understanding of societal and systemic oppression. At times, it is easier for students to consider social identity and issues of oppression from an intellectual, academic perspective alone—without connecting it to their own lives. While the intellectual perspective is important, course facilitators challenge students and themselves to explore in greater depth the interpersonal and personal responsibility layers of social identity development. Student learning occurs when discussion of theory is connected to real life situations in the classroom, residence hall, and community service learning course projects. The class explores how a student may take action and make change simultaneously on multiple levels. This multi-layered change model helps students work for liberation, community development, and civic engagement with the goal of participation in social justice and societal change. Equity and action take precedence as the individual level becomes but one portion of the greater understanding of community development, systemic oppression, and the cycle of change. Asnani, MCSP RA and UC 102 section facilitator, describes what he witnessed in the program.

*I have also seen many of my residents take part in a number of community development projects. Residents become involved in the MCSP Programming Board, which allows them to take on a leadership role by coordinating various social, cultural, and educational programs. MCSP creates a safe, multicultural learning experience throughout the UC 102 sections, first-year seminars, and residential community. In each of these experiences, students meet people from various backgrounds, cultures, and communities. Such a diverse community allows students to indirectly test many of the fundamentals learned in UC 102. The classroom discussions on identity, social justice, and community are often coupled with students openly discussing their personal backgrounds and identities. Some have admitted to never being in a classroom with people from such a wide range of backgrounds. This environment encourages students to learn about other ethnicities, cultures, and identities. For example, there were two students from Singapore in one of my sections. Other students talked about wanting to learn more about what life is like in Singapore. The class would often ask the two students questions about government, education, life, and culture in Singapore. Following these sorts of discussions, I would notice diverse friendships developing throughout the residence hall.*

*Another example is found in the dining hall. When eating in the dining hall, I often see about 20 students of all different backgrounds sitting together. Men, women, Asian Americans, African Americans, Caucasians, Latinos, and international students, all of which are MCSP students, talk, eat, and enjoy each other's company. This is often different from what I see in other dining halls on campus.*

## Community Development

UC 102 contributes to the strong sense of student community in MCSP in two ways. First, the course material and group discussions model community development with academic readings, exercises, and pointed questions about "what is a community?" and "what role does conflict play in communities?" Chapters and articles such as *Ritual and Community* by Malidoma Patrice Somé (1993), *Black Walls* by Lui Xinwu (1994), and *On Being a Good Neighbour* by Martin Luther King, Jr. (1963/1994) prompt students to discuss what it means to develop community while they lived a strong and developing community on the residence hall floors. Intense interaction often accompanies conflict and controversy, connections and shared experiences, and many late night discussions. Exercises such as "hurt words," identifying words or phrases that are hurtful to various communities, along with an in-depth discussion of these words' origin, current ramifications, and action strategies to confront the people who choose to use such words, are critical at this point both in the classroom and in community development. Informed and intentional language usage becomes apparent both inside and outside of the classroom.

Second, UC 102 provides a perfect opportunity to contribute to the necessary development of community. Each discussion section has about 6-15 first-year students from the program. The students can choose any section that fits into their fall schedule and this allows for each section to consist of students from different floors, various majors, different social identities, and an array of community service interests. This mixture initiates interactions between students who might not otherwise connect. The connections made during intense classroom conversations carry over onto the residence hall floors of the living-learning community and students are often found traveling between floors. Asnani shares an example.

*Eventually, students share and display what they are learning in the classroom through their involvement in the community. For example, several of my residents were also students in UC 102 sections that I facilitated. In our weekly sections, I noticed one particular student show deep interest in civil rights and social justice issues. He would often talk about initiating change in his community. His ideals about equality and justice were clearly mentioned in his writings and participation in class. After class one day, we walked up to the floor together and he asked me for more information on how to get involved with the community. I gave him several resources and noticed that he really meant what he said in class. That provoked me to find out whether he would really do what he said. Throughout this year, I have witnessed him participate in the MCSP Drama Troupe, the Civil Rights March in Detroit, the Detroit Project and other numerous community service and social justice events. Through UC 102, students learn that if they want to implement change, they must take initiative in their community.*

## Academic Community Service Learning

Community service learning is one of the core principles of MCSP. UC 102 incorporates intentional academic community service learning into the curriculum to support this aspect of the mission.

Several key aspects of community service learning defined by Torres, Sinton, and White (Campus Compact, 2000) include: reciprocity, community voice, collaboration, reflection, orientation, training and service, communication, accountability, and assessment. It is easy for community service programs to overlook one or more of these key elements, but each is prevalent in MCSP. Reflection, for example, is one component borrowed from Campus Compact and is utilized in the curriculum.

Significant to the academic component of community service learning, students participate in extensive conversations both before and after service-learning experiences. Students share personal stories and relate these experiences to theoretical course concepts. Some students connect this reflection to past service work. Class discussion and writing assignments help students probe deeply into the issues. This reflective process enables students to integrate their community learning experience and peers' personal stories, to real life in the residence halls and their home communities. Through these reflective exercises, students learn to connect issues of social justice with community engagement.

Students are expected to voice their thoughts on the readings and to relate the written material to 1) their personal experiences and 2) the lives of the community members they serve. For example, one service-learning opportunity involved working with community organizations to organize and to participate in a local AIDS Walk. The event lasted for one day, but pre- and post-reflections stay with our students for a lifetime. Many students considered AIDS far removed from their daily experiences. However, by understanding the issue on multiple levels through their learning on ableism, classism, heterosexism, sexism, racism, and other forms of oppression, students were able to more thoroughly appreciate their efforts. As the students walked through the streets of campus, they had the opportunity to acknowledge that many in their own communities are infected with HIV or AIDS. Knowledge of social issues, self-awareness, and community participation together helped the MCSP students realize that their coordinated efforts are necessary in their communities, and reflection is an important step in the process.

After completing the community service learning opportunities during fall semester, student interest in continuing service-learning programs through the co-curricular MCSP student-led Programming Board typically increases. Students initiated and implemented ongoing service events such as: the MCSP Drama Troupe, which teaches drug and alcohol education in local schools; the 30-hour famine, which heightens awareness about local and international hunger issues; and participating in Habitat for Humanity weekends in the tri-state area. Additional information on co-curricular activities and the student-led Programming Board are provided in the student leadership chapter of this book entitled, *Leadership and Empowerment: Working to Make Change.*

# Course Structure

The course structure is much like the nature of the MCSP as a whole; it encompasses several different techniques of teaching and learning to meet students' needs. In this section, the logistics, lectures, small group discussions, and community service learning components will be described in more detail. The lessons we have learned over many years—with incredible student leaders—are also shared in each section.

## Logistics

To receive academic credit, students must satisfy the attendance requirement for both the lectures and weekly discussion sections, fulfill the community service learning component, and complete four writing assignments. According to the College of Literature, Science, and the Arts guidelines for living-learning community introductory courses, students do not receive letter grades for the course. Instead, students either earned credit or no credit for the course, which provided challenges for the instructors on various levels. It was difficult to balance numerous course materials with the limitations of a one-credit course. Another issue was that of student commitment to outside readings. We found that often UC 102 was placed on the back burner if students were crunched for time.

Each writing assignment allows students to expand on one or more of the broader course goals. The writing assignments ask students to use specific university resources, explore their own social identities, or reflect on community issues and community service learning experiences.

## Large Group Lectures

The program director teaches the lecture to engage students in specific issues relevant to the campus community and broader concepts of the definition of community. MCSP first-year students, RAs, and PAs all attend these lectures. Traditionally, the first large group meeting is designated as the MCSP kick-off event, during which time students are greeted by the program's student leadership team, faculty, and staff. Designated faculty and students share their individual experiences and understanding of community with the students. After faculty, staff, and student staff introductions, all first-year students are asked to share more about themselves through a group exercise tailored to a large audience. The event is followed by a reception to encourage faculty, staff, and student interaction. Energy is high, as this event usually has an air of excitement and enthusiasm for the program. First-year students often reflect on their first few days on campus and share about how MCSP has already helped to make a smooth transition to college.

The remaining lectures have changed over the years, depending on the instructors' vision and the course material for the year. For example, in partial response to a hate crime against a student who was perceived to be gay, one lecture consisted of viewing, *The Laramie Project* (2002), during which students were encouraged to take note of how the Laramie community responded to the brutal murder of Matthew Shepard. The film was followed by testimonials from three members of the Lesbian, Gay, Bisexual, and Transgender Affairs (LGBTA) Office Speakers Bureau and a period during which students asked questions regarding hate crimes and the campus community. A similar lecture was conducted a few years earlier when the movie *Not in Our Town* (1995) was shown with follow-up facilitation about our own MCSP community and how to make change within the community in order to stop hate crimes and model the program's inclusive goals. The movies had a strong and significant impact on first-year students, and allowed them to make the connections between theory and practice.

The final large group meeting at the end of the term has been designated as the MCSP poster session, during which MCSP students and faculty visually display their academic and community work. Every MCSP first-year seminar, English course, UC 102 section and the student-led Programming Board present their work. Posters, performances, and Web site displays are scattered throughout the residence hall, and the event is open to the public. Each course poster describes a definition of community and shares community service learning efforts. Community partners, University administration, and other campus community members are invited. The poster session enables each MCSP community member to view every aspect of the program at once, increasing understanding of the program's seamless nature. It also serves as a snapshot of all that the program offers, taking a celebratory approach to the end of the semester, and enabling students to share their work with a sense of accomplishment.

## Small Group Structure

Most individual student engagement occurs during the small group discussion sections. Each section meets for one hour per week, and is facilitated by a trained MCSP RA. These small group sections consist of discussions on the course materials and objectives, exercises to complement the readings or lectures, and reflection about how material relates to real life individual and community experiences. Discussions include a range of topics such as multiple identities, identity privilege, altruism, community service experiences, systemic oppression, and the transition to college. Exercises are designed to deepen the learning of the current course topic and allow students to further reflect on how issues relate to real life situations. Alefiyah Mesiwala, MCSP Resident Advisor, shares what it was like to facilitate the small sections of the UC 102 course.

*"Whatever, women complain too much. They don't deserve to have the same pay for the same amount of work. A woman just ends up spending all the man's money so a man definitely deserves to earn more," retorted one of my students while in the midst of a classroom discussion about gender oppression. Taken aback by the comment, I searched the classroom, hoping that some of the other students would disagree to the bias. Unfortunately, the male majority in the class grunted in agreement while the only females turned their heads, afraid to combat such a powerful statement. Refusing to let the last 15 minutes of discussion end like this, I began to assert my own views. Immediately, my input fueled a lively dialogue among the students about the relevant topic.*

*Imagine a group of young men who always feel that women are their dependents and women who feel they do not have a voice. These were the prevailing attitudes that the students held entering the classroom I facilitated. That day my students encountered numerous viewpoints—ideas that they probably were never challenged to consider. A fortunate few were able to confront ideas before they consciously experienced gender oppression for themselves, whereas for others, this discussion may have illuminated what was already present in their lives. One hopes the students walked away that day taking something more with them—a realization that the world may be different than it appears.*

*Perhaps it is helping first-year students explore these issues that fuels my dedication to the UC 102. Upon reflection, as a teacher, mentor, peer, and student within MCSP, I have the awesome responsibility of trying to lead people to become better individuals and in effect, contribute to the larger society. While I do not necessarily think about this as the year progresses, it is the maturity and growth of my students that I have observed over the year that attests to my claim. MCSP students are leaders—I see them becoming involved in their communities, leading programs, and actively engaging in building an environment that is inclusive and safe. The UC 102 is a powerful part of this process.*

## Community Service Learning Component

The community service learning component has been structured in two different ways. For the first two years, a PA for community service was paired with each RA's class section. Together the RA and PA facilitated the course and the RA took the lead with facilitation, course material, and conducting the exercises. The PA led the facilitation on the community service learning pre- and post- conversations, and organized the opportunity itself. Each PA worked with students in their section to choose a community service learning project of interest for the class to complete together.

Outside of the classroom, the MCSP community coordinator worked with PAs each week to assist them toward implementing the projects and creating a format for in-depth discussions. This format allowed each peer advisor to tailor the service-learning project to each classes' interest and assist the RA with course discussion. It also served as a strong training ground for PAs to become future RA's. However, at times there was tension between RA and PA pairs about how to facilitate the course and/or a community service learning project, which tended to arise from different styles of leadership and facilitation as well as personality conflicts. Conversations with the program director and community coordinator often helped to work through these conflicts. In addition, not only are the RAs serving as facilitators for the course but also as advisors on floors in which the PAs live, creating tension about the various and sometimes conflicting roles. These difficulties led to changes in the organizational structure after the second year.

The second structure provided an opportunity for each first year student to choose one of several one-time community service opportunities offered through the course and our community partners. Students registered for different sections were able to interact with one other and with different RAs and PAs. A PA arranged and facilitated each community service opportunity, and the experiences were outside of designated class time. Opportunities included building a local Habitat for Humanity house, creating mittens for the homeless, participating in the local AIDS

Walk, and working with children from University Family Housing to offer a "parent's night out." The PA, with assistance from an RA, conducted the pre- and post- service-learning conversations. For example, before attending the Habitat for Humanity build-day, students met as a group with the peer advisor to learn more about Habitat for Humanity, the area and family for which the house was being built, social and political issues surrounding the circumstances, and appropriate dress and logistics for the day. After completing the project, students were asked to reflect on their experiences while considering several course readings. Academic service-learning reflection was conducted through small group discussions and in the final writing assignment.

In retrospect, the first organizational structure operated much more successfully than the second, providing a more seamless experience for the students and course facilitators. Students under the first organizational structure were able to attend their community service learning opportunity as a class, which furthered group discussion and learning outcomes. The community service learning opportunities were not pre-determined, but designed specifically to meet the needs and interests of students in each section. The PAs were able to participate in each class discussion, furthering their understanding of how to facilitate a course if selected as RAs the following year. In this manner, the first structure was a stronger training session for the PAs as potential RAs and future course facilitators as well as provided deeper learning for first year students.

# Student Leadership Training and Ongoing Learning Process

Cultivating strong student leaders, where "leadership" is broadly defined, is a significant aspect of the program as shared in the chapter of this book entitled, Leadership and Empowerment: Working to Make Change. The RA initial training and ongoing learning process will be discussed in this section. The process is shared through the eyes of an RA. In addition, a description of the training process for the community service PAs, and challenges encountered, is offered.

### Resident Advisor Training and Learning Process

While the program director administers course material and group lectures, RAs and PAs are essential to administering and fulfilling the goals emphasized by UC 102. The RA facilitators for the introductory course are usually juniors or seniors selected after a rigorous, yet supportive interview process to become leaders for MCSP and university housing. RAs are student leaders who are engaged with first-year students on many levels. Primarily, RAs are responsible for developing dynamic living-learning communities in the residence hall and reporting to the hall director. MCSP RAs, in addition to their university housing commitments, are also MCSP leaders and in particular, facilitate UC 102. The RAs undergo extensive training before leading a UC 102 course section. The MCSP training is multi-faceted—including developing community, honing classroom skills, and providing feedback and evaluation.

The program director trains RAs both before and throughout the semester. Three weeks before MCSP students arrive to campus, RAs begin a comprehensive, challenging schedule of various training exercises to prepare for students' arrival. This first training segment primarily outlines and establishes overall UC 102 course goals and the RA's role. Intentional training covers topics such as establishing course ground rules, responding to body language, asking open-ended questions, and balancing participation with facilitation. While the RAs are introduced to course objectives and practice teaching through role-play, the focus of the training is community development. This is accomplished through various activities and exercises that elucidate the problems and challenges of establishing an ideal community in which students feel safe, where they can openly discuss issues, and may excel both academically and socially. The philosophy of the training is that if RAs can 1) understand community, 2) learn how to build community, and 3) model community among themselves, they can attempt to teach the MCSP students what it means to be an engaged community member. The RAs then attend the residence education's staff training process designed by the associate directors of the department and hall director of the residence hall.

The training process is tested early as RAs establish themselves with MCSP students in the first few weeks of school. Many MCSP RAs agree that this is a stressful and exciting time of the year. For most, it is about finding their classroom style, establishing themselves as leaders and peers in the residential community and classroom, and balancing personal commitments outside of the RA role. Alefiyah Mesiwala, Resident Advisor, describes her experience.

*As overwhelming as this responsibility can be, the RAs are bolstered by the support of the program director and the PAs for community service. All the RAs meet with the program director on a weekly basis in order to reflect on the past week of classroom discussion and lectures and collectively help each other prepare for the upcoming week in the classroom. The weekly meetings led by the program director are used as ways in which facilitators are able to share experiences in the sections, offer feedback on successful facilitation techniques or exercises, and ask for feedback from other facilitators. It also provides a time for RAs to practice activities and discussion skills with each other before implementing them in the classroom. Furthermore, the weekly meetings allow time to discuss areas for improvement and express individual concerns about the course.*

In addition to this weekly supervision, each RA also meets with the program director individually throughout the semester. The meetings provide the RA with one-on-one guidance and time to problem solve about specific course issues. The program director observes each facilitator once during the beginning of the semester to offer feedback on strengths and weaknesses of individual facilitation styles and further the RAs course facilitation skills.

## Reflective Comments written by Alefiyah Mesiwala, Resident Advisor

*The arduous process that RAs undergo to become effective student leaders and facilitators results in increased growth and maturity. In particular, juggling the positions of classroom facilitator and community-builder not only broadens our perspective as RAs, but also helps us as successful student leaders.*

*Serving as a facilitator in the classroom enriches personal growth while we are students at the University of Michigan. Many of my peers agree that the issues discussed in UC 102 are topics that all college students will encounter and reflect upon. The UC 102 course personally challenged me to reconsider and expand my thinking about many issues I was trying in the classroom to confront with first-year students.*

*My personal growth from teaching the course was tremendous. Perhaps the greatest challenge I faced as a facilitator was learning to listen to students, and then challenging them to go beyond their perceptions. For me to encourage my students to think about different perspectives or force them to consider a different point of view, I personally had to understand the different sides to many of the subject matters that we discussed. This forced me to reevaluate and reconsider my opinions. Many times, I would prepare by reading in advance, attend a talk, or reflect on my opinions before facilitating a particular discussion. It became necessary that I was familiar about various aspects of an issue—only then could I teach different sides of an issue and be a resource to my students for new information.*

*The teaching experience helped me and many other RAs grow intellectually, but it also provided us with the invaluable experience of being a role model. In particular, we began to understand how influential our leadership could be, both in the classroom and community. Our experiences and growth made us realize that we were beginning to embody one of MCSP's essential goals—to be dynamic, engaged community members that effect social change by collectively working with others to improve society.*

*I felt it was important that students had a role model who was knowledgeable about a subject and could also express opinions and attitudes about a particular issue. My example taught the students how to hold an opinion, express it in an appropriate manner, and consider opposing views. In retrospect, I realize how important of a responsibility I had in the classroom. On my residence hall floors, I see how students respect each other, yet are not afraid to express their opinions. I see how people really do participate in their communities and the initiative to do things. When you realize how little sometimes you need to do to be influential, you begin to think about all the things that you could help change for the better.*

*Perhaps the greatest lesson that we as RAs have learned through facilitation has been the importance of flexibility, even when one has a set course of goals and direction. Flexible leadership has meant learning to think spontaneously, keep an open mind, and most importantly, assess the needs of people being led. These practices are essential to the success of UC 102 sections, but also critical for other leadership positions.*

*Even if I am motivated and interested in the material that I want my students to think about, it is important for me to actually take into account my particular class dynamics. During the semester, I tried to be receptive to student feedback about course activities, readings, and discussions. When my students knew that I was listening to them, they gave more feedback. In the long run, this helped me develop a stronger, more understanding relationship with students. I learned to work with them. Rather than always following my syllabus or my prescribed classroom "objectives," I allowed my students to help shape the direction of our classroom discussions. This not only made it easier for me, but it also engaged them in such a way that UC 102 didn't seem like another academic exercise.*

*Through our experiences with MCSP and UC 102, we RAs definitely have strengthened our commitment to social activism, service, leadership, and a lifelong commitment to learning, while learning the skill and importance of encouraging others to do the same.*

### Peer Advisor Training Process

Much like the RA training, PAs for community service are trained and supported both before and throughout the semester. Three days prior to MCSP first-year student move-in, the PAs for community service, along with peer mentors and PAs for the student-led Programming Board, begin training. The first days of training cover broad topics relevant to all MCSP student leadership positions, such as student leaders' various roles in the program, and program components and offerings. Each leadership group is then asked to focus on their specific program role. For the PAs who work on community service, this is a time to review UC 102 responsibilities and course goals, build relationships with RAs, and work out course logistics. Throughout the semester, the PAs for community service meet with both the program director and the community coordinator as a group and individually.

In-depth training on facilitating community service learning opportunities is provided along with logistical training on how to actualize a quality service-learning event. Pre- and post-service experiences are related to course material and created based on the academic community service learning topic. Again, the students experienced a challenge when the PAs were removed from the individual sections and each facilitated a large group community service learning event. While it is more time consuming for the program director and community coordinator to have PAs paired up with each RA section, the benefits to students and student leaders far outweigh the costs.

## Conclusion

The MCSP introductory course UC 102 reflects the overall MCSP goals through concentrating on transition of first-year students from high school to college, academic excellence, social identity exploration, community development, and community service learning. The course material and structure has evolved to further reflect the program growth, programmatic vision, and student evaluation responses. Each year, RAs, PAs, and students bring their own perspectives and interests to the large lectures, small group discussions, and community service learning opportunities.

UC 102 is also meant to be fluid enough to reflect current community issues facing under-graduates, such as specific hate-crime incidents, affirmative action policies, local issues (e.g., low income housing in Ann Arbor and Detroit communities), and global issues (e.g., military conflicts and war). The theoretical readings, interpersonal explorations, and community service learning opportunities help to bridge critical thinking and community action. UC 102 serves as one model for living-learning programs hoping to bridge social justice issues and community service learning for undergraduate students and student course facilitators. It also provides one place for living-learning students to come together, share perspectives, challenge one another on issues, and develop a strong sense of community. As Danny Asnani, a former MCSP Resident Advisor, Peer Advisor, and first-year student in MCSP during his entire four years at the University of Michigan, states:

> *I believe MCSP is a program with a great mission. The program challenges students by providing a diverse environment, which allows interaction in the classroom as well as in [residence] hall communities. MCSP creates an environment that displays many characteristics of an ideal community and the UC 102 course is instrumental to the program. UC 102 is where students bond and create connections. I really believe that the course adds a sense of community and a place for students to grow personally and with the program.*

## Notes

1. This exercise was drawn from the Project Community resource binder developed by the Edward Ginsberg Center for Community Service and Learning.
2. This exercise was adapted from a presentation by Maura Cullen at a student affairs conference at Ithaca College in Ithaca, NY during the 1993-1994 academic year.

## References

Adams, M. (1997). Pedagogical frameworks for social justice education. In M. Adams, L.A. Bell, & P. Griffin (Eds.), *Teaching for diversity and social justice* (pp.30-43). New York: Routledge.

Adams, M. (2000). Conceptual frameworks. In M. Adams, W.J. Bluenfield, R. Castaneda, H.W. Hackman, M.L. Peters, & X. Zuniga (Eds.), *Readings for diversity and social justice* (pp. 5-9). New York: Routledge.

Baldwin, D. (Producer), & Kaufman, M. (Director). (2002). *The laramie project* [Motion picture]. United States: HBO Home Video.

Bell, L. A. (1997). Theoretical foundations for social justice education. In M. Adams, L.A. Bell, & P. Griffin (Eds.), *Teaching for diversity and social justice* (pp. 3-15). New York: Routledge.

DeGrauw, W. P., & Norcross, J.C. (1989). Students coping with psychological distress: What they do and what works. *Journal of College Student Psychotherapy, 4*(2). Binghamton, NY: Haworth Press.

Delgado, R., & Stefancic, J. *Critical White studies: Looking behind the mirror.* Philadelphia: Temple University Press, 471-474.

Gardner, J., & Jewler, A. J. (1997). *Your college experience: Strategies for success.* Albany, NY: Wadsworth.

*Gratz v. Bollinger,* 123 S. Ct. 2411 (2003).

*Grutter v. Bollinger,* 123 S. Ct. 2325 (2003).

Freire, P. (2000). *Pedagogy of the oppressed.* (30th anniversary ed.). New York: Continuum. (Original work published 1970).

Griffin, P. (1997). Introductory module for the single issue courses. In M. Adams, L.A. Bell, & P. Griffin (Eds.), *Teaching for diversity and social justice.* New York: Routledge.

Gurin, P. (1999). New research on the benefits of diversity in college and beyond: An empirical analysis. Diversity in higher education: Why corporate American cares. Retrieved October 29, 1999 on http://www.inform.umd.edu/DiversityWeb /Digest/Sp99/benefits.html

Gurin, P. (1999). Selections from The Compelling Need for Diversity In Higher Education, expert reports in defense of the University of Michigan: Expert report of Patricia Gurin. In *Equity and Excellence in Education*, 32(2), 37-62.

Gurin, Patricia, Dey, Eric L., Hurtado, Sylvia, and Gurin, Gerald. (2002). Diversity and higher education: Theory and impact on educational outcomes, *Harvard Educational Review. 72*(3), 330-366.

Hardiman, R., & Jackson, B. (1997). Conceptual foundations for social justice courses. In M. Adams, L.A. Bell, & P. Griffin (Eds.), *Teaching for diversity and social justice* (pp.16-29). New York: Routledge.

Harro, B. (2000). The cycle of socialization. In M. Adams, W.J. Bluenfield, R. Castaneda, H.W. Hackman, M.L. Peters, & X. Zuniga (Eds.), *Readings for diversity and social justice* (pp.15-21). New York: Routledge.

Helms, J.E. (1990). *Black and White racial identity development: Theory, research and practice*. Westport, CT: Greenwood.

Inkelas, K. (1999). *A Tide on which all boats rise: The effects of living-learning program participation on undergraduate outcomes at the University of Michigan*. Ann Arbor, MI: University of Michigan Housing Research Office.

Jones., S., & McEwen, M.K. (2000). A Conceptual model of multiple dimensions of identity. *Journal of College Student Development, 41*(4), 405-413.

King, M.L., Jr. (1994). On Being a Good Neighbor. In G. Albert (Ed.). *Service-Learning reader: Reflections and perspectives on service* (pp. 197-202). Alexandria, VA: National Society of Experimental Education. (Original work published 1963).

Marrs, J. (1997). Growing up (What) in America (pp. 36-37)? In R. Delgado, & J. Stefancic (Eds.). *Critical White studies: Looking behind the mirror*. Philadelphia: Temple University Press.

McIntosh, P. (1992). White privilege and male privilege: A Persona account of coming to see correspondences through work in Women's Studies (pp. 70-81). In M.L. Andersen, & P.H. Collins (Eds.). *Race, class and gender: An anthology*. Belmont, CA: Wadsworth.

Obear, K. (2000, December). *Developing a positive identity*. Paper presented at the meeting of the Social Justice Training Institute, Springfield, MA.

O'Neill, P., & Miller, R. (Producers). (1995). *Not in our town* [Motion picture]. Oakland, CA: California Working Group.

Pincus, F.L. (2000). Discrimination comes in many forms: Individual, institutional and structural. In M. Adams, W.J. Bluenfield, R. Castaneda, H.W. Hackman, M.L. Peters, & X. Zuniga (Eds.), *Readings for diversity and social justice* (pp. 31-35). New York: Routledge.

Reynolds, A.L., & Pope, R.L. (1991). The complexities of diversity: Exploring multiple oppressions. *Journal of Counseling & Development, 70*(1), 174-180.

Somé, M.S. (1993). *Ritual: power, healing, and community*. New York: Penguin Group.

Tatum, B. (1997). *"Why are all the Black kids sitting together in the cafeteria?": And other conversations about race*. New York: BasicBooks.

Xinwu, L. (1994). Black walls. In G. Albert (Ed.). *Service-learning reader: Reflections and perspectives on service* (pp. 243-248). Alexandra, VA: National Society ofExperimental Education.

Young, I. M. (2000). Five faces of oppression. In M. Adams, W.J. Bluenfield, R. Castaneda, H.W. Hackman, M.L. Peters, & X. Zuniga (Eds.), *Readings for diversity and social justice* (pp. 35-49). New York: Routledge.

Zinsser, W. (1988). College pressures. *The Norton Reader* (pp. 234-241). New York: W.W. Norton.

# Chapter 15

## COLLABORATIVE LEARNING ABOUT SUSTAINABILITY: MAJOR PROJECTS TO EMPOWER ONGOING LEARNING AND ACTION

**Susan Santone** and **James Crowfoot**

Today's college students face unprecedented challenges to their future well-being and security. The combined impacts of population growth, consumption, social instability, and other factors are undermining the natural systems that support all life. A growing global consensus of scientists, policymakers, and citizens view these conditions as "unsustainable" because they threaten vital ecological and human systems for future generations (Annan, 2000; Lee, 2002; Tibbs, 1999; Vitousek, Mooney, Lubehenco, & Meillo, 1997).

In response, "sustainability" (or "sustainable development") seeks to remedy conditions of unsustainability and create individual and collective well-being within the planet's ecological limits. A transdisciplinary field, sustainability recognizes the need to address social, ecological, and economic problems as connected systems and to equip citizens and professionals with the requisite knowledge, skills, and motivation for individual and collective action (Kirk, 2003; Krizek & Power, 1996; Rees, 1996).

The Michigan Community Scholars Program (MCSP) offers a course on sustainability as one of the required first-year seminars. As described in a companion article elsewhere in this book, Collaborative Learning About Unsustainability: An Interdisciplinary Seminar to Help Achieve Sustainability, the course provides a 'global' perspective on sustainability, examining economic, environmental, and social conditions as well as implications for the Ann Arbor/Washtenaw County/southeast Michigan region and other localities.

To link the seminar ideas with MCSP's intellectual, democracy, and service goals, students undertake an independent project focused on research and/or application of sustainability in the community.

This article will describe the independent project as a major element of the seminar pedagogy, how it advances individual and collective learning and empowerment, and incorporates students' individual interests, learning styles, and preparation for challenge and risk taking. The article will also describe the role of the instructors and community partner as advisors in the project development process, discuss pedagogical considerations for working with first-year students, and compare two projects regarding student learning and growth. The article concludes with feedback and suggestions from students, and reflections from the authors, Jim Crowfoot, the main course instructor and Susan Santone, the community partner.

## Project Overview

The seminar project is a major course element that requires students to undertake independent research on a sustainability topic and then present their findings to the other seminar members. The project accounts for 30% of students' grades.

During the first month of the seminar, students gain sufficient basic background about unsustainability and sustainability to begin to select possible foci for their projects. Students then conduct their projects over a two month period that leads up to an oral presentation and written report. The most important features of the project are:

- Projects can be research-based, hands-on, or a combination of the two types.
- An individual project should take about 40 hours to complete and a two-person project should take about 80 hours.
- While basic criteria and requirements are provided, students have much latitude in the way the project unfolds. Students utilize feedback from the instructors, community partner, and other students to develop their topics and ideas.
- Students select a topic that they want to pursue and develop a project plan in consultation with other seminar members and the instructors. Often students choose a topic that they were already interested in before learning about sustainability. For the project, this interest is typically reframed based on its connections and potential contributions to sustainability.
- Students must grapple with how unsustainability and sustainability are connected to their work, placing it within the context of the available knowledge on sustainability, and then arriving at their own learnings and conclusions to be shared in their presentations.
- Throughout a two-month research period, students individually (or in teams of two) plan and carry out their project, preparing for their final presentation and written work. During this time students regularly share with the seminar their progress and problems and receive feedback.
- Each student or team is assigned to a project advisor—one of the instructors or the community partner. The advisors are available to meet with students about their projects; both students and advisors initiate these meetings.
- Students work and learn independently as they implement their project. This requires that they manage their time, direct their own progress, and maintain focus.
- Students become problem-solvers through their inquiry and conclusions from experiences, analyses, thinking, and visioning. As they move into the role of presenting their results, students become semi-autonomous teachers and experts within the seminar.

## Choice of Topics

Students are strongly encouraged to select a topic that truly interests them. Sometimes such topics are rooted in the academic concentrations that students are considering or already committed to. Other times these topics emerge from volunteer experiences and other out-of-school experiences. Current events, new ideas stimulated by the seminar or other college courses, and invitations from public announcements or friends to engage in activism are other sources of potential topics. To encourage that high-interest topics are selected, team projects are limited to two persons; earlier experiences with larger project-groups were mixed in that not all students were strongly interested in their topics.

From its beginning, the seminar stresses the social, economic, and ecological aspects of the different themes, including local and global significance. This approach to framing sustainability is embedded in the project criteria. Students must develop their topic with this transdisciplinary, global perspective, and consequently advancing their and the seminar's understanding of unsustainability and sustainability.

Over the four years the seminar has been offered, students' topics have been quite broad, ranging from organic food use on campus to affirmative action's role in a sustainable society. Other examples of topics included hydrogen-fueled vehicles, micro credit and female poverty, consumption patterns in residence halls, environmental health in Central America, how wars are sustainable and unsustainable, local land and water policies in communities with exemplary sustainability policies and practices, campus-based arts projects and sustainability, sweat shops and clothing worn by women college students, and many other challenging and interesting topics.

# Project Types

Projects fall into three broad categories; research-based, hands-on, and a combination of the two. As the names imply, some projects focus on direct service or action to bring about change while others center on research, utilizing a combination of existing written resources and the student's own data gathering. Other projects combine both service/action and research elements. Reflection, self-evaluation, and peer feedback are vital components for all projects.

### Research-Based Projects

In the research-based project, students choose a topic of interest and begin by framing the issue in terms of unsustainability and sustainability. For some topics, the connections to sustainability are obvious (e.g., comparing and contrasting the land and water use policies and practices pursued by Olympia, Washington [Thurston County], Burlington, Vermont [Crittendon County] and Ann Arbor, Michigan [Washtenaw County]). Other topics do not necessary derive from sustainability (e.g., local voting patterns of younger and older citizens) but are reframed and broadened to address it (e.g., examining voting patterns in terms of civic participation, democracy, and their impacts on the social fabric).

A central question drives each research-based project. Examples include: What are the market barriers to hydrogen-fueled cars? What are the promises and realities of micro credit for reducing female poverty? How can the university increase its use of organic produce in the residence hall dining rooms? and What defines a sustainable business and what actual examples exist?

To answer these questions, the students conduct surveys, observations and other research— library and Internet based—relevant to their project's community or regional focus. The hybrid car team for example, surveyed customers at a car dealership about their criteria for purchasing a car and perceptions of how hybrid cars reflect these features. To gather further data, the team put its survey online and interviewed other on-campus students. Using Excel, they tallied their results and created tables to display findings.

In the micro credit project, the student began with a review of governmental statistics on female income, land ownership, education, and other indicators of women's status in the United States and internationally. Citing lack of political, social, and economic power as primary factors in female poverty, the student then described case studies and evaluated the existing research on micro credit to determine how well it has addressed these root causes. To provide a local parallel, she compared micro credit efforts abroad to domestic poverty reduction programs.

The student working on the topic of sustainable business began by reviewing literature on economic sustainability and businesses' role in a more sustainable economy. He then described what businesses are doing to achieve sustainability and compared and contrasted case studies of exemplary businesses. This sparked an interest in "greenwashing," the practice of claiming to operate sustainably in advertising but not pursuing these goals in actual practice. Further research in this area enabled the student to differentiate between businesses that are seriously pursuing sustainability from the much larger number of "greenwashers."

### Hands-On Projects

Hands-on projects often focused on personal aspects of sustainable living, especially in terms of the campus. One student, for example, monitored energy usage and recycling behavior in her residence hall by interviewing students about their behaviors and attitudes towards environmentally-conscious choices. To gain a broader view, she spoke with university staff in the housing and facilities programs about campus-wide sustainability efforts, particularly those focused on recycling and energy conservation. Finally, she developed strategies to increase student awareness of, and participation in, efforts to reduce consumption and waste.

Two students working as a team conducted a different hands-on project in their residence hall. These students wanted to communicate to their peers what they considered valuable concepts from the seminar. They first surveyed students in their hallway to determine their knowledge about sustainability, level of general interest, and specific questions they had on these topics. They then analyzed and used this information to develop three bulletin board displays the team posted in its hall over six weeks. Each board had unsustainability and sustainability as its frame and featured a different topic—water, land use, and consumption. After displaying these boards, the team again interviewed their hall mates to determine the effects of exposure to this information.

A student activist working for the Michigan Public Interest Research Group conducted a hands-on project with an off-campus focus. Her project grew from two specific campaigns on which she worked—improving implementation of the Clean Water Act and improving youth participation in voting. She framed these campaigns in relation to addressing unsustainable practices and what is needed to achieve sustainability, evaluating her own participation in these campaigns based on her own vision and commitment to sustainability.

### Combination Projects

Combination projects involved a community service element backed with a paper on the underlying concepts, research, and global aspects of the work. Projects of this type took place in different community institutions, (e.g., education, parks, businesses, etc).

Because of students' interests in education, seminar participants are frequently interested in school-based projects. Two students interested in sustainability education visited a local classroom to present activities about energy used in food production, then wrote a paper considering global sustainability education efforts, which included examples from other countries.

An art major from a small Lake Michigan community provided a second example of a school-based project. Working with middle school students in her hometown, the student combined an in-class quilt making project on the local importance of the Great Lakes with research and presentations on related local and global water issues. Her project included an on-campus display of the quilt and how it was created, followed by display at the school where it was done. To conclude the project, she donated the quilt to a museum in her hometown focused on the Great Lakes.

Two students interested in ecological restoration conducted another example of a combination project. Working with other community volunteers in the Ann Arbor Natural Area Program, they removed invasive species from a local preserve and collected seeds from native species. The seeds were then used to restore an area degraded through human activity. For their paper, the students researched the ecology of the field site and the larger ecological restoration movement at local and global levels.

# Role of the Instructors and Community Partners: Reflections from Jim and Susan

The instructors for the course included Jim Crowfoot, the main instructor; two upper-level undergraduate student assistants; and the community partner, Susan Santone, director of a nonprofit organization focused on sustainability and antidiscrimination education. For the independent projects, each student or team was assigned to one of the instructors based on a match between the project topic and instructors' individual specialties. The advisor then worked with the student to provide feedback and support throughout the two-month project development phase. Students typically met with their advisors outside of class time or communicated with them via e-mail and/or phone.

We (Jim and Susan) have found it very valuable to work as an instructor team in planning and implementing this part of the seminar. We have different teaching foci and experiences; Susan has focused on training and curriculum for K-12 teachers and students, and Jim has focused on graduate students and upper-level undergraduates. Our complementary differences affect our approach to the independent project in terms of structuring the process, requiring intermediate check-ins, and the progress and quality of work being done.

Within our individual styles, our approach to advising individual students and teams varied further depending on their requests, the type of project, and most importantly, individual pedagogical considerations. Factors such as students' previous topic knowledge, readiness for challenge, and ability to direct their own learning greatly impacted the degree of support and direction.

In the following section, Susan will consider these issues by comparing two student projects. In the first example, a pair of students focuses on educating children about sustainability. In the second, a student grapples with affirmative action, racism, and the role of social equity in sustainability. To provide a more reflective view of the project development process, the author speaks in the first person.

## Pedagogical Considerations as Examined through Two Case Studies by the Community Partner

### First Steps in the Project: Assessing Students' Knowledge

What do students already know about their topic and where are their knowledge gaps? What assumptions do they bring to the issue? What are their skills in conducting independent research? These are the questions I had to answer in assessing students' readiness for their chosen project.

Kelly and Kaitlin were two students interested in education, believing that children offer a fresh and receptive audience for instilling the ideas of sustainability. While Kelly and Kaitlin's grasp of the sustainability education field was sketchy, I felt they could gain enough knowledge within the scope of the assignment to complete a worthwhile project.

I first provided the students with state educational standards, examples of curriculum, articles, Web sites, and other resources to provide an overview of the educational landscape, specifically sustainability education. The students were self-directed and clear about their interests, and after just one meeting, felt ready to begin research, and develop an outline and project timeline. For the next several weeks they worked independently with only a few e-mail messages between us.

The approach with Jeremy was less straightforward. Race and affirmative action are charged topics and learners often bring more emotion than analysis to the issue. When exploring such divisive issues, learners may selectively seek out resources that reinforce their views (Johnston, 1996). Thus I needed to find out what Jeremy understood about racism and how this might affect his ability to critically assess new information and ask the right questions.

To help clarify Jeremy's motivations and understanding, I asked him questions such as: What makes you want to study affirmative action? What is your understanding of the goal of affirmative action? How would you define racism? What does it have to do with sustainability?

Jeremy's responses brought to light his interest in the social equity element of sustainability. Clearly, he understood that racism was a problem in education and undermines social stability. As a college student, education and affirmative action figured prominently on campus due to the high-profile University of Michigan admission lawsuits. But on how all of this fit together he was less sure, and struggled to develop a strong question to frame his project.

It became clear that Jeremy was having difficulty defining the problem and separating causes from symptoms. Before he could accomplish his goal—to evaluate affirmative action as a potential solution to racism—he needed better understand the scope of the problem and its root causes.

As a first step, I recommended resources that would provide historical perspective on institutionalized discrimination and its continuing legacy in K-12 education. I wanted to avoid ideologically-charged sources, so I compiled data and resources from the Department of Education, National Council on Educational Statistics, Office of Civil Rights, and other credible institutions addressing these issues. My goal was not to prove a certain viewpoint, but rather help Jeremy gain a more complete understanding of institutional racism. Jeremy took a few weeks to sort through the information before we met again. In the meantime, I met again with the education project team.

## Sustainability in the Classroom

Kelly and Kaitlin wanted to work directly with students in a classroom setting. Having been a teacher, I knew the challenges involved in a setting up a classroom visit: meeting with the teacher, finding out the schedule, and then developing activities that will fit within the planned units. My concern was that time required to coordinate the project would outweigh time for actually doing it. As it happened, Kelly knew a first-grade teacher who was willing to work with them, removing major logistical obstacles.

To plan their classroom visit, Kaitlin and Kelly had to figure out how to link sustainability to the scheduled curriculum unit, plant lifecycles. Seeing an easy fit with sustainability, the team focused on the lifecycle of growing, harvesting, processing, and transporting food. Their goal was to demonstrate for students how much energy is used in these processes, and that locally-grown food uses less energy while benefiting the local economy.

Fortunately, Kelly and Kaitlin had experience working with youth and utilized some engaging and developmentally-appropriate activities. For example, they had the students act out the stages of food production (growing, harvesting, transporting, processing). Then they compared the energy used in the stages to the gas, coal, and electricity used in the actual processing activities. The children drew pictures of the various processing steps and connected the pictures in a visual 'web.' After discussing impacts of transporting food and energy saved by eating locally-grown products, students decorated paper bags from a local grocery store with a "buy local" message. The sequence of activities provided opportunities for the young students to raise questions, make connections, reflect on learning, and take positive steps—key elements of sustainability education (and, not incidentally, of the seminar and MCSP as well).

For their written reports, Kelly and Kaitlin researched the state of sustainability education around the world and provided examples of projects and initiatives from Australia to Europe. They also identified some opportunities for incorporating sustainability education into the U.S. system via science or social studies courses, or through hands-on projects such as school-wide composting or recycling. While the paper did not address some of the institutional barriers affecting sustainability education (such as the political climate and its impact on policy), the work was overall well-written and clearly-cited. Most importantly, it emerged from the students' authentic interests and made connections between global events and a single local classroom.

Throughout their project, Kelly and Kaitlin identified specific research topics and found appropriate resources, in part because their topic was quite focused. Jeremy's project, on the other hand, centered on the mammoth issues of affirmative action, racism, and education. As such, the process of developing the project and focusing the topic unfolded differently than with Kelly and Kaitlin.

## Jeremy's Journey

After Jeremy's initial research on racism in education, we met and again tried to develop a focus question for his project. As he shared what he had learned, it was clear that he had a better sense of the racism landscape. At the same time, he still struggled to identify how individual pieces fit together or what the real questions were. In short, Jeremy was not coming up with a viable outline, and time was quickly running out. Sensing Jeremy needed more structure, I suggested he focus on three things: the legacy of racism in education, its impacts, and affirmative action's viability as a solution. Clearly, this was more direction than I provided to other students; in those cases, I offered feedback on outlines they had constructed. But each student has different needs, and I decided that this was appropriate to help Jeremy's project progress.

The approach seemed to help; by the end of our next meeting, Jeremy had a decent outline built around a few solid questions: What racial inequalities exist in the educational system? How does this affect students' opportunities? To what extent is affirmative action effective in addressing this?

At that point, I provided Jeremy with additional resources and he said he felt ready to begin writing. Over the next few weeks he did not respond to my inquiries and I hoped that meant everything was going well. In fact, by the next time I heard from him, the paper was done.

Instructors want to see their students learn and grow. From reading Jeremy's paper, it was clear that he had learned to connect social, political economic, and historic points he had never before considered. The paper included an historic overview of the racism in education, covering post-Emancipation and the major court cases on segregation, busing, and equal rights. He provided data on racial inequalities in terms of educational funding, 'tracking,' and access to quality teachers and college-prep courses. He supported his claims with data from the U.S. Department of Education, National Council on Educational Statistics, and U.S. Census. He linked educational with economic opportunity and drew connections between racism and classism.

Citing inequality throughout the K-12 system, he advocated that solutions included equal educational opportunities for all children from the beginning. Moreover, he wrote that early intervention would address systemic inequalities more effectively than affirmative action, which he described as "12 years too late" for most students. At the same time, he acknowledged affirmative action's role as a valid policy to address the legacy of White privilege. This ability to consider multiple viewpoints and base them on concrete facts, rather than ideology, demonstrated how far he had come in understanding racism. There were some holes in his arguments, missing citations, and undefended assumptions. But the point for me as an instructor was that some clear ideas and connections had replaced his fuzzy notions about racism. In short, it was evident that he had learned how to learn about this difficult topic.

### Lessons Learned

The process of working with first-year students in the seminar has yielded important lessons about independent projects as a learning strategy. We (Jim and Susan) have shared some of these ideas below. The reader may find that what we learned from the project experience is applicable to learning communities and service-learning in general:

- Students benefit from developing their interests and ideas through feedback from peers and instructors. This is especially true in a seminar on sustainability, which emphasizes relationships built on mutual support and collaboration.
- Projects can engage students at intellectual and emotional levels. The instructor should be prepared to support students in grappling with the "hands, head, and heart" of learning. This means acknowledging students' experiences and reactions as valid, while at the same time helping them ground their beliefs in a firm factual and theoretical basis.
- The instructor must consider what the student brings to the project in terms of prior knowledge, biases, assumptions, and motivations. Preconceived ideas, whether accurate or not, may keep students' vision about the topic narrow. Instructors should be ready to help students clarify their knowledge limitations and in doing so, ready the learner to accept new ideas and perspectives.
- Students differ in their abilities to work independently, pose focused questions, and develop a project on their own. Instructors should adjust their approach and provide each student with the appropriate level of support.

## Students' Reflections about the Independent Projects

Over the four years the seminar has been offered, students have had multiple opportunities to evaluate their learning experiences and suggest possible changes. Such reflection and evaluation promotes several key seminar goals: to help students acquire critical awareness of their own learning needs, and empower them to advocate for themselves and the group as a whole.

At the end of the April 2003 seminar, students were surveyed about their project experience. Responses include:

- "The major project was awesome—it was a great excuse for me to research something I had already been interested in."
- "It has been a great tool to increase my awareness of environmental issues and issues of sustainability as a whole."
- "I learned a lot from my research and I really enjoyed talking about it to the class."
- "Very important. I have become a recycler."
- "This research project has been invaluable to me as a learning experience. I have learned as much about sustainability during the research project, and all by myself. After completing most of the project, I felt more confident in my own ability."
- "It is a great learning experience..."
- "I thought the major presentations were a valuable asset to individual learning. It challenged us to delve into topics of our choice and to figure out where our interests lie."
- "The project gave me an opportunity to present to my peers the work and history of a cause that I was already committed to. [It] also allowed [me] to look deeper into the cause and analyze its work and how it links to sustainability."
- "The project was easily the most educational part of the class."
- "It has been extremely helpful to me in allowing exploration of [my] level of dedication and [possible] choice [of] a field [to concentrate in]."

This sample provides some indication of students' enthusiasm for these projects and what they gained from them. An in-depth, independent evaluation of the effects of such projects on students is a needed research area for the field of education for sustainability.

## Students' Suggestions for Strengthening the Independent Projects

Student feedback serves as continuous motivation and guidance for the instructors to improve the course. The unfolding process of learning and mutual inquiry enables us to become more effective teachers and accountable partners in the collaborative learning culture of this seminar. In sharing students' suggestions, we aim to underscore that while the projects are valuable and important in introductory teaching and learning for sustainability, they are, like all good collaborative inquiry, "works-in-progress."

Like the previous set of comments, the following suggestions for improving the independent projects were provided in April 2003:

- "I thought the major projects ran very well. Possibly having a rough draft of the paper due early, freeing individuals to get on top of writing so that they won't be so overwhelmed during exam time."
- "For projects on topics we had discussed in class, could non-seminar members be invited so they could learn more. The amount of work at the end is a little overwhelming with the long paper and the evaluation paper."
- "Force partnership [it] builds better presentations."
- "The only change to the major project should be earlier planning of possible ideas. Requirements for major project should be given a lot earlier."
- "...It should maybe be spread out a little more throughout the semester and [have] due dates for parts of the project to be turned in."

- "I think it would have been easier and better to possibly start the projects sooner or maybe be more structured with when things are due. It would have been better for the students to be reminded and know exactly where we should be an any given time."
- "I feel like more guidance could be given to students when trying to develop their projects...I don't know, I guess that was kind of hard for me. Collaboration with others, not necessarily partners may help."
- "Perhaps past examples of previous presentations and reports, so we get a better idea of what is expected of us."
- "...Clear description of the intended result of project, samples of the things that might be a 'project thesis.'"
- "Sometimes when given a length on essays you tend to repeat yourself. An open number of pages would be good because your paper might be better shorter than longer."

Students have suggested that independent project presentations be spread out throughout the seminar, even though this would result in students having different lengths of time to work on these projects. Other suggestions include setting aside a full day at the end of the semester for project presentations rather than using the final weekly meeting times of the seminar, as has been done.

# Conclusion

The independent project is a significant element of the sustainability seminar offered to first-year students in the MCSP. The project approach reflects key principles of sustainability pedagogy while supporting MCSP goals. Through techniques such as independent inquiry, collaborative learning, peer feedback, and community-based work, the independent project provides an opportunity for students to develop at multiple levels in a community of supportive co-learners.

From the students' suggestions and our experience, it is clear that independent projects of this kind have both strengths and weaknesses. These projects also have substantial flexibility in how they can be defined, planned, and implemented within a specific course. Our approach to the projects has evolved over four years, informed by student feedback and our own changing ideas. We intend to continue using independent projects in our teaching about sustainability. In doing so, we will work with the students to experiment, adapt, and strengthen the project as an integral part of the seminar learning experience.

## References

Annan, K.A. (2000, October). Sustaining the earth in the new millennium: The UN Secretary-General speaks out, *Environment*, 20-30.

Johnston, L. (1996). Resisting change: Information seeking and stereotype change. *Europoean Journal of Experimental Social Psychology, 26*, 799-825.

Kirk, C.M. (2003). Sustainability: Taking the long view [Special issue]. *Planning for Higher Education, 31*(3), 1-185.

Krizek, K.D., & Power, J. (1996). *A planners guide to sustainable development*. Chicago, IL: American Planning Association.

Lee, M. (2002). State of the planet, *The Ecologist, 20*(7), 6-11.

Rees, W.E. (1996). Revisiting carrying capacity: Area-Based indicators of sustainability, *Population and Environment: A Journal of Interdisciplinary Studies, 17*(3), 11-31.

Tibbs, H. (1996). Sustainability, *Deeper News GBN (Global Business Network), 3*(1), 1-76.

Vitousek, P.M., Mooney, H.A., Lubchenco, J., & Meillo, J.M. (1997). Humandomination of earth's ecosystems, *Science, 277*, 494-499.

# Chapter 16
## TEACHING AND LEARNING ABOUT DEMOCRACY, DIVERSITY AND COMMUNITY

David Schoem, Dorian Daniels, Erin Lane,
Jeff Nelson, Byanqa Robinson, and Vanessa Vadnal

## Introduction

This chapter focuses on the First-Year Sociology Seminar course, Democracy, Diversity and Community. To understand a course, it is important not just to look at the syllabus or ask the instructor what he/she taught, but also to hear from the students about what they learned and how they experienced the course. We will attempt to offer those different perspectives in this chapter.

David Schoem, the faculty member, first writes about the goals of the course, including discussion of content, teaching method and processes, assignments in the community, and dialogue. Second, he discusses his view of the challenges and successes of the course.

Students who have taken this course in each of the past three years then write about their experience, what they learned, and the influence of the course on their subsequent experiences at the University of Michigan, including thinking about social identity, civic engagement and diverse democracy. These students came to the class from different backgrounds and experiences, and their writing offers insightful stories and perspectives on their experience and what they have taken from it into their lives subsequent to the class.

## The Faculty Perspective: David Schoem

Not long after the tragedy of September 11, 2001, a *Newsweek* reporter and photographer came to my MCSP First-Year Sociology Seminar to learn and write about the mood on campus. "Generation 9/11" would be how they defined this group of college freshmen in their Nov. 12, 2001 cover story.

With the reporter present, the students in my class, as usual, talked openly about their varying opinions and perspectives on what had taken place on September 11. What most struck and surprised the reporter was the ease and thoughtfulness with which this very diverse group of twenty students openly and sensitively discussed their conflicting and passionate points of view with one another about such difficult and emotional issues. The class included White, African-American, Korean, Pakistani-American, Christian, Jewish and Muslim students, men and women, students from Seattle, New York, Detroit and places in between. I am a White, Jewish man. Speaking with the reporter after class helped reaffirm for me that while what my students and I were experiencing was just a typical class discussion, it represented, in fact, a rather unique experiment for much of America.

## Course Goals

The course, Democracy, Diversity and Community, is offered through the Sociology Department in conjunction with the Michigan Community Scholars Program (MCSP) as part of the College of Literature, Science, and the Arts' First Year Seminar Program. It is my attempt to engage students in thinking critically about diverse democracy in the United States and to practice deliberative democracy in the classroom. What I attempt to achieve every semester in this class is to take a group of young people from many different backgrounds, most of whom have lived in racially, economically, and religiously segregated neighborhoods, and develop a safe learning environment and a sense of community. My goal is that in this class' learning environment, the students will feel sufficiently comfortable and trusting of one another to learn deeply and express openly and honestly their feelings, insights, and differences.

I want immediately to emphasize the word "attempt" in the preceding paragraph, because every semester I have a new group of students, new challenges, and varying levels of success and failure.

Nevertheless, it is my hope that this course, much like the mission of the MCSP program, gives students a chance to fully appreciate the enormity of the promise of the American dream, to understand our serious historical shortcomings as a society in actually achieving this dream, to experience a taste of what the dream might feel like, and to feel empowered to go forward in their own lives to make the dream a reality. It's heady stuff, very challenging, and can also be tremendously rewarding.

## Course Content and Process

The course works sequentially through the three foci, diversity, democracy and community, during the fourteen week semester. We begin, at least in this most recent year, with a review of the Declaration of Independence, the Constitution, and consideration of what "America" means to students. We read Langston Hughes' poem, "Let America Be America Again" (1992) as an entrée to the discussion.

We then move onto the start of a semester-long process of intergroup dialogue and related activities and exercises (Schoem & Hurtado, 2001). I have been fortunate that my course description draws a fairly diverse group of students each year. Most recently my class of twenty was comprised of five African Americans, one mixed Indian (Asian) and White American, one Indian (Asian), one Chinese American, one Mexican American, and eleven White students of various ethnic backgrounds. There were four Jewish students, one Muslim, and fifteen Christian students. There were five men and fifteen women.

I immediately begin work to have students build a sense of community within the class and form a degree of trust among one another. We share very modest stories about ourselves and information about our styles of presentation in class, and we discuss how we are most likely to learn and respond most constructively to comments from classmates. Students immediately see the wide range of similarities and differences that exists within the group and welcome the opportunity to be gently prodded to engage with such a diverse set of people.

We quickly move on to in-depth exploration of issues of social identity, with particular emphasis on racial identity, racism, and race relations. We read Alex Kotlowitz's *The Other Side of the River* (1998) to gain a sense of perspective on these issues, asking students of diverse backgrounds which side of the river is the "other" side. Students continue this area of study, reading Beverly Tatum's *Why Are All the Black Kids Sitting Together in the Cafeteria?* (1997) and selections from Allan Johnson's *Privilege, Power and Difference* (2001). Students see films such as "True Colors" (1991) and "None of the Above" (1993), and read authors such as Cornel West (1993), Harlon Dalton (1995) and Frank Wu (2002) from a coursepack.

During this part of the class, at an opportune moment I will invite students to discuss social identity issues using the fishbowl dialogue method. I also have students discuss issues using a rotating concentric circle exercise, play an exercise game on power, and other kinds of methods of encouraging dialogue (Schoem, Frankel, Zuniga, & Lewis, 1995). All of this attention to dialogue does, in one sense, take time away from the formal content of the course. On the other hand, the attention to these process issues deeply enriches every discussion of the content and enables students to think more critically and with greater perspective and insight than they would ever approximate in a traditional classroom format. Not only do students listen more carefully to one another, but they read more analytically, take a greater personal interest in issues pertaining to their own social identity as well as their classmates' social identity, and they take the classroom discussion to the cafeteria and the residence hall floors in the evening.

Students have a writing assignment in this part of the semester that requires them to write about their own social identity. It is a shortened version of the semester-long "ethnic identity paper" (Schoem, 1991) that I have used in the past that resulted in publishable student essays. I have students submit a first draft, discuss my comments with them, and then have them revise and rewrite a final draft. These papers allow students to probe parts of their lives that have often gone unspoken or remained invisible to them until this time. White students invariably have never explored their white identity. Students of Color are much more in touch with their racial identity, but have had few if any opportunities to have their life story, as they describe it in these pages, studied and discussed as valued and embraced text.

Depending on the year, I organize short case studies on topics such as affirmative action, education, or segregation, to give students an opportunity to apply some of their learning. In 2002, I also invited a group organized by the campus's Office of Lesbian, Gay, Bisexual, Transgender Affairs to discuss sexual orientation and identity issues.

We then move on to a study of democracy, not in traditional political science terms, but more in terms of social relations and social structures. We read Robert Putnam's work on "Bowling Alone" (1995), John Leo's (1993) challenge of social responsibility over extreme individualism, and Kevin Phillips' writing in *Wealth and Democracy* (2002) on what he sees as the dangerously wide economic gap between the very rich and very poor in the United States. We turn to articles from Ellis Cose (1997, 2002), Tatum (1997), Bernice Reagon Johnson (1992), and Martha Nussbaum (1996) for potential models to consider how to build a strong, diverse democratic society.

Finally, we close the semester with a section looking at community. There are a number of aspects of community that I like to cover in this section of the course. First, I like students to get a sense of the different views of community—ideals of community and realities of community life. Students look back on their own experiences with community and communities. We watch the movie, *Smoke Signals* (1999) We also bring the issue of dialogue into the discussion, because students have come to understand that conflict is present in every community, and the communities that do best are often those that are most skilled at managing conflict in a constructive and just manner. We also return to Putnam's (1995) concern for the decline in civic engagement, particularly in this group's generation, and the importance of being involved in organizations, community, political processes, etc. We read from Paul Loeb's *Soul of a Citizen* (1999) and Laurent Parks Daloz et al.'s *Common Fire* (1996) to study examples of people living lives of commitment, and we skim through Ellis Jones' *The Better World Handbook* (2001) for a series of concrete suggestions for doing work for the public good. We also see short films from *Seeds of Peace* (1996), the University of Michigan's Program on Intergroup Relations, Conflict, and Community (1993), and the PBS documentary, *Not in Our Town* (1995), all of which portray intergroup dialogue and/or communities standing together against hate.

Finally, in place of a take-home essay exam, students write an integrative essay on one of the class themes, using numerous references from the assigned books and coursepack articles.

# Community Involvement

Community involvement is an integral part of the course. Although it is integrated into the course as I teach it, for the purposes of this paper I have decided to set it apart to provide some focused discussion on this component of the class.

I require my students to take part in seven community involvement activities and write a short paper about them. My hope is that students will 1) have a real life experience on campus moving them beyond their comfort zones, 2) gain some perspective on the social dynamics of their own social identity group and begin to see more clearly the dynamics of other social identity groups, 3) observe and experience in-group/out-group dynamics, 4) gain experience and insight on being an engaged citizen by virtue of participating in a governmental body or organization both in the Ann Arbor community and in the University of Michigan campus community, and 5) learn that they can participate effectively in a substantive conversation about a difficult issue with someone from a different social background, that they can live through that difficult experience, and that not only can the conversation go well but that they can develop even better skills for such dialogues. For many students, this part of the course is one of the most meaningful experiences they have during the semester.

The specific assignments are as follows:

1. Attend three activities in total, including one activity organized by one of your social identity groups and two activities organized by a social identity group different from yours.
2. Attend two meetings or activities demonstrating democracy in practice from the following categories:
   a) A meeting, event, or service activity of a community agency/organization such as the Ann Arbor City Council or the Ann Arbor School Board.
   b) A meeting of any UM student government or organizations such as the Michigan Student Assembly or Michigan Community Scholars Program Board.
3. Make two attempts at serious conversations about issues of social identity with people from different social identity groups.

In addition to these activities, students also write a final group paper that I call the multicultural organizational change paper. I ask students to identify some organization that they have participated in during high school or college, such as a club, a school, a job, a leadership group, etc. Students must define for themselves what they mean by "multicultural" and write a short history of the organization in terms of its multicultural past. They then develop their vision of what the organization would look and act like if it, indeed, were multicultural, and offer concrete steps as to how to change the organization from what it currently is to what it might become. Students complete the assignment by writing an endnote on what role, if they so chose, they could play in bringing about change.

In completing this paper, my goal is for students to gain insight into social change processes in the community and in organizations, and also gain a sense of empowerment. I hope that they will learn that as involved citizens in a democracy they are capable of bringing about change, as they see fit, in public and private organizations now and in the future. There are some students every term who report to me later in the year that they have actually gone back to the organizations they have written about and attempted to make some of the changes they have written about.

## Challenges, Successes, and Lessons Learned

### Creating the Community We Study

One of the greatest challenges—and successes, when achieved—is to move the class to a point where we model what we are learning from the course content. First, I attempt to develop a sense of community in the classroom, where people listen to one another, learn from one another's perspectives, work through conflicts and disagreements as they arise, and develop a personal interest in one's classmates. Second, the community we build in this class is invariably one that is highly diverse demographically and intellectually. Third, we attempt to incorporate some of the lessons of democracy, including engagement, participation, involvement, and a feeling of ownership—of the class, for the class, and by the class. If my students can come away from this class feeling that they've studied, experienced, and participated in a diverse, democratic class-room community, then I feel great hope for what they have learned and what they can accomplish in the future.

## Dialogue Across Difference

The practice of dialogue is a very difficult one, particularly because it is not something that any of us are intentionally or formally trained to do. My sense is that one of the aspects of the class that students most appreciate is the emphasis on the dialogue and discussion that takes place. Sometimes it can be time consuming and frustrating to develop the trusting climate that allows people to feel open enough to fully express their views and be taken seriously by their peers, but in the end it is these open and in-depth conversation that students remember from the class. They recall the opportunity to hear an intellectual or political view expressed thought-fully and sincerely that differs from their own, and their own ability to speak up and respond forcefully and sensitively with another view. To get to this point requires constant attention and work, but the results are exhilarating.

## This Course and MCSP: A Unique Opportunity

The themes of this course are the themes of the Michigan Community Scholars Program. For most of the students who take this course, like other students at Michigan and at most college campuses, this is one of the only opportunities they will have—or will take—to study about and engage in a deep, serious, and sustained way with peers from different racial and ethnic back-grounds. If students can come away from the class with deeper and broader thoughtfulness about the course issues, and gain new insights about the possibilities of engaging with others across difference in the future, then the class has been a great success for these individuals and for the prospects of a successful diverse, democracy.

## Different Approaches to Learning

Although the course and this chapter do focus on dialogue and discussion, in fact, I inten-tionally emphasize a variety of learning approaches and skills in the class. Students do a great deal of reading, writing, and oral presenting. They go out into the community to learn through experience and by doing. They graphically present posters of their learning. Over the years, they have written journals, essays, research papers, change papers, and take-home final essay exams. Different students come to the class with a variety of specialized skills and it's important for each one to stretch, and gain experience and skill in a range of learning approaches.

## Theory Practice, and the Personal

At the heart of my teaching philosophy is the notion that theory informs practice, and prac-tice informs theory. The theoretical meaning of the readings are best accessed and understood as students apply those insights to their personal experience. When students can see theory in practice, they begin to own the insights, shaping and making sense of them for themselves. Sim-ilarly, when students examine their personal experience as text, they begin to own the theoretical ideas they are studying, and give new meaning and insight to the theory. This approach helps students engage with the course in deep and profound ways that they take with them into their lives far beyond what a strictly theoretical or personal approach could provide.

## Covering It All

Frankly, it is very difficult to adequately address the three themes of democracy, diversity and community. The issues of race, racism, and racial and other social identities are so new and demanding for traditional eighteen year-old, first-year college students, many coming from seg-regated backgrounds, that the in-depth discussion and reflection takes a great deal of time and can be emotionally exhausting. At the moment we begin to move on to the other topics I sense that students are tired and weary. Although I attempt to make a clear linkage between all the topics, I think students feel as if they need a little vacation before they're ready to start on a new course theme. And, I, as the instructor, feel that time is moving by quickly and the rhythm of the semester says it's past the midway point.

## Maintaining Focus

One of the ongoing challenges of teaching courses on diversity is to include a focus on as many social identity groups as possible while still maintaining any focus at all. I don't care much for the approach of studying each group separately because it too easily leads to an essentialist and disconnected understanding on the part of students. Yet when I try to draw connections between and intersections of race, class and gender, as I often do, some students may feel, probably correctly, that I've still emphasized one racial group over another. Or, if I focus on race more than gender, students may regret that more time was not spent on gender. I do try to include reference and representation of many groups through readings, discussion, and films, and I encourage students to focus their paper assignments on any group for which they have particular interest. But I also appreciate the disappointment of students of a particular social identity background if they find themselves less than fully and explicitly represented in the syllabus compared to others in the class.

## The Mix of MCSP and Non-MCSP Students

By agreement with the College's Deans, MCSP holds 10-15 of the 20 spaces in its seminar classes for MCSP students and the remaining spaces are open to any first-year student in the university. For the most part the arrangement works well. The MCSP students invariably are a much more diverse group, given the program's representation. MCSP students also come to the class with experience and commitment to civic engagement and community service. The non-MCSP students usually fit in well and are motivated to keep up to speed by the MCSP students' interests and commitments. They also bring a broader campus experience to the class since they live outside of MCSP and often experience campus life differently. Only on occasion, and it is noticeable, are there non-MCSP students who have enrolled in the class without careful forethought and are not prepared nor interested in the kind of serious discussion and dialogue that the others anticipate and expect.

## Longterm Learnings

The greatest success I have is when I hear from students at the end of the term or, more often, when they are juniors or seniors or well into their professional careers, who tell me about the influence that this course has had upon their life. In these cases, the course has opened up a space for new thinking, new direction, exploration of the here-to-fore unexamined or secret, and allowed them to begin a journey of intellectual and personal freedom with respect to diversity, democracy and community. Some students discover themselves in this class—their personal and their social identity—and they learn to value and appreciate just who they are. Other students gain important learning skills—critical thinking, writing and revision, research and presentation. Still other students are empowered to change the world, whether that means their personal relationships, family, community, or society at large. Finally, some students report that they take control of their lives regarding these topics, perhaps recognize the prejudices that have been ingrained into them, and choose intentionally to move beyond that. Many students build close friendships about substantive conversations through the course and continue those friendships with a diverse group of people long into the future.

## One Student's Story

This past year I had one student who came from a more rural and lower economic background than many of her classmates. She didn't speak up that much in class, perhaps because she was intimidated by the class differences or perhaps because of the strong personalities present. But this student wrote her "change" paper about the party store where she worked at home, a business that served as a gathering place for many in the surrounding communities. She wrote how the owner, a White woman she knew well, had been previously unwilling to hire people of color. My student had the strong sense that if there were people of all races and backgrounds working at the party store, it would send a strong and influential message about diversity and tolerance that would be heard widely through several neighboring counties. This student, quiet in our class, but with great internal fortitude and strength, took it upon herself to have one of the substantive conversations we had practiced in class with her boss, the owner of the party store, after the end of the semester. After the winter break, the student approached me to tell me just what she had done. Incredibly, because of this student's courage, skill, and determination, the owner hired two African Americans and a Hispanic person just in time for the Christmas shopping season. It was the first time in the history of this business that a person of color had been employed there. I hear that all went very smoothly and the impact was palpable.

### What I Learn from Teaching the Course

The topics of democracy, diversity and community are as complex as they are important. Every semester I learn more about the theory of these topics from teaching this course and, of course, the application of the theory to my personal experience and practice. I learn even more, perhaps, through the effort to build and model a diverse, democratic learning community in the context of the course. The effort to do so is the work of a lifetime, and the moments of insight and awareness in the midst of the complexity and struggle, whether on my part or the part of my students, bring a flash of hope and optimism that the effort is indeed fully worthwhile.

Ultimately, I love my students and I love to teach. Teaching these subjects can be difficult, conflict-ridden, and challenging. However, the relative intellectual innocence, hopefulness, and eagerness to engage and learn on the part of students in their first semester of college is about the best teaching experience one can hope for. As the student voices that follow make clear, it is a joy to learn and grow with each new class and generation of students.

# The Student Perspective—Year Three: Dorian Daniels

### College Welcome Week

When I consider my experiences from Democracy, Diversity and Community, two aspects of the class that immediately come to mind are class discussions and assigned readings. Since arriving at college in August, I have been very aware of my social identity as a Black female. Not even in my neighborhood, where my family is the only Black one for at least four blocks in any direction, or my high school, where there were only five Blacks in a graduating class of forty-six, was I so painfully aware of being Black. I say painfully not because I am ashamed of being Black or wish that I were something else, but because my racial identity has negatively affected my experiences at college more than anywhere else.

I came to college with an open mind, but it seemed like few others did the same, because I was repeatedly judged based on my race. Except for one White guy who was really friendly, every fellow student with whom I interacted during my first two months of college was Black because they were the only people who even acknowledged my presence. In the residence hall and in my classes, I found myself drawn to other Black students, not necessarily because we had similar experiences or interests, but out of acceptance and non-judgmental attitudes toward each other that I had not found among any other students thus far. So, although I had been very excited about taking Democracy, Diversity and Community before my arrival at college, I grew increasingly anxious about it up until the first day of class. While I had been looking forward to the discussions, my experiences around campus caused me to fear that I would have to endure the same kinds of comments in class that I had been hearing around campus.

## The Class and Fall Semester

However, as I look back on the class discussions, I am relieved to remember that the comments I heard in class were not as ignorant as I had expected they would be. While I was occasionally offended at the insensitivity expressed by some students during class discussions, I know that no one purposely made comments so malicious that I would be upset for days to come. Over the course of the semester, I learned one very fundamental fact that has dramatically helped me in my college experience: people are the product of their environment; they know nothing less and nothing more than they have experienced. This fact leads to my discussion of the readings for the class, which provided a different "experience" for me to develop new ways of considering certain situations.

Even before I came to campus and was swamped with information about the University's affirmative action lawsuits, I knew that affirmative action was something that I should support. Any program that attempts to give equal opportunity to disadvantaged and underrepresented groups seemed like a great idea to me. However, after reading pieces by Cornel West (1993), Frank Wu (2002), Ellis Cose (1997, 2002), and William Bowen and Derek Bok (1998), I decided that affirmative action is not only an excellent idea, but a necessary action to address persisting societal inequalities.

From in-class discussions and conversations with some of my White hall mates, my conclusion about the link between people's beliefs and their experiences was supported. When presented with readings and other evidence, people were able to look at situations from a different angle. Witnessing this, I was able to do the same thing, looking at affirmative action from the perspective of a poor White friend, or racial profiling in the eyes of a wealthy White classmate. Particularly memorable was a movie that we watched in class that followed two men, one Black and one White, on their search for housing, employment, a car, and clothing in a city. The White man was consistently treated better than the Black man, and the discussion that ensued was particularly heated. Some students could not believe what happened, and some justified it by saying that the footage looked old and that would not happen today, or that Whites are typically wealthier than Blacks so they are treated better because of economics, not race. One conclusion that I reached from the discussion that followed the movie is that some people saw something they had never seen before, and thus were able to look at a situation differently. Conversely, the core of others' beliefs was so shaken that they had to justify the situation to avoid extreme inner turmoil.

## Winter Semester

My conclusion not only helped me in class (to not be offended by people's ignorance or denial of the continued existence of racism and other forms of discrimination), but also greatly assisted me in other aspects of college life, and continues to do so today. As I learned to adjust to differences in upbringing and others aspects of a person's background, I was able to acquire a more diverse group of friends. I resisted friends' assertions that a White guy who rarely spoke to them was a closet racist and remembered that he is from a small town and had probably never even met any Black people before coming to the University. From class, I grew to understand the power of dialogue, so I took time to discuss important issues with him, and learned more than I ever would have if we had shared a similar background and life experiences. From these dialogues, I realized that not only had my friend made some assumptions about my friends before really getting to know them (as they had done to him), but I also realized that I had secretly held some stereotypes about him, as well. So, not only was he a product of his environment, but I was a product of mine.

Democracy, Diversity and Community has helped me understand the power of stereotypes, especially unconscious ones that I hold. Thus, I have worked hard to avoid making unsubstantiated conclusions about people. Corresponding with the goals of MCSP, I have been able to learn at a deeper level because I am aware of different views, and I try to consider them when constructing my own opinions. My group of friends is larger and more diverse now than I could have ever hoped for, if I had allowed myself to fall into the patterns of stereotyping and prejudice that limited my first couple of months at Michigan. Reflecting on my ideal community, the people with whom I live, study, eat, and socialize form a very diverse group. We each contribute positive aspects of our social identities to the group, making everyone's experiences richer. The people with whom I interact on a daily basis do not agree with me on issues such as politics, affirmative action, or the U.S.-Iraq conflict. However, we all hold strong beliefs and opinions on those issues, and we are able to have pretty lively discussions only because we do not agree. We are all committed to equal opportunity for all people, although we disagree on how that may be achieved.

Without Democracy, Diversity and Community, I would not describe my experiences at college as positively as I can now. Undoubtedly, it would be impossible to endure the ignorance expressed by some students without taking it personally, if I did not realize that it is not their fault, because they only know what they have been taught. I love the University of Michigan, and I am here to develop intellectually and emotionally into a mature and responsible adult, but being at Michigan is difficult at times. I am constantly reminded of my social status as a Black female, and if it were not for classes that allow me to discuss issues with students whose views differ from mine, and share my beliefs and opinions so that I am not silenced while being forced to hear those of the majority, I would probably choose to attend a different institution of higher education.

### My Plans for the Future

When I consider what led to my desire to be a social psychologist and work with underprivileged and at-risk youth, I know that it was my experiences in the class and other aspects of MCSP that gave me the faith that I can "be the change I wish to see in the world." I value opinions different than mine, and I actually enjoy hearing them. From these discussions, I am able to develop and modify my own opinions to fit my new knowledge and experiences. I am a firm believer in the ability of individual power to effect dramatic change in society, if that one person is truly committed to the goal and is able to communicate it effectively to others. In closing, the class allowed me to look at different issues and consider my interactions with others in a more honest, open, and considerate manner than I was able to do before, and would have otherwise. I have a great understanding of the methods in which one's community inhibits or promotes understanding and acceptance of diversity, and how that contributes to the person's core beliefs, which in turn, affect opinions, statements, and actions.

# The Student Persective—Year Two: Erin Lane, Byanqua Robinson, Vanessa Vadnal

### Social Identities

*Erin* For the first nine years of my life, I lived on the west side of Flint, Michigan as one of the few white girls in a black neighborhood. My parents raised me with the principle that all people are created equal and skin color has nothing to do with a person's character. Many of my good friends were black, but it never seemed extraordinary; we didn't think of ourselves as being any different from each other. Then in fourth grade I moved to white suburbia and I was shocked by the intense racism that I encountered. I would hear my white friends' parents make racist remarks and be too scared to retort. I knew that what they were saying was wrong, and I felt like a bad person for not speaking out. I began feeling guilty for being around them, for not speaking up, and for just being white. I started to feel very tense about the subject of race.

*Byanqa*  Until I was twelve, I lived in an ethnically diverse, middle-class community in Milwaukee, Wisconsin. It wasn't until after I moved to Detroit that I experienced racial prejudice. It is the most demeaning and shocking thing that has ever happened to me. It's unsettling to have someone just look at me, and solely based on the color of my skin, decide that I am less of a person than they are. I didn't know what to do or how to think. I wanted to change their minds and show these people that I am human just like they are.

With my acceptance to the University of Michigan came feelings of uncertainty. I had heard of the racial tension and difficulties that were present, and was unsure of how I would be received. I applied to MCSP with the hope of finding a diverse, receptive community and environment.

*Vanessa*  When I came to live in the MCSP community, I thought of myself as a Seattle native and recent graduate of a small private school. Many people would scoff at that self-definition because it lacks the characteristic that often means the most in America—race. Yet, I did not identify with being "white" because I was not sure what that meant. Although I grew up in a predominantly white suburb, I had attended a racially diverse school for eight years. For nearly half my life, anyone who was important to me attended this school. My closest friends were minorities. However, taking Democracy, Diversity and Community, I began to understand how my skin color affected my life.

## Experiences

*Erin*  In Democracy, Diversity and Community, I had the opportunity to express my feelings of guilt about race with my black classmates. After doing so, I felt a powerful sense of relief. I had always been afraid to talk about race with non-whites. Our discussions broke down this racial barrier and allowed me to look inward and admit what I was feeling. I let out feelings that had been trapped inside for the past nine years, feelings that I hadn't previously given myself a chance to rationalize because I felt so disgusted with myself over them. By reading Beverly Tatum's (1997) book, *Why Are All the Black Kids Sitting Together in the Cafeteria?*, I was able to objectively view my feelings and see ways to overcome them. My experiences in this class have allowed me to maintain better friendships with people of other races and feel comfortable again in my white skin.

*Byanqa*  The discussions were the most forceful and memorable part of Democracy, Diversity and Community. Never before had I been allowed to speak so openly on the taboo topics of race issues and stereotypes with anyone outside of my family and friends. I had imagined an interaction of this type being impossible. An uncontrollable worry of it being wrong to talk about these issues remained buried within me. I'm not even sure what was wrong about it, or even what I thought would happen had I spoken. But I feel these fears are reasonable in a sense, given my past experiences. I guess I just expected white people not to believe or respect my experiences, where I came from, and to deny that any problems even existed. The course gave us a neutral ground, an outlet to speak and discuss our thoughts and experiences. I left the course with a sense of relief to release and share my feelings; and a loss of fear of speaking.

*Vanessa*  David Schoem's class helped me begin to understand what it meant to be white in America. American pop culture told me that it meant that I was a poor jumper and bad dancer. This narrow view changed radically after riveting class discussions about the "white system of advantage." Prior to enrolling in this class, although I recognized that minorities were "disadvantaged," I had never flipped this statement in order to see that whites were "advantaged." Even if I thought this advantage was unfair and did not want it, I had it. As Harlon Dalton (1995) said in his article *Racial Healing: Confronting the Fear Between Blacks and Whites*, "like it or not, their [Whites'] fate as individuals is tied in complex ways to the fate of Whites as a whole" (p.

6). Suddenly, I saw this system of white advantage operating everywhere. I could go shopping without fear of being hassled. When I took standardized tests (or any other measure of academic ability), I did not have to worry that my performance would reflect upon my race. And the list continues.

Before David's class I applied my own standards of equity and justice when I thought about how America perceived race. I came from an open-minded family, school, and city. I had had close relationships with minorities and did not rely on media stereotypes when judging "the other." David's class opened my eyes to the ubiquity and depths of this system of white advantage. And from that I gained a much clearer understanding what my "whiteness" meant.

### Living Together

After meeting in David's class, the three of us decided to live together. We rented a house near campus along with two other girls in MCSP, and we have been living there for the past year. In most respects, our living situation is no different from any other college student household. Our differing racial backgrounds haven't slowed our friendships, in large part because we learned how to feel comfortable about race with one another. We study together, we watch movies together, and we sit on the porch together to discuss all the things that college students discuss, from our social lives to politics. Race seems to find its way into many of our conversations, and we can get through these conversations without feeling awkward and self-conscious. From David's class, we learned how to make our atypical living situation feel natural.

## The Student Perspective—Year One: Jeff Nelson

### The Impact of Awareness

I took David Schoem's class Democracy, Diversity and Community during my freshman year at the University of Michigan, Ann Arbor. I took the class in conjunction with the Michigan Community Scholars Program, which was a living-learning community on campus that provided an outlet for social service work and social justice action. By the conclusion of the year and subsequently, the conclusion of the class, I knew that my perspectives and opinions had been altered through the class, but I was not able to realize the true severity of that alteration until my semester abroad program my junior year.

This past semester I participated in the Semester at Sea program through the University of Pittsburgh. On this program, I, along with 100 faculty and staff and more than 600 students from across the globe, traveled the world to seven different nations while studying in the ports and on the ship. We ported in Cuba, Brazil, South Africa, Tanzania, India, Japan, South Korea, and Canada. In four short months, I experienced extreme diversity and complexity of the world beyond what I could have ever previously imagined. The people I met and the interactions in which I participated stimulated emotional and intellectual inquiry like I never experienced before. I lived and tasted the poverty of India, I participated in diversity workshops in post-Apartied South Africa, and I discussed political inequalities with Fidel Castro. This voyage of discovery enriched my heart, my mind, and my soul. Since the conclusion of the voyage, I have come to the realization that my abroad program was significantly enhanced because of my participation in the Democracy, Diversity and Community class and my MCSP experience.

To understand diversity one must experience it. Furthermore, discussions and dialogues focused on the topics of diversity exponentially advance one's understandings. MCSP and David Schoem's class gave me the invaluable combination of experience and discussion. In Democracy, Diversity and Community journaling, a unique component to education is added into the equation. Throughout the semester we wrote reflective journals that included insights from the readings. My understanding of the concept of diversity was increased dramatically when I was forced to search within myself for answers to these difficult questions and relate personal experiences to my answers. I found that during my Semester at Sea voyage there were endless situations where I found it valuable to step back and deal with myself intellectually by writing out my thoughts.

Another aspect of David's class that I have grown to cherish since my freshman year was the racial identity development component. While on Semester at Sea, we did a substantial amount of work delving into the complexity of racial identity development. The apex of this studying culminated in writing a paper, at which point I truly felt that I had a solid grasp on the material.

Since then I have witnessed my own racial identity develop throughout various experiences and in parallel, on this voyage, I have gone through massive progress in this intellectual/emotional development. David's class taught me that having one's opinions and perspectives challenged is quite possibly the most difficult yet rewarding situation that can occur within the educational experience. Through David's class I learned to embrace this complex feeling and pursue challenges for these very reasons.

Countries such as India and Japan challenged my perspectives in ways I had never dreamed. I knew that my ideology was Westernized in many ways, but I had never really experienced anything truly Eastern with which to compare and contrast my own perspectives. Then I lived in India for nine days. While MCSP broadened my awareness, and Democracy, Diversity and Community enhanced my understanding, nothing could have fully prepared me for India. Gender, religious, racial, ethnic, and sexual relations are intensified by the sub-continent's diversity. During a social service project in a Dalit village, I was able to witness the pivotal role that the caste system plays in daily Indian life. Through home-stay experiences I felt the religious tension between Hindus and Muslims, and furthermore, I was able to gain a feel for the consequences of arranged marriages on Indian women. Although these experiences were educationally incomparable, the intellectual and character development resulting from David's class enhanced my appreciation and understanding of these interactions.

The slogan for the Semester at Sea program is "the voyage of discovery." By engaging in exploration and cultural exchanges, students on this voyage discover a wealth of new knowledge about different cultures, different people, and different experiences. At the conclusion of the voyage though, it seems for many students that this voyage of discovery focused more on self-exploration than anything else. This was true of my experience, and I also realized that my previous experiences of self-discovery in MCSP and David's freshman seminar, dramatically improved the way I grew and matured on this voyage two years later.

## References

Alvarado, D. (1999). Multiracial student experience: What faculty and campus leaders need to know. *Diversity Digest, 3*(2), p.2-3

Bowen, W., & Bok., D. (1998). *The shape of the river.* Princeton, NJ: Princeton University Press.

Chesler, M. (1993). *Perceptions of faculty behavior by students of color.* CRLT Occasional Papers. Ann Arbor, MI: CRLT/UM.

Cose, E. (1997). *Color-Blind.* New York: Harper Perrenial.

Cose, E. (2002). *The envy of the world.* New York: Washington Square Press.

Dalton, H. (1995). *Racial healing: Confronting the fear between Blacks and Whites.* New York: Doubleday.

Dizard, R. (1993). A tale of two colleges. *Change, 25*(4), p. 27-31

Eyre, C. (Director), & Alexie, S. (Writer). (1999). *Smoke Signals* [Motion picture]. United States: Miramax Films

Farley, R., Danziger, S., & Holzer, H. (2000). *Detroit divided.* New York: Russell Sage

Gurin, P. (1999). Expert report of Patricia Gurin. Retrieved from www.umich.edu/~newsinfo/Admission/Expert/opinion.html.

Hughes, L. (1992). Let America be America again. In G. Columbo, R. Cullen, & B. Lisle (Eds.),

*ReReading America* (776-779). Boston: St. Martin's Press.

Intergroup dialogues. (1993). Ann Arbor, MI: The University of Michigan, Program on Intergroup Relations, Conflict, and Community.

Johnson, A. (2001). *Privilege, power and difference.* Mountain View, CA: Mayfield Publishing.

Jones, E., Haenfler, R., Johnson, B., & Klocke, B. (2001). *The better world handbook.* Gabriola Island, Canada: New Society Publishers

King, M.L., Jr. (1986). Letter from Birmingham City jail. In J. Washington (Ed.). *A Testament of hope* (289-302) New York: Harper San Francisco.

Kotlowitz, A. (1998). *The other side of the river.* New York: Anchor Books.

Leo, J. (1993). Community and personal duty. In S. Walker (Ed.). *The graywolf annual ten: Changing community* (29-32). St. Paul, MN: Graywolf Press.

Loeb, P.R. (1999). *Soul of a citizen: Living with conviction in a cynical time.* New York: St. Martin's Griffin.

Massey, D., & Denton, D. (1993). *American apartheid: Segregation and the making of the underclass.* Cambridge, MA: Harvard University Press.

McIntosh, P. (1997). White privilege: Unpacking the invisible knapsack. In B. Schneider (Ed.). *Race: An anthology in the first person* (120-126). New York: Three Rivers Press.

Kantrowitz, B., & Naughton, K. (2001, November 12). Generation 9-11. *Newsweek*, P.46-56

Nussbaum, M. (1996). *For love of country.* Boston: Beacon Press.

O'Neill, P., & Miller, R. (Producers). (1995). *Not in our town* [Motion picture]. Oakland, CA: California Working Group.

Parks Daloz, L. (1996). *Common fire.* Boston: Beacon Press.

Phillips, K. (2002). *Wealth and democracy.* New York: Broadway Books.

Putnam, R. (1995). *Bowling alone: The collapse and revival of American community.* New York: Simon & Schuster.

Reagon Johnson, B. (1992). Coalition politics: Turning the century. In M. Andersen & P.H. Collins (Eds.). *Race, Class and Gender* (503-509). Belmont, CA: Wadsworth.

Rist, R. (1973). *The urban school.* Cambridge, MA: MIT Press

Rodriguez, R. (1997). Asians. In B. Schneider (Ed.). *Race: An anthology in the First Person* (59-73). New York: Three Rivers Press.

Schoem, D. (1991). *Inside separate worlds: Life stories of young Blacks, Jews, and Latinos.* Ann Arbor, MI: University of Michigan Press.

Schoem, D., Frankel, L., Zuniga, X., & Lewis, E. (1995). *Multicultural teaching in the university.* Westport, CT: Praeger.

Schoem, D., & Hurtado, S. (2001). *Intergroup dialogue: Deliberative democracy in school, college, community and workplace.* Ann Arbor, MI: University of Michigan Press

Takaki, R. (1993). *A different mirror.* Boston: Little, Brown.

Tatum, B.D. (1997). *Why are all the Black kids sitting together in the cafeteria?* New York: Basic Books.

West, C. (1993). *Race matters.* Boston: Beacon.

Wu, F. (2002). *Yellow.* New York: Basic Books.

# SECTION FOUR
## Participant Voices of Insight and Experience

# Chapter 17

## MICHIGAN COMMUNITY SCHOLARS PROGRAM AND ITS COMMUNITY PARTNERS: DEVELOPING A SERVICE STRATEGY AS A VOLUNTEER ORGANIZATION

Richard Carter

This past year I had an opportunity to serve as evaluator of the year-long Michigan Community Scholars Program (MCSP) social capacity-building process—of building linkages between faculty, community partners, students, and staff. What MCSP was attempting was intensive and far reaching, and something that many campuses are beginning to think about—how to build strong, sustained, healthy relationships between campus and community partners. The primary suggestion of this chapter, emanating from my experiences with MCSP and years of working in this area, is that campus partnerships with the community should be organized and conceptualized in ways that are very similar to that of traditional volunteer organizations and their volunteer partners.

## Partnership Organizations as Volunteer Organizations

Partnership organizations are very similar to traditional volunteer organizations. The only differences between them may be that in volunteer organizations there may possibly be a higher expectation of working in a collaborative environment, and there may be a likelihood that partnerships bring together individuals that share fewer similarities in their life experiences. These individuals might include people such as the civic-minded inner-city housewife and university political science professor, or a community recreational instructor and graduate student in social work. However, in both organizations participants would fit very neatly into Webster's (1993) definition for volunteer: "one who serves or acts out of their own free will." Building on this definition, let's use as a working definition for volunteer organization: "A group of volunteers who organize themselves to achieve some stated purpose." If we were to profile the majority of people participating in human service and academic community partnership programs and traditional volunteers, we would probably find they: 1) have primary responsibility to a number of constituencies; 2) derive no financial benefit; and 3) joined under their own initiative. Also, we would quickly discover that both types of organizations require the same kind of support services to meet their objectives.

Administratively, volunteer organizations are, or should be, designed to provide the types of services that are conducive to creating and sustaining involvement of people from diverse backgrounds. Generally, these organizations consist of individuals with professional expertise, and understand the needs and limitations of the volunteer (partners). These professionals are adept at addressing or assisting with issues the partners are likely to face. Included among these issues are: reasonable expectations, keeping commitments, need for respect, feelings of making a contribution, clear communication, effective staff support. The focus of this chapter will be dedicated to helping staff develop a service strategy (which consists of expertise and perspectives) that assists the partners in reaching their objectives.

A sound service strategy incorporates some, if not all, of the following components: 1) sharing the big picture, 2) accepting that partners have their own agendas, 3) having reasonable expectations, 4) assisting in keeping commitments, 5) respecting partners, 6) communicating clearly, 7) recognizing contributions, and 8) fostering group cohesion.

## Sharing and Understanding the Big Picture

More often than not, many of us feel over worked and under appreciated. We have heard people from various professions lament their lack of time and the feeling of being over committed. Often people are reluctant to get involved with organizations because they are not entirely clear what joining a particular group will entail or what they may be asked to do.

Understanding the big picture is very important to most people. More likely than not, they are being asked to join other groups, such as professional associations, and church and civic groups. Consequently, they are constantly weighing where to give their time. By providing potential members with a good cross-section of information, they may help them determine how to best contribute to the organization, or determine if they want to affiliate with the organization at all. Potential partners need to know such things as: What is the organization's mission? How does the organization function? How is leadership developed? How are decisions made? How do various areas of the organization interface? How is the organization financed? How does the organization sustain itself? And, what are some of the past accomplishments of the organization? In short, the answer to these questions give potential partners some idea if this partnership is going to be a good fit for them.

By having a deeper understand of the organization's infrastructure, culture and history, partners are better able to create a vision that will, in part, fuel their level of participation and assist them in shaping their organizational aspirations.

## Accept that Partners Have Agendas

While partners may not seek a financial benefit, it is not unusual for them to come to the organization with their own agenda that includes expectations of some benefits. Partnership organizations are symbiotic in nature: that is to say, while they may not be seeking financial benefits, they are seeking to derive some non-financial benefit from their affiliation. These benefits can take on any number of aspects and characteristics, such as feelings of altruism (raising money for charity), personal gain (access to a mailing list), self-esteem (leadership in a civic club), or the furtherance of social values and constructs (involvement in a political organization). It is extremely important that these desired benefits are recognized and acknowledged. Even though the characteristic of these two communities (human service and academic communities) may be very different, particularly in areas of status and power, the need to derive mutual benefits from the partnership is no different than other traditional relationships. Whether it is between husband and wife, coach and player, employer and employee, if any relationship is to be sustained, all parties involved have to get something out of it. Regardless of what motivates them, it is essential that their unique needs be met if their participation is to continue.

## Reasonable Expectations

Community partners who choose to join the partnership generally have some expectations of how much time they have to commit to the organization. As was stated earlier in the chapter, partners represent a number of constituencies from the communities. Each has primary responsibility to other constituencies outside of their relationship to the university partnership. Therefore, it is important to understand what limitations the community partners have. The best way to determine their limitations is to ask them. The one mistake that is often made is to assume what tasks partners are willing to undertake. For instance, an organization might wrongly assume that "he/she is a doctor so we won't ask him/her to drive the kids." More often than not, we don't ask enough of the partner. It is not unusual for partners to feel that they are not needed because either they're being ask to do nothing, or so very little, that they are left feeling that their time would be better spent somewhere else. In effect, the expectations they brought with them to the organization were not being met.

I like to think that partners go through three stages of involvement. Stage 1) "How did I ever allow myself to get involved with this organization?" This is when the partner really come to grips with the reality that there are other things they have put on hold to do this task. Pressures could be coming from any number of sources, such as spouses, job, children, scheduling issues, etc. Stage 2) "I'll be glad when this is over." This is the stage that one is simply glad when the task is over. There is a feeling that, no matter how worthy the task, there's just not enough time in the day to get everything done. Stage 3) "I'll be more than happy to do it again." If the partner has had a gratifying experience from a job well done, along the way they have bonded with staff and other partners. And, most importantly, if their initial expectations have been met, then it is very likely they will want to continue their involvement with the organization.

Certainly partners bring various levels of expertise and abilities. Some are experienced volunteers, have a wealth of experience, and a great deal of flexibility with their time. However, there are others that may be lacking in many of these areas. They may not have time flexibility, the luxury of a support staff, or any number of attributes that enhance volunteer service. Their biggest assist may be just a willing heart. However, if staff is providing quality support to partners, there is nothing wrong with staff expecting quality service from partners. If staff is keeping their commitments they should expect that, at the least, partners will do their best to reciprocate. As always, it starts with staff setting the tone.

It is worth repeating that partners join an organization with some expectations of what will be required of them. By joining, they are essentially committed to making an effort to fulfill those requirements. It is up to the staff to meet or even exceed those expectations held by partners.

## Keeping Commitments

The strength of the organization is often determined by how well partners keep their commitments. There is an old saying, "The pathway to hell is paved with good intentions." There are few truer statements that guide the support needs of community partners. Partners who accept an assignment generally do so in good faith and feel that they can complete the task in the prescribed time frame. However, in more cases than not, if left to their own devices, they will wait until the last minute to try to get the task done. If they don't live in a perfect world, and most of us don't, there is a reasonable likelihood that a chain of unforeseen events, such as family situations, job responsibilities, or something as simple as a computer malfunction, may create difficulty in completing the task. Good staff work can often short-circuit this chain of events. Particularly in newly formed organizations, staff should be very vigilant regarding how well partners are following through on their commitments. Staff should ask themselves questions such as: am I communicating with the community partners at regular intervals? Are the partners completing tasks in a timely manner, and how invested am I (staff) in their success? These are all important questions that should be answered in the affirmative if partners are to receive appropriate assistance.

Providing adequate lead-time is crucial in assisting partners toward keeping their commitments. Partners need to fit these additional responsibilities into what is perhaps an already tight schedule. Lead time allows them to prioritize other things that are on-going in their lives while not diminishing what needs to be done for the organization. Also, building lead-time into an organization's overall service strategy will enable staff to monitor the progress of partners and lend assistance when necessary. It is helpful to set a couple of deadlines as to when tasks are to be completed. The first deadline indicates when the tasks should be completed and allows for enough cushion so that even if completion is running late it does not affect the overall outcome of what is to be accomplished. The second deadline, the "drop-dead" deadline, is the time that the task must be completed. This deadline is not necessarily shared with partners.

Keeping commitments is not only important for the individual partner; it is also a primary contributor to how the organization will be viewed both internally and externally. Staff who are welling to go the extra mile to assist partners in keeping their commitments are deeply appreciated, and are true assets to the organization. Additionally, partners are far more likely to accept assignments if they have been given adequate lead-time and have enjoyed rewarding experiences in the past.

## Need for Respect

There was a song written and recorded in the 1970s by Aretha Franklin, entitled "Respect." There is a line in the song that goes, "R-E-S-P-E-C-T, find out what it means to me." Partners, and for that matter, anyone involved in the organization, wants to feel respected as individuals. They want to feel valued as a contributing partner and asset of the organization.

The notion of showing respect to people may seem very obvious. Yet, it has been my experience that a lack of regard for individuals can and does happen more than one might expect. I can recall an instance when a dinner program was being organized. The organization's staff invited various people to fill certain roles, e.g., master of ceremonies, speaker, etc., and put together what seemed to be an excellent program. However, the one thing that the staff didn't do was to check with the community partner who was also assigned to organizing the program. You can imagine the outrage of the Partner! This is just one example of not showing respect for another's perspective; however, in the organizational milieu this dynamic repeats itself frequently in area such as financial decisions, committee appointments, and program development.

I would suggest that one reason this may be happening its because some people confuse the definition of being *polite* with that of showing *respect*. One can be polite by making a proper appearance e.g., expressing appreciation, appropriate acknowledgment etc. However, if partners are going to be shown respect it requires a deeper more engaging interaction between individuals. To facilitate such an interaction, there are a few basic things that staff could do, such as making partners feel they are listened to, seeking their input during the decision making process, and making them feel valued.

Partners, like anyone else, want to know that they are not just being heard, but they are genuinely being listened to. They want to feel confident that their suggestions and input are really being considered during the decision-making process and not just being ignored. Though they may never openly admit it, they want to see some of their ideas incorporated into the final decisions. Staff should remember that there is seldom one right way to do most things. To the extent that staff can give up ownership of an idea, and purposefully allow room for the input of others, the more likely they are to create an environment that nurtures a strong and sustaining organization which values its partners.

Staff should proactively seek the input of the organization's partners. It is of vital importance that all partners feel a sense of participation in the decision-making process, particularly in those areas that have a direct relationship with their involvement in the organization. Asking partners to give their opinions on substantive issues facilitates a strong relationship and bond between themselves and the organization. One of the best means of getting maximum effort from the partners is for them to see themselves as custodians of the organization. By providing adequate opportunities for them to get involved, this perspective is encouraged. If input is sought in a meaningful and sincere way, a strong and collaborative environment can be created.

## Clear Communication

Sometimes what may seem to have been a minor oversight can turn into a major bone of contention. One way to avoid such situations and misunderstandings is to limit surprises. This was alluded to in the discussion of respect earlier in the chapter. In collaborative relationships, community partners want to feel that they are involved in the decision-making process. Whether the ultimate decision was the right one or not is not the only important matter. The important thing is that partners must have the feeling of participating in the process. In the earlier scenario of the dinner program, it didn't matter that the program was excellent! What mattered was that the partner was not given the opportunity to participate in deciding who was going to be on the program. Sometimes events may not allow for as much input from partners as may be desired. In those instances it is a good practice to inform these partners as soon as possible. There are few things more embarrassing for partners than to be informed about a decision, particularly in their area of responsibility, from someone not directly connected with the process. Understandably, it could make them feel that others see them as being not informed, not valued by the organization, and bringing into question their competence.

Partners come to an organization with many different styles of communication. Some can be very diplomatic while others are just downright rude. Some can make the sinking of the Titanic seem like finding a cure for some dreaded disease, while others could make finding a cure for cancer akin to starting World War III. Some people learn how to work though positive reinforcement, while other have mastered the art of intimidation. Obviously, most of us would prefer to work with the more positive styles. However, in every life a little rain must fall, and from time to time you will find yourself working with the more negative styles.

One mark of a seasoned professional is the ability to disarm partners using these negative styles. There are several ways to do this: do not take them or yourself too seriously, maintain a sense of humor, and seek input on important matters. The goal is to get people to communicate with you, and possibly other partners, in a less confrontational manner. The one realty that must be accepted is that sometimes, no matter how hard you try, there is nothing you can do about such people and situations.

Having a personal relationship with partners can be a real asset in both effective communication and the overall climate in the organization. Such relationships often encourage an ambiance that is fun to work in and be associated with. In such settings, community partners look forward to spending time together, and they tend to be much more collaborative and concerned about outcomes. Partners are far more likely to see themselves as organizational custodians. In most case (whether in organizations, or in personal relationships) "people do things for people." That is not to say that people only do things for folks they know, or that they will not do things because they are not meritorious in there own right. However, after the worthiness of an undertaking has been satisfied, when it come down to a question of one's willingness to go out of their way at considerable inconvenience to themselves, the decision to do it or not will often hinge on who is making the "ask." Also, members of these organizations are often people who share a common passion. Therefore, it is no surprise that many lifelong friendships have begun as a result of relationships started in collaborative organizations. Building a personal relationship with partners can serve you well, both in moving the organization forward and also in being personally rewarding.

Increasingly we are moving toward a de-personalized society. It is not unusual for us to not have personal contact with individuals in the transaction of much of our daily business. Today we can conduct many our dealings through a series of recording (voice messages) and email communications. Most of us have had the exasperating experience of calling a service provider and being directed through a series of commands, to press various numbers on the telephone keypad, getting far more information than we want or need, until we reach the intended service provider or only to find out that we have to call back later. And, we hang up the phone feeling that we have wasted our time and/or we've been treated like we're nothing but a number.

In the best-case scenario, we are increasingly utilizing the email system. This form of communication has enabled us to transact our business without ever coming into direct contact with one another. While I have come to appreciate the benefit of email, if taken to the extreme, it could easily negate the need to establish a personal rapport in the traditional sense. As previously stated, people do things for people. In my judgment, personal contact should be an important consideration in an overall service strategy. However, to expedite communication, it is becoming more acceptable by some and even preferred by others to use email. This is a judgment call for individual staff. I would just caution that the ultimate decision should be driven by the value of quality service.

## Making and Recognizing Contribution

It is important that people who join collaborative organizations feel that they are contributing to the organization. For most people, this is one of the foremost reasons for joining and staying involved in the organization. I would wager, that if asked the question why one belongs to an organization, most would answer they hope to make some kind of contribution. To facilitate this sense of making a contribution, partners need to have a clear understanding of what is expected of them, and how this responsibility fits into the overall mission of the organization. This information is usually passed on during an orientation sessions for new members. These sessions give members an opportunity to receive assignments, get background material, ask questions and become acquainted with the current leadership. Having a clear sense of mission and organizational responsibilities gives direction to new members, and sets them on the road toward a rewarding experience.

There is no substitute for bringing good people to the organization. Desirable community partners have qualities such as: good character, the ability to handle multiple tasks, being a self-starter, and attention to detail. However, these individuals can also be very demanding for staff. They tend to be highly motivated and expect equally high levels of performance from colleagues and support staff. These people are not your ordinary volunteers. Most partners may have some but not all the characteristics listed. However, good partners possess at least a couple of these attributes and can be assets to the organization. The synergy created between highly motivated partners and good staff can create a very productive and rewarding experience for both.

Throughout the world, people who volunteer are critically important to moving organizations and institutions forward. About 59 million people in the United States did volunteer work from September 2001 to September 2002 (U.S Bureau of Labor Statistics). Among the areas in which volunteers contribute to are: finding cures for diseases, improving education, protecting the environment, helping the indigent, caring for the elderly, improving public health and safety, just to name a few. The point is that volunteers provide a tremendous asset to the overall quality of life in this nation and the world. Volunteers are valued people in moving society forward and deserve to be treated with special care, and when appropriate, receive recognition for their contributions.

## Fostering Group Cohesion

It is important that each partner feel they are a part of the collective organization. I have already mentioned the need for partners to develop a "custodial" relationship or attachment to the organization. Often a precursor to this organizational attachment is the comfort level they have with current members of the organization, and perhaps to a lesser extent, the depth of their institutional knowledge. While having a sense of camaraderie with fellow members is often central to partners remaining active in an organization, it is also important that they have an appreciation of the history of the organization. It is essentially the responsibility of the staff to provide opportunities that are inclusive enough to both promote interaction and educate members about the organization. There are several things that staff can do to promote this sense of awareness, including: hosting social functions, making the membership aware of the organization's history, and respecting and acknowledging contributions of past members.

The most obvious way to promote interaction between members is to host social functions at various intervals during the times the group meets. These opportunities are generally structured around the times meals are being served, e.g., breakfast, lunch, and dinner. Due to scheduling issues, it is often difficult to arrange gatherings outside these occasions. Evening receptions, before or after dinner, therefore, seem to be optimal times for these gatherings. These opportunities allow partners not only to get to know one another on a more personal level, but also allow them time to have informal discussions that can cover a range of issues regarding the organization as well as other interests they may have in common. Most importantly, this venue allows for more linkages and increases bonding to the organization. Passing along the institutional history of the organization provides important building blocks in structuring its longevity. This knowledge serves as the bridge that connects past, present, and future generations in their understanding of the institutional ethos that becomes part of the organization's fabric. It helps current members appreciate the contributions of past members, it assists past members in feeling a continued connection to the group, and it provides an environment that encourages past and present members to constructively dialogue and jointly move the organization forward.

In educating its members about the organization's institutional history, staff create common ground and experiences between its members. This commonality can bring a sense of continuity and cohesiveness that will immeasurably strengthen the organization. One of the cornerstones of a strong partnership organization is for its past members to feel an allegiance and continued commitment to the well being of the organization.

## Summary

Good staff is the key to having a strong, viable organization. Staff is positioned to have the broadest perspective within the organization, and generally the first to know of potential problems and what can be done to resolve them. They are among the prime sources of the institutional memory in the organization. Additionally, staff is the main source of recruiting, supporting and maintaining a strong membership.

In order to effectively serve the collective membership, and thus the organization, a sound service strategy should be developed. A sound service strategy incorporates some, if not all, of the following components: sharing the big picture, accepting that partners have their own agendas, having reasonable expectations, assisting in keeping commitments, respecting partners, communicating clearly, recognizing contributions, and fostering group cohesion.

While these suggestions primarily come from the year-long MCSP social capacity-building activities and retreat, the ideas expressed in this chapter would be effective for many other colleges. If staff do their job well, they can facilitate a successful experience for the volunteer community partners. Such an experience creates long lasting personal, professional, and organizational relationships that will continue to help the organization prosper for years to come.

### References

Merriam-Webster, Inc. (1993). *Merriam-Webster's Collegiate Dictionary* 10th Edition. Springfield, MA: Merriam Webster.

Bureau of Labor Statistics. (2002). *News: Volunteering in the United States Summary*. Washington, D.C: U.S. Department of Labor, *Dec. 18*, pp. 1-4.

# Chapter 18

## A COMMUNITY PARTNER LOOKS AT MENTORING PRACTICES

Mary Ann Dunn

Mentoring is a beneficial practice for all ages of students. Particularly today in our society when many families have both parents working, and other families consist of a single parent who must work, manage the household, and supervise the children. These families are, more often than not, in a serious state of crisis. They usually are not aware of the potential problems facing their children, or do not have the ability to improve their lives. Mentoring programs can change not only the child's life, but can make very positive impacts upon the entire family of the child being mentored. There are thousands of children nationally who lack the supervision and attention that can guide that child to reach their potential. Mentors can instill in children good work habits and ethics, and help them with the normal childhood problems of growing up, and just be a friend who will not judge, grade (as a teacher), or punish them. A mentor: a person who will accept you as you are, and at the same time, give you gentle guidance toward bettering yourself.

## Mentors and Mentoring: Serving the Mission and Goals of the Michigan Community Scholars Program (MCSP)

While working with and directing a middle school program that matched "at risk" students with collegiate and adult community members as mentors, I had the privilege of observing the results of our mentoring programs over a six-year period as a MCSP community partner. I will be sharing my thoughts from that perspective.

MCSP's four identified goals are: deep learning, engaged community, civic engagement, and diverse democracy. Comparing several sub goals in these major areas to the benefits of mentoring will show that mentoring is an excellent fit.

### Deep Learning

Take a moment to consider the definition of a mentor from above: a person who will accept you as you are, and at the same time, give you gentle (subtle) guidance toward a betterment of yourself.

This mentor can engage you with ideas, teach you critical thinking, help you explore intellectually and at the same time engage you in learning which is active and fun, and teach you that lifelong learning is a goal to constantly pursue. It is also a way for a student to become familiar with various viewpoints on a particular subject through dialogue with a mentor.

I am reminded of a student I worked with several years ago; I will call him Conrad (all names are fictitious to protect identity). Conrad first came to my attention early in the school year as I was on my way to the main office. About halfway down the hall from the office door, I first heard someone yelling, and moments later, a student came storming through the door, yelling with profanity interspersed that his father would sue this school, and he wasn't going to spend one more minute in that classroom with that teacher. He screamed he was tired of the school screwing up his life, and continued down the hall to the lobby. As he came to the lobby doors, he kicked the door open with his foot and at the same time slammed it with his fist as he went through the door, still screaming. He plopped himself down on a bench at the entrance doors, crossed his arms over his chest, and hung his head down. Although he stopped screaming, he continued to mutter under his breath about the evils of the school, teachers, principals, and school board. This was a pattern we would witness several times a week for months.

I later learned that Conrad was in sixth grade and lived with his father. He had not heard from his mother since he was four years old, and could not really remember much about her. His father, Jack, worked as an independent painter, and was occasionally unemployed. Jack always talked about how school was not really important, and his son, Conrad, really did not need to learn all of "that stuff." By law Conrad had to stay in school until he turned 16, but he planned to leave school then. Because of Conrad's frequent outbursts of anger, our office was asked to work with him. Our office was the Teaching-Learning Communities (T-LC) room. We served students "at risk." They came from all different types of families, single parents, two parents—both working, some on welfare, some highly educated, and undereducated (no high school or GED). We would assign tutors and/or mentors to students sent to us. Mentors sometimes attended class with the student and would meet with the student in our office. Mentors met with the student(s) in our room either during or after school.

Conrad was quite a challenge. When he came to our room, he was always angry, and needed to calm down. The first year, only our staff worked with him. By the time he was in seventh grade, his temper tantrums had subsided to the point that he still stormed down the hall, but the screaming was now a low muttering about all the injustices he was suffering. He was spending more time in his classes and being less disruptive. We assigned a mentor to Conrad in the middle of seventh grade. An MCSP student was asked to help him with his homework, in our office, where they could divert from the assignment and just talk about things on any subject that happened to come up.

It wasn't long before Conrad could actually see that learning could be fun, and it was easy to learn when you had others to learn with. He also realized that there are different ways of learning, and he learned much about himself. He came to understand that his anger towards the school was a substitute for the anger he felt about his mother leaving and his father's attitudes toward the entire situation.

At the end of Conrad's junior year in school, he came to see me and tell me how much more he liked school and how much he had learned about himself and life. He thanked me for the mentors and was looking forward to graduating and going on to college! He also confided in me that he had become very successful in controlling his anger, so he no longer disrupted his classes and the school by his outbursts. He did sheepishly admit to still muttering to himself once in a while, but said he no longer did it when others could hear him. Conrad thanked me for helping him improve his life and declared that he was going to become a mentor when he became an adult so he could give back to his community what he had gotten from them.

## Engaged Community and Civic Engagement

Conrad's story also fits well with the second MCSP goal: engaged community. Conrad felt comfortable in our room because he felt it to be a safe and accepting environment. We did not judge him, we were not there to grade him, accepted him as he was, cared for him as an individual, and then helped him explore his own personal and social identities. His mentors helped him study, learn, and finally guided him towards understanding different perspectives because of their different backgrounds.

MCSP's third goal is meaningful civic engagement/community service learning. Mentoring programs fit into this category extremely well. MCSP mentors learn about school systems and the many problems and successes that are a part of any society. They often learn a lot about themselves. One of the MCSP student mentors who worked with a group of sixth-grade students on writing a newspaper for the school said to me near the end of his assignment,

> *I had no idea there were so many issues involved in running a school or so many needy children. I came from a well-educated two-parent family with one sibling and we were just expected to go to college. Money (tuition) was not a concern. If we didn't get academic scholarships, my parents could afford to send us to any school we wanted to attend. When I was in school, my friends were all from the same type of families...well educated and very prosperous. We never had to worry about where our next meal would come from! I came to college thinking that all students were from the same type of family as mine.*

This MCSP student obviously learned much about civic life, social problems, themselves, and society during his brief assignment in our middle school. One of the students in the group he worked with was from a two-parent home but both parents worked long hours and were seldom home to spend any time with their children. Another lived with their mother who had to work two jobs just to have enough to pay rent and provide scant necessities. She was often home alone with very little adult guidance from an adult. Three-fourths of the group had no idea if they would go to college, or what it would take to get there. The mother of one of the other students was a teacher, but she neglected her own children. The daughter usually came to school with no lunch, lunch money, dirty clothing, and poor hygiene. Her brother often had no lunch or lunch money and usually wore the same clothes all week. The daughter was in the newspaper group and the MCSP student learned that there are often problems even when parents are educated. This is a good reason to have sustainable partnerships between the students, universities, community partners, and businesses. It shows the need to develop and maintain long-term commitments between these groups to help provide the unmet needs of our young children.

## Diverse Democracy

The final goal is a commitment to a diverse democracy, intercultural understanding, and dialogue. MCSP students help broaden younger student's "social and intellectual 'comfort zones' beyond their own social identity groups" (MCSP Mission and Goals statement). Mentoring will encourage both younger and older students to stay involved in their communities to strengthen both themselves and their communities. Many of the MCSP mentors expressed the desire to become and stay involved in their own communities after graduation. The desire to stay involved is also instilled in the mentees. Many of our former mentees have kept in contact and informed us that they are so grateful for the mentors who gave them the incentive to become better persons.

One example is Idella, who wrote several years ago to say thanks for arranging a mentor. She had finally finished college and was working on a teaching certificate because she wanted to become a guiding influence on young people who lacked guidance and direction. She felt she could do this as a teacher who could encourage mentoring programs in any school in which she worked. She was so grateful for the mentor who had inspired her to make more of her life than being a "school drop-out." Participating in public life and civic organizations will help create strong communities dedicated to building and maintaining diverse democracies committed to intercultural understanding and social justice.

From my perspective as a collaborating community partner with MCSP, I observed that working with young adults and matching them up with younger students, to provide the younger ones direction and an opportunity to thrive and grow, benefits everyone from the smallest group of one (self) to all of society. From deep learning experiences inside and outside the classroom, to understanding the joy of learning, engaging in ideas, and learning how to think critically, to becoming engaged in the community with ideas, perspective, and a safe and accepting environment with a focus on both the individual and the group provides the basis for meaningful civic engagement which prepares students to become leaders and actively participate in their communities throughout their lives. I observed that the younger students' intellectual and social "comfort zones" were broadened which advanced the idea of a diverse democracy and intercultural understanding. Like the pebble thrown in a pond, the concentric circles formed will continue to grow and touch many lives, not just locally, but nationally and even globally.

## Final Thoughts

There are a few challenges to overcome such as finding the personnel who are willing and will take the time necessary to manage the program, setting priorities, finding and training mentors, and dealing with schedules. The most challenging aspects were scheduling the mentoring sessions to fit the college student's class schedules, and involving teachers who may not feel that Johnny has a problem, ("he's just lazy, has trouble concentrating, or should be on a drug for his hyperactivity behavior," etc.). However, these were some of the very reasons why that student needed a mentor!

Nevertheless, with some basic training as that given in the MCSP, many people who never thought about mentoring have outstanding experiences with the MCSP. They learn that exchanging differing viewpoints, guiding young at-risk students to set, and reach for, larger goals such as academic success, reflective learning of self and society, and providing a safe and accepting environment are not only beneficial to the young mentee, but most people find they too have grown personally and in social understanding and commitment to their own communities. Thus, they provide more meaningful civic engagement in their entire adult lives.

# Chapter 19
## FROM STUDENT TO COMMUNITY PARTNER
Cassie Lapekas

*"Recognizing the dignity and beauty of every person we pledge intelligent and practical action to overcome racism, poverty and injustice. And to build a metropolitan community where all people may live in freedom, harmony, trust and affection. Black and white, yellow brown and red from Detroit and its suburbs, of every economic status, national origin and religious persuasion we join in this covenant" (Focus: HOPE Mission Statement, Adopted March, 1968).*

## University Life

As a graduating senior at the University of Michigan, I was exhausted by the thought of one more class. I was looking forward to commencement and all that would follow—though I must admit that I had few definite plans in place with only three months remaining before I was slated to enter the "real world." As a result, in spring 2001, I began looking for a classroom experience that would take me into the community and workplace in a fairly structured setting and simultaneously offer me the opportunity to reflect on my experiences. The Michigan Community Scholars Program (MCSP) was the opportunity I was looking for and, though I didn't know it then, the one that would change my life and the path of my career forever.

As a high school student, I was highly involved in service and civic participation. I was the president of my high school's community service organization and therefore spent the vast majority of my extracurricular hours organizing volunteers to serve at after-school programs, Special Olympics events, and shelters for at-risk teens. I thoroughly enjoyed my community involvement in high school and planned to pursue similar interests in college.

However, in an educational environment as enormous as the University of Michigan, I initially felt lost in a sea of students and never sought the level of community involvement I had previously enjoyed. Moving from a small farming town to a new city, I felt particularly detached from my surroundings; I assumed that I would only temporarily reside in Ann Arbor and never truly became invested in the city. I planned to move out of state upon graduation and the demands of schoolwork, political internships, and part-time employment quickly engulfed my time; I found myself at the end of my academic career feeling as though I had lost an extremely important part of my personal life—my commitment to community.

I discovered the MCSP course in a search for a class that would bring me back to the concept of civic engagement in a tangible way. Though I'd heard of the MCSP in passing, I knew only that it was a living-learning environment at the university that supported student community involvement; I was completely unaware of the program's broader goals and mission, and even more unaware of how those goals were met. The online course description for the MCSP class that interested me promised an internship with HARC, a local HIV/AIDS resource center, or

Focus: HOPE, an organization with which I was unfamiliar. With few expectations, I arrived in class the first morning and was quickly slotted into a position with Focus: HOPE, which I learned is a human and civil rights organization in metro Detroit. I left with a syllabus, a first reading assignment, and contact information for Colleen, who would be supervising my internship from the Focus: HOPE perspective.

Since arriving in Ann Arbor three years prior, my ventures into Detroit—only 45 miles away—had been brief, infrequent, and limited. I never spent an extended amount of time in the city and rarely strayed far from local freeways during my visits. Over the years, my perceptions of the city had evolved into a strange mix of curiosity and fear; I'd heard that Detroit was dangerous, destitute, and beyond hope and repair. In a number of my undergraduate classes, however, I learned about many of the factors involved in the city's decline and became aware of another possibility—the possibility that Detroit is in no way beyond repair and that hope and potential are everywhere in the city, even if they are oftentimes hidden. The theories I learned as an undergraduate would have remained theoretical in my mind if not for my internship; MCSP was about to offer me the opportunity test what I'd been told and learn more than I ever could have seated behind a desk in Ann Arbor. This would be my chance to develop my own theories.

## Focus: HOPE

I left for Focus: HOPE on the first day of my internship not certain what I would find, but not expecting much from a nonprofit civil rights organization in Detroit. I envisioned a handful of people in a ramshackle office with mismatched furniture. Off the highway, in northwest Detroit, I passed boarded-up houses, vacant businesses, and littered parks. When I finally spotted Focus: HOPE, I was truly taken aback. What I found was no ramshackle office; it was a business and a state-of-the-art engineering facility encompassing the space of nearly five city blocks. Furthermore, Focus: HOPE wasn't a handful of people; it was hundreds of people.

From the moment I walked in the front door of the Focus: HOPE Resource Center, I was inundated with knowledge and the spirit of the organization. What I found there was innovative and inspiring. I was immediately fascinated. Founded in 1968 by a seemingly unlikely pair—a priest, Father William Cunningham, and a suburban homemaker, Eleanor Josaitis—the organization was originally a response to the Detroit riots and an attempt to find racial harmony within the city. Cunningham and Josaitis met through their parish and were both moved to action by the riots and all they represented and entailed—violence, anger, and inequality in Detroit.

Focus: HOPE first sought to address the issue of nutrition within the city. At the time of the riots, food was scarce for many Detroit residents and the quality of the food found within the city was often low. Researchers at the time were beginning to fully understand the permanent effects of malnutrition on the development of infants and toddlers, and soon realized that inadequate nutrition within the first three years of a child's life resulted in significant, irreversible effects on a child's brain capacity. Low-income mothers and children under the age of six were immediately identified as individuals at high risk for malnutrition. Cunningham, Josaitis, and numerous volunteers lobbied the federal government and were eventually able to offer low-income Detroit mothers and children access to nutritional food supplements in conjunction with the Department of Agriculture. After a lengthy battle for funding, senior citizens, many of whom were surviving on intolerably low fixed incomes, were added to the program. Today, with the cooperation of the federal government, the Focus: HOPE food program serves over 45,000 women, children, and senior citizens in the Metro Detroit area each month.

Though it remains the most well known aspect of Focus: HOPE, the food program was just the beginning of what would become an absolute phenomenon in urban education. In an attempt to holistically address Detroit residents' needs, Focus: HOPE began a machinist training program in the early 1980s with the intention of offering education and employment to many who had traditionally been denied access based on gender, race, or other socioeconomic factors. The Focus: HOPE Machinist Training Institute (MTI) successfully trained primarily women and minorities to enter the financial mainstream with an emphasis on both machining skills and work ethic; MTI trained students to become quality employees in every sense and therefore became a respected source of labor for Ford, General Motors, Chrysler, and a number of other manufacturing institutions.

After the establishment of MTI, Focus: HOPE continued to respond to the changing needs of its constituency. The Center for Advanced Technologies (CAT) currently allows students to earn associate or bachelors degrees in engineering; the CAT, however, is no ordinary collegiate engineering program. CAT students learn all that may be learned through engineering textbooks, but they also have the opportunity to gain experience in the field through a unique, hands-on approach. The students play essential roles in operating a tier-I manufacturing shop floor while earning their degrees. Through intricate partnerships with local universities and hard-earned manufacturing contracts with the Department of Defense and major auto manufacturers, CAT students are able to immediately apply the theories learned in the classroom—and simultaneously turn a profit. The profits of their hard work pay for the costs of their education and health insurance, and even afford them a paycheck every two weeks. The experience they gain makes them exceptionally marketable in the world of engineering and such a creative arrangement allows students to simultaneously go to school and earn a paycheck.

Leaving Focus: HOPE after only a few hours with such inspiring newfound knowledge, I was astounded and excited, for I knew I was looking forward to an amazing, intense experience.

Colleen rotated me through intern positions in all of Focus: HOPE's programs to ensure that I would be well aware of what each offered. Soon, however, I found myself drawn to one particular project, a market research analysis. The goal of the project was to research comparable educational options in the local geographic area to determine Focus: HOPE's competitive edge and highlight areas of potential improvement. Such work required that I first gain a thorough knowledge of what Focus: HOPE offered, so I spent much of my time observing and interviewing appropriate staff and instructors.

Though I thoroughly enjoyed my market research project, which gave me the unique opportunity to learn a great deal about Focus: HOPE in a relatively short period of time, that research was only the beginning of my internship experience. My surroundings in Detroit were completely foreign to me, and I learned as much—if not more—from my struggle to understand and become accustomed to my new environment. Having been raised in a small-town community, I was beyond surprised to find bulletproof glass in front of the register at McDonald's and witness drug transactions in local parks. I was admittedly sheltered and naïve and, though I loved the work I was doing and the people I was meeting at Focus: HOPE, I was almost ashamed to realize how fearful and uncomfortable I initially felt in the Detroit community.

As I began to deal with my fear and discomfort, my primary source of support was MCSP. At critical stages in my internship, my MCSP instructors and classmates were available to help me make sense of my experiences. I always knew I had the complete support of my classmates and instructors. In the classroom, my thoughts, feelings, and ideas were always validated, yet I was constantly encouraged to learn as much as a possibly could; I am certain that my internship experience would not have been nearly as valuable without the challenge and support of the MCSP educational environment.

Our class met once a week and I found myself looking forward to each meeting as an opportunity to reflect on what I was learning about Detroit, Focus: HOPE, and myself. I eagerly anticipated the chance to give and receive feedback on my internship experiences and those of other students. As a class, we explored our own social identities and actively chronicled our experiences in journals. Through the journals, I began to see my thoughts and actions differently and even began to reevaluate my goals upon graduation. Thinking about my social identity and those around me reminded me to respect differences, but understand that we are all fundamentally much more alike than different. As a combined result of my internship and work in the classroom, my world was expanding and I finally began to recognize my role and responsibility in community at every level.

I realized how easily fear could hinder my growth and understanding and dealt with it as directly as possible, pushing myself into situations that were safe but just beyond my realm of comfort. I formed friendships with a number of Focus: HOPE colleagues and began to explore the Detroit community outside the safe haven of the Focus: HOPE campus. My appreciation for Detroit and the unbelievable dedication and vision of those in my midst at Focus: HOPE grew consistently. I was thoroughly impressed with the mission of the organization and forever changed by the idea that two people with such unbelievable resolve could enact such enormous change. I witnessed colleagues and volunteers from vastly different backgrounds uniting for common causes in a manner I did not even know to be possible. During my time at Focus: HOPE, I was increasingly inspired and connected to the fight for social justice.

As the semester progressed, I found myself dreading the culmination of my internship. I knew that I would miss the people and the environment of Focus: HOPE terribly and I began volunteering my time there beyond the expectations of the MCSP program. My former excitement at the prospect of moving out of state and pursuing a career in the political realm was waning, and I was beginning to rethink my criteria for job selection. I thought it impossible to enjoy full-time employment as much as I enjoyed my internship.

## Working at Focus: HOPE

Then, as my work at Focus: HOPE was coming to an end, I was surprised to learn that Colleen, my internship supervisor, was planning to leave to pursue an alternate career. The decision to apply for her available position was not an easy one for me, nor was it a choice that immediately presented itself as a viable option. I began by questioning Colleen about her job responsibilities and the best—and worst—aspects of her job. As a senior ambassador, Colleen's position included: providing visitors with detailed, knowledgeable tours of the Focus: HOPE campus, serving as a liaison between Focus: HOPE and the Detroit community, assisting in the planning of special events; and orchestrating annual holiday assistance for Detroit families in need.

Armed with essential information and my experience with the organization thus far, I consulted family, friends, and my MCSP instructors for advice and guidance. Though none of my career plans for the upcoming months and years were definite, I had envisioned a professional future somewhat different than the one I found myself seriously contemplating. I was uncertain and having difficulty reconciling all the possibilities that graduation brings. Throughout the decision process, my MCSP support system was instrumental in making choices that were best for me; even when my class was technically over, my instructors and classmates remained unfailingly available and encouraging. My instructors, in particular, were always willing to help me define my options and understand the consequences of my decisions.

I interviewed for the available position, was offered the job ... and happily accepted within a matter of two weeks. All of my confusion and uncertainty were erased upon beginning the orientation process. The first step in orientation was meeting with Eleanor Josaitis and my fellow new colleagues. In this critical first meeting with Eleanor, we learned her story and the history of the organization, of the obstacles the organization had faced and triumphs they had earned over the years. I was mesmerized by Eleanor's passion, commitment, and determination—and she informed us that she expected nothing less of each of us. We read the organization's mission statement, and were then asked if we had any philosophical differences with the statement. Eleanor was heartfelt and straightforward; she was looking for true ambassadors for civil and human rights. Nothing less would do.

# Professional Growth

During my year as an ambassador at Focus: HOPE, I grew, learned, and developed personally and professionally more than I ever thought possible. In providing tours of campus, I learned detailed information about the organization as a whole and each of its training programs individually. My public speaking skills developed rapidly and I learned to cater my presentations to a wide variety of audiences; indeed, during my time at Focus: HOPE, I was involved in tours and volunteer initiatives at all levels—for senators, executives, college students, and young children—with varying goals at stake.

I developed service programs and orchestrated volunteer experiences for hundreds of volunteers; the volunteer activities I planned benefited the volunteers, Focus: HOPE, and Detroit. With the help of such volunteers, I co-managed an annual holiday program to provide holiday assistance to local families in need and helped organize an annual Walk for Diversity, modeled after the peace marches of Dr. Martin Luther King, Jr. In the process of working with volunteers to meet the community needs, my vision of Detroit changed drastically. Any fear or discomfort I previously felt vanished and I found myself with a renewed, realistic sense of hope for my surroundings and vastly strengthened dedication to social and economic justice. I knew that my job made a difference—even if only in a very small way—and that was enough to allow me to enjoy going to work each morning. I found a more rewarding job difficult to imagine.

Almost ironically, part of my job was to supervise and provide a quality experience for the next year's MCSP interns at Focus: HOPE. As an MCSP community partner, working with the students was initially a very surreal experience for me; the realization that I was in their exact position only one year prior was shocking. The students, though at times challenging, were ultimately a joy to work with and a personal testament to how much I had changed in the time since graduation. Having been through the MCSP classroom and internship experience, I was in an ideal position to provide the students with the best possible internship scenario; I was aware of the material they would cover in class, the reactions they might have to their experiences at Focus: HOPE, and some of the most effective ways to integrate the two. The time I spent working with MCSP students in their own internship setting was also an amazing period of personal reflection for me. It helped me define who I was, where I was going, and where I eventually wanted to be in terms of my career and personal commitment to the tenets of social justice.

For me, supervising MCSP students and having an active role in their learning processes solidified the purpose of the program and the goals it accomplished. I found that many of the students initially felt much the way I did when I visited Focus: HOPE for the first time; some felt uncomfortable or unsafe in the city and were ashamed by such feelings. I understood their fear and embarrassment from my own experience, and was thereby able to genuinely encourage them to acknowledge their feelings without compromising their learning. Students who felt uneasy were assigned projects with fellow classmates to make tasks and interactions seem less daunting. As frequently as I could, I accompanied students on first-time activities, such as food delivery to homebound seniors, in order to ease their concerns. Before long, I witnessed students—who were once reluctant to leave the social safety of fellow classmates—comfortably engaging neighborhood families in conversation at the Focus: HOPE food centers. It was then that I realized how tangibly different community learning is. These were not students memorizing (and quickly forgetting) facts and statistics for an upcoming exam; they were instead living their lessons, and I can personally attest to the fact that lived lessons make the greatest impact.

Not all of the students, though, were uncomfortable or reluctant at Focus: HOPE. A few, in fact, were very almost immediately very insistent about the type of internship assignments they would—and would not—do. Soon after the students started their work at Focus: HOPE, the manufacturing arm of the organization requested assistance with an important, time-consuming data entry project. Focus: HOPE does not differ from other nonprofits in the sense that they are always understaffed and the interns immediately came to mind as a group who might be able to help the organization fill this immediate need. Some of the students, however, described data entry as too "menial" a task and requested reassignment. This sense of entitlement surprised me because, as an intern, it had never even occurred to me to challenge one of Colleen's assignments; I believed I was there both to learn and to serve the organization in the most helpful possible manner. Some of my interns instead seemed to believe that the organization and I were there solely to serve them as an educational resources, and were at first unable to appreciate the symbiotic relationship between a nonprofit and its interns.

Having recently been an intern, I understood the tiring nature of repetitive tasks and promised the students that I would limit their time spent on projects like data entry. I also explained, however, that the success of Focus: HOPE relied heavily on the efforts of volunteers, interns, and employees alike, that running a nonprofit required many kinds of work, and that not all of them were fun. Through our conversations and subsequent discussions with their instructors, I believe the students came to a much deeper understanding of nonprofit work, the real purpose of nonprofit enterprises, and what it means to serve.

## Full Circle

As a community partner, I relished my opportunity to work with the students while simultaneously providing feedback and input to the program's directors. As a member of the MCSP community on a new level, I was introduced to the outstanding web of resources that contributes to the success of the program as a whole. I met fellow community partners, additional faculty members actively instructing in the MCSP classroom, and the MCSP, who work logistically and ideologically to allow the program to function. The new acquaintances and perspectives of those I have encountered in conjunction with my MCSP affiliation continue to be a source of outstanding connections, information, ideas, and opportunities.

I often wonder how different my life would be today had I not walked into an MCSP classroom. My journey has truly come full circle and I have had the distinct privilege of involvement in MCSP at a number of levels. As a result of the path I chose after my exposure to MCSP faculty, staff, students, and philosophy, I have found a truly rewarding personal mission and professional tract. I am so very grateful for the unbelievable, lifelong relationships I formed at Focus: HOPE and the unique experience I found there—the opportunity to love my job and respect my work.

I left Focus: HOPE in the summer of 2002 to investigate my interest in nonprofit fundraising at United Way Community Services, but have continued to work with and fully support both Focus: HOPE and MCSP. My commitment to civil and human rights and the city of Detroit has never been stronger and I remain in touch with many of my former colleagues at Focus: HOPE. I continued to deliver food to homebound seniors through their food program and was thrilled to witness the success of the 2002 Annual Walk for Diversity. As an independent consultant for MCSP, I continued to share my perspective and input with the program and learned from their ongoing growth and evolution as a leader in university-community relations.

Only in retrospect can I truly appreciate the goals and mission of the MCSP at work. MCSP learning is far deeper than I originally thought. It does not simply support student community involvement; it provides the route and the resources to allow it to happen. Through the collaborative efforts of students, faculty, staff, and community partners, the program combines theory and practice to provide students with optimum learning. Through books, course-packs, and lectures, I might have understood the history of Detroit, but I never would have *felt* the lasting effects of that history or the difference that an organization such as Focus: HOPE can make. Without feeling and involvement, one would be hard-pressed to find dedication to the cause of social justice and community. MCSP offers students what it takes to find that commitment and the foundation to become leaders for endeavors that truly matter.

My greatest hope for the MCSP is that its students continue to gain even half as much from their involvement as I did. My MCSP experience presented me with an entirely new set of life possibilities and my only wish is that I would have become involved earlier in my academic career. I believe so strongly in the goals and successes of the program because they've been so vastly influential in my own life. I look forward to seeing where this journey takes me next, but I will never lose sight of where it began.

# Chapter 20

## LEADERSHIP AND EMPOWERMENT: WORKING TO MAKE CHANGE

Penny A. Pasque, Sedika F. Franklin, and Sarah A. Luke

*"Never doubt that a small group of thoughtful,*
*committed citizens can change the world.*
*Indeed, it is the only thing that ever has."*
Margaret Mead, 1901 - 1978

The Michigan Community Scholars Program (MCSP) students have energy, strength, and commitment toward working to make change in the world. Each student voluntarily chooses to enroll in this living-learning program at the University of Michigan, which focuses on diversity, community service, leadership, and deep learning. First-year students meet the challenges of their new campus lives while working to translate passions into action. In MCSP, students learn how to be effective leaders and build community in this diverse and dynamic environment. Simply stated, *students* create the daily reality of this undergraduate living-learning program.

MCSP is a collection of classroom, residential community, and off-campus experiences that challenge new thinking and awareness for students to become leaders and active community participants with power to change the program's cocurricular structure. This structure and philosophy shapes student perspectives, attitudes, and behaviors through deep learning while simultaneously creating a memorable and interconnected experience for undergraduates. Participation in the program means 24-hour involvement with this daily, immersive culture. MCSP is reflected in the sense of community on the residence hall floors, group ownership in programmatic decision-making, availability of the student-led programming board and leadership positions, inclusion of all members in event planning, nightly organized and spontaneous events, participation in late night conversations over pizza, and a feeling of belonging to the program.

It was very difficult for us, the authors, to write an article that would honestly reflect the breadth, and in particular, the depth of the student leadership experiences in the program. Every year, there are such rich feelings of belonging and commitment to the program and its participants. The students care deeply about one another and the communities by which they are served — and in which they serve themselves. We decided to approach the process of communicating the intensity of the program through this article by determining a MCSP theme to discuss each week, taping and transcribing our conversations. We met for an hour each week during the course of the semester. Many memories and stories were shared, with laughter, conflict, tears, and feelings of triumph as we communicated the vast scope of the cocurricular program. Portions of the taped conversations are woven throughout the article to relay this strong sense of community and student ownership of the program. MCSP students are strongly committed to the program's survival, excellence, and sustainability of the established student empowerment models. This commitment is reflected in program attendance, participation in student leadership meetings, number of applications, recruitment for student leadership positions, and the high level of student involvement in the program as a whole.

This article describes the MCSP student leadership initiatives through bridging theory, observation, and stories, including some challenges in building a strong, student-empowered, and inclusive living-learning program. Four sections of the cocurricular experience in MCSP are included: leadership opportunities and student empowerment (where subtopics about the program are offered), diversity in student leadership, community service learning and leading, and transforming theory into practice. Each section describes the program, provides examples, and analyzes best practices. It is worth noting that the authors have collectively held positions, including first-year student leader, peer advisor (PA) for community service, PA for programming board, peer mentor (PM) coordinator, resident advisor (RA), and program director. We approached these discussions and writings on student leadership with these perspectives in mind.

## Leadership Opportunities and Student Empowerment

Gaining skills and competencies is critical to becoming a strong leader. MCSP offers many leadership opportunities to approximately 150 undergraduates each year. At the heart of the program is student participation, ownership in decision-making, leadership skill building, and community action. Sedika Franklin, former MCSP first-year student, PA for community service, PM coordinator, and RA describes her perspective.

> *[MCSP] really is more than the classroom. I mean, the classroom's important. And on top of that is this whole sense of, "We are creating this program. We are in charge of it. We can make decisions. We know these are the nights we have for programs, this is the money we have, these are the classes we have to take, and everything else is up to us to create." So the more we put out to the group, "You come in and decide, you come and make the decisions." The more the group got involved and took ownership, the more they did things that as staff we could never imagine: like the drama troupe, like the spring break Habitat for Humanity Trips, and everything. I mean, all these things that were created: the PM program, the whole PM coordinator position. All those things were things that as one person you can't necessarily make up. It's not about [Penny] or me, it's about empowering everybody. And the more you get everybody involved, the greater that it possibly is . . . That's kind of the magic of the program to me, the cool piece, that it is student directed and student owned. And when you go up on the floors, you know it's a community. People look out for each other.*

This section describes the various MCSP leadership positions, discusses student involvement in programmatic decision-making, and the MCSP leadership course, defines the oral tradition of the MCSP buddy program, and analyzes conflict within community as related to leadership.

### Leadership Positions

There are a number of volunteer and paid student leadership positions within MCSP. The volunteer leadership positions include: first-year student involvement in the programming board, sophomores and juniors serving as a volunteer PMs for first year students, assisting with recruiting opportunities, and presenting at regional and national conference presentations. Paid student leader opportunities include: PA for the programming board, PA for community service, PM coordinator, and RA. Undergraduates are also provided with opportunities to facilitate courses.

Peer mentors help first-year students with the transition from high school to college by attending orientation with the first-year students, answering questions about college life, and planning various events for students to get to know one another. Each mentor is connected to a small group of first-year students who usually reside on the same living-learning floor. The PM coordinator oversees the PMs, helps develop mentoring skills, and organizes the PM activities. Peer advisors for the programming board work with first-year students on student organizing and on planning various community service learning opportunities, speakers series, social events and diversity initiatives. Each PA for the programming board has a specific role defined by the group each year, which often includes treasurer, secretary, coordinator, and various other roles deemed important by that year's student leaders. The peer advisors for community service work with the RAs who facilitate small sections of the MCSP introductory course in conjunction with the program director. Each PA for community service organizes academic community service learning events for a small section of the class, conducts pre- and post-discussions about the event, and implements various cocurricular service-learning events in collaboration with the programming board.

The resident advisors are responsible for fulfilling residence education responsibilities as outlined by the hall director. In addition, RAs have responsibilities with MCSP. RAs help develop a strong sense of community in the entire learning community as linked with the MCSP mission and goals. RAs serve as role models for student leaders throughout the program and also facilitate small sections of the MCSP introductory course, UC 102, during the fall semester in conjunction with the program director. Each of the RAs also serves on an MCSP committee during the winter semester; these committees include student recruitment, staff selection, community development, and academic support. The RAs have often created their own committee to serve on as a leader, based on the needs of first-year students enrolled that year. During one year, for example, two RAs created a medical mentoring program between current University of Michigan medical students and MCSP first-year students. Communicating community service opportunities within the medical center was one valuable aspect of the initiative, in addition to mentoring about how to apply to medical school.

Furthermore, MCSP student leaders have the opportunity to gain valuable teaching experience at the university level beyond the UC 102 course. Students may facilitate sections of academic community service learning courses offered in MCSP through the Ginsberg Center for Community Service and Learning and the sociology department. After completion of an intergroup dialogue course offered in MCSP through Intergroup Relations (IGR), an MCSP student may apply to facilitate one of the dialogue courses during their sophomore, junior, or senior years. These courses offer students a safe place to discuss issues surrounding social identity such as ability, class, ethnicity, gender, race, religion and sexual orientation.

Each of these positions enables students to develop a solid foundation for developing leadership skills and to test assumptions and techniques throughout the year. Sedika, Sarah, and Penny provide two such examples during their conversation:

*Sedika:* I think MCSP helps people to get out there and do more. Because you start with MCSP, my freshman year we came up with a lot of ideas. So, we'd go to Penny [program director] and say, "We want to go to the African American museum and the Holocaust museum. How can we do this?" And then, all of a sudden that branched out and we planned, and we went. The seven of us, we were the leaders that year. And then, our sophomore year people went on to be presidents of CAMEO and the MMAC [students of color organizations on campus] and go on to do the MPA [Minority PA] roles and stuff like that. So I think MCSP plays a major role in allowing people to feel comfortable and confident, so they can feel more comfortable getting involved around campus.

*Sarah:* Yeah, you're right. I was the chair of the programming board, but before then I never really envisioned myself as a chairperson. I thought I could help on the board and plan programs, but in terms of the setting agendas and calling meetings to order—I didn't know how I would do that because I didn't feel like that was part of my personality. But I think that it helped me learn that leadership isn't necessarily a personal characteristic, but that anybody can be a leader. I think that we were effective that year in the programming board. I think we ran it differently than other people would have. I think we had a different style. But we got things done, and I think we had fun! It was effective.

**Penny:** And was awarded student organization of the year [at the University of Michigan] that year! [laughter] Don't sell yourself short!

**Sedika:** Right! [laughter]

**Sarah:** That's true. We got a lot accomplished together. Yeah, so I guess I never really thought of myself in that kind of a role because I am a quieter person.

## Student Involvement in Decision-Making

Student leaders in MCSP are involved in decision-making in many different aspects of the program, including choosing student leaders for future years, accepting incoming first-year students into the program, and participating in leadership training. This helps current leaders to be a part of the regeneration process to strengthen the program beyond their tenure. Leaders encourage first-year students with potential to continue with the program. Sedika elaborates on this point: "I think you really have a lot of people in the program that advocate for you. They'll say, 'You'll be perfect for this job!' Although you may not even realize it."

Student empowerment is built into the MCSP's structure. These processes provide a foundation for future sustainability. Student leaders are aware of processes, timelines, decision-making procedures, and the MCSP culture, so it is possible for the students to recreate a strong program in following years, make changes, or even implement effective techniques in other student organizations. Students then take this sense of empowerment and their leadership skills elsewhere, as MCSP student leaders tend to be leaders and community activists all over on campus and in their home communities.

One best practice example offered here is the student leadership selection process. Current student leaders interview, evaluate, and select future leaders for MCSP. This is no easy task, as issues always arise about different interview techniques and confidentiality. The leadership selection process includes an application with essay, two interviews, two small group exercises, and a personal reflection on how the candidate viewed his/her own participation in the selection process. The small group exercises place students in various situations and ask them to work together to determine outcomes. For example, one such exercise is a forced-choice problem. Candidates receive descriptions of different individuals who have needs from a community service agency. Individually, and then as a group, the candidates determine who will receive time, energy and commitment from the MCSP programming board over the next few years. There is no "correct" answer; the exercise asks applicants to grapple with typical MCSP decisions in terms of time, energy, and financial contributions as well as the challenge of determining which agency to work with for community-service. It also inevitably creates conflict between students. While this is a simulation of a real-life dilemma, the exercise allows current student leaders to glimpse how applicants may interact in various small group situations. Student leaders complete evaluations, which are added to the candidates overall file.

After the interview process is complete, a selection committee consisting of student-elected leaders (one representative from each group of student leaders) and some of the MCSP staff members reviews applications and selection process materials. As a team, the selection committee chooses leaders for the next academic year. Student leaders have disagreed with program and faculty directors during this process and have felt comfortable challenging others' opinions in a confidential setting.

MCSP prides itself on actualizing student empowerment in programmatic decisions to develop a strong student organization. The following conversation analyzes the selection process:

**Sedika:** I think [the student leader selection process] was really well planned and really well implemented, because it really gave us the opportunity to see how people would react to certain situations and deal with different problems that they might see in the future. And it gave them the insight, "Maybe this isn't the position I really want," or, "this is perfect for me." So it really works for both sides. We really got to see, "OK, these people would work wonderfully in the programming board. These others would work with community service. Maybe these people should be here, because they've already worked with this part of the program. Maybe we should let them see what they can do in the other part of the program."

***Penny:*** Did the process help to make you feel valued as a student leader because your opinion, or your view on who should be hired, was the basis for the selection process?

***Sedika:*** Yeah, definitely. Coming in and being there for the first two-and-a-half years, and then feeling that your input had a lot to do with who would be in the program, who was going to be in what position, and how you were going to help them. It was really nice to see. I thought it was a wonderful part of selecting our leaders. And just being more active, this was something I really wanted to do.

From the moment I heard about this process, I was like, "Yep, I'm going to be there to select new leaders."

***Sarah:*** I think it helped me feel a sense of ownership for the program. It was fun thinking about whom I would get to work with next year and just got me excited to see what the next year might be like. You feel like you're really a part of things. Because I remember even this year being really excited and thinking, "Oh! Who are going to be the PAs? And I wonder who is going to work with my UC 102 [MCSP introductory course] section?"

***Sedika:*** Even this year since I'm graduating, being a part of the interviewing, I thought, "OK, I want to know that these people who are coming in after me are going to take care of the program." So it really is a sense of ownership. You know you don't want to go out and leave the program deserted. You want to make sure these people know what they are doing.

***Sarah:*** And, that it can be as good of an experience for first-year students as it was for you.

## Course on Leadership and Community

MCSP provides a community leadership course taught each winter term by the program director. The course enables students to consider various theoretical frameworks for leadership and decision-making, and link these concepts to civic responsibility, personal leadership styles, social justice, and community action. The course assists in building a sense of community between the MCSP first-year students interested in continuing with the program as leaders during their sophomore year. It also provides a foundation for leadership development.

This course considers various theoretical perspectives on leadership through such sources as Komives, Lucas, and McMahon's *Exploring Leadership for College Students Who Want to Make a Difference* (1988), Bolman and Deal's *Leading with Soul* (1995), and Johnson & Johnson's *Joining Together: Group Theory and Group Skills* (2000). In addition, students compare and contrast numerous personality indicators. A contemporary movie, *American History X* (1998), is viewed and analyzed utilizing the theories discussed in the course. This movie helps students to unpack the various theories together after observing the same case study, in this instance, a contemporary movie. Students also apply these theories to student organizations in which they belong and process their weekly observations through written assignments and course discussions. Applying the theories to the movie, student organization experiences, and MCSP community leadership experience deepens the leadership training and strengthens the connections between theory and practice.

This intentional leadership course is considered an MCSP best practice. During the one year this course was not offered (the program's first year), student leaders were less prepared for leadership positions within the program. Students completing the leadership course approached their MCSP leadership positions with a greater sense of responsibility and understanding of their own leadership styles. The students were able to articulate and act upon the many ways they could affect change in MCSP and the community. The impact of this course was also evident through an increased number of quality, student-initiated programs as well as through a stronger sense of community among student leaders, and within the learning community as a whole.

## Buddy Program as Oral Tradition

Student affairs administrators are challenged annually to communicate information between different classes, or "generations," of student leaders. How does the organization transfer knowledge from one generation of student leaders to the next in order to avoid starting over every year? The buddy program is MCSP's "best practices" answer to this question: MCSP student leaders transmit valuable information from one generation of students to the next and this process becomes even more valuable than the packet of training and information materials students receive.

The timeframe for selecting students for leadership positions was established to facilitate the passing of information from one generation of students to another. The buddy program begins during the middle of winter semester each year, after leaders for the following fall semester are selected. This program overlaps with the course on leadership and community. In the buddy program, every current student leader is paired up with a newly chosen student leader. This encourages incoming RAs to discuss course facilitation and community building with current RAs, incoming PMs to discuss mentoring with current PMs, and so forth. The program culminates at the end of the academic year when all leaders gather for a special event to recognize the tireless efforts of the outgoing staff and welcome the incoming staff. The buddy program transfers formal and informal culture-awareness and procedures from one generation of students to the next and equips new leaders with a wealth of knowledge for the upcoming year. Examples of this effective oral tradition and how it aids student leadership are provided in the narrative below:

> *Sarah:* I think that students effectively mentor one another within the program.
>
> Like when I was a PA, [Sedika], Kisha, and Destiny kind of helped me and taught me, "Ok, this is what you have to do," and, "if you need help with this, I can help you out." I really believe that I was more prepared because of the advice [Sedika] gave me. We have the buddy program so people have someone to rely on, but then it seems like everybody helps each other out.
>
> *Sedika:* Yeah. I really liked when that was started, the whole buddy program. It was really effective in that this person had been through it and now they're going to help me through it.
>
> *Sarah:* And they have specific advice about issues that they had to deal with in the past.
>
> *Penny:* It helps to transmit information, the struggles, and the "I would do it differently now because," from generation to generation. There is only so much a job description can tell you. The passing down of information is so important and this initiative prevents us from loosing the information when people graduate.
>
> *Sedika:* Right, right.
>
> *Sarah:* And I think even because our classes teach people the ideas of identity development and social justice, they teach an important part of what it means to be a good leader: knowing who you are and knowing how to help people who don't identify the same way that you do. In that way, I think that MCSP as a whole, instead of just putting people in positions, gives them the tools to be successful in those positions.

### Conflict in Community

The program has a number of responsible and strong community leaders. Student leadership also includes conflict and mistakes. Two examples of such conflict are reflected below along with the programmatic change that resulted from the conflicts. The following example took place in the first year of the program, when a RA did not take his position as seriously as he should have during a volunteer program that led students out of state.

*Sedika:* For community service we were planning a trip to Cleveland for Habitat for Humanity. We had some stumbling blocks on our trip that kind of warranted some new planning strategies for community service, how things should be done strategically, how leaders should take on their role, and how they should be more open and honest. And I think that that's one thing that we've changed throughout the years. I've sat down with [Penny] and said, "OK this is the plan. And you've shared the guidelines we created and need to follow." And that's something that we've changed throughout the year and now it's kind of stable. That wasn't the way things were my first year.

*Penny:* What happened was an RA took students on a community service trip and then went to the bar that night. It was the first year of the program.

*Sedika:* Yeah. It was kind of a whole weird deal. We were downtown and it was 2:00 am in the morning. We were supposed to drive back to the church where we stayed overnight so that we could do our community service in the morning. So we go back to the meeting spot and he was not there.

*Penny:* And you were first year students!

*Sedika:* Right! I was like, "Oh! I'm in a strange place. I don't know where we are." We finally found him, but it was scary.

As Sedika mentioned, this was an opportunity for learning and change. MCSP has made considerable changes to procedures for service-learning events, and the first-year students helped implement these changes so the above experience would never happen again. Examples of changes include preconversations that occur before every community service learning trip. Logisitics covered in preconversations include liability forms, an itinerary, and emergency contacts.

Another conflict situation arouse when the university police called the program director one day. After completing a community service program and dropping off the first-year students, two sophomore student leaders took the MCSP van to the United States/Canada border and attempted to go to Windsor, Canada, for an evening on the town. The border patrol observed that the vehicle was registered to the University of Michigan, and contacted the university. The two students were instructed to return the van to campus. Upon arrival, they met with the program director. The two students were extremely apologetic, owned their mistake, and vowed that this, or something like it, would never happen again. The students learned quite a bit from this experience and both immediately and visibly altered their leadership skills for the better. In this instance, both students held to their word and served MCSP as stellar role model leaders throughout their MCSP careers. In fact, one of these students was later hired as a RA for the program, served as a capable leader, and followed the MCSP procedures when checking out the van for community service events.

At the time, it was clearly written in the MCSP van use instructions that every student must drive directly to the community service site and directly back to campus. Currently, MCSP stresses this aspect of the van usage and requires students to both read and sign the van expectations.

# Diversity in Student Leadership

Students attend universities at a critical developmental period when they define themselves in relation to others, and experiment with different social roles, before making commitments to majors, social groups, and intimate relationships (Gurin, 1999). The Michigan Community Scholars Program offers many opportunities to explore diversity. MCSP is racially and ethnically diverse compared to the University of Michigan as a whole. Through its inclusive recruitment techniques, MCSP attracts a diverse student body within the program. All incoming first-year students can apply to the program. MCSP actively recruits high school student leaders, students with community service-learning experience, students of color, and international students. From this multicultural group of students emerges a strong cohort of student leaders who reflect the program's diversity each year. For example, during the 2001-2002 academic year, MCSP included 60% students of color and 40% white students from nine different countries. Approximately 5% more women than men were enrolled in the program from eight different schools and colleges at the university. Every applicant to the program that year was accepted.

During the MCSP's first year, volunteer student leaders were primarily African American. In subsequent years, a conscious change took place and the student leadership has come to reflect the entire program's diversity, including African American, White, Asian American, Latina/o, multi-ethnic, and international students. We believe the diversity of the student leadership, coupled with a foundation in social justice, equity, and community service learning, has enabled MCSP students to develop a strong model program at the University of Michigan. Reflecting the success of the program's cocurricular foundation, the MCSP programming board was awarded the Student Organization of the Year award by the Office of Student Activities and Leadership in 2001-2002. This recognition reflects the day-to-day student commitment to the program's success.

A diverse student population alone does not guarantee that students will have meaningful interactions and increase social identity awareness. Social identity theory and the complexity of participation in a diverse society are found throughout the curriculum and cocurricular experiences for undergraduate students. The frequency and quality of intergroup interaction, or informal interactional diversity (Gurin, Dey, Hurtado, & Gurin, 2002), is required to impact educational outcomes and predominately takes place outside the classroom. For Gurin et al., benefits from classroom diversity occur when students learn both content and knowledge about diverse people and gain personal experience with diverse peers. The simultaneous impact of conversations and interactions inside and outside the classroom profoundly affects student perspectives. These interactions aid students in applying theoretical material to their residence hall lives, student organizations, and community service opportunities outside of the classroom.

In the MCSP introductory course and other MCSP courses, students learn about social identity development theories, explore their own identities, gain knowledge about identities of those different from themselves, and work to understand individual identity within society. Grappling with these issues in the classroom enhances students' willingness to utilize theoretical knowledge of social identity in the community and cocurricular experiences. Students use this added skill base in multiple situations beyond the classroom. For example, Sarah Luke—a first-year student in the program, former PA for the programming board, and current RA—discusses how diversity in leadership issues personally affected her, her leadership abilities, and MCSP first-year students' lives.

*My older brother tells my parents, "You send Sarah to U of M and she comes back a liberal." And I never realized that I thought differently about things but I think I have the tools to think critically. When people say things, I think about where they are coming from. I see it in my residents too. I have a couple residents from the Detroit area and one is from an area where there are a lot of Arab Americans who own stores and there is some tension in the community about which stores to go to. One of them was joking around saying how she didn't like to go to the "Chaldean stores" because she didn't like how the people smell. Another resident who is African*

*American looked at her and said, "Yeah, just like how Black people smell. Well that is the same thing that could be said about me." It just showed me that this woman was making the connection and confronted her friend on it. I think part of it is the classes but I also think part of it is living in an environment where people are trying to be socially conscious as well. That puts you in check. People feel comfortable enough to tell each other and respect each other enough to say, "Hey, do you know what it sounds like when you say that?" That's how you learn—by messing up in a safe environment.*

The program's social justice and community involvement focus raises student awareness of issues pertaining to intergroup relations and possible conflicts that may arise. The curricular and cocurricular experiences equip students with skills to deal with conflict proactively. Thus, the student leadership experience in MCSP teaches students to work cooperatively and successfully in a multicultural context. This diverse student body, combined with leadership training and experience, strengthens students' ability to serve and lead in an increasingly diverse world.

## Community Service Learning and Leading

John Dewey is often regarded as one of the founders of community service learning pedagogy. Dewey (1900/1990) wove together concepts such as community service, engagement, and learning. Cognitive reflection in pre- and post-service discussions is a key element of intentional service-learning. The MCSP cocurricular programming board provides short- and long-term opportunities for MCSP students to engage in intentional community service learning based on the Dewey model.

The MCSP introductory course, UC 102: The Student in the University, provides a foundation for MCSP students to engage in meaningful community service learning rather than simply volunteering. The students apply this approach to their community work outside of the classroom through the various activities they initiate through the programming board. The MCSP drama troupe, Students Helping Others to Choose Knowledgably (SHOCK), exemplifies the intentionality of community service programs that MCSP students conduct. Students created SHOCK in response to the absence of substance abuse awareness programs in the Ann Arbor public school system and intentionally utilize the Dewey model in their practice. MCSP students isolated a specific community need, discussed the idea with community leaders in the school system, and then took action. This year the drama troupe received a program award honoring their work from the Ginsberg Center for Community Service Learning at the University of Michigan. SHOCK is one of the many MCSP student community service learning initiatives.

Sarah Luke describes another example of a student-initiated community service learning opportunity, which was also a model of student activism, the 30-Hour Famine.

*Yeah, I participated in the 30-Hour Famine last year. It was actually pretty amazing. It was the first year. It was almost all first-year students from the MCSP programming board figuring out how to put together this campus wide event. They had statistics like, "for every $2 you raise, someone has a sandwich." They had equivalents like a family could buy a sheep in this country if you raise this much money. And there was the education piece, the video from World Vision. The programming board took time to make their own video, and their posters would always have some fact about world hunger. I personally learned a lot about the issue and have been involved ever since. I also think just seeing the diversity in the leadership team that put together the Famine together was pretty amazing. You'd see people from all different backgrounds coming together for this one cause, world hunger. They really helped solidify the event because everyone had different strengths and ideas about how it should be done. I think that made it come together to be a really wonderful event. And one of my residents was the activities chair this year and she was telling me how exciting it was and how the number of people that came to their* *activities grew from last year. It was a really good experience and I think part of that was because of the educational component that they incorporated.*

Community service learning through MCSP's cocurricular aspects is a significant part of daily life in the living-learning program. Students take responsibility to determine student interest, identify community needs, then thoughtfully plan and implement various service-learning programs, including pre- and post-service conversations. MCSP students are often found planning a parent's night out for university family housing, participating in alternative spring break, organizing a trip to build a house with Habitat for Humanity, helping with environmental sustainability initiatives, and much more. Student-initiated community service learning programs are organized on a weekly or bi-weekly basis during the semester, excluding the final exam period.

## Transforming Theory into Practice

One foundational element of the MCSP is that students utilize the theory from the classroom in day-to-day decision-making, community engagement in the living-learning program, community service opportunities, and interacting with the greater society. The stories we have communicated here serve as examples of classroom theory translating into MCSP participant actions. MCSP students are often in each other's rooms with the doors open or convening in the floor lounge. On the residence hall floors is where this sense of community forms and overflows into the MCSP classrooms. For example, student leaders in one room were known for informally writing a topic on the wipe-board on their door each week, such as "gender issues and dating," or "race and religion," and then the community would come together at night to discuss the topic. These informal events were regularly attended, helping facilitate discussions and a feeling of connectedness. These dynamic conversations were not a part of residence hall or MCSP programming, but grew from student initiative and leadership.

Another example of transforming theory into practice happened when a MCSP community member was faced with a hate crime; derogatory words were placed on a student's door. The MCSP community—including a first-year seminar, the programming board, and the floor community—all pulled together to take action. Responses included a student-designed sign, advertising that hate crimes are not tolerated in the MCSP community, which was distributed for people to display on their doors and in windows. Similarly, the faculty, staff, and community partners sent a letter to students denouncing hate crimes and supporting a just and equitable community. In addition, the students watched a movie on communities that had faced hate crimes and had community meetings to discuss the situation. A MCSP faculty member, Charles Behling, prompted students to be conscious about taking responsibility off the hate crime victim and holding the entire community accountable for the community response to the hate crime.

The community members also responded to one another when facing issues around inappropriate language, when including all people in community events, and when following through on the daily, lived practice of the program. Transforming theory into practice extends beyond the MCSP residence hall floors. For example, Sedika discusses the impact of the MCSP introductory course, UC 102, on her personal identity and college career:

*First off, MCSP gave me a deeper understanding of who I am and what I believe in. In part, UC 102 focuses on identity and understanding your own identity and being able to be open minded about other people's identities. So coming from a diverse background already but not knowing everything, I was thrown in and it was an experience that I really enjoyed. I took quite a bit from the program and act on it. It's like my first year made me who I am right now. I have learned and moved up in leadership positions so much that I can apply what I have learned through UC 102, training and interacting with people and being able to sit and talk to some-*

*one about anything. A strong and effective leader: that's what I have become.*

# Conclusion

The MCSP started as a small living-learning program with a focus on transition from high school to college, social justice, community service, student leadership, and academic excellence. It has become a significant living-learning program at the University of Michigan where students, staff, and faculty work together to form strong in-depth courses on identity and community and where students have the opportunity to utilize what they learn in every aspect of the program. The diverse community strives to nurture academic leadership, personal student needs within a safe environment where mistakes can be made, and a place where transformative change may occur. In MCSP, deep learning is lived by empowering students through leadership and ownership of the program. Through emphasizing student leadership and ownership in diverse learning communities, students can continue to change the curricular and cocurricular programs, and grow as activists to influence and change the world.

## References

Bolman, L.G., & Deal, T. E. (1995). *Leading with soul: An uncommon journey of spirit.* San Francisco, CA: Jossey-Bass.

Dewey, John. 1900/1990. *School and society.* Chicago: University of Chicago Press.

Griffin, P. (1997). Introductory module for the single issue courses. In Adams, M., Bell, L.A., & Griffin, P. (Eds.), *Teaching for diversity and social justice.* New York: Routledge.

Gurin, P. (1999). New research on the benefits of diversity in college and beyond: An empirical analysis. Diversity in higher education: Why corporate America cares. Retrieved October 29, 1999, from http://www.inform.umd.edu/DiversityWeb /Digest/Sp99/benefits.html

Gurin, P., Dey, E. L., Hurtado, S., and Gurin, G. (2002). Diversity and higher education: Theory and impact on educational outcomes, *Harvard Educational Review. 72*(3), 330-366.

Hess, J., & McKenna, D. (Producers), & Kaye, T. (Director). (1998). *American History X* [Motion picture]. United States: New Line Cinema.

Johnson, D.W., & Johnson, F.P. (2000). *Joining together: Group theory and group skills.* Fifth Edition. Boston: Allyn and Bacon.

Komives, S, R,, Lucas, N,, & McMahon, T.R. (1988). *Exploring leadership: For college students who want to make a difference.* San Francisco: Jossey-Bass.

Mead, M. (2001). *Why remember Margaret Mead.* Retrieved December 2, 2002, from www.mead2001.org

# Chapter 21

## PROGRAM EVALUATION AND RESEARCH DESIGN: INTEGRATING SERVICE-LEARNING, DIVERSITY, AND LEARNING COMMUNITIES

David Schoem, Josie Sirineo, Carly M. Southworth and Stefani Salazar

## Introduction

It is only in recent years that there has been serious and focused interest in the assessment of learning communities (Shapiro and Levine, 1999). The same lack of interest has been true, to an even greater extent, with regard to residential learning communities (Shapiro and Levine Laufgraben, 2004). It is significant, therefore, that although the Michigan Community Scholars Program (MCSP) at the moment of this writing has no hard assessment data to report, it has in fact developed a fully planned program evaluation and research design for use in the coming years.

When the MCSP first opened its doors to students, its overall purpose was set but the program's vision and activities were not yet in place. As a result, it is not surprising that all of the early attention of the program was directed towards program development. However, in the third year of the program, with funding support from the University of Michigans Provost's Committee on Education for Diverse Democracy and the Office of the Vice President for Research, and with additional consultative support from the Dean's Office of the College of Literature, Science, and the Arts and University Housing, MCSP embarked upon an effort to develop a program evaluation and research design.

This chapter will first provide a brief discussion of the process and content of developing the program evaluation and research design. It will then provide separate discussions for the program evaluation and the research design, including the specific evaluation surveys and research design instruments. Finally, it will discuss the next steps that are anticipated for both the program evaluation and the research design.

## Process and Content of Developing a Program Evaluation and Research Design

In a very short time in the young history of the Michigan Community Scholars Program, it was apparent to those of us closely involved in the program that there were very exciting things happening for MCSP students. We saw first-hand and heard testaments from MCSP students that their lives had been changed by virtue of participating in MCSP. Students reported that they would not have graduated without the benefit of the program, that their majors, careers and life choices had changed, evolved, and deeply developed as a result of the contacts, relationships, courses, and vision of the program. We were thrilled with these reports and began to make claims about the program as a result. At the same time, we were aware that we needed good evaluation data to substantiate the claims that we started to make on the basis of these reported experiences.

As we began talking we found that we were interested in two kinds of assessment. First, we wanted to document and evaluate the success of the program in terms of the mission and goals statement. This would provide us with data to help identify programmatic areas that we could strengthen and build upon in an ongoing process of change and improvement from year to year. Second, we were also interested in collecting data on the impact of the program on the attitudes and behaviors of individual MCSP students in the short term and longitudinally in terms of learning, civic engagement, and diverse democracy measures. We wanted to know, most importantly, whether and how this program makes a difference in the lives of individual students.

Funding for program assessment is not typically built into university budgets and such was the case with the MCSP budget. However, we had the flexibility to make internal reallocations and, therefore, we made some hard choices to carve out funding to conduct a program evaluation from our existing budget as this was a very important priority. We knew we could not find enough funds within our existing budget to conduct a longitudinal research project, so we decided that the research project would be dependent upon our identifying support from external sources. Funding we hope to receive from these external sources will pay for graduate student research assistant support, survey materials, as well as any additional administrative costs incurred towards the implementation of the research design, data collection, and subsequent data analysis.

We are fortunate at the University of Michigan to have extensive resources in terms of research design and program evaluation expertise. Everyone we met with was more than willing to be of help. We received assistance and consultation from the assistant deans for undergraduate education from the College of Literature, Science, and the Arts (LS&A), the associate director of University Housing, the assessment consultant from the Center for Research on Learning and Teaching, directors of other learning communities, including the Undergraduate Research Opportunity Program, Women in Science and Engineering Residence Program, the Health Science Scholars Program, and the MCSP Advisory Board (1).

For the research design, we also relied heavily on existing surveys that colleagues on campus were developing and using and we consulted with them at different stages of the research design development. These colleagues included faculty and staff from the Program on Intergroup Relations for surveys on intergroup dialogue, the Office of Multicultural and Academic Initiatives for the "Michigan Study," the School of Education's Center for Higher and Postsecondary Education for the "Diverse Democracy" survey, the research office of the Office of the Vice President for Student Affairs who work with the "CIRP" study, the research office of University Housing for their "Residence Environment Survey" survey, and the School of Education for help with "NSSE." We also read and consulted with numerous books and articles on assessment of civic engagement and service learning and assessment more generally (2).

Finally, we were assisted in our efforts by various national partners and colleagues. Experienced assessment specialists from Portland State University and Temple University periodically read and reviewed our various plans and draft documents. We met with other learning community colleagues from around the country whose programs have a focus on service learning from the University of Maryland, the College of William and Mary, George Mason University, and Portland State University to discuss and share best practice. We also participated in assessment conversations with the eight campuses represented in an AAHE/Ford Foundation Planning Grant on "The Engaged Campus in a Diverse Democracy" (3).

At our starting point, we quickly observed that most of the early learning community studies, notably Tinto and Goodsell (1993) and many who have followed them, focused primarily, even exclusively on grade and retention data. While we were interested in that information, our interest went well beyond those measures. We also were clear that, at least in the program evaluation, that it was important that we not only evaluate the experience of our students but of our faculty and community partners as well.

Much like the slow start in doing assessment work, we had never developed a mission and goals statement for the program. Many of those we consulted with looked immediately for that statement to give direction to our work. Further, we felt we would be able to develop our survey questions much more clearly with the goals before us. Thus, as part of our process of developing the program evaluation and research design, we worked with our faculty, community partners, staff and student to come up the mission and goals statement and have used that "living document" to guide us in our work (4).

# The Program Evaluation

The evaluation includes three components: program characteristics, academic achievement components, and surveys. Each of these components is described below.

## Program Characteristics and Academic Achievement Components

The program characteristics component focuses on the collection of general program characteristics of MCSP, including demographic data of MCSP students and faculty as well as the cataloging of the course offerings, community service opportunities, and social activities that MCSP offers its students each year. The academic achievement component focuses on the collection of data on the academic success of MCSP students as incoming freshman and throughout their college career.

In order to effectively and consistently keep track of the program's characteristics, a master file was created to catalogue each year's program participant demographics, course offerings, community service opportunities, and social activities. The file will be updated each year with the numbers of students, faculty and community partners, as well as characteristics such as race, gender, department (for faculty), etc. For courses, MCSP currently offers a variety of first-year seminar courses from multiple disciplines such as psychology (I Too Sing America: A Psychology of Race and Racism), sociology (Democracy, Diversity and Community), and a required introductory, "membership" course (The Student in the University). Community service opportunities are also varied and can be one-time activities such as Habitat for Humanity or Alternative Spring Break, or semester long courses focusing on education with tutoring of local elementary and high school students. This master file will be updated annually and will ultimately serve as a measure for analysis of the program's growth and development as well as changes based on student input from the evaluation surveys and other emerging developments over the years.

Information on the academic achievement of MCSP students will come primarily from M-Pathways data. M-Pathways is the University of Michigan's university-wide database used for student admissions purposes. From this data, information will be collected on the race, ethnicity and gender makeup of each incoming MCSP cohort, as well as their average incoming high school GPA and SAT/ACT scores. Additionally, M-Pathways data allows us to follow each MCSP cohort through to graduation, and therefore GPA, career path (school of degree, major), and retention data will also be collected on each MCSP cohort. Finally, each MCSP cohort will be compared to a control group of university students drawn from the College of Literature, Science, and Arts (LSA). Our original intent was to compare MCSP students to a control group with similar characteristics drawn from the entire university, but who did not participate in similar types of programs. This ultimately proved infeasible due to the nature of the M-Pathways system and inconsistencies in record keeping within MCSP and across living-learning programs in general.

M-Pathways is a data entry system designed to facilitate the input of student admissions data. The process of entering this data, however, can vary widely across departments and programs. This revelation came when comparing M-Pathways data on each cohort to MCSP's records. Wide inconsistencies were found in the number of students actually considered part of the program by MCSP and those recorded as members of the program in the M-Pathways data. This inconsistency exists because students in the university who take MCSP courses do not necessarily have to be a member of MCSP, yet they are still entered into the M-Pathways system as such. And this turns out to be a fairly common practice across similar university programs. However, determining who is a member of each living learning program on campus is essential to creating a university-wide control group that seeks to exclude such students. Due to the lack of standardization in determining program membership across programs and the lack of time and resources to devote to such an endeavor (while we could manually determine which students in our records were actual members of MCSP and which were just taking courses, we cannot do this for other living learning communities on campus), our original intentions for a university-wide comparison were hampered. After consulting with the LS&A information manager about this dilemma, we decided to compare MCSP students more broadly to students with similar characteristics in LS&A. Though the comparison is broader than we had hoped for, it is not all together uninformative as over eighty percent of MCSP students are also in LS&A. Thus, we can still glean some useful information about MCSP students in comparison to other university students.

## The Survey Component

Attached are the actual instruments for the program evaluation component, including student, faculty, and community partner experience surveys. In order to evaluate the success and implementation of all components of MCSP, the surveys touch upon several areas such as satisfaction, sense of belonging and ownership, classroom experience, perceived diversity and inclusiveness, and program support. The questions included in the three surveys were shaped from the values stated in the newly developed program mission and goals statement.

In an attempt to capture as many completed surveys as possible, the faculty and community partner surveys will be distributed at the end of the fall semester, when most faculty and community partners are more heavily involved with the program. We then plan on reporting out the data collected and facilitating small focus groups at the beginning of the winter semester. This will also give us the opportunity to use this smaller population as a test run before implementing the student survey. It is our hope to have the student surveys completed in early March, a time chosen based on the academic calendar, implementation of other university surveys, and other relevant events. Students will have multiple opportunities to complete the survey via hall meetings, Programming Board meetings, and through the MCSP office.

## Michigan Community Scholars Program: Student Satisfaction Survey
### BACKGROUND/DEMOGRAPHIC INFORMATION

**What year are you?**

Freshman _____ Sophomore _____ Junior _____ Senior _____

**How many years have you been in MCSP?**

One _____ Two _____ Three _____ Four _____

**Are you currently a student leader?**

a. I am not currently a student leader as described in b, c, d, or e.
b. I am a Peer Advisor
c. I am a Peer Mentor
d. I am a Resident Advisor
e. I am a Class Facilitator

**Have you decided on a major?**

No _____ Yes (Please specify: _____)

**Student status**

a. In-state student from _____ *(City, County, Township, etc.)*

b. Out-of-state student from _____ *(State)*
c. International student from _____ *(Country)*

**Race/Ethnicity:**
a. African American/Black
b. Hispanic/Latino/Chicano
c. Asian/Asian American/Pacific Islanders
d. White/Caucasian
e. American Indian/Alaskan Native
f. Multi-racial/Multi-ethnic (Please specify: _____)
g. International student

**Gender:**
Male_____        Female _____        Transgender _____

**Sexual orientation:**
Bisexual _____        Heterosexual _____        Homosexual _____

**Religion:** _____

**Estimated parent's income last year:**

| | |
|---|---|
| a. Less than $10,000 | f. $50,000-$69,999 |
| b. $10,000-$14,999 | g. $70,000-$99,999 |
| c. $15,000-$19,999 | h. $100,000-$149,999 |
| d. $20,000-$29,999 | i. $150,000-$199,999 |
| e. $30,000-$49,999 | j. $200,000 or more |

### THE MCSP COMMUNITY

**About how often have you done each of the following: during the current school year?**

1 = Never     2 = A few times a semester     3 = A few times a month     4 = Once or more a week

| | 1 | 2 | 3 | 4 |
|---|---|---|---|---|
| Studied with other MCSP students outside of class. | | | | |
| Attended MCSP social events/programs. | | | | |
| Attended MCSP educational events/programs. | | | | |
| Spent my leisure time socializing with other MCSP students. | | | | |
| Interacted with my assigned Peer Mentor. | | | | |
| Interacted with my Resident Advisor. | | | | |
| Attended MCSP Programming Board meetings. | | | | |
| Stopped by the MCSP office. | | | | |

**On the whole, interaction between students within the MCSP community is:**
a. Positive
b. Generally positive
c. Neither positive nor negative
d. Generally negative
e. Negative

**I have planned or helped plan an MCSP social event:**
a. Never
b. Once
c. A few times a semester
d. A few times a month

**I have planned or helped plan a student-initiated community service project:**
    a. Never
    b. Once
    c. A few times a semester
    d. A few times a month

**Indicate the extent to which you agree or disagree with the following statements.**

1= Strongly agree    2= Agree    3= Neither agree or disagree    4= Disagree    5= Strongly agree

| | 1 | 2 | 3 | 4 | 5 |
|---|---|---|---|---|---|
| I feel a sense of belonging to the MCSP community. | | | | | |
| It is easy to find people in MCSP who share my background and experiences. | | | | | |
| I feel comfortable in the MCSP community. | | | | | |
| MCSP is comprised of people from diverse social backgrounds and perspectives. | | | | | |
| During my leisure time, I enjoy spending time with other MCSP students. | | | | | |
| MCSP is a safe and accepting environment for people from diverse social backgrounds and perspectives. | | | | | |
| I understand the role of MCSP student leaders (i.e. Peer Advisors, Peer Mentors, Resident Advisors). | | | | | |
| I am aware of most social and community service activities available to MCSP students. | | | | | |

**In a few words, please describe your experience living in the MCSP community.**

**What was your favorite MCSP social event/program?**

**Your least favorite social event/program?**

**CLASSROOM EXPERIENCE**

**How many MCSP courses have you taken this academic year?** _____

**Please list the courses.**

**About how often have you done each of the following during the current school year?
(Place a check in the appropriate box)**

1= Never     2 = A few times a semester     3 = A few times a month     4 = Once or more a week

| | 1 | 2 | 3 | 4 |
|---|---|---|---|---|
| Asked an MCSP instructor for information related to a course you were taking. | | | | |
| Visited informally with an MCSP instructor before or after class. | | | | |
| Visited with an MCSP instructor during their office hours. | | | | |
| Discussed personal problems or concerns with an MCSP instructor. | | | | |
| Had lunch or dinner with an MCSP instructor in the dining hall. | | | | |
| Participated in community service with MCSP faculty. | | | | |
| Went to a cultural event (e.g., concert or play) with an MCSP instructor or class. | | | | |
| Utilized tutoring and other academic support services provided by MCSP. | | | | |
| Talked about academic plans with an MCSP faculty member or advisor. | | | | |
| Worked with an MCSP instructor on an individual class project. | | | | |
| Worked with an MCSP instructor involving his/her research. | | | | |
| Applied MCSP course content to solve a real-world problem. | | | | |

**I would consider MCSP courses among the best I have taken here at the University.**
   a. Strongly agree
   b. Agree
   c. Neither agree nor disagree
   d. Disagree
   e. Strongly disagree

**I would rate the MCSP faculty among the best here at the University.**
   a. Strongly agree
   b. Agree
   c. Neither agree nor disagree
   d. Disagree
   e. Strongly disagree

**MCSP provides the academic support I need to succeed at the University.**
   a. Strongly agree
   b. Agree
   c. Neither agree nor disagree
   d. Disagree
   e. Strongly disagree

*Please answer the following questions in the space provided.*

**Some MCSP courses have outside community members (known as MCSP community partners) that assist faculty members in teaching MCSP courses. If you have classroom experience with an MCSP community partner(s), did that community partner(s) contribute significantly to your understanding of the course material? Why or why not?**

**What was your favorite MCSP course? Why?**

## COMMUNITY SERVICE EXPERIENCES

I volunteered in my community before coming to UM and participating in MCSP.
- a. Never.
- b. A few times a year.
- c. A few times a month.
- d. Once or more a week.

Please list all of the community service activities you participated in this year through MCSP.
*(Circle those that were course related or required.)*

Have you participated in community service activities outside of MCSP this year? Please list.

I can apply the concepts and discussions of my MCSP courses to my community service experiences.
- a. Strongly agree
- b. Agree
- c. Neither agree nor disagree
- d. Disagree
- e. Strongly disagree

I am satisfied with the variety of community service opportunities MCSP provides.
- a. Strongly agree
- b. Agree
- c. Neither agree nor disagree
- d. Disagree
- e. Strongly disagree

I have had positive experiences with the staff and/or supervisors at the community service sites at which I have served.
- a. Strongly agree
- b. Agree
- c. Neither agree nor disagree
- d. Disagree
- e. Strongly disagree
- f. I have not interacted with staff and/or supervisors on site.

I think about community service differently now than in high school.
- a. Strongly agree
- b. Agree
- c. Neither agree nor disagree
- d. Disagree
- e. Strongly disagree

*Please answer the following questions in the space provided.*

What was your favorite community service experience with MCSP? Why?

What was your least favorite? Why?

**GENERAL QUESTIONS**

Each item below describes a goal or value of MCSP. Please tell us how important these experiences are for you and to what extent you agree or disagree that MCSP has met these goals for you.

How important do you consider the following? (check appropriate box)

1= Very important     2= Somewhat important     3= Neutral     4= Somewhat unimportant     5= Very unimportant

| | 1 | 2 | 3 | 4 | 5 |
|---|---|---|---|---|---|
| Learning about community and social issues | | | | | |
| Long-term commitment to learning | | | | | |
| Academic success | | | | | |
| Exploration of personal and social identities | | | | | |
| Living in a community comprised of people from diverse backgrounds | | | | | |
| Living in a safe and accepting environment for all people | | | | | |
| Providing high quality community service | | | | | |
| Developing leadership skills | | | | | |
| Reflecting and learning from community service experiences | | | | | |
| Learning from people of different backgrounds and cultures | | | | | |
| Making a difference in the world | | | | | |

Considering your experience with MCSP, do you agree or disagree that MCSP has met these goals?

1= Strongly agree     2= Agree     3= Neither agree or disagree     4= Disagree     5= Strongly agree

| | 1 | 2 | 3 | 4 | 5 |
|---|---|---|---|---|---|
| Learning about community and social issues | | | | | |
| Long-term commitment to learning | | | | | |
| Academic success | | | | | |
| Exploration of personal and social identities | | | | | |
| Living in a community comprised of people from diverse backgrounds | | | | | |
| Living in a safe and accepting environment for all people | | | | | |
| Providing high quality community service | | | | | |
| Developing leadership skills | | | | | |
| Reflecting and learning from community service experiences | | | | | |
| Learning from people of different backgrounds and cultures | | | | | |
| Making a difference in the world | | | | | |

Overall, how satisfied are you with your experience in MCSP?
- a. Very satisfied
- b. Somewhat satisfied
- c. Neither satisfied or unsatisfied
- d. Somewhat unsatisfied
- e. Very unsatisfied

**How well has MCSP met your expectations?**
- a. Much better than expected
- b. Better than expected
- c. About what I expected
- d. Worse than expected
- e. Much worse than expected

**My involvement in MCSP has helped make my transition from high school to college a smooth one.**
- a. Strongly agree
- b, Agree
- c. Neither agree nor disagree
- d. Disagree
- e. Strongly disagree

**My involvement in MCSP has helped me connect to the broader campus community.**
- a. Strongly agree
- b. Agree
- c. Neither agree nor disagree
- d. Disagree
- e. Strongly disagree

**MCSP administrative/office staff are supportive of student needs.**
- a. Strongly agree
- b. Agree
- c. Neither agree nor disagree
- d. Disagree
- e. Strongly disagree

**I would recommend MCSP to incoming students.**
- a. Strongly agree
- b. Agree
- c. Neither agree nor disagree
- d. Disagree
- e. Strongly disagree

**In a few words, please tell us what you have enjoyed most about your experience with MCSP?**

**What have you enjoyed least?**

**What suggestions do you have for new or different:**
  *Social events/programs?*
  *Educational events/programs?*
  *Community Service opportunities?*
  *MCSP courses?*
  *Do you have any other suggestions for changes?*

## Faculty Satisfaction Survey

As part of our efforts to evaluate the Michigan Community Scholars Program, we are conducting this brief satisfaction survey. We would greatly appreciate your participation in this process. This survey should take no more than 15-20 minutes to complete. Your participation is considered completely voluntary and you do not have to answer any questions that make you feel uncomfortable.

Thank you for your participation!

SA = Strongly Agree    A = Agree;    N = Neutral    D = Disagree    SD = Strongly Disagree    N/A = Not Applicable

| General Program Experiences | SA | A | N | D | SD | N/A |
|---|---|---|---|---|---|---|
| Overall, I am satisfied with my experience with MCSP. | | | | | | |
| My expectations of MCSP have matched my experiences with MCSP. | | | | | | |
| Participating in MCSP is worth my time and energy. | | | | | | |
| I look forward to MCSP faculty seminars and other opportunities to get together with other MCSP faculty. | | | | | | |
| I have positive interactions with other MCSP faculty. | | | | | | |
| I look forward to participating in MCSP in the future. | | | | | | |
| I feel like a member of the larger MCSP community. | | | | | | |
| The program and its staff are supportive of my specific teaching needs. | | | | | | |
| **Classroom Experiences** | SA | A | N | D | SD | N/A |
| My experience teaching within MCSP has been a positive experience for me. | | | | | | |
| MCSP provides opportunities for my professional development. | | | | | | |
| MCSP encourages innovative teaching. | | | | | | |
| I feel that MCSP students are developing deeper understandings about community, social identity, and social issues within society. | | | | | | |
| **Community Experiences** | SA | A | N | D | SD | N/A |
| Teaching within MCSP makes me want to be more involved in my community (through volunteering, fundraising, political involvement, etc). | | | | | | |
| If you work with a community partner, please answer the following questions. | | | | | | |
| My community partner(s) has enhanced my ability to teach my course. | | | | | | |
| Students respond positively to my community partner(s). | | | | | | |
| I have a strong relationship with my community partner(s). | | | | | | |
| I feel the relationship between the students in my course and my community partner(s) has been a mutually beneficial experience. | | | | | | |

### Please answer the following questions in the space provided:

1. What have you enjoyed most about your experience with MCSP?
2. What have you enjoyed least?
3. What do you see as the strengths of MCSP?
4. What do you see as its weaknesses?
5. In the space below please share any other comments or suggestions you may have regarding your satisfaction with MCSP.

## Community Partner Satisfaction Survey

As part of our efforts to evaluate the Michigan Community Scholars Program, we are conducting this brief satisfaction survey. We would greatly appreciate your participation in this process. This survey should take no more than 15-20 minutes to complete. Your participation is considered completely voluntary and you do not have to answer any questions that make you feel uncomfortable.

Thank your for your time and participation!

SA = Strongly Agree    A = Agree;    N = Neutral    D = Disagree    SD = Strongly Disagree    N/A = Not Applicable

| General Program Experiences | SA | A | N | D | SD | N/A |
|---|---|---|---|---|---|---|
| Overall, I am satisfied with my partnership with MCSP. | | | | | | |
| My expectations of MCSP have matched my experiences with MCSP. | | | | | | |
| Participating in MCSP is worth my time and energy. | | | | | | |
| I look forward to participating in MCSP in the future. | | | | | | |
| I feel like a member of the larger MCSP community. | | | | | | |
| MCSP and its staff are supportive of my specific community agency needs. | | | | | | |
| **Experiences in the Classroom** | SA | A | N | D | SD | N/A |
| If you assist in teaching an MCSP course, please answer the following. | | | | | | |
| I have a good relationship with my faculty partner. | | | | | | |
| I feel I have contributed a good amount to student learning. | | | | | | |
| MCSP students are receptive to my contribution to the course. | | | | | | |
| I feel that MCSP students are developing deeper understandings about community, social identity, and social issues. | | | | | | |
| My organization has benefited from my partnership with an MCSP faculty member. | | | | | | |
| Overall, I benefited from my classroom experiences with MCSP. | | | | | | |
| **Experiences on Site** | SA | A | N | D | SD | N/A |
| If MCSP students serve as volunteers for your organization, please answer the following questions. | | | | | | |
| My organization has benefited from the service of MCSP students. | | | | | | |
| MCSP students provide high quality community service. | | | | | | |
| I feel that MCSP students are developing deeper understandings about the community my organization serves and its issues. | | | | | | |
| The service provided by MCSP students is crucial in assisting my organization in reaching its goals. | | | | | | |

### Please answer the following questions in the space provided:

1. *What have you enjoyed most about your partnerships with MCSP?*
2. *What have you enjoyed least?*
3. *What do you see as the strengths of your partnership with MCSP?*
4. *What do you see as its weaknesses?*
5. *In the space below please share any other comments or suggestions you may have regarding your satisfaction with MCSP.*

## The Research Design

Developing the research design for the Michigan Community Scholars Program involved a process that is easily adaptable to institutions or programs of varying size and complexity. The first step in completing such a design is to use the program's structure as a starting point. The four major components of MCSP are deep learning, engaged community, meaningful civic engagement/community service learning and diverse democracy/intercultural understanding and dialogue. Collecting data on the participants' perceptions and experiences in relation to these areas should provide sufficient evidence of the impact the program has on its participants.

The second step is to design the tool that will measure attitudes and behaviors. This step prompted us to collect existing surveys dealing with themes consistent with MCSP. The selected surveys were:

- National Survey of Student Engagement (NSSE) 2003
- Michigan Student Study
- Residence Environment Survey 2002-2003
- Diverse Democracy Project
- Community-Based Learning Student Survey
- Cooperative Institutional Research Program

We very carefully sifted through each survey and selected questions that were consistent with MCSP's themes, mission or goals. Once these questions were amassed, they were diagrammed to depict their survey source, relevant theme, and its measurement scale. The following illustration is an example of such mapping.

NSSE 1 - Ways of knowing: learning and teaching through traditional, experiential, discovery and other innovative means; learning across disciplinary boundaries; learning collaboratively in the classroom and outside the classroom.

| Example: In your experience at your institution during the current school year, about how often have you done each of the following? | |
| --- | --- |
| | Ways of knowing: learning and teaching through traditional, experiential, discovery and other Innovative means; learning across disciplinary boundaries; learning collaboratively in the classroom and outside the classroom. |
| **NSSE** | Very often, Often, Sometimes, Never<br>G. Worked with other students on projects during class<br>H. Worked with classmates outside of class to prepare class assignment<br>I. Put together ideas or concepts from different courses when completing assignments or during class discussions |

In the above example, the selected question is "In your experience at your institution during the current school year, about how often have you done each of the following?" The question is measured on a Likert type scale where respondents can estimate how frequently they were engaged in the given activities. "NSSE 1" is a marker that indicates the question's origin. In this particular case, it is the first question presented on the National Survey of Student Engagement (NSSE). The text featured above the question is the pertinent MCSP goal that is being measured. Please note that only items G, H, and I were chosen for this particular question.

At the third step, the researcher can determine how well the instrument assesses the impact on the program's participants. Current questions can be tailored to the nuances of the program while additional questions can be developed for areas that have not yet been addressed. Questions that are duplicates or are unclear can be eliminated.

The fourth step encourages the researcher to present the drafted survey to interested parties both on and off campus for feedback. The feedback gained from this exercise will be valuable but it is important to relay to reviewers the systematic process in place. Knowledge of such process will help keep the instrument focused. Given that the survey is close to being finalized, permission from the authors of the original survey questions should be acquired in this step.

The final step is to pilot a study of the new survey to ensure that the questions are clearly worded and the instrument is valid.

## Michigan Community Scholars Program
## Matrix of Outcomes

| Deep Learning Outcomes | Engaged Community Outcomes | Community Service Outcomes | Diverse Democracy Outcomes |
|---|---|---|---|
| *Engagement with ideas* <br>• Performance on critical thinking tests <br>• Intellectual exploration | *Scholarly community* <br>• Close interaction between program and participants | *High quality service learning* <br>• Understanding of how service fits needs of community <br>• Percentages of students participating in community | *Diverse community* <br>• Substantial percentages of diverse people in program <br>• Evidence of different types of diversity |
| *Ways of knowing* <br>• Traditional/innovative teaching and learning <br>• MCSP faculty and their disciplines <br>• Frequency of learning collaboratively per semester | *Safe and accepting environment* <br>• Perception of safe environment | *Reflection* <br>• Excerpts from journals and assignments written by students <br>• Transcripts of participant interviews | *Participation in ID* <br>• Number of students participating in ID <br>• Evaluation of ID <br>• Application of ID experiences |
| *Transition to college* <br>• Listing of available academic and social support services <br>• Mentoring <br>• Offering and evaluation of MCSP orientation | *Involved, participatory community* <br>• High retention of students by semester and year <br>• High retention of faculty from year to year <br>• High retention of community partners from year to year | *Leadership development* <br>• Student participation in leadership activities <br>• Leadership roles for faculty, CP and staff | *Commitment to strong democracy* <br>• Perception of democratic commitment <br>• Participation in civic organizations |
| *Academic success* <br>• MCSP students identify college expectations <br>• GPA performance of MCSP students <br>• GPA comparison of MCSP students and non-MCSP students | *Focus on individual and group* <br>• Foster sense of responsibility for each other | *Sustainable partnerships* <br>• Tracking of partnerships between university and community sites <br>• Cultivation of current and new partnerships <br>• Document recruitment network | *Reflection on social justice* <br>• Successful completion of courses dealing with diversity and democracy <br>• Reflective writings on the subject |
| *Learning about community* <br>• Learn about social identities <br>• Learn about other socio-cultural groups and their histories | | *Long term commitment* <br>• Expectation of future civic engagement <br>• Actual percentages of participation from alumni surveys | *Model good practice* <br>• Comparison of students' initial and final visions of diverse democratic community practices <br>• Report of student activities |

## Michigan Community Scholars Program
## Research Design Survey

**DEEP LEARNING**

**1. How often have you done each of the following in the classroom in the past year?** *(Circle one for each.)*

Once or more a week - 4
Few times a month - 3
Few times a semester - 2
Never - 1

| | | | | |
|---|---|---|---|---|
| Talked about current news events | 1 | 2 | 3 | 4 |
| Discussed major social issues such as peace, human rights, and justice | 1 | 2 | 3 | 4 |
| Talked about different lifestyles/customs | 1 | 2 | 3 | 4 |
| Held discussion with students whose religious beliefs were different from your own | 1 | 2 | 3 | 4 |
| Discussed your views about multiculturalism | 1 | 2 | 3 | 4 |
| Talked about art, music, theater or other cultural-aesthetic pursuits | 1 | 2 | 3 | 4 |
| Held discussion with students whose political opinions were different from your own | 1 | 2 | 3 | 4 |

**2. How often have you done each of the following outside the classroom in the past year?** *(Circle one for each.)*

Once or more a week - 4
Few times a month - 3
Few times a semester - 2
Never - 1

| | | | | |
|---|---|---|---|---|
| Discussed something learned in class | 1 | 2 | 3 | 4 |
| Talked about current news events | 1 | 2 | 3 | 4 |
| Discussed major social issues such as peace, human rights, and justice | 1 | 2 | 3 | 4 |
| Talked about different lifestyles/customs | 1 | 2 | 3 | 4 |
| Held discussion with students whose religious beliefs were different from your own | 1 | 2 | 3 | 4 |
| Discussed your views about multiculturalism | 1 | 2 | 3 | 4 |
| Talked about art, music, theater or other cultural-aesthetic pursuits | 1 | 2 | 3 | 4 |
| Held discussion with students whose political opinions were different from your own | 1 | 2 | 3 | 4 |
| Read books on your own (not assigned) for personal or academic enrichment | 1 | 2 | 3 | 4 |

**3. About how often have you done each of the following during the current school year?** *(Circle one for each.)*

Once or more a week - 4
Few times a month - 3
Few times a semester - 2
Never - 1

| | | | | |
|---|---|---|---|---|
| Asked your instructor for information related to a course you were taking | 1 | 2 | 3 | 4 |
| Visited informally with an instructor outside of class | 1 | 2 | 3 | 4 |
| Communicated with your instructor using email | 1 | 2 | 3 | 4 |
| Discussed personal problems or concerns with instructor | 1 | 2 | 3 | 4 |
| Went to a cultural event (e.g. concert or play) with an instructor or class | 1 | 2 | 3 | 4 |
| Talked about academic plans with a faculty member or advisor | 1 | 2 | 3 | 4 |
| Worked with an instructor on an independent project | 1 | 2 | 3 | 4 |
| Worked with an instructor involving his/her research | 1 | 2 | 3 | 4 |
| Applied course content to solve a real-world problem | 1 | 2 | 3 | 4 |
| Worked on a paper or project where you had to integrate ideas from various sources | 1 | 2 | 3 | 4 |
| Worked in groups or small teams | 1 | 2 | 3 | 4 |

**4. Please indicate the level to which you agree with the following statements.** *(Circle one for each.)*

Strongly agree - 4
Agree - 3
Disagree - 2
Strongly disagree - 1

| | SD | D | A | SA |
|---|---|---|---|---|
| I frequently question or challenge professors' ideas before I accept them as right | 1 | 2 | 3 | 4 |
| I'd rather figure something out for myself than simply have it explained to me | 1 | 2 | 3 | 4 |
| I prefer courses requiring me to organize and interpret ideas over courses that ask me only to remember facts or information | 1 | 2 | 3 | 4 |
| I consider the best teachers to be those who can tie things learned in class to things that are important to me in my personal life | 1 | 2 | 3 | 4 |
| I enjoy discussing issues with people who don't agree with me | 1 | 2 | 3 | 4 |
| There have been times with which I have disagreed with the author of a book or article that I was reading | 1 | 2 | 3 | 4 |
| I try to explore the meaning and interpretations of the facts when I am introduced to a new idea | 1 | 2 | 3 | 4 |
| A good way to develop my own opinions is to critically analyze the strengths and limitations of different points of view | 1 | 2 | 3 | 4 |
| When I discover new ways of understanding things, I feel even more motivated to learn | 1 | 2 | 3 | 4 |
| I am a person who is eager to try new experiences | 1 | 2 | 3 | 4 |
| Something I learned in one class helped me understand something in another class | 1 | 2 | 3 | 4 |
| I try to look at everybody's side of a disagreement before I make a decision | 1 | 2 | 3 | 4 |
| I enjoy the challenge of learning complicated new material | 1 | 2 | 3 | 4 |
| I often have discussions with other students about ideas or concepts presented in classes | 1 | 2 | 3 | 4 |
| I enjoy taking courses that challenge my beliefs and values | 1 | 2 | 3 | 4 |
| I enjoy courses that are intellectually challenging | 1 | 2 | 3 | 4 |
| I sometimes find it difficult to see things from another person's point of view | 1 | 2 | 3 | 4 |
| I have critically analyzed the accuracy of information from web sites | 1 | 2 | 3 | 4 |
| I have applied material I learned in a class to other areas in my life, such as my job, internship, or interactions with others | 1 | 2 | 3 | 4 |
| I really enjoy analyzing the reason or causes for people's behavior | 1 | 2 | 3 | 4 |
| I prefer simple rather than complex explanations for people's behavior | 1 | 2 | 3 | 4 |
| I believe it is important to analyze and understand our own thinking processes | 1 | 2 | 3 | 4 |

**5. During the current school year, how much of your coursework emphasized the following mental activities?** *(Circle one for each.)*

Very much - 4
Quite a bit - 3
Some - 2
Very little - 1

| | VL | S | QB | VM |
|---|---|---|---|---|
| Applying theories or concepts to practical problems or in new situations | 1 | 2 | 3 | 4 |
| Memorizing facts, ideas, or methods from your courses and readings so you can repeat them in pretty much the same way | 1 | 2 | 3 | 4 |
| Analyzing the basic elements of an idea, experience, or theory, such as examining a particular case or situation in depth and considering its components | 1 | 2 | 3 | 4 |
| Synthesizing and organizing ideas, information or experiences into, new, more complex interpretations and relationships | 1 | 2 | 3 | 4 |
| Making judgments about the value of information, arguments, or methods such as examining how others gathered and interpreted data and assessing the soundness of their conclusions | 1 | 2 | 3 | 4 |
| Applying theories or concepts to practical problems or in new situations | 1 | 2 | 3 | 4 |

**6. In you experience at your institution during the current school year, about how often have you done each of the following?** *(Circle one for each.)*

Once or more a week - 4
Few times a month - 3
Few times a semester - 2
Never - 1

| | | | | |
|---|---|---|---|---|
| Asked questions in class or contributed to class discussions | 1 | 2 | 3 | 4 |
| Made a class presentation | 1 | 2 | 3 | 4 |
| Prepared two or more drafts of a paper or assignment before turning it in | 1 | 2 | 3 | 4 |
| Worked with other students on projects during class | 1 | 2 | 3 | 4 |
| Worked with classmates outside of class to prepare class assignments | 1 | 2 | 3 | 4 |
| Put together ideas or concepts from different courses when completing assignments or during class discussions | 1 | 2 | 3 | 4 |
| Participated in a community service project as part of a regular course | 1 | 2 | 3 | 4 |
| Used an electronic medium (list-serv, chat group, Internet, etc.) to discuss or complete an assignment | 1 | 2 | 3 | 4 |
| Discussed ideas from your readings or classes with faculty members outside of class | 1 | 2 | 3 | 4 |
| Worked with faculty members on activities other than coursework (committees, orientation  student life activities, etc.) | 1 | 2 | 3 | 4 |
| Discussed ideas from your readings or classes with others outside of class (students, family members, coworkers, etc.) | 1 | 2 | 3 | 4 |

**7. Which of the following have you done or plan to do before you leave the University of Michigan?** *(Circle one for each.)*

Have done & plan to do more - 4
Have done - 3
Plan to do - 2
Haven't done & don't plan to do- 1

**Academic**

| | | | | |
|---|---|---|---|---|
| Work on a research project with a faculty member outside of course or program requirements | 1 | 2 | 3 | 4 |
| Independent study or self-designed major | 1 | 2 | 3 | 4 |
| Take a course devoted to diversity issues in your first year of college | 1 | 2 | 3 | 4 |

**Extracurricular**

| | | | | |
|---|---|---|---|---|
| Practicum, internship, field experience, co-op experience, or clinical assignment | 1 | 2 | 3 | 4 |
| Participate in a learning community or some other formal program where groups of students take two more classes together | 1 | 2 | 3 | 4 |
| Study abroad | 1 | 2 | 3 | 4 |
| Community service or volunteer work | 1 | 2 | 3 | 4 |
| Get elected to student leadership position | 1 | 2 | 3 | 4 |
| Work at least part-time while in college | 1 | 2 | 3 | 4 |
| Join a social fraternity or sorority | 1 | 2 | 3 | 4 |
| Participate in student protests | 1 | 2 | 3 | 4 |
| Participate in groups and activities reflecting your own cultural-ethnic background | 1 | 2 | 3 | 4 |
| Help members of the community get out to vote in elections | 1 | 2 | 3 | 4 |
| Join an organization that promotes cultural diversity | 1 | 2 | 3 | 4 |
| Challenge others on racially derogatory comments | 1 | 2 | 3 | 4 |
| Challenge others on sexually derogatory comments | 1 | 2 | 3 | 4 |
| Make an effort to educate others about social issues (ex. AIDS prevention, homelessness, etc.) | 1 | 2 | 3 | 4 |
| Make efforts to get to know individuals from diverse backgrounds | 1 | 2 | 3 | 4 |

**ENGAGED COMMUNITY**

**8. How much interaction did you have with people in each of the following groups before coming to college?** *(Circle one for each.)*

|  | Substantial interaction - 4 | Some regular interaction - 3 | Little interaction - 2 | No interaction - 1 |
|---|---|---|---|---|
| African Americans/Blacks | 1 | 2 | 3 | 4 |
| Hispanics/Latinos/Chicanos | 1 | 2 | 3 | 4 |
| Asian Americans/Pacific Islanders | 1 | 2 | 3 | 4 |
| Whites/Caucasians | 1 | 2 | 3 | 4 |
| American Indians/Alaskan Natives | 1 | 2 | 3 | 4 |
| Multi-Racial/Multi-Ethnic individuals | 1 | 2 | 3 | 4 |
| Gay/Lesbian/Bisexual/Transgender individuals | 1 | 2 | 3 | 4 |
| People with disabilities | 1 | 2 | 3 | 4 |
| People with different religious beliefs | 1 | 2 | 3 | 4 |

**9. In the past year at Michigan with which groups below, other than your own, have you had the most interactions and contact? After you answer this question, answer question #10 about this group.** *(Circle one.)*

| | |
|---|---|
| African Americans/Blacks | 1 |
| Hispanics/Latinos/Chicanos | 2 |
| Asian Americans/Pacific Islanders | 3 |
| Whites/Caucasians | 4 |
| American Indians/Alaskan Natives | 5 |
| Multi-Racial/Multi-Ethnic individuals | 6 |

**10. To what extent have you done each of the following with individuals from the group you selected in question #9?** *(Circle one for each.)*

|  | Quite a bit - 4 | A little - 3 | Some - 2 | Not at all - 1 |
|---|---|---|---|---|
| Had tense, cautious interactions | 1 | 2 | 3 | 4 |
| Felt comfortable sharing your personal feelings and problems | 1 | 2 | 3 | 4 |
| Spent personal time (ex. share a meal, attend social events together) | 1 | 2 | 3 | 4 |
| Participated in meaningful discussions about race relations outside of class | 1 | 2 | 3 | 4 |

**11. We are all members of the different social identity groups (e.g. gender, race, ethnicity, sexual orientation, socio-economic class, etc.). How often do you think about your social identity?** *(Circle one for each)*

|  | Often - 4 | Sometimes - 3 | Rarely - 2 | Never- 1 |
|---|---|---|---|---|
| Gender | 1 | 2 | 3 | 4 |
| Race | 1 | 2 | 3 | 4 |
| Ethnicity | 1 | 2 | 3 | 4 |
| Sexual orientation | 1 | 2 | 3 | 4 |
| Physical or learning disability | 1 | 2 | 3 | 4 |
| Socio-economic class | 1 | 2 | 3 | 4 |

**12. Mark the box that best represents the quality of your relationships with people at UM** *(Circle one for each.)*

|  | Unhelpful |  |  | Helpful |  |
|---|---|---|---|---|---|
| Other students | 1 | 2 | 3 | 4 | 5 |
| Faculty members | 1 | 2 | 3 | 4 | 5 |
| Administrative personnel and offices | 1 | 2 | 3 | 4 | 5 |

## MEANINGFUL CIVIC ENGAGEMENT/COMMUNITY SERVICE LEARNING

*Please skip to Question #14 if you are not involved in any community service*

**13. What are your attitudes toward community involvement? (Circle one for each.)**

Strongly agree - 5
Agree - 4
Neutral - 3
Disagree - 2
Strongly disagree - 1

| | | | | | |
|---|---|---|---|---|---|
| I was already volunteering in my community before coming to UM | 1 | 2 | 3 | 4 | 5 |
| I probably won't volunteer or participate in my community in the future | 1 | 2 | 3 | 4 | 5 |
| Performing work in the community helped me clarify which major to pursue | 1 | 2 | 3 | 4 | 5 |
| The skills I gained from my community service work have made me more marketable in my chose profession when I graduate | 1 | 2 | 3 | 4 | 5 |
| I think a lot about the influence that society has on other people | 1 | 2 | 3 | 4 | 5 |
| I think a lot about the influence that society has on my behavior | 1 | 2 | 3 | 4 | 5 |
| I have met people at UM who have inspired me to be a better leader | 1 | 2 | 3 | 4 | 5 |
| My college experiences encourages me to pursue leadership roles either on campus in my chose profession when I graduate | 1 | 2 | 3 | 4 | 5 |
| The community work I participated in this year made me aware of some of my own biases and prejudices | 1 | 2 | 3 | 4 | 5 |
| Participating in the community helped me enhance my leadership skills | 1 | 2 | 3 | 4 | 5 |
| Doing work in the community helped me to become aware of my personal strengths and weaknesses | 1 | 2 | 3 | 4 | 5 |

**14. In your role as a responsible citizen in this society, how important are each of the following to you?** *(Circle one for each.)*

Essential - 4
Very important - 3
Somewhat important - 2
Not important - 1

| | | | | |
|---|---|---|---|---|
| Working to end poverty | 1 | 2 | 3 | 4 |
| Paying taxes to support public services | 1 | 2 | 3 | 4 |
| Using career-related skills to work in low-income communities | 1 | 2 | 3 | 4 |
| Contributing money to a political cause | 1 | 2 | 3 | 4 |
| Supporting a strong military | 1 | 2 | 3 | 4 |
| Promoting a racial tolerance and respect | 1 | 2 | 3 | 4 |
| Contributing money to a charitable cause | 1 | 2 | 3 | 4 |
| Defending the right to own a gun | 1 | 2 | 3 | 4 |
| Voting in national elections | 1 | 2 | 3 | 4 |
| Creating awareness of how people affect the environment | 1 | 2 | 3 | 4 |
| Working to minimize government involvement in individual affairs | 1 | 2 | 3 | 4 |
| Making consumer decisions based on a  company's ethics | 1 | 2 | 3 | 4 |
| Speaking up against social injustice | 1 | 2 | 3 | 4 |
| Volunteering with community groups or agencies | 1 | 2 | 3 | 4 |

**15. We would like to know your thoughts in a variety of situations. For each item, indicate how well it describes you.** *(Circle one for each.)*

|  | Not at all like me<br>1 |  |  |  | Very much like me<br>5 |
| --- | :---: | :---: | :---: | :---: | :---: |
| I really enjoy analyzing the reason or causes for people's behavior | 1 | 2 | 3 | 4 | 5 |
| I prefer simple rather than complex explanations for people's behavior | 1 | 2 | 3 | 4 | 5 |
| I believe it is important to analyze and understand our own thinking processes | 1 | 2 | 3 | 4 | 5 |

## DIVERSE DEMOCRACY/INTERCULTURAL UNDERSTANDING AND DIALOGUE

**16. People often have differences in perspectives. Indicate how much you agree or disagree with each statement.** *(Circle one for each.)*

Strongly agree - 4
Agree somewhat- 3
Disagree somewhat- 2
Strongly disagree - 1

|  |  |  |  |  |
| --- | :---: | :---: | :---: | :---: |
| There are at least two sides to an issue | 1 | 2 | 3 | 4 |
| Conflict is a normal part of life | 1 | 2 | 3 | 4 |
| I am afraid of conflicts when discussing social issues | 1 | 2 | 3 | 4 |
| Democracy thrives on differing views | 1 | 2 | 3 | 4 |
| Conflict between groups can have positive consequences | 1 | 2 | 3 | 4 |

**17. Many colleges have diversity programs for diversity education. Indicate whether you support or oppose each of the following:** *(Circle one for each.)*

Strongly support - 4
Support somewhat- 3
Oppose somewhat - 2
Strongly oppose - 1

|  |  |  |  |  |
| --- | :---: | :---: | :---: | :---: |
| Incorporating writings and research about different ethnic groups and women into courses | 1 | 2 | 3 | 4 |
| Requiring students to complete a community-based experience with diverse populations | 1 | 2 | 3 | 4 |
| Offering courses to help students develop an appreciation for their own and other cultures | 1 | 2 | 3 | 4 |
| Requiring students to take at least one cultural or ethnic diversity course in order to graduate | 1 | 2 | 3 | 4 |
| Offering opportunities for intensive discussion between students with different backgrounds and beliefs | 1 | 2 | 3 | 4 |

**18. Please indicate the extent to which you agree or disagree with each of the following statements.** *(Circle one for each.)*

Strongly agree - 5
Agree - 4
Disagree - 3
Strongly disagree - 2
Haven't thought about this - 1

|  |  |  |  |  |  |
| --- | :---: | :---: | :---: | :---: | :---: |
| Since coming to U of M, I have learned a great deal about other racial/ethnic groups and their contributions to American society | 1 | 2 | 3 | 4 | 5 |
| I have gained a greater commitment to my racial/ethnic since coming to U of M | 1 | 2 | 3 | 4 | 5 |
| My relationships with students from different racial/ethnic groups at U of M have been positive | 1 | 2 | 3 | 4 | 5 |
| Since coming to college, I have become aware of the complexities of inter-group understanding | 1 | 2 | 3 | 4 | 5 |
| I think this campus' focus on diversity puts too much emphasis on the differences between racial/ethnic groups | 1 | 2 | 3 | 4 | 5 |
| My social interactions on this campus are largely confined to students of my own race/ethnicity | 1 | 2 | 3 | 4 | 5 |
| At times, it is important to be with people of my own racial/ethnic group for the chance to be myself | 1 | 2 | 3 | 4 | 5 |

**19. Indicate the extent to which you agree or disagree with the following statements.** *(Circle one for each.)*

Strongly agree - 4
Agree somewhat- 3
Disagree somewhat- 2
Strongly disagree - 1

| | | | |
|---|---|---|---|
| I try to keep up with current events | 1 | 2 | 3 | 4 |
| I enjoy getting into discussions about political issues | 1 | 2 | 3 | 4 |
| Racial/ethnic discrimination is no longer a major problem is the U.S. | 1 | 2 | 3 | 4 |
| It's fair to give preference in college admissions to children of alumni | 1 | 2 | 3 | 4 |
| Many Whites lack an understanding of the problems that people from different racial/ ethnic groups face | 1 | 2 | 3 | 4 |
| Colleges should support women's athletics as much as they support men's athletics | 1 | 2 | 3 | 4 |
| Our society has done enough to promote the welfare of different racial/ethnic groups | 1 | 2 | 3 | 4 |
| A high priority should be given to see that students of color receive financial aid for college | 1 | 2 | 3 | 4 |
| Hiring more faculty of color should be a top priority of UM | 1 | 2 | 3 | 4 |
| The system prevents people of color from getting their fair share of good jobs and better pay | 1 | 2 | 3 | 4 |
| State hate crimes laws are needed to protect people from harassment based on race, gender or sexual orientation | 1 | 2 | 3 | 4 |
| A person's racial background in this society does not interfere with achieving everything he or she wants to be | 1 | 2 | 3 | 4 |
| Colleges should aggressively recruit more students of color | 1 | 2 | 3 | 4 |
| Enhancing a student's ability to live in multicultural society is part of a university's mission | 1 | 2 | 3 | 4 |
| Colleges do not have a responsibility to correct racial/ethnic injustice | 1 | 2 | 3 | 4 |
| Emphasizing diversity contributes to disunity on campus | 1 | 2 | 3 | 4 |
| Some degree of inequality is necessary in a society that wants to be the best in the world | 1 | 2 | 3 | 4 |
| If people were treated more equally we would have fewer problems in this country | 1 | 2 | 3 | 4 |
| It is not really that big a problem if some people have more of a chance in life than others | 1 | 2 | 3 | 4 |
| I often think about how my personal decisions affect the welfare of others | 1 | 2 | 3 | 4 |

**20. How would you rate yourself in the following areas?** *(Circle one for each.)*

A major strength - 5
Somewhat strong - 4
Average - 3
Somewhat weak - 2
A major weakness - 1

| | | | | |
|---|---|---|---|---|
| Communication skills | 1 | 2 | 3 | 4 | 5 |
| Ability to work cooperatively with diverse people | 1 | 2 | 3 | 4 | 5 |
| Knowledge about my own culture | 1 | 2 | 3 | 4 | 5 |
| Racial/cultural awareness | 1 | 2 | 3 | 4 | 5 |
| Openness to having my views challenged | 1 | 2 | 3 | 4 | 5 |
| Ability to see the world from someone else's perspective | 1 | 2 | 3 | 4 | 5 |
| Knowledge about the cultural backgrounds of others | 1 | 2 | 3 | 4 | 5 |
| Ability to discuss and negotiate controversial issues | 1 | 2 | 3 | 4 | 5 |
| Tolerance of others with different beliefs | 1 | 2 | 3 | 4 | 5 |

21. Indicate the extent to which you agree or disagree with the following statements. *(Circle one for each.)*

Strongly agree - 4
Agree somewhat- 3
Disagree somewhat- 2
Strongly disagree - 1

| | | | | |
|---|---|---|---|---|
| It is important for me to educate others about the social identity groups to which I belong | 1 | 2 | 3 | 4 |
| I like to learn about social identity groups different from my own | 1 | 2 | 3 | 4 |
| I want to bridge differences between social identity groups | 1 | 2 | 3 | 4 |
| If I found out someone I knew was gay, lesbian, or bisexual, I'd be accepting and supportive | 1 | 2 | 3 | 4 |

## DEMOGRAPHICS

Student ID: _____

Race/Ethnicity: *(please check only one box)*
☐ African Americans/Blacks        ☐ Hispanics/Latinos/Chicanos
☐ Asian Americans/Pacific Islanders   ☐ Whites/Caucasians
☐ American Indians/Alaskan Natives   ☐ Multi-Racial/Multi-Ethnic individuals
☐ International Students

Major(s):  Primary _____
             Secondary _____

Gender:            ☐ Female        ☐ Male          ☐ Transgender

Sexual Orientation:  ☐ Bisexual      ☐ Homosexual     ☐ Heterosexual

Political views:    ☐ Far left       ☐ Liberal        ☐ Middle of the road
                     ☐ Conservative   ☐ Far Right

Religion: _____

Estimated family income last year:
☐ Less than $10K        ☐ $50K-59,999
☐ $10K-14,999            ☐ $60-74,999
☐ $15K-19,999            ☐ $75K-99,999
☐ $20K-24,999            ☐ $100K-149,999
☐ $25K-29,999            ☐ $150K-199,999
☐ $30K-39,999            ☐ $200K-249,999
☐ $40K-49,999            ☐ $250K or more

Student status:     ☐ In state      ☐ Out of state    ☐ International

Current grade point average (GPA): _____

## MCSP STUDENTS ONLY:

Are you currently a student leader? If yes, which one?
☐ Peer Advisor      ☐ Peer Mentor      ☐ Resident Advisor   ☐ Class Facilitator

## MCSP Research Design: In-Depth Interviews for Longitudinal Study

These in-depth interviews will be administered to a random sample of MCSP students when they first enter college. We will follow-up with this single set of students at the end of each year of college until graduation, one year after graduation and at five-year intervals beyond college.

The interview questions will be very similar for each administration of the in-depth interviews. The content areas of the questions will always be the same, but individual questions will be specifically tailored to reflect the different experiences of the interviewees at their different stages of schooling and life. For example, students first entering college will, of course, not be asked respond to questions about their interactions with faculty and college courses they have completed, and students five years out of college will not be asked about college or MCSP courses they have taken in the past year.

The questions presented below have been prepared as a model for students who are completing their first year of college. All the questions below will be asked of every interviewee, but they are organized here in terms of distinct question sets according to their link to the MCSP mission and goals. For the purposes of this chapter, only the interview questions are listed from the five bullet points below.

- Introductions
- Information about the Research
- Permissions and Human Subjects Approval
- Demographic Information
- Interview Questions

### Question Set A - Deep Learning

1. Please tell me what courses you have taken and which ones were your favorites? Were any of these MCSP courses? What kinds of topics or subjects are you most interested in?
2. Describe your idea of a good class? Of a bad class?
3. Describe a class which really make you think hard or re-examine your existing notions about a topic? Were any of these MCSP classes?
4. Do you talk about your course topics with friends or others outside of class? What kinds of things do you talk about with friends outside of class?
5. Do faculty know you by your name? Are any of these MCSP faculty?
6. How would you describe the faculty you like best at college? How many people like this are there?
7. Describe your transition from high school to college - academically and socially? Any particular highlights or challenges? Do you feel your grades are an accurate reflection of your feelings about your transition?
8. Ideally, what do you hope to gain from your college education? What would make you look back and feel like it was a good experience for you (courses, ideas, jobs, etc.).

### Question Set B - Engaged Community

1. When you think about community, what comes to mind? What does that term mean to you?
2. What have you learned about yourself and your social group identities this year? What about other social identity groups?
3. Describe your past experiences with people from different backgrounds. What is your comfort level being with people who are different from you - racial, ethnic, sexual orientation, religion, disability?
4. Have you had a chance to stretch your "comfort zone" this year at college? Have you had many interactions with people from different backgrounds? What's it been like to live in Couzens/MCSP with people from many backgrounds?

5. Describe a time you talked in-depth with someone from a different background about an issue you both disagreed about; or agreed about? Did this take place in MCSP or with other MCSP students? Have you found you've learned things from people who are from different backgrounds than you? Give an example.
6. What activities have you participated in this year? At college, in the community? Did you join any organizations? Which ones?
7. How many close friends do you have at college? Did you meet any of these close friends in MCSP? What percent are from backgrounds that are the same or different from your own?

### Question Set C - Meaningful Civic Engagement/Community Service Learning

1. Describe your activities outside of the MCSP and university community this year? - Volunteering, community service learning, voting, internships, student organizations, change efforts, political groups, fundraising?
2. Why do you get involved in these activities? Why do you do community service? What do you get out of it?
3. Do you see yourself continuing to do these kinds of activities throughout college? Throughout your life? Are they an important priority for you?
4. What leadership roles have you had in college (within MCSP/outside MCSP)? What does being a leader mean to you? Why do you take leadership roles? What do you try to accomplish as a leader?
5. How would you describe the contributions you make through your community service commitments? Do you work very hard at what you do in the community - how high is the quality of service you deliver?
6. Why do you get involved in community service work - more for your own benefit or for the benefit of people in the community?

### Question Set D - Diverse Democracy/Intercultural Understanding and Dialogue

1. What does "democracy" mean to you? How about "diversity?" Do these terms fit together for you in any meaningful way, as in "diverse democracy?"
2. What are your thoughts about equality and inequality in society? In what ways do you think you have more or fewer privileges than others?
3. What does the term social justice mean to you? How about injustice?
4. What is your vision of a just society, Or a just, diverse democracy?
5. What kinds of things do you do to try to live up to your vision of a just, diverse democracy?
6. Do you feel there are enough people who model good practice? Whom do you identify as the models of good practice and what qualities do you they embody?

### Next Steps for the Evaluation and Research Design

The process of developing the evaluation and research design over the past year was both productive and educational. The program evaluation will be implemented in the coming year and, in addition to learning more about the experience of participants in MCSP, we also anticipate that we may refine the various instruments as we learn from the first process of implementation. In the case of the research design, we will now seek funding to support the longitudinal research. In doing so, we anticipate that we may collaborate with other units on campus to study together the impact of programs that have a related vision and focus (which will necessitate some change in the survey and interviews) in order to understand better the differential impact on students of other community service programs, service-learning programs, and programs that have an even more intensive level of involvement than MCSP, all in comparison to students who do not participate in any of these types of programs. All of this speaks to the importance of ongoing evaluation and research in programs like the Michigan Community Scholars Program, and we look forward to what we will learn in the years ahead from the data collected about the program and about its impact on the lives of individual students over time.

## Notes

1. *Consultations for Program Evaluation*

   We wish to thank the following for their helpful comments and feedback in the development of the program evaluation: Wallace Genser, Sandra Gregerman, Marjorie Horton, Mary Hummel, Michelle O'Grady, Mary Piontek, Stella Raudenbush, Sally Sharp, Evans Young.

2. *Consultations for Research Design*

   We wish to thank the following for their helpful comments and feedback in the development of the research design: Eric Dey, Patricia Gurin, Sylvia Hurtado, John Matlock, Malinda Matney, Rena Murphy.

3. *Consultations with National Partners and Colleagues*

   We wish to thank the following individuals and the representatives from the listed institutions participating in the American Association of Higher Education (AAHE) Engaged Campus for Diverse Democracy Project for their helpful comments and feedback in the development of the evaluation and research design: Heather Woodcock Ayers, Karen Inkelas, Jodie Levine Laufgraben, Kathy McAdams, John O'Connor, Judith Patton, Chandler-Gilbert Community College, Collin County Community College, Evergreen State University, George Mason U., North Carolina A&T, Portland State University, Wagner College.

4. *MCSP Mission and Goals Statement*

   **Mission Statement***

   The Michigan Community Scholars Program (MCSP) is a residential learning community emphasizing deep learning, engaged community, meaningful civic engagement/community service learning and intercultural understanding and dialogue. Students, faculty, community partners and staff think critically about issues of community, seek to model a just, diverse, and democratic community, and wish to make a difference throughout their lives as participants and leaders involved in local, national and global communities.

   **Goals**

   1. Deep Learning

      - *Engagement with Ideas:* Critical thinking; Intellectual exploration; Active learning; Joy of learning; Long term commitment to learning; Exchange of differing viewpoints.
      - *Ways of Knowing:* Learning and teaching through traditional, experiential, discovery and other innovative means; Learning across disciplinary boundaries; Learning collaboratively; Learning in the classroom and outside the classroom.
      - *Transition to College:* Successful academic and social transition from high school to college and throughout their years with MCSP; academic and social support services and mentoring; providing an orientation to the resources of the wider university.
      - *Academic Success:* Each student getting the most of what he/she wants from a college education; GPA performance of students equal to or better than a comparable cohort of UM students.
      - *Learning about Community:* Developing complex understandings about community and social issues in society; Learning about self, social identities, and a wide range of socio-cultural groups and histories.

   2. Engaged Community

      - *A Scholarly Community:* Close faculty-student-community partner-staff interaction; Respecting each community member as both educator and learner; A focus on community members coming together to teach, study, learn, understand, and engage with ideas from different disciplinary perspectives and with people from different backgrounds.
      - *A Safe and Accepting Environment:* Comprised of people from diverse social backgrounds and with diverse perspectives; Intercultural understanding, interaction and dialogue across groups. A place and set of people who enjoy being with one another.

- *An Involved, Participatory Community:* High levels of commitment, short term and long term, to building community and participating within the community.
- *A Focus on the Individual and the Group:* A community that cares for each individual yet fosters a sense of responsibility to community; exploration of personal and social identities of self and others.

3. **Meaningful Civic Engagement /Community Service Learning**
   - *High Quality Service-Learning:* Providing service fitting the needs of the community; preparation of students to participate effectively in the community; participation in the community through long term and short term projects, including service learning, internships, social change efforts, political participation, volunteering, and fundraising.
   - *Reflection:* Reflective learning about democratic processes, civic life, social problems and social justice, self, and society.
   - *Leadership Development:* Preparing students to be active participants and leaders in civic life; training for students through courses and workshops; student leadership through peer facilitation of courses, peer advising and mentoring, peer control of student program planning and budget; leadership roles for faculty, community partners, and staff.
   - *Sustainable Partnerships:* Meaningful, mutually beneficial, and long-term partnerships between university and community.
   - *Long Term Commitment:* Develop long term commitment to civic engagement for the public good; broad dissemination of experience and insights from MCSP community.

4. **Diverse Democracy, Intercultural Understanding and Dialogue**
   - *A Diverse Community:* A commitment to maintaining a diverse community among students, faculty, community partners and staff; a commitment to working with diverse individuals and communities outside MCSP.
   - *Participation in Intergroup Dialogue:* Deep intercultural engagement; Understanding and dialogue across groups; Broadening students' social and intellectual "comfort zones" beyond their own social identity groups.
   - *Commitment to Strong Democracy:* Developing a commitment to strengthening democratic practice and participating in public life and civic organizations locally and globally.
   - *Reflection on Social Justice:* Linking notions of diversity with democracy; Reflection on issues of social justice and injustice, equality and inequality (including historic legacies of inequality).
   - *Model Good Practice:* Developing a vision of a just, diverse democracy; Modeling diverse democratic community practices in the short term that can be replicated long term beyond college.

\* *This is a Working Document of the MCSP Mission and Goals. We view it as a living document, offering us an opportunity to educate and engage one another in discussions about the values of this statement, and to make changes to the document when the community deems appropriate.*

## References

*CIRP Freshmen Survey.* (2003). http://www.gseis.ucla.edu/heri/cirp.html.

*Diverse Democracy Project.* (2003). http://www.umich.edu/~divdemo/.

Gelmon, Sherril, Barbara Holland, Amy Driscoll, Amy Spring, and Seanna Kerrigan (2001). *Community-Based Learning-Student Survey.* http://www.compact.org.

Gelmon, Sherril, Barbara Holland, Amy Driscoll, Amy Spring, and Seanna Kerrigan. (2001). *Assessing Service-Learning and Civic Engagement.* Providence, RI: Campus Compact.

Inkelas, Karen K. 1999. A tide on which all boats rise: The effect of living learning participation on undergraduate outcomes at the University of Michigan. Ann Arbor: University of Michigan.

*Michigan Student Study.* http://www.umich.edu/~oami/mss/index.htm.

*National Survey of Student Engagement.* (2003). http://www.indiana.edu/~nsse/.

Shapiro, Nancy and Jodie Levine.1999. *Creating Learning Communities*. San Francisco: Jossey-Bass.

Shapiro, Nancy and Jodie Levine Laufgraben. 2004. *Learning Communities in Context*. San Francisco: Jossey-Bass.

Tinto, Vincent and Goodsell, Anne. 1993. *A Longitudinal Study of Freshman Interest Groups at the University of Washington*. University Park, PA: National Center for Postsecondary Teaching, Learning and Assessment.

# About the Authors

ZACH ABRAMSON is a pre-med student at the University of Michigan majoring in computer science. When he is not studying, he enjoys working out, playing tennis, or just playing on his computer. From time to time, he has been known to draw a little.

DANNY V. ASNANI is a graduate from the University of Michigan. He received a B.A. in economics in April 2003. Danny joined MCSP at its inception in 1999 as a first year student. Throughout his undergraduate career he was a peer and resident advisor for the program.

NANCY BALOGH has taught in Detroit Public Schools for 23 years. She has an M.A. in bilingual education from Eastern Michigan University. She is currently the Title I-reading specialist teacher at John Logan Elementary School in Detroit.

EDGAR BECKHAM, dean of the College Emeritus of Wesleyan University in Middletown, Connecticut, is currently a senior fellow at the Association of American Colleges and Universities. He is also scholar in residence at Miami University's Center for American and World Cultures. After 28 years of service at Wesleyan, including 17 as dean of the College, Beckham joined the Ford Foundation in 1990, coordinating its Campus Diversity Initiative until 1998. Mr. Beckham has chaired the Connecticut State Board of Education, and the boards of Middlesex Hospital, the Rockfall Foundation, the Connecticut Housing Investment Fund, and the Connecticut Humanities Council. He currently chairs the Board of the Donna Wood Foundation and is a Trustee of Mt. Holyoke College. He is also a member of the Institute on Higher Education Project on the Future of Higher Education. Credentials include: 1958, B.A., Wesleyan University; 1959, M.A., Germanic Languages and Literatures, Yale University; 1997, Doctor of Humane Letters, Olivet College; 2000, Doctor of Humane Letters, Clark University.

AMY BORER is a student at the University of Michigan Business School. Having obtained the NASD General Securities Representative (Series 7) license in 2003, she plans to pursue a career in finance. In 2003, Amy was honored by the Office of Student Activities and Leadership as the University of Michigan's Outstanding New Member for her work in developing an original substance abuse prevention program for use in the Ann Arbor Public Schools.

KATE BRADY is the director of community relations for University Preparatory High School and Academy, a public charter school in Detroit based on the "big picture" model of schools. Kate has served in this capacity for 2.5 years, and has worked with students in the Lives of Urban Children and Youth (LUCY) Initiative during two of those years, both during the school year and as part of an intensive summer internship program.

STEPHANIE D. BROWN is a third year psychology major/CAAS minor. She is from Detroit and was an MCSP member in her freshman and sophomore years. Stephanie is still active in MCSP through the drama troupe and alumni committee created in 2003. Stephanie has moved on to become a facilitator for intergroup dialogue, another form of experiential learning.

RICHARD CARTER obtained Bachelor's and Master's degrees in Education at U-M. He joined the University of Michigan staff in 1970, and served for many years with the Alumni Association, leaving the position of associate executive director to become an associate dean of students. He currently service as associate director of State Outreach in the Office of Government Relations. Throughout his career, Carter has worked to bring groups of people from diverse backgrounds and experiences together. He's initiated programs for students, alumni and non-affinity groups that provide them valuable information and service opportunities to the University of Michigan.

GEORGE COOPER is a longtime writing composition teacher, with each course teaching him something new about writing and students. His relationship with the community minded teachers and students at MCSP has helped him understand that freshman composition cannot be conducted in the service of the university alone. Cooper believes that students need to see writing beyond its importance in gaining good grades: they need to see good writing as a way of changing and improving their world.

JAMES CROWFOOT is a faculty member in MCSP and the Program in the Environment. He is also an emeritus professor of natural resources and urban and regional planning in the University of Michigan's School of Natural Resources and Environment.

DORIAN DANIELS is a psychology and African American studies major interested in education and social justice. After graduate or law school, she plans to return to her hometown, Chicago, and work toward fair education, employment, and housing for underprivileged people.

JEN DENZIN's dedication to service-learning stems from her undergraduate work as a creative writing instructor, tutor to inmates, and peer facilitator with Project Community. This work, coupled with mission trips as a youth, encouraged Jen to serve as a Peace Corps Volunteer with her husband, Drew. Upon return, Jen was hired as LUCY's program associate to act as a liaison between students and community partners, and co-teach courses in the LUCY sequence. Jen is currently teaching English at Northville High School.

K. FOULA DIMPOULOS, M.S.W., came of age while working at Students for Appalachia at Berea College. While at Berea, she was the program manager of Girls Only, a guest speaker at the National Governor's Association Annual Meeting, and the Kentucky hub coordinator for the Campus Outreach Opportunity League (COOL). As a student at the University of Missouri, St. Louis, she was co-organizer of Stop the Hate Week and served as co-director of Anytown. In her short time at the University of Michigan, she was a guest speaker at the Division of Student Affairs panel on LGBT students, co-facilitator at Leadership Connection, co-facilitated the Office of LGBT Affairs' Speaker's Bureau training, and guest speaker at the School of Social Work all school event. Her background in community service, service-learning, organizing, and social work continue to influence and fuel her vision of the world as it could be. As an activist, advocate, organizer, public speaker and social worker, she endeavors to make the corners of her world more just and equitable.

MARY ANN DUNN has worked with and been interested in the inter-relationship between young children, youth, and seniors for several decades. She has taught school in Indiana and Michigan and has a B.S. degree from Eastern Michigan University where she majored in sociology. Because of her interest in "children at risk," she has many experiences working with low achieving students and encouraging them to set higher goals for themselves.

Mary Ann was involved with MCSP for five years as a coordinator of the Michigan Mentors Program in the Teaching-Learning Communities Program through the Ann Arbor Public Schools. This opportunity provided experience in setting up relationships between young students and seniors, and between middle school students and college students in MCSP.

As a firm believer in community, Mary Ann has always been active within the communities in which she lives by serving with numerous groups and in a variety of positions within the group.

SEDIKA F. FRANKLIN recently completed her B.A. in psychology at the University of Michigan. She was an active member for MCSP for all four years of her undergraduate career. She is thankful to be blessed with wonderful friends and family, yet she is most thankful for God's love through many trials and tribulations.

JOSEPH A. GALURA is the director of Project Community/Sociology 389, co-director of LUCY: the Lives of Urban Children and Youth Initiative, a faculty associate in Asian/Pacific Islander American Studies and a field instructor in the School of Social Work at the University of Michigan. Joe founded the OCSL Press and edits the *Praxis* series on service-learning, with Jeff Howard. Additionally, he has written *Filipino Women in Detroit: 1945-1955* (2002) and *Tapestry: Filipinos in Michigan, 1900-1950* (forthcoming), with Emily P. Lawsin.

ANNALISA HERBERT is a Ph.D. candidate in American Culture at the University of Michigan. As an undergraduate student at San Francisco State University she had the opportunity to run a class similar to Sociology 389 for two years through the Community Involvement Center and was inspired through that experience to work on building bridges between the community and university. As graduate student she was able to continue that work at the University of Michigan, by training undergraduate students to be class facilitators through Project Community, and MCSP.

JEFFREY HOWARD is the associate director for service-learning at the University of Michigan's Edward Ginsberg Center for Community Service and Learning. He has taught, conducted research, and published work on academic service-learning for more than 25 years. He is founder and editor of the Michigan Journal of Community Service Learning and edits the *Praxis* series on service-learning with Joe Galura. He is a member of the National Advisory Council for Campus Compact, and the National Review Board for the Scholarship of Engagement Project. His latest publication, funded by the Corporation for National Service, is the *Service-Learning Course Design Workbook*, which provides a model for designing a service-learning course from start to finish; there are more than 6,000 copies in circulation. He has offered workshops on service-learning pedagogy at dozens of colleges and universities around the country.

KRISTEN MICHELLE JOE is a senior sociology major at the University of Michigan. She has been a student coordinator for MCSP for two semesters.

TERENCE JOINER is a clinical assistant professor of pediatrics at the University of Michigan Medical School. Throughout his career, he has had an interest in serving underserved children. Dr. Joiner started his career at a community health clinic with the Wayne County Health Department. In 1987, he moved to the Henry Ford Health System, where he worked in Ann Arbor and Detroit. In 1993, he founded the Pediatric Free Clinic at the University of Michigan. In 1993, this clinic was renamed the Marshall H. Becker Memorial Clinic. In 1994, Dr. Joiner helped establish Ypsilanti Pediatrics. This was a collaborative program with the Washtenaw County Health Department. The primary goal was to serve underserved children in south Ypsilanti. Presently, Dr. Joiner has taught in MCSP since 2002. He has been a guest lecturer for classes in the Health Sciences Scholars Program, another living-learning program at U-M. He also teaches medical students in the medical school.

NJIA KAI, Detroit-born mother of four; Howard University graduate; filmmaker/videographer; cultural activist; founder and director of CAMP Detroit, DV Studio and The Cinema Cafe.

JEAN M. KLEIN is a lifelong resident of the east side of Detroit. Klein attended Detroit Public Schools. She has a B.M. degree from Michigan State University. She received her teaching certificate and 18 hours of graduate studies in education from Wayne State. She has taught in Detroit Public schools, and Church of the Messiah Daycare and Kindergarten. She has been a member of Church of the Messiah since 1977, and executive director of its human service agency, The Boulevard Harambee, since 1996. She has three daughters, including Laura, a former LUCY student, and now sociology major at U-M.

ERIN LANE is a junior at the University of Michigan. She is majoring in economics with a math minor and hopes to pursue a career in sustainable developmental economics.

CASSIE M. LAPEKAS graduated from the University of Michigan in August 2001 with a B.S. in political science. While a student at U-M, Cassie participated in an MCSP internship course, and subsequently worked as a senior ambassador at Focus: HOPE in Detroit. Cassie has served as a community partner and consultant to MCSP and was most recently employed in resource development at United Way Community Services in Detroit. She is currently employed by Smith Bucklin, an association management company in Chicago.

SARAH LUKE has enjoyed four years of involvement in MCSP while pursuing a B.A. in psychology at the University of Michigan. She is thankful for the support of her family and friends, and her faith in God, which have empowered her to excel both within MCSP and the broader university community. Upon graduation, she will begin a juris doctorate program at the University of Michigan School of Law in the summer of 2004.

SHEYONNA MANNS is a second year LSA student studying English and political science, specializing in political theory. Two-time Coordinator of MCSP Sociology 389, Manns has been involved in Bursley family residence hall multicultural council, Michigan Gospel Chorale, and writes for the Black Student Union newsletter, The Spectrum.

GREGORY B. MARKUS is a research professor at the Institute for Social Research and a professor of political science at the University of Michigan, where he received his Ph.D. in 1975. His areas of specialization include urban politics, civic participation, and social research methods. For more than 30 years, Markus has worked with initiatives at the local, state, national, and international levels that build the capacities of individuals, organizations, and communities to address public issues democratically.

DAVID MAURRASSE is an assistant professor in the School of International and Public Affairs and the Urban Planning Program at Columbia University, and president and CEO of Marga Incorporated, a consulting firm, with various clients including foundations and nonprofit organizations. He was also founder and director of the Center for Innovation in Social Responsibility (CISR), which promoted research and dialogue toward more effective partnerships between major institutions/industries and communities. David is author of *Beyond the Campus: How Colleges and Universities Form Partnerships with their Communities*, and is working on a new book, *Listening to Harlem: Gentrification, Community, and Business* to be released in 2004. He is also editing *A Future for Everyone: Innovative Social Responsibility and Community Partnerships*. David has also held positions at Yale University, the Rockefeller Foundation, and Community Resource Exchange.

KELLY E. MAXWELL, Ph.D. has been involved with intergroup dialogue for the past seven years and in the higher education community for more than a decade. As associate director of the Program on Intergroup Relations at the University of Michigan, she teaches courses on intergroup issues including social identity, privilege, oppression, and power. In addition, her research interests include policy and intergroup relations issues in higher education, particularly related to critically examining white privilege and its role in maintaining systems of inequity in education.

YVONNE W. MAYFIELD is the principal of Bellevue Elementary School in Detroit. She has been an educator for 32 years, beginning as a middle school teacher in Highland Park, MI after graduating from Eastern Michigan University in Ypsilanti. After completing her M.A. in the teaching of reading, Ms. Mayfield became a reading coordinator, an educational consultant for the J. B. Lippincott Company, and a demonstration teacher in the Detroit Public Schools. In the late 1980s, Mayfield gained experience as an administrator through her positions as an administrative unit head in a middle school and assistant principal of a K-8 school prior to becoming the principal of Bellevue. Mayfield's love of education was inspired by her parents, especially her father, who is a retired teacher.

In addition to being an avid reader, Ms. Mayfield enjoys traveling and playing her organ and piano. She is an ordained deacon at Hartford Memorial Baptist Church in Detroit. Mayfield has received two special awards: Principal of the Year from Communities In Schools, and an outstanding leadership award from Junior Achievement.

ALEFIYAH MESIWALA is a graduate from the University of Michigan Honors biochemistry program and new alumni of MCSP. By teaching undergraduate courses, doing extensive research, and involving herself in the community, she has demonstrated her effort to integrate a passion for science with social activism. Following these interests, she began the dual M.D./Ph.D. degree program at the University of Michigan in fall 2003.

LOUIS NAGEL has been on the faculty at the University of Michigan School of Music since 1969. He is a prominent concert artist and lecturer, and his students are noted as performers and teachers nationally and abroad. Devoted to the concept of the community musician, he serves as director of the Music School Performance Outreach program, in collaboration with his wife, psychoanalyst and musician Julie Jaffee Nagel, in programs for the Michigan Psychoanalytic Institute and the American Psychoanalytic Association. Since 1999, he has served as faculty for MCSP.

JEFF NELSON's life still revolves around social service work and social justice initiatives. In summer 2003, he was an intern with Illinois Governor Rod Blagojevich working specifically with the director of special projects on community development and other social justice projects. The rest of his time is taken up by his most recent venture, "Race For A Chance." He is training for the Fairfield Marathon and raising money for a family that he stayed with in Cape Town during a semester abroad. His goal is to raise enough money to pay for the children's tuition for the next few years so all three of the kids can stay in school. He hopes to join Teach For America or the Peace Corps after graduating in 2004.

JOHN O'CONNOR was the founding dean of New Century College (NCC) at George Mason University in Fairfax, VA. NCC awards undergraduate degrees in integrative and individualized studies, offers an interdisciplinary curriculum based on learning communities and portfolio assessment, and administers Centers for Service and Leadership and Field Studies. Previously at George Mason University, he was vice provost for Information Technology, and director of the Instructional Development Office. At AAHE, John is a senior scholar for the AAHE field of inquiry "Organizing for Learning" and directs projects on the "Engaged Campus." These projects support the public engagement of colleges and universities in their communities and preparing students for their civic responsibilities. He co-directed with Gene Rice the 2002 Forum on Faculty Roles and Rewards, "Knowledge for What? The Engaged Scholar" and with Susan Engelkemeyer the AAHE 2002 Summer Academy. John is also a Pew Foundation fellow with the Washington Center for Improving the Quality of Undergraduate Education for the National Learning Communities Project. He has written and presented on learning communities, higher education and democratic engagement, and teaching and learning with technology.

CHIBUZO OKAFO is a junior at the University of Michigan. He is majoring in political science. He has been a member of MCSP for three years and currently is a resident advisor. He is also a facilitator for the Sociology 389 course.

PENNY A. PASQUE was the program director of MCSP as the program was established and served in this role for a few years before starting the Ph.D. program at the Center for the Study of Higher and Postsecondary Education at the University of Michigan. Currently, she is a research assistant at the National Forum for the Public Good. Prior to her arrival at U-M, Penny coordinated the Faculty Programs at Cornell University with over 100 faculty members connecting the faculty with undergraduate students. Penny has served as a faculty member and keynote speaker on issues of social justice for PaperClip Communications and National Association for Student Personnel Administrators Leadership Conference Series in Pittsburgh, PA, Tampa, FL, Chicago, Atlanta, GA and San Francisco, CA. She has presented at statewide, national, and international conferences in the field of higher education. Nationally, Penny served on the Executive Council of the American College Personnel Association (ACPA) as the chair of the Standing Committee for Women and currently serves as a member of the ACPA Research Task Force and ACPA Ethics Committee. Locally, Penny serves on the Social Justice and Educational Equity graduate student committee for the School of Education at the University of Michigan.

KEVIN PERERIA is an international student from Hong Kong, in his freshman year at the University of Michigan. Having always had an interest in community service, MCSP, and this assignment, in particular, served as a great introduction to learning about a community that he had joined.

STELLA RAUDENBUSH is a member of the faculty of University of Michigan School of Education where she teaches courses on urban issues and social justice, and directs the Lives of Urban Children and Youth Initiative. She holds a B.A. in sociology from Cardinal Cushing College and an Ed.M. from Harvard University. Her career as a community activist, teacher, and spiritual seeker spans more than 30 years. Her first public political act was to hand out flyers at Boston's market district to support the United Farm Workers' boycott of lettuce.

She later worked as a social worker in Boston, academic counselor in a desegregation initiative, and a community organizer with low-income women and children. Her work with undergraduate students is derived from studying youth subcultures from cross-cultural perspectives. She is a national trainer for the Service-Learning National Clearinghouse, senior fellow at the National Youth Leadership Council, and consultant to school districts and community organizations in multiculturalism, diversity and youth development initiatives across the nation.

Her manual for K-12 service-learning continues to influence the growing service-learning movement. Her book, *A Gathering of Elders: Wisdom Teachings for the Service-Learning Movement* is forthcoming in 2004.

BYANQA ROBINSON is a junior psychology major at the University of Michigan. She hopes to get a master's degree in psychology and work as a family counselor.

MARTI R. RODWELL, executive director, HERO of Washtenaw County, has devoted much of the past decade to empowerment work, ranging from her affiliation with the Federation of Child Care Centers of Alabama to pre-employment goal-setting with Washtenaw Community Corrections. Her message is always based on the underlying principle that external oppression is difficult enough to overcome, but internalized oppression is an even greater threat to the well being of people everywhere.

STEFANI SALAZAR graduated with her B.A. from Colorado State University in 1996. She came to the University of Michigan in 1999 and is currently a Ph.D. candidate in sociology. She is currently working on the research team for the Detroit Area Study and the Detroit Arab American Study.

SUSAN SANTONE is a community partner in MCSP. She is executive director of Creative Change Educational Solutions, a nonprofit organization providing curricula, training, and programming in sustainability, ecological economics, and anti-discrimination. Her educational writing includes articles on teaching methods and a curriculum on discrimination developed for the United Nations.

DAVID SCHOEM has been the faculty director of MCSP since its inception in 1999. He teaches in Michigan's Sociology Department and has served as assistant dean for Undergraduate Education and assistant vice president for Academic and Student Affairs, working on issues such as founding the Program on Intergroup Relations; developing learning communities; establishing a diversity requirement; and implementing the First-Year Seminar Program. He is a PEW National Learning Communities fellow. He has led faculty institutes on diversity issues through the American Association of Colleges and Universities, Ford Foundation, Washington Center, and at numerous colleges and universities. He has written extensively on topics in higher education, including his recent article, "Transforming Undergraduate Education: Moving Beyond Distinct Undergraduate Initiatives" (*Change* Magazine), and recent books, *Intergroup Dialogue: Deliberative Democracy in School, College, Community and Workplace* (University of Michigan Press), *Multicultural Teaching in the University*, (Praeger Publishers), and *Inside Separate Worlds: Life Stories of*

*Young Blacks, Jews and Latinos* (University of Michigan Press). His newest book, forthcoming, is *College Knowledge: 101 Tips for the College-Bound Student* (University of Michigan Press).

NANCY S. SHAPIRO, associate vice chancellor for Academic Affairs at the University System of Maryland, was the founding director of the College Park Scholars living-learning program at the University of Maryland. Her publications include two co-authored books, *Creating Learning Communities* (Jossey Bass, 1999), and *Scenarios for Teaching Writing* (NCTE, 1996); numerous articles and reviews on a variety of undergraduate education topics, including learning communities, general education, and K-16 issues; and an edited collection of essays on K-16 statewide initiatives in *Metropolitan Universities* (1999). Her forthcoming co-authored book, *Expanding and Sustaining Learning Communities* will be published by Wiley & Sons in 2004. She is the principal investigator and director of three large federally funded projects including U.S. Department of Education Title II Teacher Quality Enhancement Partnership Grants, an NSF/Math Science Partnership Grant. Dr. Shapiro is a National Learning Communities Project fellow.

JOSIE SIRINEO is a graduate student in the Center for the Study of Higher and Postsecondary Education at the University of Michigan. In 1998, she received her bachelor's degree in sociology and education at UCLA. Post graduation she was employed in institutional research at Mount St. Mary's College in Los Angeles. Her professional interests include research design, methodology and the ethics of conducting research.

CARLY M. SOUTHWORTH, MCSP 2002-2003 interim program director, is from Muskegon, Michigan and earned her M.S.W. from the University of Michigan. She is passionate about issues of social justice and equality, specifically around race and class, and has worked in various diversity programs and initiatives at the University and throughout various communities. She has a passion for photography and is a member of Zeta Phi Beta Sorority. Carly is currently serving as Living Center Director at Grand Valley State University.

NANCY THOMAS (nancy.thomas@uconn.edu) is an associate vice provost at the University of Connecticut and director of the Democracy Project for the Society for Values in Higher Education (www.svhe.org). She works with colleges, universities, and educational associations to advance deliberative dialogue and democratic practices on campus and in partnership with communities. Dr. Thomas graduated from St. Lawrence University (AB Government, 1979) and Case Western Reserve University School of Law (J.D., 1984). She practiced as a university attorney before completing a doctorate in educational leadership at the Harvard Graduate School of Education (Ed.D., 1996). Since then, she has served as special assistant to the president for legal and policy affairs at Western New England College; director of Listening to Communities for the American Council on Education; adjunct faculty member (teaching legal issues in higher education) at the Graduate College of Education, University of Massachusetts Boston; and, senior associate at the New England Resource Center for Higher Education (NERCHE). Dr. Thomas is the author of multiple book chapters and articles on educating for democratic leadership and citizenship, colleges and universities as institutional citizens, and legal issues in higher education.

AARON TRAXLER-BALLEW is the program coordinator for the Program on Intergroup Relations at the University of Michigan. He has been involved with intergroup dialogue as a student, staff member, and instructor. As a student in the Residential College, Traxler-Ballew also participated in service-learning activities within a living-learning community. He has co-facilitated intergroup dialogues on gender, race, sexual-orientation, and socioeconomic class, and trained and coached intergroup dialogue facilitators.

VANESSA VADNAL will be a junior in fall 2003 at the University of Michigan. After getting her B.A. in psychology, she plans either to earn a Ph.D. in clinical psychology or go to law school.

CARMEN WARGEL began working as a social justice activist in high school and continued that work through her undergraduate program in Interdisciplinary Studies in the Western College Program at Miami University of Ohio. She graduated with a focus in Strategies for Social Change in the U.S. Contemporary Feminist Movement(s). After graduation, Carmen worked as an organizer with the Indiana National Organization for Women, Indiana University GLBT Student Support Services Office, and the Governor's Commission for a Drug-Free Indiana. She is currently a graduate student in the University of Michigan School of Social Work, studying community organizing. Her field placement is with two Ginsberg Center programs: the LUCY Initiative and Project Community.